Urban and Regional Prosperity in a Globalised New Economy

Urban and Regional Prosperity in a Globalised New Economy

Edited by

Roger Sugden

University of Birmingham (UK) and L'institute

Rita Hartung Cheng and G. Richard Meadows

University of Wisconsin-Milwaukee (USA) and L'institute

IN ASSOCIATION WITH L'INSTITUTE (INSTITUTE FOR INDUSTRIAL
DEVELOPMENT POLICY), UNIVERSITIES OF BIRMINGHAM (UK),
FERRARA (ITALY) AND WISCONSIN-MILWAUKEE (USA)

Edward Elgar
Cheltenham, UK • Northampton, MA, USA

Published by
Edward Elgar Publishing Limited
Glensanda House
Montpellier Parade
Cheltenham
Glos GL50 1UA
UK

Edward Elgar Publishing, Inc.
136 West Street
Suite 202
Northampton
Massachusetts 01060
USA

A catalogue record for this book
is available from the British Library

Library of Congress Cataloguing in Publication Data

Institute–Milwaukee Workshop on Urban and Regional Propserity in a Globalised
    Economy (1st–2nd : 2000–2001 : University of Wisconsin/Milwaukee)
    Urban and regional prosperity in a globalised new economy / edited by Roger Sugden, Rita
    Hartung Cheng and G. Richard Meadows.
        p. cm.
    This volume comprises papers that were requested from various authors . . . at the First and
    Second L'Institute–Milwaukee Workshop on Urban and Regional Prosperity in a Globalised
    Economy.
        Published in association with L'institute (Institute for Industrial Development Policy),
    Universities of Birmingham (UK), Ferrara (Italy) and Wisconsin–Milwaukee (USA).
        Includes bibliographical references and index.
        1. Regional economics—Congresses. 2. Economic development—Congresses. 3.
    Wisconsin—Economic policy—Congresses. 4. Globalization—Congresses. I. Sugden, Roger.
    II. Cheng, Rita H. (Rita Hartung), 1952– III. Meadows, G. Richard. IV. Title.

HT388.I575 2001
338.9—dc21   2003046373

ISBN 1 84376 389 3 (cased)

Typeset by Cambrian Typesetters, Frimley, Surrey
Printed and bound in Great Britain by MPG Books Ltd, Bodmin, Cornwall

Contents

PART I

PART II

v

Figures

Tables

Contributors

Marco Bellandi, University of Florence and L'institute

J. Robert Branston, University of Bath and L'institute

Rita Hartung Cheng, University of Wisconsin-Milwaukee and L'institute

John M. Connor, Purdue University

Keith Cowling, University of Warwick

Marco R. Di Tommaso, University of Ferrara and L'institute

Kaye G. Husbands, Williams College

G. Richard Meadows, University of Wisconsin-Milwaukee and L'institute

Mark A. Mone, University of Wisconsin-Milwaukee

Donald A. Nichols, University of Wisconsin-Madison

James Peoples, University of Wisconsin-Milwaukee and L'institute

Kris Piwek, University of Wisconsin-Milwaukee

Stuart O. Schweitzer, UCLA

Timothy R. Sheehy, Metropolitan Milwaukee Association of Commerce

Stanley Siebert, University of Birmingham

Roger Sugden, University of Birmingham and L'institute

Philip R. Tomlinson, University of Bath

Sammis White, University of Wisconsin-Milwaukee

Johan Willner, Äbo Akademi University

James R. Wilson, University of Birmingham and L'institute

Nancy L. Zimpher, University of Wisconsin-Milwaukee

Foreword

G. Richard Meadows and Roger Sugden

MULTINATIONAL NETWORKING IN RESEARCH AND LEARNING

The activities that have resulted in this volume have been undertaken under the auspices of L'institute, a joint venture between the Universities of Birmingham (UK), Ferrara (Italy) and Wisconsin-Milwaukee (US). Established in 1997, L'institute was born and has grown out of a multinational network of scholars engaged in the study of regional economic development. It strives to engage international scholars in the process of such development. Whilst doing so, it is also evolving a multinational networking process that stimulates open scholarly interaction in the search for policies that recognise and foster region-specific development goals. The current volume is a reflection of both of these concerns.

The roots of L'institute lie particularly in two Summer Research Workshops hosted jointly by the Universities of Warwick and Birmingham (UK) in the early 1990s. These two workshops may be seen as constituting the first phase of a long-run, evolving process. The aim was to provide a small yet expanding group of scholars – drawn from across Europe and to a more limited extent from the US – with the time and space to discuss emerging issues in industrial development policy. It was on these foundations that an approach was made to the European Commission for Human Capital and Mobility funding to take the project into its next phase. As a result, a partnership spanning nine institutions across eight European countries succeeded in attaining support for a series of workshops and graduate research initiatives over the period 1994–97. This project led to the creation of the European Network on Industrial Policy (EUNIP), which soon grew to encompass many institutions and well over 200 individual scientists, mostly in Europe and the Americas. Its aims, objectives and payoffs were neither designed nor realised exclusively for the advantage of the core partners in the original Human Capital and Mobility project, and the intention was to create links between scientists in an emerging environment of mutual cooperation and support.

Building on these initiatives, the project moved into a third phase. Most notably, in 1997 EUNIP was given independent life through the establishment of its Annual Conference (see www.eunip.com for further information). In the same year and based on the emergence of EUNIP, L'institute (Institute for Industrial Development Policy) was established.

The aim of L'institute is to provide an ongoing focal point for analysis and discussion of industrial development processes, and to give a stimulus to the dynamic networking that goes beyond the confines of specific, self-contained projects by opening new possibilities for scholarly interaction and cooperation. Moreover, by creating an organisation that sits firmly within established universities, vital roots are provided; they give networking a concrete presence, lifting it beyond comparatively short-run initiatives and abstract theorising. The intention is to nurture multinationalism amongst scholars and others concerned about industrial economic development and public policy.

The activities of L'institute are grounded in the scholarship of the individual people involved rather than the institutional objectives of the three sponsoring universities. Likewise, to foster openness, L'institute has a minimal structure that enables and facilitates individuals drawn from a far wider set of organisations than those that are its formal sponsors. The emphasis on multinationalism implies a coming together of individuals across nations, a process based on and respecting the different experiences, histories, traditions and cultures of various localities in various parts of the world. These differences are seen as a source of strength, providing opportunities for mutual benefit, and for identifying and pursuing efficient ways forward. Such multinationalism is arguably in stark contrast to the transnationalism of today's typical global corporations; to transnationalise is to have a transverse structure that crosses nations and localities, taking advantage of opportunities to serve sectional interests without being rooted in the localities that make up those nations. The benefit of multinationalism is in the quality of research and learning, in unique and otherwise unobtainable outputs. (See Sugden, 2000 on one interpretation of the implications for multinationalism versus transnationalism in the pursuit of efficient and equitable industrial development policy.) L'institute draws together varied expertise from across nations, rooting the research and learning agenda in the concerns of those nations, and in the interests of the peoples of those nations.

Moreover, it is recognition of those regional interests that drives another of the prime aims of L'institute: the desire to include international scholars in the process of regional economic development, bringing to bear multinational expertise that might be able to offer new insights into the development possibilities that might satisfy the aims and objectives of the people of a region.

Among the specific projects that have been pursued by L'institute have been two workshops at the University of Wisconsin-Milwaukee. (For details of further activities, and more on the strategy and operation of L'institute, see www.linstitute.org.) An initial intention was to extend and reinforce the networking process in North America by recreating the environment of the aforementioned Warwick–Birmingham Summer Research Workshops of the early 1990s; the First L'institute–Milwaukee Workshop on 'Enterprise strategies and regional growth policies in the new global economy', held in July 2000, was intended to tighten and extend links between scholars in North America and Europe. Moreover, the success of the event led to the Second L'institute–Milwaukee Workshop on 'Urban and regional prosperity in a globalised economy', held in July 2001. Again, there was concern to nurture the multinational network. In addition, however, the Second Workshop was intended to explore the ways in which an international group of scholars might contribute to processes of regional economic development being discussed within the specific context of the current challenges facing South-eastern Wisconsin.

This volume is an outcome of these two workshops. It is a reflection both of multinational networking, and of the attempt to participate in the process of regional economic development. It is also a contribution to both of those concerns.

REFERENCE

Sugden, R. (2000), 'Small firm networking and the internationalisation of universities: a multinational approach', L'institute Discussion Paper 7, Universities of Birmingham, Ferrara and Wisconsin-Milwaukee. Available at www.linstitute.org. Original version presented at the First L'institute–Milwaukee Workshop, University of Wisconsin-Milwaukee, July 2000.

Preface

Nancy L. Zimpher

UNIVERSITY IN THE COMMUNITY

Over the last two years, business, government and education leaders in Wisconsin have focused on building a regional strategic plan for economic development. Led by the University of Wisconsin System and Board of Regents, Wisconsin Economic Summits were held in 2000 and 2001, drawing more than 900 leaders from business, labour, government, education and the non-profit sectors together to consider Wisconsin's economic condition and establish a collaborative vision. The Summits served as a turning-point in thinking about the future direction of Wisconsin's economy. Although a coordinated, vibrant and realistic business plan for economic development is yet to be developed, the work of the Summits is continued by various regional groups. The agenda for growth includes initiatives to attract, develop and retain Wisconsin's workforce, preserve Wisconsin's economic backbone, expand the biotechnology/biomedical sector, identify and develop other significant industry clusters, build public/private partnerships, and develop other regional solutions. Lessons learned from neighbouring states and our multinational network of academic scholars will contribute to the success of Wisconsin's regional economic development.

The University of Wisconsin-Milwaukee has a significant role in strengthening Wisconsin's place in the emerging global marketplace. Drawing on its unique strengths as a premier urban research university, the University of Wisconsin-Milwaukee has an institutional commitment to serve Milwaukee and Wisconsin by providing a wide range of research and service expertise and by maintaining strong and dynamic partnerships with the various communities and organisations in the region. The scholarly and business perspectives of participants in the L'institute Workshop as reflected in this volume are excellent examples of the wide range of research and service contributions of this university to local economic development. The work of L'institute complements and contributes to the existing and ongoing focus on Wisconsin economic development. The volume also contributes in a meaningful way to broader issues of urban and regional prosperity in a globalised economy.

Acknowledgements

The volume comprises papers that were requested from various authors, who exchanged ideas and provided each other with critical comments at the Second L'institute–Milwaukee Workshop on 'Urban and regional prosperity in a globalised economy'. Each of the contributions has been revised as a result of this rigorous process. Moreover, the initial choice of requested papers was a product of the First L'institute–Milwaukee Workshop on 'Enterprise strategies and regional growth policies in the new global economy'. This volume is accordingly an outcome of a process involving researchers at both workshops, and the editors would like to acknowledge the contribution of each of those participants. They were as follows:

John Addison	Susan Gupta	Kanti Prasad
Bart Armah	Thomas Hefty	Georgia Saemann
Swarnjit Aurora	John Heywood	Richard Schuler
Moshen Bahmani	William Holahan	Stuart Schweitzer
David Bailey	Candace Howes	Timothy Sheehy
Harminder Battu	Kaye Husbands	Stanley Siebert
Marco Bellandi	Noel Kavanagh	Wayne Talley
Robert Branston	Richard Marcus	Ana Teresa Tavares
Maria Callejon	Mark Mone	Philip Tomlinson
John Connor	Samar Mukhopadhyay	John Torinus
Kirsten Daniel	Donald Nichols	Josh Whitford
Lisa De Propris	Beth Norris	Johan Willner
Marco Di Tommaso	James Peoples	James Wilson
Susan Donohue	Laura Peracchio	Jonathan Zeitlin
Abera Gelan	Richard Perlman	Nancy Zimpher

Amongst these, it is especially pertinent to highlight and acknowledge the role of Susan Donohue, William Holahan and James Peoples, who were part of the organising committee.

Last but not least, the editors would particularly like to acknowledge the contribution of Marcela Valania, who took overall responsibility for administering each of the workshops, and to thank administrative staff at the University of Wisconsin-Milwaukee's Department of Economics (College of Letters and Science) and School of Business Administration, hosts of both workshops.

Urban and regional prosperity in a globalised new economy: an overview

Roger Sugden, Rita Hartung Cheng and G. Richard Meadows[*]

There is currently a popular view that the world is undergoing profound changes in the relationships through which it is organised. In particular, there is widespread talk of a 'globalised' economy, facilitated by and associated with 'new' technologies and practices. There is a further consensus that within this globalised, 'new' economy, regionalisation of some form is important. The aim of this volume is to address these topical issues, presenting perspectives from which they can be analysed and understood, and exploring specific aspects in greater detail. We provide a framework for analysing and understanding current trends, and suggest approaches that highlight appropriate ways forward in the context of opportunities and dangers. In doing so, we discuss specific cases and explore detailed policy possibilities, including the prospect of stimulating change through multinational engagement and debate.

Part I of the volume comprises a chapter by Roger Sugden and James R. Wilson. It has two aims. The first is to provide a general introduction to some of the issues and a reference point for later contributions. It reports a set of questions, topics and themes, what might be considered an introductory agenda. The objective is in part to position subsequent chapters in the broader context from which they were derived. It is also to provide a springboard for further questioning and understanding. The second aim of the chapter is to explore a perspective on concepts that provide the basis for the analysis of urban and regional prosperity in a globalised new economy. The intention is to begin to explore items underlying the initial agenda in a manner that provides an overall perspective. In essence, the focus is on aspects of the conceptualisation of 'urban', 'regional', 'prosperity', 'globalised' and 'new' economy.

Having distinguished between *democratic globalisation* and *elite globalisation*, the chapter presents notions of urban and regional prosperity as part of the same process. The idea is of a virtuous circle where 'localities' are feeling their way forward, evolving towards paths along which they can govern themselves. It is argued that the ultimate challenge is to move towards a scenario where all actors in each locality, and in the communities within and across localities, participate in the democratic governance of their development. Achieving this would imply that urban and regional prosperity is rooted in the inclusion of each person in a globalised new economy; there would be opportunity and ability for everyone to access and shape the globalisation process, and in this sense to be 'citizens of the world'.

Part II of the volume explores specific issues. Its range is very wide, encompassing deindustrialisation, industrialisation, labour market flexibility, enterprise formation, cartels, concentration and the clustering of economic activity.

In Chapter 2, the prime focus of Keith Cowling and Philip R. Tomlinson is that aspect of a globalisation process accounted for by large Japanese firms, the impact on smaller Japanese firms and thus the consequences for regions within Japan. They discuss the problems of 'hollowing out' using a case study of the machinery sector. Their contribution explores the roots of Japan's present crisis by focusing on the role played by the country's large transnational corporations. These corporations are seen as central actors, controlling a significant proportion of manufacturing. It is their strategic decisions – those decisions that determine the level and location of investment, employment and output – which ultimately shape the development path for Japanese industry.

In recent years, Japan's large transnationals have become engaged in the process of (what Part I of this volume characterises as) *elite globalisation*, pursuing their own interests at the expense of domestic Japanese industry. Japan's firms have established *new* (overseas) *keiretsu*, comprising large Japanese transnational corporations and their core domestic suppliers. Increasingly, these new *keiretsu* have been used by the large transnationals as substitutes for investment and production in Japan. As a result, smaller Japanese firms have been placed in a weaker bargaining position with their main contractors, who have had increasing access to global supply chains. Consequently, Japan's smaller firms have experienced declining order books and have had to accept lower profit margins. The result has been an unprecedented rise in the number of small-firm bankruptcy cases.

The chapter views the strategic decisions made by Japan's elite corporate hierarchies as being incompatible with the wider Japanese public interest, which is concerned with promoting domestic employment and encouraging regional industrial growth and vitality. This fundamental insight is argued to be crucial for designing appropriate policy responses to arrest Japan's current industrial decline. It is further suggested that the lessons from Japan's experience might show policy-makers elsewhere, in regions concerned with their future industrial development, the effects of globalisation and the problems of hollowing out.

An apparently very different sort of economy is the subject of Chapter 3, the discussion of Mexico by Kaye G. Husbands. Nevertheless, the topic of foreign direct investment again figures prominently, and there are parallel concerns about indigenous smaller firms being pushed out of supply chains. Moreover, for both chapters the issue might be characterised as a concern with failures to industrialise appropriately, in the case of Japan because the sort of industrialisation has ultimately resulted in a deindustrialisation, and in the case of Mexico because industrialisation has been at best stunted.

The chapter identifies and contemplates a critical question: does economic growth in the likes of Mexico depend on the viability of indigenous Mexican firms, or does production by foreign firms contribute as much or even more to the Mexican economy? More precisely, its concern is technological change and innovation: is there a reduction in indigenous innovation that critically impairs future growth, when foreign firms supplant indigenous firms under liberalised trade and ownership rules? Husbands reviews wide-ranging literature. She concludes that globalisation might foster the upgrading of technology within particular regions by facilitating freer trade and linkages across trading partners. However, latecomer developers – such as Mexico – can better reap the benefits if they possess local systems of technology development. Moreover, she also points to the desirability of indigenous innovation within localities for areas of the world more widely. It is argued that indigenous innovation in 'developing countries' could have positive spillover to 'developed nations'; for example, firms from the US, Japan and Europe might find that access to very distinct technology processes in, say, Mexico, spurs the development of new products and processes that are not only utilised in Mexico but also in their other markets in different parts of the world. This is illustrated with particular cases, especially the automobile industry, and explored in terms of potential public policy by considering industrial and technology clusters, and the role of education programmes.

Chapter 4 is by Johan Willner and is entitled 'Economic activity, market structure and public policy'. It moves the discussion in different directions, albeit also concentrating on different types of enterprise and discussing technological change. Willner's starting-point is the frequent argument that high wages, a large public sector, unionisation, and job security lead to lower output and employment and that this explains why unemployment in Europe is higher than in the US. However, his overview of recent research throws doubts on this popular 'eurosclerosis' hypothesis. Social insurance and the public infrastructure may in fact have a favourable effect on economic activity. Wage flexibility may have a limited effect on employment. Profit opportunities seem to be of limited importance for explaining entry, as compared to a preference for being self-employed, while access to credit may be essential for both entry and survival.

The chapter includes an oligopoly model with and without free entry and credit rationing. While there may indeed sometimes exist a trade-off between desirable objectives such as high wages (and indirectly unionisation and high income taxes) and job security on the one hand, and employment and enterprise formation on the other, the relationship turns out to be more complex than usually believed. Better job security may in fact reduce marginal costs, which increases employment in an oligopoly with a fixed number of firms. Higher wages may even lead to increased enterprise formation and have no negative effect on employment if access to credit is an important barrier to entry. Moreover, public production will then lead to an increase in the number of private firms in a mixed oligopoly, and can also offset possible negative effects of higher job security if there is entry and exit under credit rationing. Overall, the implication of Chapter 4 is that an industrial policy may be counterproductive when, in the name of increased profit opportunities, it excludes large segments of the population from the prosperity that high economic activity is supposed to generate.

The chapter by Stanley Siebert continues with the topic of labour market flexibility, discussing the 'eurosclerosis' hypothesis in further detail. It highlights a conceptualisation of the new economy that emphasises a rise in skilled-labour-using technologies, coupled with increasing global competition. Siebert argues that these factors reduce the demand for unskilled labour in the 'developed world', suggesting a lengthening of the lower tail of the earnings distribution. In other words, increased global competition is said to mean that unskilled workers in, say, the UK, need to earn somewhat less so as to be able to compete in the world market. He argues that, in these circumstances, labour market institutions that prevent a widening of earnings differentials may have more of a displacement effect on unskilled workers. Therefore, the rise of the new economy means urgently investigating two important questions. First, do public policies that cut the bottom off of the earnings distribution – for example, minimum wage laws, encouragement of unionisation – merely push people into the bottom of the income distribution? Second, what weight ought to be placed on movements into and out of the bottom of the earnings distribution?

Siebert's analysis of these questions is empirical, considering data from Western Europe, the US and Japan. His findings indicate that labour regulation strengthening unions and/or imposing good working conditions eliminates 'bad' jobs. Such regulation therefore causes unskilled workers (those without the skills to compete for good jobs) to suffer. His findings also indicate that the reason for the suffering is that the average unemployed person would much rather have a job, even a 'bad' job, than remain on welfare. The chapter contemplates the potential for constructing corporatist institutions that might permit more favourable outcomes. Whilst pessimistic, it considers such possibilities to be important on the basis that freedom of association, like freedom of the press, is part of a democratic society. Trade unions have been in the forefront of the fight for democracy in many countries, for example South Africa. Siebert concludes that simply wishing trade unions away is neither possible nor desirable; searching for the happy medium for union power is accordingly a central political issue.

Another change of direction is taken in Chapter 6; the broad subject is large firms and globalisation, an issue that repeatedly arises throughout the volume, but the particular topic addressed by John Connor is antitrust and global cartels. He discusses what might be seen as a dark side to globalisation. More specifically, he explores certain effects of the new economy on collusive international business schemes, and describes the responses of competition-law agencies to the growing threat of global cartels. The chapter points to the resurgence of global cartels that began in the 1980s, refers to a number of cartels discovered and prosecuted since 1995 and pays especial attention to the case of lysine, one of the first and most successful biotechnology industries to emerge since 1945.

Connor sees the nexus between cartel formation and the new economy as perhaps subtle and speculative, but nonetheless real. He describes the emergence of a cartel when Archer Daniels Midland Co. (ADM) entered the lysine market, and presents estimates of the global (overcharge and deadweight) losses to customers. These are compared to the penalties exacted from ADM in a calculation of the deterrence effect. His conclusion is that the crime was not made to pay but that the loss in global net revenues was relatively small. As is typical in such situations, ADM was not punished to the full force of the law. Had it been, the firm's losses would have run into billions. The chapter also points to a tendency towards recidivism, and to diversity amongst global corporations as a cause for concern: when diversified corporations benefit from a cartel in one line of business, they are also likely to participate in a cartel in another line. The lower costs of modern means of transport and communication are identified as factors facilitating new economy cartels, but also as responsible for increasing convergence amongst national jurisdictions with respect to the content and execution of competition laws. Connor concludes with a particular warning for regional economies looking to base their success on clusters of activity in particular sectors; the benefits from clustering might vanish if antitrust rules are violated.

This last point is particularly pertinent as regional concentration in particular sectors of economic activity, 'clustering' of one form or another, is a key concern in many debates on economic development at the current time. It is also the focus of the next three chapters of the volume.

For James Peoples, the globalisation of business activity makes it imperative that firms adopt strategies that enhance their competitive advantage. He considers one possible strategy to be regional concentration of business operations, and presents evidence to show that many industries in the US are geographically concentrated; for example, he indicates that more than 40 per cent of US aircraft are manufactured in Los Angeles, Seattle or Fort Worth.

Chapter 7 argues that regional concentration may enhance the productivity of businesses. It is hypothesised that, in part, the explanation for productivity improvement might be that locating operations at a few metropolitan areas facilitates the development of centres of expertise. It is further argued that the competitive advantage associated with high productivity also contributes to regional prosperity by lowering employees' risk of job loss, and by providing these employees with high paying jobs. In contrast, it is suggested that the potential for improved industrial performance might not present firms with a sufficiently significant advantage to warrant concentrating their operations; firms might favour geographical dispersion, to avoid high transportation costs and to limit their reliance on any one local labour market. Peoples utilises worker and industry information on manufacturing industries to examine the issues. He concludes that the findings indicate that industry productivity levels are highest when the four major production localities employ 40 per cent of the industry workforce. Further analysis is also said to reveal greater educational attainment by workers employed in these centres of activity; the argument is that local employment of a highly educated workforce helps explain high productivity at such locations. The chapter lends support to municipalities' efforts to help their regions become centres of expertise, and indicates that efforts to develop such centres are well served by municipalities investing in their institutions of higher education.

The topic of Chapter 8, by Stuart O. Schweitzer and Marco R. Di Tommaso, is clusters in new high-technology sectors, including biotechnology. They too have an interest in institutions of higher education, asking whether universities, amongst other things, are important in the clustering process.

The chapter begins with some considerations regarding geographical agglomeration over time, drawing out concerns in the 'old economy' and pointing towards what is additionally relevant about the 'new economy'. It identifies two themes explaining clustering by firms. The first refers to specific factors that draw particular firms to certain localities. In the old economy these place-specific geographic endowments included ease of transportation, the pull of raw materials and the lure of product markets. It is argued that in the new economy the situation is somewhat different; changes in information and communication technologies suggest that transportation costs have been largely eliminated as an important consideration, and 'commerce' is now more a case of transmission of digitised information over the Internet than of exchanges of physical outputs. The second theme emphasises synergies among firms, the advantages of physical proximity. These might include access to a local market for skilled labour, or to specific technical or market knowledge. The authors suggest that in modern, high-technology industries, experience in the likes of Silicon Valley implies that physical proximity to other firms and in particular to other similar, specialised and complementary firms can offer great benefits. At issue are not only the passive exploitation of other firms' presence, but also the active development of strategic relationships.

The role of proximity is pursued in a discussion of the life-cycle of biotechnology firms. This leads to the hypothesis that universities are significant location determinants, because they are sources of knowledge and of scientifically skilled personnel. The emphasis of Schweitzer and Di Tommaso is on research-oriented universities, not educational institutions in general. They conclude that if their depiction of the life-cycle is accurate, and is consistent with the model by which firms cluster together in proximity to research universities, an important policy instrument is clearly suggested: the creation of a network of strong research-oriented universities that are structured so as both to support high-technology firms, and even to promote spin-offs.

In Chapter 9, Marco Bellandi also discusses clustering in the new economy. The motto of Marshall's *Industry and Trade* (1919) is: 'the many in the one, the one in the many'. For Bellandi, it may also be read: 'the global in the local, the local in the global'; global tendencies enter into the life of localities, but any global tendencies emerge as the result of the peculiar manifestations characterising different local contexts.[1] Whilst arguing that Marshall considered this particular ramification, Bellandi also sees it as more evident nowadays, with the diffusion of new information and communication technologies, the widespread activity of private and public transnational organisations, the re-emergence of local and regional contexts of social and economic activity, and innovation.

From such inspiration, Chapter 9 focuses on four concerns. First, it reviews some general points about clustering by considering the experiences of Italian industrial districts, commenting especially on large corporations, external economies, and small-to-medium specialised firms as engines of growth. Second, attention turns to the wider role of clusters in economic development; Bellandi considers the concept of a cluster, its association with territories – explicitly returning the analysis to the idea of localities introduced in Chapter 1 – and the contexts in which clusters emerge and prosper. Third, the chapter contemplates the significance of the new economy for the nature and impact of clustering processes. Fourth, the specific case of South-eastern Wisconsin is discussed, raising queries relevant to many parts of the world about the desirability of clusters as a route to economic success. Concern with this particular case also provides an effective bridge into Part III of the volume.

One aim of Part III is to consider a specific case in further detail, moreover the case that was at the heart of initial discussions motivating the request for contributions to this volume. Another is to draw together aspects of the relevance and applicability of the analysis in Parts I and II: whereas Part I provides anchor points for subsequent chapters, one intention in Part III is to present material that draws on arguments in earlier chapters to discuss experiences and possibilities in a particular case, seeing this as illustrative of more widely applicable points about urban and regional prosperity in a globalised new economy. A third aim of Part III is to reflect on the processes underlying (amongst other things) the publication of this volume.

Throughout the previous chapters, the volume refers to examples from areas in various countries. Included in this, there are periodic, brief references to the state of Wisconsin (US). That case is considered in greater depth in Part III, which accordingly opens with a chapter by Donald A. Nichols providing a detailed discussion of the situation facing a traditional manufacturing area looking to prosper in the modern, global economy. This outlines the current position in the particular case and identifies what its author sees as especially crucial issues at this point in time. The analysis is more widely relevant not least because the people of Wisconsin are facing problems that are shared by many other regions throughout the world as they embark on a new century of change.

Nichols sketches how the new economy and globalisation have affected manufacturing, and notes the challenges posed for the future. It is argued that the first step in recognising these challenges is to understand if there really is such a thing as a 'new economy', and if so, whether it has openings into which a set of 'old economy' industries can be incorporated. Specifically, can an area like Wisconsin use its traditional industries as stepping-stones to join the new economy and enjoy its benefits? Nichols concludes that it can, because in many instances it is the old economy that provides the market for new economy products. The chapter concentrates most of its attention on the large and volatile machinery industry, which provides over half of Wisconsin's exports and which is the sector most sensitive to export fluctuations and import competition. This industry is concentrated in the South-eastern part of the state. Nichols describes what South-eastern Wisconsin might be like if it remains the hub of some old economy machinery industries, but operates in the new economy mode of entrepreneurial venture capitalism while developing new technologies for its traditional industries.

The attention on South-eastern Wisconsin is maintained in Chapter 11. Mark A. Mone reflects on attempts by the University of Wisconsin-Milwaukee to enhance economic development in the area over the period 1998–2002. He describes the context for these efforts, looking at the involvement of the university in a variety of initiatives, and reports on specific outcomes; the chapter includes a detailed report on South-eastern Wisconsin as an Appendix, written by Nancy L. Zimpher, Mark A. Mone, Sammis White, Timothy R. Sheehy and Kris Piwek. The chapter also offers personal conclusions and suggestions about the process of university involvement.

Varied opinions on the role of a university are considered and the lack of a universally agreed approach is noted. Mone argues that a sense of social responsibility and of self-preservation ought to impel universities to engage in issues of local economic development. He discusses the need for different constituencies to be suitably represented, and the implications of absence. The chapter also considers the reactions to a university attempting to take a lead and concerns about leadership more generally. Alluding to the commonly held view in management literature that different skills are required to launch as compared to expand a business, it is suggested that the start of a local economic development process that brings together many and varied constituencies might need the skills of a visionary champion. This would be someone capable of marshalling the different constituents, gaining commitment to overarching themes and goals, and having the connections to bring the necessary resources to bear. To then sustain these efforts, other skills are necessary, those that would ensure that an appropriate infrastructure is resourced and effective. There are potential problems of turf wars as well as of defensive attitudes to change and alleged threats, for example from those already employed in positions of economic development responsibility. He argues that key stakeholders need conviction in the process, and there must be practical forms of collaboration. As for a university in particular, it is concluded that any academic institution involved in local economic development has a significant responsibility. The university must feature a sustained and resourced commitment, a concomitant restructuring of its activities, and understanding and acceptance amongst its academics and administrative staff.

The concluding chapter also provides, as an Appendix, a report that discusses economic prosperity in South-eastern Wisconsin. This report is authored collectively by participants at the L'institute–Milwaukee Workshop on 'Urban and regional prosperity in a globalised economy'. It is entitled 'International perspectives on South-eastern Wisconsin's economic development' and, as detailed in Chapter 12, was first-drafted and debated by participants during the course of the workshop. The report implicitly draws on material presented in earlier chapters of this volume and, like Chapters 10 and 11, is relevant to wider localities.

Moreover, Chapter 12 provides a personal reflection on the process that led to the publication of this volume and the writing of the report, both of which are part of a deliberate attempt to involve international expertise in debates about economic development in particular regions. They are aspects of a process of stimulating change through multinational engagement and debate. Such multinationalism is itself a response to the challenges that regions currently face. What might be advocated is that a like-minded process be introduced in similar circumstances elsewhere, as part of a strategy for ensuring urban and regional prosperity in a globalised new economy. The chapter attempts to draw lessons from experience that might aid future initiatives.

More specifically, in Chapter 12, J. Robert Branston, Roger Sugden and James R. Wilson explore the aims of the L'institute–Milwaukee Workshop as initially conceived, and ask whether these aims have been realised. The chapter seeks to identify problems that were encountered, and make tentative suggestions as to how these might be overcome. The motivation for such an analysis lies in an ongoing concern to become part of the process of economic development in particular localities. In this regard, the current volume is not an end-result. Crucially, then, the chapter concludes with thoughts on how and where the process might develop from here. Amongst the lessons to be learned, special focus is given to the 'insider'/'outsider' issue; that it is not for outsiders to come into town for a couple of weeks and pretend to understand local conditions and desires, let alone attempt to start telling local people how to run their economy. It is emphasised that, if development is to be based on the aims, objectives and actions of the people of a locality, and if those outside the locality might be able to contribute ideas and suggestions for locals to act upon as they decide, then both insiders and outsiders need to be aware of each other's roles, respectful of each other, and willing to learn together as the process unfolds. This is a point that is also relevant to the activities of various international organisations, for example the World Bank, and successfully taking it into account is a prerequisite if economies are to benefit from multi-national interaction. One of the motivations for this volume is to bring such benefits closer to realisation.

NOTES

* This contribution to the volume is presented as a form of abstract. It draws freely from correspondence with authors and from the words of each chapter, using those words without quotation marks (the inclusion of which might have made the overview less easy to read). The aim is to assist the reader by providing a sort of summary. In no circumstances ought this contribution to be quoted in its own right; quotation ought always to be from the specific chapters that follow. It is of course the case that any misrepresentations and errors in this overview are the sole responsibility of its authors.

1. This is a point emphasised by Bellandi in his presentation at the Second L'institute–Milwaukee Workshop.

REFERENCE

Marshall, A. (1919), *Industry and Trade*, London: Macmillan.

PART I

1. Economic 'prosperity' and 'globalisation': an agenda and perspective

Roger Sugden and James R. Wilson[*]

1. INTRODUCTION

The principal aim of this volume is to provide interesting insights into the determinants of urban and regional prosperity in a 'globalised', 'new' economy. This is a subject that raises numerous issues that can be addressed from many dimensions. The intention is not to be exhaustive, rather it is to contribute to a better understanding of possible ways forward by analysing particular topics. In doing so, the volume uses examples drawn from experiences throughout the world, although it concentrates (especially in Part III) on the case of Wisconsin.

As a starting-point, the contributors – and more generally the participants at the Second L'institute–Milwaukee Workshop from which the volume is derived – were asked to consider topics from a set of questions. These were identified out of an assessment of the past, present and future for Wisconsin manufacturing in the globalised economy. The questions drew very heavily on Nichols (2000), a slightly revised version of which is published as Chapter 10 of this volume. The organisers of the workshop prepared the questions.[1]

Several key issues were highlighted as the overlapping and interrelated themes around which analysis was structured and on which contributions were requested. These and some of the questions that they suggest are outlined in Section 2 of this chapter. In part, the objective of reproducing the starting-point in Section 2 is to position subsequent contributions to the volume explicitly in the broader context from which they were derived. It is also to provide a springboard, a stimulant to further questioning and understanding in the future.

The objective of subsequent sections in this chapter is to begin to explore items underlying this initial agenda in a manner that provides a perspective on the overall problem of ensuring urban and regional prosperity in a globalised new economy. In essence, we focus on aspects of the conceptualisation of 'urban', 'regional', 'prosperity', 'globalised' and 'new' economy.

Section 3 analyses 'globalisation' and 'new' economy. We identify an approach that is broad – encompassing the economic, social, political and cultural – and that suggests a particular concern with transport, communication and information technologies, and with knowledge and learning. We suggest both a broad definition of globalisation and a more focused approach. Production governance is argued to be a key issue. This suggests that economic democracy and effective voice are fundamental to an understanding of 'prosperity' in modern economies, to an understanding of what is meant by 'prosperity' and of how it can be attained. The link between globalisation, the new economy and a concern with urban and regional settings is pursued in Section 4. We argue the appropriateness of analysing development in terms of 'localities', a perspective that implies that prosperity in both urban and regional areas be seen as part of the same process. Attention is also focused on the significance of networking and some of the points are illustrated by examples of city development. Conclusions to the chapter are presented in Section 5.

2.   INITIAL QUESTIONS

- *What are the distinguishing features of the new economy, and how might these be managed to ensure urban and regional prosperity?* For Nichols (2000), the distinguishing feature is the role and nature of information, including information technology, industrial technology and branding, although some might argue that there are other characteristics that need to be highlighted. Nichols argues that information technology costs are rising as a share of total manufacturing costs, that information is the key component of value added and that the way information is handled is fundamental to the generation of wealth. However, what is the evidence for the significance of information, including information technology costs? How will information technology change the supply chain and distribution channels? What will be the impact of peer-to-peer (P2P) technology, not least on how firms might cooperate with each other and with customers? Is information the key, or is it really knowledge and learning? What would information, knowledge and learning requirements imply for workforce development, and correspondingly for needs in education and training?
- *Even if the new economy raises fresh issues, are there 'old' concerns that remain critical and that necessitate attention?* One view is that, in any economy, the determination of production strategy is the key issue; the ability to make the strategic decisions is fundamental to welfare. In fact, by definition, to make the strategic decisions is to determine the

aims of production; to explore the aims raises fundamental questions about the desires of the people of a region, fundamental questions about what is meant by the term 'prosperity'. The significance of strategy can also be illustrated by the 'hollowing out' problems that were faced by Wisconsin and elsewhere in the 1980s (see for example the chapter by Keith Cowling and Philip Tomlinson on Japan's machinery industries). Strategic decisions were made within firms to locate manufacturing activity outside of the older industrialised areas. What are the implications for different models of strategic decision-making for the new economy? Is hollowing out still an issue? Does the conduct of firms headquartered outside a region (or, more generally, without a clear commitment to a particular region) raise questions about future prosperity? Another long-running concern in the old economy has been the gains that might be had from mixing and balancing various types of organisation and activity. For example, public and private enterprises (see Johan Willner's chapter on enterprise formation); non-government and government, local, national and supranational public bodies; manufacturing and service enterprises. To what extent do these remain key issues for urban and regional prosperity in the twenty-first century, and to what extent does the new economy face new problems in these respects? Does urban and regional prosperity depend upon manufacturing success? Put differently, must localities and regions stimulate export-producing industries to prosper? Is it wise for a region to focus on a particular sector(s) and, if so, how should the sector(s) be chosen? Nichols (2000) advocates that Wisconsin focuses on the machinery sector because it has a long and successful tradition in this industry, and because nationally the industry has concentrated in the state. Is national concentration in the past a key issue for today and the future, and does concentration matter at all? (See the chapters by James Peoples on concentration in the US, and John Connor on global cartels.) Further, if selected sectors are chosen, how do we ensure that the required labour force is available? (On this, see the chapters by Stanley Siebert and Johan Willner.) Associated with this, does manufacturing in certain sectors of the new economy leave a place for skilled craftwork (as Nichols suggests it does)? If so, how does that impact on workforce development?

- *Does a locality's relationship and linkage to the wider world, both to different parts of the same country and to different countries, have an impact on urban and regional prosperity, and if so how might this impact be influenced?* Nichols (2000) focuses on the maximisation of value added in a region's manufacturing, and emphasises links through international trade (especially manufacturing exports) and through global financial markets (as a determinant of general economic conditions and thus of industrial development). Is it appropriate (also) to focus on relationships and linkages other than trade and finance? For example, are relationships based on the accumulation of knowledge and learning opportunities especially important? (See the chapter by Kaye Husbands discussing technological development in Mexico, also those by Mark Mone and Rob Branston et al. on universities and university activity.) Nichols suggests that there might be links between Wisconsin and Silicon Valley to develop leading-edge information technology for the machinery sector. This prompts the possibility of other such links around the world, all as part of an attempt to maximise value added from manufacturing in a particular region. It also points to the need for a workforce with certain sorts of skills and attributes, which therefore has implications for the availability of appropriate education and training opportunities.

- *Is the presence of clusters, agglomerations and/or networks crucial for urban and regional prosperity and, if so, how might beneficial outcomes be stimulated?* One of the most prominent concerns of researchers in industrial economic and business development over recent years has been the grouping of enterprises and organisations, and the relationships within these groupings. (In this volume, see the contribution by Marco Bellandi, amongst others.) Nichols (2000), for example, refers to the 1990s 'transformation of the old Midwest manufacturing economy from a group of loosely connected factories into a tightly integrated network of quality-conscious, customer-driven managerial teams'. He goes on to emphasise the creation of particular sorts of network, supply chains, as critical to Wisconsin's success: 'whole new industries of supply chain management have emerged, led by the trucking firms who specialise in minimising the costs of coordinating production activities over great distances'. What characteristics of clusters, agglomerations and/or networks are required for urban and regional prosperity? (See, for example, the chapter by Stuart Schweitzer and Marco Di Tommaso on clustering amongst biotechnology firms.) Is networking a way to reduce production costs? What form(s) of the supply chain is (are) required? How is networking best served by P2P technology? What are the generally applicable lessons to be taken from an understanding of the experiences of particular industries and/or particular geographical areas? What is the possibility for a network spreading across localities and indeed nations, and how might this be stimulated by public policy? Are networks a source of economies of scale? Nichols suggests that economies of scale in information can be reaped by individual firm growth or by merger/takeover.

However, the literature on networks suggests that smaller firms have cooperated to achieve scale economies. Is interfirm cooperation typically possible and, where it is, what are the implications for antitrust as applied to urban and regional prosperity? Are there also possibilities for cooperation to yield economies of scope?

- *In the new economy, what is the best mix and what are the optimum relationships between firms of different geographical 'origin' and between firms of different size?* Nichols (2000) emphasises the importance of competition from outside, for example the influence of foreign competition forcing local manufacturers to become 'lean and mean'. He also focuses on the influence of non-US transnational corporations and recent takeovers of local firms, suggesting that it would have been more desirable if the takeovers and therefore the control had gone the other way. 'Far better for Wisconsin, for example, if Case had bought New Holland than that New Holland bought Case. Far better for Wisconsin, for example, if Giddings and Lewis had purchased the machine tool division of Thyssen than that Thyssen bought Giddings and Lewis.' What about localities other than Wisconsin, would it have been better for them? Is there a possibility for urban and regional prosperity that might benefit all localities? Is the impact of production being controlled from outside (but in the same nation) different to the control being from another nation? What sort of outside investment is most desirable and how can it be best attracted? Vital in this respect, can a region brand or rebrand itself so as to achieve its aims? As for firm size, some might argue that the relationship between large firms and SMEs (small and medium-sized firms) is one of the determinants of urban and regional prosperity. In Wisconsin there has been concern about large firms buying up the small but this is a wider issue; other regions face similar quandaries, not least because of the potential effects on innovation and industrial dynamism. To what extent is it necessary for urban and regional prosperity that there is a vibrant small-firm sector? What are the prospects for smaller firms avoiding dependence on their large-firm rivals and customers? Do large firms necessarily dominate supply chains? Is the presence of large firms essential? How might prospects be swayed by public initiatives? What are the consequences for the optimum mix across firm size for workforce development? For example, what are the educational and training requirements to ensure a vibrant supply of entrepreneurs able to establish new businesses? Is the activity of 'serial entrepreneurs' in creating small firms a key factor for prosperity in each and every region?

3.   'GLOBALISATION' AND THE 'NEW' ECONOMY

Multidisciplinarity, Geography and Technology

To begin to explore some of these questions, an important foundation is to consider the concept of globalisation. For some considerable time, globalisation has been a fashionable topic. It is currently difficult to read a newspaper, watch a television documentary or study an academic article without frequently encountering some reference to the concept, and it is clear that the framework of analysis in many spheres is becoming heavily influenced by so-called globalisation. The subject of 'economy and globalisation', for example, has recently spawned a huge literature;[2] its importance essentially stems from acknowledgement that past, present and future globalisation processes undeniably have strong implications for how problems of economic development are analysed.

The popularity of globalisation, however, brings with it the danger that, in increased use, there is a failure to articulate exactly what is meant by the term and by the changes to which it refers. Indeed, Scholte (2000) notes that 'in spite of a deluge of publications on the subject, our analyses of globalisation tend to remain conceptually inexact, empirically thin, historically and culturally illiterate, normatively shallow and politically naive. Although globalisation is widely assumed to be crucially important, we generally have scant idea what, more precisely, it entails' (Scholte, 2000, p. 1). Clear definitions are crucial with such a broad and potentially complex phenomenon, so as to set the context and parameters for debate. Yet they are often overlooked, due to the very nature of globalisation as difficult to confine to one sphere, and thus to define precisely or to measure empirically.

Globalisation is a multifaceted phenomenon, with implications that encompass not just the economic but also the social, political, cultural and geographical. Radice (2000), for example, notes that 'globalisation has been a prominent topic among geographers and sociologists as well as economists and political scientists, and is studied within every paradigm, from neoclassical economics to postmodern social theory to realist international relations theory to Marxism' (Radice, 2000, p. 6). In this regard, Vellinga (2000) comments that it has the characteristics of a 'theoretical umbrella', in a similar way to dependency theory.

One approach to the problem of definition is to follow Kudrle's (1999) suggestion that globalisation be considered with regard to the specific intent of those using the term.[3] Economic definitions of globalisation, for example, are frequently rooted in market analysis; De la Dehesa (2000, p. 17) defines it as 'a dynamic process of growing liberty and world integration in the markets for labour, goods, services, technology and capital'.[4] It is likely, however, that scholars in different fields would choose to root their definitions in alternatives to the market, focusing instead on cultural, social, spatial or political factors, or indeed on non-market aspects of the economy.

Waters (2001), for example, argues that *the* key figure in the formalisation and specification of the concept of globalisation is the sociologist Robertson. For Robertson (1992, p. 8), globalisation refers 'both to the compression of the world and the intensification of consciousness of the world as a whole', a definition that is clearly distinct from the market-centred perspective of the economist. From the geographer's perspective the definition differs yet again, with the focus shifting to the scale and scope of territories such as cities or regions. In discussing the rescaling of urban governance in the European Union, for example, Brenner (1999, p. 432) conceives globalisation as 'a reterritorialisation of both socioeconomic and political-institutional spaces that unfolds simultaneously upon multiple, superimposed, geographical scales'.

Leaving aside, for a moment, the issue of definition, further debates rage around the extent, impact and consequences of globalisation, the forces and causes behind globalisation, the policies to be pursued in response to globalisation, and even the chronology of globalisation.[5] With regard to the latter, for example, many authors question whether globalisation is a new phenomenon. De la Dehesa (2000) notes that a similar process, of a form almost as intense as that which we see now, was evident between 1870 and 1914. Hirst and Thompson (1999, p. 2) go further and state that 'in some respects, the current international economy is *less* open and integrated than the regime that prevailed from 1870 to 1914'. Such arguments clearly depend on the definition of globalisation that underpin them. If the issue is 'market' globalisation then these authors may have a strong case. In contrast, if the issue encompasses wider factors, then it would be difficult to deny that those commentators claiming globalisation to be a 'new' phenomenon, influenced by the likes of jet travel and computers, also have some degree of credibility to their arguments.

What is perhaps clear above all else, however, and arguably what most people consider when they think of current globalisation, is that throughout the world there is a development towards levels and forms of global interaction that are significantly *different* from previous intercourse at international level. The difference is highlighted by Scholte (2000, p. 3) in terms of the importance of relations that transcend borders. He argues that globalisation is a 'new and distinctive' phenomenon only when it is conceptualised in terms of 'deterritorialisation'. He suggests that 'the proliferation and spread of supraterritorial – or what we can alternatively term "transworld" or "transborder" – connections brings an end to what could be called "territorialism", that is, a situation where social geography is *entirely* territorial'.[6] Scholte's use of 'trans' as a prefix is based upon the notion of transcending territorial space.[7]

Unfortunately, perhaps, the prefix also has connotations of a transverse structure, one that merely crosses territories. The latter has very different implications to transcending, and connotations that might better describe what Scholte (2000, p. 53) terms the 'tens of thousands of global companies', the transnational corporations. Moreover, he does not explore the implications of *multi-territorial* activity, an example of which might be the multinationalism advocated in Cowling and Sugden (1999). This multiterritorialisation can be argued to imply 'of many territories, rooted in and growing out of many territories'. It can also be seen as a route to transcending territories.

The importance of transcending borders is also associated with recognition of recent advances in transport, information and communication technologies. These advances have markedly eased previous difficulties inherent in interaction over large distances. Not only have the costs (both actual and time) of long-distance transport and telecommunications fallen dramatically, but the last decade has seen the advent and evolution of email and the Internet. These new technologies herald the cheap and almost instantaneous transfer of vast amounts of information across the entire wired-up world, and create the potential (as yet only partially realised?) for a new 'layer' of market and non-market activities that are detached from physical localities.[8]

Economic activity focused around these developments is commonly termed the 'new' economy, although there is a degree of confusion as to what, exactly, this constitutes. For some authors the phrase new economy is used in a relatively narrow sense, to refer simply to technological advances. Gordon (2000, pp. 71–2), for example, defines it as 'the post-1995 acceleration in the rate of technical change in information technology together with the development of the Internet', and seeks to compare it with the great inventions that have previously transformed economies. For others, however, the new economy is a wider phenomenon, encompassing both new technologies, and the emerging global economic relationships that they help to facilitate and that in turn condition their use.[9] In this sense the new economy is something deeper, with roots fundamentally in the capitalist organisation of economic activity. Reich (2001, p. 1), for example, points to a society where 'we can get exactly what we want from almost anywhere at the lowest price and highest value'. The roots of such developments are seen to lie in modern capitalism, although advancements in technology combine in driving them to a 'new' level, primarily because it becomes increasingly easier to transfer information, and thus, it is claimed, to compare, contrast and make informed decisions.[10] This has similarities to the argument in Radice (2000, p. 13) that 'globalisation can best be understood as an aspect of capitalism'. Indeed, it is difficult to separate either globalisation or the new economy from the capitalist context in which they have evolved and are evolving, and thus also difficult to separate them from one another.[11]

Drawing these ideas together, a useful starting-point is to define globalisation broadly, capturing its cross-disciplinary character, recognising its roots in a changing geography and identifying its association with alterations in transport, information and communication technologies. In essence, we suggest that:

> globalisation is a multidisciplinary process in which a new geography and new technologies imply changes in activity and behaviour.

In more detail:[12]

> globalisation is a process in which the constraints of geography on economic, political, social and cultural activity and behaviour change, becoming less territorialised and more trans- or multi-territorial; it is a process that stimulates and that is stimulated by alterations in transport, information and communication technologies; and it is a process in which people are more or less aware of the changes, implying that their activity and behaviour is therefore modified.

The focus is on how people respond to the processes that are occurring, processes that include movements towards a new economy as an integral part of globalisation and that, more generally, are rooted in modern capitalism.[13]

Knowledge and Governance

Whilst such a broad conceptualisation provides a solid foundation for analysis, it has a strength that is also a weakness. The definition we have provided encompasses many perspectives but in so doing fails to identify and highlight all that we see as especially crucial. This probably makes it more widely acceptable but at the same time less interesting.[14] However, the purpose of definitions is not simply to gain consensus, rather it is to provide an appropriate analytical foundation. It is for this reason that we suggest the broad definition of globalisation can be usefully refined, narrowed to provide a more insightful foundation for analysis. In this respect, we return to Kudrle (1999) and advocate a conceptualisation that accommodates the concerns of its users. More particularly, for an analysis of the implications of globalisation for economic development we suggest that the conceptualisation of globalisation needs to incorporate two key, related issues: knowledge and governance.

Knowledge (and learning) is a key driver behind the ability to respond to the changes that are occurring with the globalisation recognised in our broad definition. This suggests that it is a fundamental concern. Indeed, it is no coincidence that knowledge has become acknowledged in the mainstream development agenda as perhaps *the* key issue at a time when the forces of globalisation have accelerated in conjunction with new technologies.[15] Given movement towards a new economy, where knowledge is seen to be the key to realising returns,[16] it has become generally accepted that education and the generation and diffusion of knowledge are vital and central components to development processes (see, amongst others, Schweitzer and Di Tommaso in Chapter 8 of this volume, Nichols in Chapter 10 and Florida, 1994). While there are hints that knowledge could play a wider role in the development of economies,[17] the standard premise for these arguments is essentially a market perspective. Knowledge is seen as important in terms of the value it can add to production processes, and crucially, therefore, the ability to attract investment, in particular foreign direct investment (FDI). Indeed, a primary concern from this perspective is with bridging knowledge gaps so that localities can 'compete' on a more equal footing, or extending knowledge gaps so that localities can enhance their 'competitive advantage'. In a sense, therefore, the argument is very similar to that for flexible labour markets; like flexible (cheap) labour, knowledge is seen as a route to competitive advantage.[18]

While we recognise the so-called competitive imperative for knowledge in a new (and global) economy, our concern is primarily from an alternative perspective. We see knowledge and learning as central to development, central to each individual (and the communities that they form) realising their potential. They are important because they afford people the opportunity to engage effectively in the decision-making processes that govern development. In turn, this enables development to reflect accurately the aims and objectives of localities, an issue of paramount importance to the meaning of development itself.

The significance of decision-making processes is argued elsewhere. Consider, for example, the governance of transnational corporations, of what Scholte (2000) calls 'global companies'. The typical modern corporation is governed by an elite, only a subset of those with an interest in its activities. To govern is to make the strategic decisions, to 'control' a corporation. It is an elite that determines a corporation's strategy and therefore its impact. The result is strategic failure: concentration of strategic decision-making power in the hands of an elite implies a failure to govern production in the interests of the community at large. To avoid such failure, the democratisation of governance is required (see, for example, Cowling and Sugden, 1999 and Branston et al., 2001, also the contribution to this volume by Keith Cowling and Philip R. Tomlinson). Achieving this would imply a shift from governance designed to yield prosperity for an elite. Rather, there would be governance in search of a prosperity that is based on the concerns of everyone interested in a corporation's activities.[19]

More generally, a similar argument for democratisation applies to all aspects of economies, and to economies as a whole. Take, as another example, the position of so-called 'developing' countries (see especially Sugden and Wilson, 2002). Since the early 1980s their economic prosperity has been largely influenced by the 'Washington Consensus',[20] an approach that emphasises policy measures such as fiscal discipline, financial liberalisation, trade liberalisation, privatisation, deregulation, and limited government intervention. The extent of convergence on appropriate economic policy to be pursued by 'less developed' and 'transition' economies has been remarkable over the last two decades.[21] Also remarkable, however, has been the perceived lack of progress. The structural adjustment programmes, through which policies have been transmitted, have been widely and heavily criticised, and for large numbers of people Washington Consensus policies are associated with continuing poverty and rising inequality. This strikes at the credibility of, and hence support for, the development agenda, something that can be seen in the collapse of World Trade Organisation (WTO) talks in Seattle in November 1999, and protests wherever the forces at the core of the Consensus meet.[22] The dwindling support for this agenda has been recognised by the institutions at the heart of the Consensus, and the World Bank and IMF have indeed made movements towards changes in emphasis and approach in their policy prescriptions.[23] However, while such re-evaluation is clearly necessary, it is important first to reflect on *why* the Washington Consensus agenda has failed to generate the necessary success and support. We suggest that the explanation is an exclusion from governance, a failure to engage people in the decisions and processes surrounding their development. Evolution of the Washington Consensus and encouragement of a certain sort of private sector economy has been associated with monopoly power and a denial of access to the 'global' economy for the vast majority of potential participants.[24] This denial not only implies an absence of provision, an absence of material welfare, it even implies a failure to include the majority in the determination of the aims and objectives of economic activity, the most fundamental of strategic decisions faced by an economy. This is an exclusion from determining the aims and objectives of development, from determining what is meant by 'prosperity'.

The especial significance of knowledge is that it is vital for the democratisation of decision-making. In particular, it helps to free people to participate fully in the governance of their locality;[25] to become involved in the (formal and informal, interrelated networks for the) governance of firms, institutions, government and other economic actors. Moreover, where effective governance does not exist, it helps to free people to ensure that it becomes established and evolves towards effectiveness.

In this sense, we view knowledge as essentially *active* and *dynamic*. The crucial issue is not one of knowledge of 'facts', rather it is far deeper. Criticising educational methods that 'discourage original thinking', Fromm (1941) argues against the 'pathetic superstition ... that by knowing more and more facts one arrives at knowledge of reality'.[26] Similarly, good governance necessitates that each interested person be able to think about and therefore

participate fully in the governance process. Each must be active, alert to the
necessity for certain types of knowledge, able to use their voice in the pursuit
of that knowledge, able to use that knowledge in influencing strategic ways
forward.[27] Moreover, while information and education give people the basic
ability and confidence to participate actively in the governance of their development, participation itself is a learning process that generates further knowledge. In particular, it generates knowledge around practical issues of
governance; it allows localities to establish what works for them, and what
does not. In turn, localities learn more about economic democracy, which may
enable improvements in governance that further increase the benefits and
incentives for participation. The idea, then, is of a virtuous circle where localities are feeling their way forward; evolving towards ways in which they can
govern themselves to ensure attainment of *their own* development aims and
objectives.

This is in line with the observation by Hirschman (1970), in comparing
'exit' and 'voice', that 'while exit requires nothing but a clearcut either–or
decision, voice is essentially an *art* evolving in new directions'.[28] He goes on
to argue that this presents an inherent bias towards exit that tends to 'atrophy
the development of the art of voice'.[29] A similar argument could be made with
regard to participation in the governance of localities; development of the
virtuous circle might be hindered by the difficulties and frustrations of ensuring democratic involvement. This also runs into Fromm's (1941) view that
freedom can be accompanied by uncertainties and fears that lead people to
seek an escape.[30] In 'free market' economies, Fromm argues that people can
react to having 'freedom from constraints' without having 'freedom to do' by
turning their backs on freedom, accepting conformity and the decisions of
others.[31] As Branston et al. (2001) suggest, it might be similarly argued that
freedom from governance by others without having the freedom to govern
oneself, runs the risk of people seeking to escape from governance alto-
gether.[32]

The challenge, therefore, is to set a virtuous circle in motion, so that the
active and dynamic concept of knowledge can be realised. Knowledge that
contributes to (and in turn is generated by) involvement in governance is
crucial to the way in which people respond to globalisation and the new economy. It essentially determines whether these broad processes can be harnessed
to further the prosperity of a locality, as defined by the locality itself, or
whether they are geared solely towards serving 'elite' or 'external' interests.

Thus we suggest a more focused definition of globalisation, reflecting these
key issues:

> globalisation is a multidisciplinary process in which a new geography and new tech-
> nologies imply changes in activity and behaviour, and in which knowledge and
> governance are fundamental to the attainment of economic prosperity.

In addition, our discussion points to a distinction between two types of globalisation:

elite globalisation, a process harnessed to further the prosperity of an elite

and

democratic globalisation, a process harnessed to further the prosperity of all people in a locality.

4.   REGIONAL AND URBAN PROSPERITY

Nations, Regions and Localities

Following from the discussion in Section 3, globalisation can be seen to present a *new level* of analysis for economic, social and political problems, or, at least, a level of analysis that is *changing significantly in its nature*. Within this new analytical context, specific territories – whether these are 'cities', 'regions', 'nations' or something different – might be argued to play an integral part in the changes currently occurring. Likewise, the responses of territories to globalisation might be considered significant.

Unsurprisingly, given the lack of consensus surrounding all aspects of globalisation, there is disagreement over the role of nations in a global and new economy. This debate is not new, and was addressed in 1918 by Bucharin, who contrasted the dual trends of nationalisation and internationalisation, arguing that the latter was built around the former.[33] More recently, authors such as Hirst and Thompson (1999), Wade (1996), Ruigrok and van Tulder (1995) and Gordon (1988) have presented the case for what Radice (2000, p. 5) terms 'progressive nationalism': 'they contest what they see as the predominant neoliberal ideology of globalism, which is used as a weapon by economic and political elites to defend their wealth and power'. For these authors, as with Bucharin, nations still have a key role to play in economic and social activity. This is in contrast to what some see as the vision of a truly global economy; a borderless world made up of fully global companies, in which nation states have little role. Kindleberger (1969, p. 207) hinted at such a scenario, asserting that 'the nation-state is just about through as an economic unit . . . containerization . . . airbuses, and the like will not permit sovereign independence of the nation-state in economic affairs'. More recently, similar arguments have been associated with authors such as Ohmae (1990, 1995) and Reich (1992), although Radice (2000) warns that their work has often been caricatured. (See also the contribution to this volume by Husbands.)

Despite these differences, a common thread in the literature is that globalisation processes are inherently associated with 'regionalisation' *of some form*.[34] For example, Ohmae (1995) argues that while traditional 'nation states' have become unnatural units in a global economy, 'region states', based on economically functional rather than political boundaries, are the right size and scale to tap into this economy. Related to this, Storper (1997) heralds the resurgence of regional economies in a globalisation framework, stressing the key role of regional communities and firms as the basic building blocks of an increasingly connected world. In some sense, therefore, there is a clearly acknowledged regional dimension to globalisation, presenting a strong premise for looking at 'regions' as important units of analysis. Moreover, the imperative is twofold, given our concern with knowledge, learning and communication. This is partly because formal channels of education and learning – such as schools, colleges and universities – are often regionally based. In addition, people communicate and learn by virtue of living in proximity to one another, including geographical proximity.[35] This implies that knowledge, learning and communication require consideration at a regional level, contributing to the need to examine in more detail what might be meant by the concept of a region.

Vellinga (2000, p. 7) argues that 'regions are mostly products of history . . . [that] cannot always be defined in a strict geographical sense. The boundaries are often not clearly delimited and may shift with changes in the development process. The formation of these regions results from the development of material interests and related social classes and power relations in a socio-spatial context. This process will often also involve the formation of communities of belief and identity'. Along with acknowledgement that regions are not *fixed* entities, there is a clear distinction made here between 'region' and 'community'. This suggests the possibility of a layered approach to the units with which we analyse development, so as to avoid rigid, fixed categorisations and so as to incorporate different notions of 'community'. In particular, we suggest that it is useful to refer to the concept of 'locality' as distinct from 'region' or 'nation', terms that often carry specific, fixed connotations. We define a 'locality' as a local geographical area characterised by certain common institutions, practices and identity, and by the relationships that these foster between actors. Such a definition gives fluidity, allowing us to consider different 'layers' of locality, and to accommodate the different communities that exist within and across these layers.

To illustrate, consider a large town or city. Whilst a geographical district within the city might be considered a specific locality, so too might the city as a whole and indeed the wider area of which the city is a part. One possibility is to think of these distinct entities as part of an interrelated whole, encompassing not one but many localities. The 'first' layer comprises localities defined around local shops and firms, churches, government, media and grass roots organisations. In the metropolitan area of Milwaukee, for example, these localities might include districts ('villages') such as Shorewood and Bayside. For each such locality, however, there are likely to be strong links in terms of employment, administration and social factors with other areas in the city (defined in the same way). What happens in one locality will affect others and in this sense each cannot be isolated. In particular, some areas within a city may be focal points for a significant firm or institution – such as a university – that is important to many other parts of the city. Similarly, the centre of the city, or 'downtown' area, may be important to other 'localities', although this is said to be changing with the new economy.[36] The idea of 'locality' can therefore be seen in terms of intertwined layers. Specific areas of a city can be 'localities', as can the city as a whole, or the geographical area encompassing nearby towns and villages that rely on the city. This is illustrated in Figure 1.1.[37] In the case of Milwaukee, this approach allows us to treat the city as a locality, but also to recognise the layers of locality that underpin the city as a whole. It also acknowledges the roles that Milwaukee and its underpinning localities play in the geographical area more widely defined, for example, in the state of Wisconsin.

Moreover, such an approach allows us to incorporate different concepts of community into the analysis. Dewey (1916, p. 5), for example, defines community in terms of common aims and beliefs, and their communication: 'there is more than a verbal tie between the words common, community, and communication. Men live in a community in virtue of the things which they have in common; and communication is the way in which they come to possess things in common. What they must have in common in order to form a community or society are aims, beliefs, aspirations, knowledge – a common understanding – like-mindedness as the sociologists say'. This can be applied to the 'first' layer of locality, existing around local shops and institutions. The people that occupy these localities are communities by nature of living together and communicating around such local institutions. A layered approach, however, also recognises that communities exist across and within these localities on work, social, religious, ethnic and other grounds. Thus there are also layered 'communities' intertwined with layered 'localities', the likelihood being that individuals are members of several different but related communities spanning different layers of locality. The fluidity of this approach is in contrast to a more rigid analysis focused on fixed historical or administrative regions, which often do not correspond naturally to social, economic or cultural relationships.[38]

From this perspective the notions of 'urban' and 'regional' prosperity can be seen as part of the same process. While the word urban conventionally relates to a city or town, the word region traditionally refers to any area

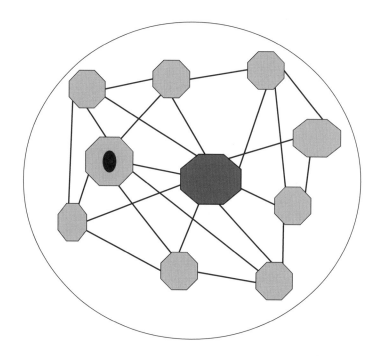

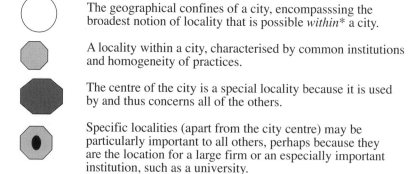

The geographical confines of a city, encompasssing the broadest notion of locality that is possible *within** a city.

A locality within a city, characterised by common institutions and homogeneity of practices.

The centre of the city is a special locality because it is used by and thus concerns all of the others.

Specific localities (apart from the city centre) may be particularly important to all others, perhaps because they are the location for a large firm or an especially important institution, such as a university.

Links between localities, thus decision-making channels for broader notions of locality.

Note: *Localities might also exist beyond a city.

Figure 1.1   Localities and linkages within a city: intertwined layers

considered as a unit for geographical, functional, social or cultural reasons.[39] Often this is a fixed administrative area in terms of government, such as a US 'state' or a European 'nation' or 'region'. It may, indeed, be a city. From the perspective developed above, however, the distinction loses some of its importance. A city or town is both a locality in its own right (comprising other intertwined localities and communities), and potentially part of a larger locality taking in surrounding areas (that may or may not correspond to a historically defined region).

Networking and Governance

Implicit in this approach is the concept of 'networking'. The 'first', most 'local' layer is defined around local institutions, and the relationships and communication that these facilitate between actors (see also the chapter in this volume by Bellandi, and those by Schweitzer and Di Tommaso, and Mone). Likewise, the concept of intertwined layers relies on networks of relationships between actors and communities across localities, both within specific urban concentrations and encompassing the wider geographical areas around them. Indeed, relationships across localities need not be confined to localities in geographical proximity. For example, in a global and new economy it might seem natural that localities, and actors within localities, could also form networks for cooperation, competition and exchange of experiences that are multinational in nature, transcending previous geographical borders. These processes, both within and across localities, might be fostered by appropriate use of the Internet.[40]

Following from our arguments in the previous section, the governance of networks is a key consideration in terms of achieving prosperity that is recognised by all actors within each interlinked 'locality'.[41] In particular, we envisage the possibility of such networks as facilitating decision-making that can move localities towards *their own* aims and objectives, in the context of the pressures and opportunities presented by the global and new economy. Within this, our concern is essentially with the governance of 'production' within and across localities, as it is production that determines the 'prosperity' of communities. Moreover, production is not confined to the production of goods and services (and hence employment, and material prosperity) but also encompasses the production of knowledge, health, and general social well-being. In turn, these form part of the virtuous circle that can facilitate greater involvement in governance networks, and a voice for everyone in their collective prosperity. This returns the discussion to the distinction between 'elite' and 'democratic' globalisation. We advocate governance networks that require more than mere cooperation and partnership across 'stakeholders',[42] that are neither designed to serve elites nor hijacked by elites, be these internal to a locality or external. Achieving this is the biggest challenge in ensuring urban and regional prosperity, especially given the prominence of transnational capital in a global and new economy, and the powerful external pressures that this places on local development.

As for the view that localities and actors could form networks in the absence of geographical proximity, in one way these are already observed; the concept of global networks of urban localities is illustrated, for example, by the growing literature on 'world cities'.[43] Fundamental to the world cities literature, however, is a hierarchical structure of city relationships; one of the theses comprising Friedman's (1986) seminal 'world city hypothesis' is that 'key cities throughout the world are used by global capital as "basing points" in the spatial organization and articulation of production and markets. The resulting linkages make it possible to arrange world cities into a complex spatial hierarchy'.[44] Such linkages are transnational in the sense that they suggest a transverse structure across localities, with transnational capital and transnational corporations as the driving force. They do not, however, imply a transcending of localities in a way that is truly *multi*national. In particular, the existence of a hierarchy serves to remove the democracy inherent in networking between equal partners. In addition, basing the relationships on *trans*national capital removes the fundamental rooting of networks in their constituent localities.

A key implication of the world cities literature is that the hierarchy of cities is determined by the location of transnational capital. For Friedman (1986), world cities are the basing points for transnational capital, implying a concentration of corporate headquarters, while for Sassen (1991, p. 324) they are seen as 'centers of finance and as centers for global servicing and management', implying a key role in servicing transnational capital. Both approaches result in a hierarchy of cities in which the location of global capital is seen as paramount.[45] Moreover, the links between cities in such a model are also defined by flows (of information, capital and personnel) between transnational firms and institutions. Indeed, Castells (1996, p. 386) focuses his analysis on *flows between cities*, what he terms the 'network society'. He argues that 'the global city is not a place, but a process. A process by which the centers of production and consumption of advanced services, and their ancillary local societies, are connected in a global network, while simultaneously downplaying the linkages with their hinterlands, on the basis of information flows'. This suggests a concept of networking between world cities that is not fully rooted locally; it crosses above the localities comprising and surrounding cities, and is dominated by the agenda of a transnational elite. The desire to attract and maintain this transnational elite has implications for the way in which cities across the hierarchical spectrum, from world cities to peripheral cities, are able to govern their own development.

The city of Birmingham (England) is an interesting example. It has under-gone a substantial transformation over the last two decades, stimulating a debate over its alleged success. In particular, Henry and Passmore (1999, pp. 61–2) show concern that in its quest to become a world city, Birmingham has rejected its local roots and instead sought to create an enclave for international capital in the city centre. They argue that the flagship development projects have created 'a space for the national and international business/tourist class, which is increasingly divorced from its regional and local context', and that 'a city is being made to show and entertain investors rather than for local people to live in'. This is the danger inherent in an approach to city development that essentially aims to attract an elite. Arguments that the wealth that this elite brings to the city will 'trickle-down' to benefit all of its citizens miss the point. What matters is that all citizens have the opportunity and ability to become involved in the democratic governance of their locality, not least to define the prosperity that they seek from development.[46] In turn, this principle must be reflected in relationships with other localities, whether in geographical prox-imity or not, so that networking is truly *multi*locational (rather than simply *trans*locational, in the sense of a transverse structure).

In the case of Birmingham, Henry and Passmore (ibid., p. 66) go on to suggest that future development should involve an embracing of the city's multicultural heritage, 'drawing on the "rooted globalisations" of Birmingham's people'. One specific suggestion is to establish a centre for cultural hybridity, which 'could overcome the prejudices which reduce partic-ipation in the present city centre and inhibit an honest engagement with our multicultural selves' (ibid., p. 64). Hubbard (2001, p. 5), while re-enforcing their concerns, takes a slightly different view of the route forward. Following Castells (1996), he argues that 'for Birmingham to become plugged into the global space of flows it needs to establish connections and manipulate flows'. A 'more radical policy', he suggests, 'would be to establish a series of Birmingham Centres for Cultural Hybridity in Mumbai, Islamabad, Chicago, Beijing and so on' (ibid., p. 5). Our response takes elements of both of these views. The fundamental emphasis on governance implies a solid rooting in localities, and therefore 'place'. However, the layered approach to locality does not see place as a rigid, fixed concept, but as a fluid arrangement of inter-twined localities and communities. Thus there is also an emphasis on 'flows' between the layers, in the form of relationships that, crucially, maintain concern with governance for all constituents.

From this approach to locality, we see the ultimate challenge as moving towards a scenario where all actors in each locality, and in the communities within and across localities, participate in the democratic governance of their collective development. Thus urban or regional prosperity would become rooted in the inclusion of each member of each community making up the global economy. This conceptualisation of urban and regional prosperity, or more accurately local prosperity, is consistent with an embracing of the global and new economy that is truly democratic; concerned with the opportunity and ability for everyone to access and shape the globalisation process.

5.   CONCLUSIONS

This chapter began with a presentation of the topics and questions that contributors to the volume were asked to consider at the start of their deliberations. The intention is that subsequent chapters will take up specific points in some detail. Even from this brief introduction, it seems clear that the subject of urban and regional development in a globalised new economy raises a myriad of concerns, and only a fraction of these are being touched upon in this volume.

Most of our discussion has focused on crucial conceptualisations. Globalisation is a commonly used word. Nearly as commonly, it is a loosely used word. We linked its conceptualisation to the new economy and suggested a broad definition based upon a multidisciplinary process, new geography and new technologies. These three characteristics are the cornerstone of what is fresh about globalisation at the current time. They are also at the heart of our more focused conceptualisation, designed to take the analysis forward albeit at the expense of some consensus. For an analysis of the implications of globalisation for economic development, knowledge and governance are fundamental. The issue is not the so-called competitive imperative for knowledge that is so widely addressed at the current time. Rather, knowledge (and learning) is important because it is the key to people having the opportunity to engage effectively – that is, democratically – in the decision-making processes that govern development. In turn, this enables prosperity to reflect accurately the aims and objectives of localities. The significance of knowledge is that it be seen in an active and dynamic sense. What matters is not knowledge of 'facts' but knowledge in terms of thinking and awareness. Equally important, knowledge is an ongoing process; participation in governance generates knowledge around practical issues, allowing localities to establish what is effective for them, and what is not. This raises the prospect of a virtuous circle, of localities evolving towards ways in which they can govern themselves to ensure attainment of their own development aims and objectives. If successful, it also implies the possibility of democratic as against elite globalisation.

Our analysis of specific territories that play an integral part in a globalised new economy introduced the concept of locality. Disagreement in the existing literature about the role, if any, of nations and regions cannot hide the common view that globalisation processes are inherently associated with regionalisation of some form. We suggested an approach that avoids rigid categorisations, focusing instead on local areas characterised by certain common institutions, practices and identity, and by the relationships that these foster between actors. We advocated a layered approach to these localities, accommodating different communities that exist within and across these layers. This identifies and structures interlinked territories – hence, urban and regional areas – from a multidimensional and fluid perspective. Moreover, implicit in this approach is a central role for 'networking', taking analysis to the significance of the governance of production networks. We envisage the possibility of certain sorts of influential networks within and across localities, therefore within and across nations and regions; these might facilitate decision-making to move localities towards their own aims and objectives, to achieve what they see as prosperity. Ultimately, there might be democratic governance, more than simple cooperation and partnership across interest groups.

At the moment, that point is some way off. Nearly 2500 years ago, Socrates saw himself as 'a citizen, not of Athens or Greece, but of the world'.[47] Since that time, the world has shrunk through technology. However, few people can meaningfully claim that they are citizens in the sense of participating fully in the governance of their economies and societies. Today's globalised new economy is characterised by exclusion, both at the level of the world as a whole, and of particular territories and entities within that world. The challenge is to ensure democratic globalisation, a situation where all actors in all localities participate in the democratic governance of their development. Then, each and every person would be in a position to proclaim: 'I am a citizen, not only of my home town and my nation, but also of the world'.[48]

NOTES

*   We are grateful to Miriam Quintana Fernandez and J. Robert Branston for comments and suggestions around earlier material underlying this chapter.
1.   In particular, by Rita Hartung Cheng, Susan Donohue, William Holahan, Richard Meadows, James Peoples and Roger Sugden.
2.   See, for instance, De la Dehesa (2000) and Scholte (2000) for recent, thoughtful and interesting contributions.
3.   He makes a distinction between 'market', 'direct', and 'communications' globalisation. Other authors, however, make different splits. Scholte (2000), for example, identifies at least five broad definitions, associated with the concepts of 'internationalisation', 'liberalisation', 'universalisation', 'modernisation', and 'deterritorialisation'.
4.   He also notes that one of the first to use the term globalisation was Levitt (1983), who used it to refer to the globalisation of markets.
5.   Indeed, Scholte (2001, p. 39) notes that 'the only consensus about globalisation is that it is contested'.
6.   Ibid., p. 46, emphasis added. His point is that 'although . . . territory still matters very much in our globalising world, it no longer constitutes the whole of our geography' (p. 46).
7.   This is clearly a topic where semantics can intrude. For Scholte (2000), 'whereas international relations are *inter*territorial relations, global relations are *supra*territorial relations. International relations are *cross*-border exchanges *over* distance, while global relations are

*trans*border exchanges *without* distance. Thus global economics is different from international economics, global politics is different from international politics, and so on. Internationality is embedded in territorial space; globality transcends that geography' (p. 49).

8. The Internet has already made it possible, for example, to order goods from CDs through to cars directly from suppliers in other parts of the world, creating a market that leaves behind (further than previous forms of international trade) the necessity of being fixed to a physical locality. On the Internet as a tool for global linking in academic and academic-related activities, see Sugden (2000) on the experience of L'institute.

9. See, for example, Reich (2001) and Atkinson and Gottlieb (2001).

10. The problems of inequality and defragmentation of society that Reich sees as the opposite side of the new economy coin are also essentially an enhancement of the problems inherent in Anglo-US capitalism, and identified as central in the Marxist-influenced dependency literature. Frank (1967, p. 9), for example, argues that 'economic development and underdevelopment are the opposite faces of the same coin. Both are the necessary result and contemporary manifestation of internal contradictions in the world capitalist system'. In one sense, therefore, the new economy facilitates an extension of the patterns of capitalist development that we have seen throughout the last century; increased ease of communication and information transfer simply enable those with power (those holding capital) greater scope to exercise it on a global basis. In another sense, however, it could be argued that the new economy has the potential to balance these powers, because it implies greater access to information for all actors, and thus an enhanced ability to hold those with power accountable.

11. See also Scholte (2000), arguing that 'globalisation has not put the structure of capitalism itself under threat. If anything, the current situation is one of hypercapitalism' (p. 4). He goes on to argue 'that capitalism has been not only a primary cause, but also a chief consequence of globalisation' (p. 130).

12. The following borrows heavily from Waters (2001), defining globalisation generally as 'a social process in which the constraints of geography on economic, political, social and cultural arrangements recede, in which people become increasingly aware that they are receding and in which people act accordingly' (p. 5).

13. Our focus is also on a multidisciplinary approach, as distinct from a mere cross- or interdisciplinary concern; it is not simply that globalisation is relevant in various disciplines, rather it is that the process can only be fully understood from a perspective that fuses various disciplines together.

14. To give an analogy, suppose there is concern with the question 'what is a transnational corporation?'. A commonly accepted answer is that a transnational is a firm that crosses national borders. This is useful insofar as it highlights the crossing of borders, a key characteristic of what most if not all would choose to identify as a transnational corporation. To a degree it is also useful because it accommodates various conflicting theories of the firm and is therefore not dependent on those theories. However, this is simultaneously a weakness because incorporating a theory of the firm would enrich the understanding of what is meant by the term 'transnational corporation'. The drawback is that it would also cause adherents to different theories of the firm to find the resultant definition of a transnational unacceptable. Similarly, if a narrower conceptualisation of globalisation is offered by further identifying what is seen as especially crucial, it will be unacceptable to those who argue that other issues need to be emphasised (instead or as well).

15. The 1998/99 *World Development Report* (World Bank, 1998), for example, is dedicated to knowledge. Moreover, Joseph Stiglitz, former Chief Economist at the World Bank, has made suggestions that the World Bank should evolve towards a 'knowledge bank'. See Stiglitz (1998b), and Standing (2000) for a critique of his suggestions. The recent concern with knowledge in development is also mirrored in other fields, with knowledge creation and knowledge management currently fashionable topics in the areas of organisational behaviour and management, see for example Inkpen (1998).

16. Putting these developments in deeper historical perspective, Dunning (2000, p. 8) argues that 'over the last three centuries, the main source of wealth in market economies has switched from natural assets (notably land and relatively unskilled labour), through tangible

assets (notably buildings, machinery and equipment, and finance) to intangible created assets (notably knowledge and information of all kinds)'.

17. Stiglitz (1998a, p. 31), for example, states that 'education – especially education that emphasizes critical, scientific thinking – can also help train citizens to participate more effectively and more intelligently in public decisions'.

18. Moreover, just as flexible labour markets have become more attractive as transport technologies have allowed goods to be produced far from where they are consumed, knowledge as a route to competitive advantage has become increasingly attractive in a new economy dominated by information flows.

19. The importance of corporations in a globalisation context is recognised by Stallings and Peres (2000, p. 17), who note that globalisation can be viewed 'as a microeconomic phenomenon led by the strategies and behaviour of corporations'.

20. On the Washington Consensus, see Williamson (1990).

21. Rodrik (1996, p. 9) argues that 'faith in the desirability and efficacy of these policies unites the vast majority of professional economists in the developed world who are concerned with issues of development'.

22. Following Seattle, the annual meetings of the IMF and World Bank in Prague during November 2000 were targeted by protesters. Likewise, the World Economic Forum in Davos during December 2000 and the European Union summit in Gothenburg, June 2001.

23. Joseph Stiglitz has been a particularly key figure in this regard. See, for example, Stiglitz (1998a, 1998b), Standing (2000).

24. Indeed, Ruigrok and van Tulder (1995, p. 151) suggest that 'what is often referred to as "globalisation" is perhaps better described as "Triadisation". The 1980s internationalisation of trade and investments was largely limited to the United States, the European Community and Japan as well as East and South East Asia ... other regions on the globe have been excluded from this supposedly "global" restructuring process'.

25. We use the word 'locality' here in order to distance our analysis from the distinct implications of other words – such as city, town, region or nation – that are often used to describe territories. We expand on our motivation for doing this, and on what exactly we mean by a 'locality', in Section 4.

26. Fromm (1941, p. 247). He continues: 'Hundreds of scattered and unrelated facts are dumped into the heads of students; their time and energy are taken up by learning more and more facts so that there is little left for thinking. To be sure, thinking without a knowledge of facts remains empty and fictitious; but "information" alone can be just as much of an obstacle to thinking as the lack of it.'

27. See Branston et al. (2001) on citizen-focused or citizen-determined governance. The relevance of different disciplines to this approach is suggested by Escudé's (1997) citizen-centric analysis of foreign policy.

28. Hirschman (1970, p. 43). From a different perspective, the philosopher Dewey (1916) appears to make a similar point in his discussion of democracy and education. He argues that 'all communication is like art. It may be fairly said, therefore, that any social arrangement that remains vitally social, or vitally shared, is educative to those who participate in it' (p. 7).

29. Ibid., p. 43, emphasis removed.

30. See also Reich (2001) on the uncertainties that people face in the new economy.

31. Such a phenomenon might explain the downward trend in voter turnout in Western economies over recent decades. For example, in perhaps the most 'free market' of economies, the United States, turnout in presidential elections has been declining since 1960, reaching just 49 per cent in 1996 although rising slightly in 2000. The recent general election in the UK also saw the lowest turnout since 1918, prompting one commentator to declare that 'disengagement from politics is one of the ineluctable trends of modern life' (leader article, *The Financial Times*, 9 June 2001).

32. A full understanding of the art of democracy as central to economic prosperity, and of escape from governance as threatening the attainment of that prosperity, both require multidisciplinary analysis.

33. He argued that 'the beginnings of the organization process that characterizes the development of industry within "national" economic boundaries become ever more evident also

against the background of world economy relations. Just as the growth of productive forces within "national" economy, on a capitalist basis, brought about the formation of national cartels and trusts, so the growth of productive forces within world capitalism makes the formation of international agreements between the various national capitalist groups . . . ever more urgent' (p. 26). He thus appeared to see the process of internationalisation as being essentially constructed from nations or 'national capitalist groups'.

34. The coexistence of globalisation and localisation trends has often been termed 'glocalisation'.

35. Dewey (1916, p. 7), for example, notes that 'not only does social life demand teaching and learning for its own permanence, but the very process of living together educates'. We suggest that 'living together' need not be confined to geographical proximity; mental proximity is important in a new economy and this might be achieved over large distances. On mental proximity, see Sacchetti and Sugden (2001).

36. Atkinson and Gottlieb (2001) argue that the new economy is leading to a decline in the importance of downtown areas: 'the common vision of the metropolitan area as a place with one economy, located among downtown skyscrapers and inner-ring factories, no longer describes the metropolis common to America' (p. 4). For example, they report that 14 000 jobs were lost in downtown Milwaukee over the period 1979–94, whereas 4800 jobs were introduced in inner-ring suburbs and 82 000 in outer-ring suburbs. Similar trends can also be observed in other cities, although the reasons may be different. In South Africa, for example, the central areas of Johannesburg, and to a lesser extent Cape Town, have seen a large-scale displacement of economic and social activity in favour of affluent suburbs such as Sandton (in Johannesburg) and Claremont (in Cape Town), which are perceived as safer and more desirable places to work and spend leisure time. However, while these shifts may be an important phenomenon in terms of the changing of geography cities, it is likely that there will remain centres, whether 'downtown' or otherwise, that are especially important from an economic and social perspective.

37. While Figure 1.1 is drawn for a city, a similar figure could be drawn to represent the relationships between village and town localities in a rural area.

38. Thompson (2000, p. 44), for example, notes that in Southern Africa '"national" borders were drawn by Europeans, who were quite ignorant of the family and community borders that they were partitioning'. In discussing the Southern African Development Community (SADC) she goes on to argue that the 'member states approach to regionalism rejects "separate development" of the individual countries, which were just as falsely (and forcefully) divided as the ethnic groups within South Africa'.

39. These definitions are derived from those in the *Collins English Dictionary*, 1986. It should be noted that some 'regions' may be largely or entirely urban. In the English context, for example, these include the West Midlands and Greater London.

40. For some time there have been websites that facilitate networking among people sharing common interests, views, beliefs, etc. Theoretically this has allowed the establishment of communities that span localities, although inclusion is limited to those that have access to the Internet. New ventures in the UK are demonstrating the potential for similar networking to take place in the context of geographical localities (see *The Independent*, 2 July 2001). A website called myvillage.com, for example, splits London into distinct villages, and provides a forum for businesses, organisations and individuals to network and share information with others in each locality. There are valid concerns here around the inclusiveness of an Internet forum and the editing of the site itself. However, such ventures demonstrate how people might network within localities in a new economy, and also provide scope for the type of networking across localities that we have suggested. Someone living in one London village, for example, could bring issues to other village forums where there may be a related interest, thus learning from and contributing to what happens in neighbouring villages.

41. Moreover, as we have suggested, effective governance is fundamentally linked to issues of knowledge and learning.

42. Atkinson and Gottlieb (2001) argue that the new economy requires new governance, more specifically cooperation and partnerships across actors and geographical areas. Democratic

governance is about more than this, simply because democracy requires more than cooperation and partnerships. Exactly what is required, however, is something that economics, or indeed other branches of social science, are not best placed to analyse alone; by nature, it requires a multidisciplinary approach, and this is a significant challenge facing practitioners across the social sciences.

43. On 'world cities', see, for example, Friedman and Wolff (1982), Friedman (1986), Sassen (1991, 1994), Beaverstock et al. (2000) and Taylor (2000).
44. Friedman (1986, p. 71), emphasis removed.
45. For a related analysis in a broader context of development, see Hymer (1972).
46. In particular, a certain route may be important for a certain culture, or even a certain city/locality. Given localities, for example, may have an attachment to certain industries, which then become important to their notion of prosperity. For example, is brewing important to the people of Milwaukee in terms of their objectives, or automobile manufacture in Birmingham?
47. Quoted in Plutarch, *De Exilio*, v.
48. Perhaps more accurately: 'I am a citizen, not only of the localities of which I am a part, but also of the world'.

REFERENCES

Atkinson, R.D. and Gottlieb, P.D. (2001), *The Metropolitan New Economy Index. Benchmarking Economic Transformation in the Nation's Metropolitan Areas*, Washington DC: Progressive Policy Institute and Center for Regional Economic Issues (Case Western Reserve University), http://www.neweconomyindex.org/metro/index.html.

Beaverstock, J.V., Smith, R.G., Taylor, P.J., Walker, D.R.F. and Lorimer, H. (2000), 'Globalization and world cities: some measurement methodologies', *Applied Geography*, **20**, 43–63.

Branston, J.R., Cowling, K. and Sugden, R. (2001), 'Corporate governance and the public interest', L'institute Discussion Paper No. 13, University of Birmingham, http://business.bham.ac.uk/linstitute/.

Brenner, N. (1999), 'Globalisation as reterritorialisation: the re-scaling of urban governance in the European Union', *Urban Studies*, **36**(3), 431–51.

Bucharin, N. (1918), *Imperialism and World Economy*, extracts reprinted as 'World economy and national economy', in H. Radice (ed.) (1975), *International Firms and Modern Imperialism*, Harmondsworth, Middlesex: Penguin Books.

Castells, M. (1996), *The Rise of the Network Society*, Oxford: Blackwell.

Cowling, K. and Sugden, R. (1999), 'The wealth of localities, regions and nations; developing multinational economies', *New Political Economy*, **4**(3), 361–78.

De la Dehesa, G. (2000), *Comprender la Globalización*, Madrid: Alianza Editorial.

Dewey, J. (1916), *Democracy and Education*, New York: Macmillan.

Dunning, J.H. (2000). 'Regions, globalization, and the knowledge economy: the issues stated', in J.H. Dunning (ed.), *Regions, Globalization, and the Knowledge-Based Economy*, Oxford: Oxford University Press.

Escudé, C. (1997), *Foreign Policy Theory in Menem's Argentina*, Gainesville: University Press of Florida.

Florida, R. (1994), 'A nation of regions: the economic geography of America', in G. Thompson (ed.), *Markets*, London: Hodder & Stoughton.

Frank, A.G. (1967), *Capitalism and Underdevelopment in Latin America: Historical Studies of Chile and Brazil*, New York: Monthly Review Press.

Friedmann, J. (1986), 'The world city hypothesis', *Development and Change*, **17**, 69–83.

Friedmann, J. and Wolff, G. (1982), 'World city formation: an agenda for research and action', *International Journal of Urban and Regional Research*, **6**(3), 309–44.

Fromm, E. (1941), *Escape from Freedom*, page references are from the 1994 edition, New York: Owl Books.

Gordon, D. (1988), 'The global economy: new edifice or crumbling foundations?', *New Left Review*, **168**, 24–64.

Gordon, R.J. (2000), 'Does the "new economy" measure up to the great inventions of the past', *Journal of Economic Perspectives*, **14**(4), 49–74.

Henry, N. and Passmore, A. (1999), 'Rethinking "global" city centres: the example of Birmingham', *Soundings*, **13**, 60–66.

Hirschman, A.O. (1970), *Exit, Voice and Loyalty: Responses to Decline in Firms, Organizations and States*, Cambridge, MA: Harvard University Press.

Hirst, P. and Thompson, G. (1999), *Globalization in Question*, Second Edition, Cambridge: Polity Press.

Hubbard, P.J. (2001), 'The politics of flow: on Birmingham, globalisation and competitiveness', *Soundings*, **17**. Circulated currently as Research Bulletin 37 of the Globalization and World Cities Study Group and Network (GaWC), found at http://www.lboro.ac.uk/departments/gy/research/gawc/ (page references from this version).

Hymer, S.H. (1972), 'The multinational corporation and the law of uneven development', in J.N. Bhagwati (ed.), *Economics and World Order*, London: Macmillan.

Inkpen, A.C. (1998), 'Learning and knowledge acquisition through international strategic alliances', *The Academy of Management Executive*, **12**(4), 69–80.

Kindleberger, C. (1969), *American Business Abroad: Six Lectures on Direct Investment*, New Haven: Yale University Press.

Kudrle, R.T. (1999), 'Three types of globalization: communication, market and direct', in R. Vayrynen (ed.), *Globalization and Global Governance*, Lanham: Rowman & Littlefield.

Levitt, T. (1983), 'The globalization of markets', *Harvard Business Review*, **83**(3), 92–102.

Nichols, D.A. (2000), 'Wisconsin manufacturing in the global economy: its past, present and future', Paper prepared for the Wisconsin Economic Summit, Milwaukee, November/December 2000. (A slightly revised version of this paper is published as Chapter 10 of this volume.)

Ohmae, K. (1990), *The Borderless World*, New York: HarperCollins.

Ohmae, K. (1995), *The End of the Nation State: The Rise of Regional Economies*, London: HarperCollins.

Radice, H. (2000), 'Responses to globalisation: a critique of progressive nationalism', *New Political Economy*, **5**(1), 5–19.

Reich, R.B. (1992), *The Work of Nations: Preparing Ourselves for 21st-Century Capitalism*, New York: Vintage Books.

Reich, R.B. (2001), 'The new economy as a decent society', *The American Prospect*, **12**(3), 12 February, Internet version, found at http://www.prospect.org.

Robertson, R. (1992), *Globalization: Social Theory and Global Culture*, London: Sage.

Rodrik, D. (1996), 'Understanding economic policy reform', *Journal of Economic Literature*, **XXXIV**, 9–41.

Ruigrok, W. and van Tulder, R. (1995), *The Logic of International Restructuring*, London: Routledge.

Sacchetti, S. and Sugden, R. (2001), 'Knowledge distribution, linkages and power in the economy. A perspective on development', Mimeo, L'institute, University of Ferrara.

Sassen, S. (1991), *The Global City: New York, London, Tokyo*, Princeton: Princeton University Press.

Sassen, S. (1994), *Cities in a World Economy*, California: Pine Forge Press.

Scholte, J.A. (2000), *Globalization: A Critical Introduction*, Basingstoke: Palgrave.

Stallings, B. and Peres, W. (2000), *Growth, Employment, and Equity: The Impact of The Economic Reforms in Latin America and the Caribbean*, Washington, DC: Brookings Institution Press.

Standing, G. (2000), 'Brave new words? A critique of Stiglitz's World Bank rethink', *Development and Change*, **31**, 737–63.

Stiglitz, J. (1998a), *More Instruments and Broader Goals: Moving Toward the Post-Washington Consensus*, 1998 WIDER Annual Lecture, Helsinki: WIDER.

Stiglitz, J. (1998b), 'Towards a new paradigm for development: strategies, policies and processes', Paper presented as the 1998 Prebisch Lecture, UNCTAD, Geneva.

Storper, M. (1997), *The Regional World: Territorial Development in a Global Economy*, London: The Guilford Press.

Sugden, R. (2000), 'The Internet as a tool for global linking', *Qualitative Market Research. An International Journal*, **3**(2), 107–9.

Sugden, R. and Wilson, J.R. (2002), 'Development in the shadow of the consensus: a strategic decision-making approach', *Contributions to Political Economy*, **21**, 111–34.

Taylor, P.J. (2000), 'World cities and territorial states under conditions of contemporary globalisation', *Political Geography*, **19**, 5–32.

Thompson, C.B. (2000), 'Regional challenges to globalisation: perspectives from Southern Africa', *New Political Economy*, **5**(1), 41–56.

Vellinga, M. (2000), 'The dialectics of globalization: internationalization, regionalization, and sub-regional response', in M. Vellinga (ed.), *The Dialectics of Globalization: Regional Responses to World Economic Processes: Asia, Europe and Latin America in Comparative Perspective*, Oxford: Westview Press.

Wade, R. (1996), 'Globalization and its limits: reports of the death of the national economy are greatly exaggerated', in S. Berger and R. Dore (eds), *National Diversity and Global Capitalism*, London: Cornell University Press.

Waters, M. (2001), *Globalization*, Second Edition, London: Routledge.

Williamson, J. (1990), 'What Washington means by policy reform', in J. Williamson (ed.), *Latin American Adjustment: How Much has Happened?*, Washington, DC: Institute for International Economics.

World Bank (1998), *World Development Report 1998/1999*, Oxford: Oxford University Press.

PART II

2. The problem of regional 'hollowing out' in Japan: lessons for regional industrial policy

Keith Cowling and Philip R. Tomlinson[*]

1. INTRODUCTION

The machinery sector plays a significant role at the centre of the Japanese industrial economy,[1] as it does in other parts of the world, for example in Wisconsin and the US Midwest. In the post-war period, the sector was regarded as being at the forefront of Japan's international success in manufacturing (see Johnson, 1982). However, while the machinery sector in Wisconsin and the Midwest has recently enjoyed something of a renaissance (see Nichols in Chapter 10 of this volume), Japan's industrial regions have experienced a long period of serious economic stagnation. During the 1990s, Japan's large transnational corporations continued to pursue strategies towards a greater globalisation of their production. Over the same period, Japan's domestic machinery sector lost in excess of three-quarters of a million manufacturing jobs and over 12 per cent of its business establishments. Real output also fell by approximately 8.3 per cent (Japanese Statistics Bureau, 2001). As the decade came to a close, both Japan's Ministry of International Trade and Industry (MITI) and economic commentators were seriously concerned that Japanese industry and the machinery sector, in particular, were in a phase of *kūdoka* or 'hollowing out' (see Cowling and Tomlinson, 2000, 2002).

It is useful to consider Japan's recent experiences as a discourse on regional industrial policy, not least because of more general lessons for regional development in various areas of the world. It is relevant in Wisconsin, for example, because of the similarities in the industrial composition, and since Wisconsin is currently considering ways forward for its own economy. The state also has its particular concerns about outsourcing, hollowing out and the appropriate design of policies to encourage sustainable business clusters. In this respect, a review of Japan's recent problems may provide insights and lessons for the direction of industrial policies in both Wisconsin and other regions.

This chapter, therefore, considers Japan's recent experiences and the problems of hollowing out using a case study of the Japanese machinery sector. In doing so, it explores the roots of the present crisis by focusing upon the role played by Japan's large transnational corporations. This is important because these corporations are the 'central actors' within the Japanese economy and they control a significant proportion of Japanese manufacturing. It is their strategic decisions – those that determine the level and location of investment, employment and output – that ultimately shape the development path for Japanese industry (see Cowling and Sugden, 1994, 1998). In recent years, Japan's large transnationals have become engaged in the process of *elite glob-alisation* (see Sugden and Wilson's chapter in this volume), pursuing their own interests at the expense of domestic Japanese industry. This is a fundamental insight that is crucial for designing appropriate policy responses to arrest Japan's current industrial decline. It is argued that the lessons from Japan's recent experience might guide policy-makers in other regions, such as Wisconsin, who are concerned with future industrial development, the effects of globalisation and problems of hollowing out.

The remainder of this chapter is as follows. In Section 2, we provide an outline of Japan's domestic machinery sector, focusing upon its development, its major industrial belts and the main characteristics of its industrial structure. Section 3 considers the globalisation of the industry and argues that this process has evolved to suit Japan's corporate elite. The hollowing out of Japan's machinery industries and the effects of this *elite globalisation* upon Japanese manufacturing is discussed in Section 4. In the light of our observations, Section 5 provides some guidelines for the future course of regional industrial policy in Japan, and also briefly considers the implications of Japan's recent experience for Wisconsin and regional prosperity elsewhere. Section 6 concludes.

2.   JAPAN'S MACHINERY INDUSTRIES

Industrial Policy and Development

Throughout much of the twentieth century, the machinery sector has been at the forefront of Japanese manufacturing industry. Today, the sector accounts for approximately 45 per cent of all manufacturing employment and over 40 per cent of total Japanese output. The machinery industries also provide 75 per cent of the economy's exports (Whittaker, 1997). Moreover, the sector has been the source of Japan's international competitiveness in manufacturing and has provided the economy with global competitors, or 'national champions', such as Toyota and Hitachi (see Section 3).

According to Johnson (1982), the growth of Japan's machinery sector, its relative importance in Japanese manufacturing and its post-war international competitiveness are the result of an active industrial policy and an institutional style of capitalism.[2] In this respect, the immediate post-war period saw the Japanese Ministry of International Trade and Industry (MITI) designate the machinery industries as being 'strategic'. This meant that MITI identified the sector as being one that would play a pivotal role in Japan's future economic and industrial development. As a result, over the last 50 years, the sector has, at various times, benefited from measures such as direct subsidies, discriminatory tariffs, preferential commodity taxes, import restrictions and favourable industry regulation. MITI's industrial policies were also supported by the development of strong institutional arrangements. A *banking keiretsu* of city banks was encouraged by the Bank of Japan, which facilitated low-cost, long-term finance for industry. To promote Japanese trading interests abroad, the Japanese External Trade Organisation (JETRO), was established. The overseas JETRO offices expanded upon the role played by Japan's general trading companies (the *sogo shosha*), by conducting extensive market research and aiding Japanese exporters to secure contracts in new and existing markets (see Johnson, 1982).

In addition to these measures, MITI has also shielded Japan's machinery industries from foreign competition. This protection has included both tariffs and quotas and until 1971, strict controls upon foreign direct investment (FDI). The controls over FDI were operational under the 1949 Foreign Exchange and Foreign Trade Control Law and the 1950 Foreign Investment Law. These laws allowed MITI to sanction all inward and outward FDI proposals, to protect infant domestic industries from the pressures of global competition.[3] MITI did, however, positively encourage machinery firms to enter into suitable licensing and joint venture agreements with foreign firms. These arrangements were usually subject to MITI's approval, but they enabled Japanese industry to gain access to the latest international technology. For Ozawa (1973), it was the remarkable ability of Japanese manufacturing to successfully adopt and improve upon these technologies that was critical in Japan's post-war international success.

Japan's 'Industrial Districts'

The data in Table 2.1 provide some information on the geographical location of domestic Japanese manufacturing and, in particular, the machinery sector. As Table 2.1 shows, over 73 per cent of output and 68 per cent of employment in the machinery industries are concentrated within 15 of Japan's 47 prefectures. In addition, these 15 prefectures also account for 63 per cent of total manufacturing output and employment. Since the Meiji Restoration of 1868, these regions have emerged to become the hub of Japanese manufacturing, benefiting from being close to major ports and a large labour force.

The most important of these prefectures are the large industrial belts of Aichi, Kanagawa, Shizuoka and Tokyo (see Table 2.1), where the major industries transport equipment, electrical machinery and electronics are concentrated.

It is within these prefectures that we find Japan's main industrial clusters. These are Japan's 'industrial districts'. Marshall (1919) defines an industrial district as an area where there is a cluster of industrial activity, which enables firms to benefit from external scale economies that are a result of their direct interdependence (see also Bellandi's contribution to this volume). These agglomeration economies include not only 'technological factors', such as labour market pooling and the sharing of local infrastructure, but also the diffusion of information such as new technology, advances in knowledge and changes in organisation. These clusters are often characterised by a propagation of small-firm activity, with firms establishing horizontal linkages between themselves, such as those evident in Emilia-Romagna – the 'Third Italy' – and Baden Württemburg, in Germany. There are also a large number of small firms in Japan's industrial districts. Indeed, small and medium-sized businesses play an important role in Japanese manufacturing and regularly account for over 99 per cent of private business establishments, employ over 78 per cent of the labour force and produce approximately 70 per cent of domestic output (Japanese Small Business Corporation [JSBC], 1998). Japan's small firms primarily operate in vertical *keiretsu* networks, acting as subcontractors to larger firms within a corporate group (the *kigyo shudan*). However, a number of Japan's smaller firms have developed other income sources and do not rely solely upon subcontracting.

In this respect, Whittaker (1997) has identified three types of industrial district that exist within Japan. The first type of district is known as the *sanchi*, which is composed of agglomerations of small independent firms, operating in small workshops. In the machinery sector, these firms primarily specialise in the low-volume production of high-tech goods. They can be found in the metropolitan centres of Tokyo and Osaka. Whittaker (1997) identifies the small-scale nature of production within the *sanchi*, as being Japan's closest example of a Marshallian industrial district. The largest industrial districts are the so-called 'company castle towns' (*kigyo joka machi*), where there are a large number of small firms, but the dominant players are Japan's large corporations. Examples of these company castle towns include Toyota City, in Aichi prefecture, where Toyota and its core suppliers (for instance, Denso and Aisin Seiki) have established their major domestic operations. Nissan has developed similar clusters within Kanagawa, Tokyo and Tochigi, while Honda's operations are primarily within the prefectures of Shizuoka, Saitama and Mie. In addition, the large electronics firms, such as Hitachi, Sony, Toshiba and NEC have also created their own *keiretsu* networks within these prefectures. Finally,

Table 2.1 The geographical concentration of Japan's machinery sector and manufacturing industry (by prefecture), 1998

Prefecture[1]	Total Manufacturing Industry			Total Machinery Sector[2]		
	Number of establishments (1998)	Share of Japan's manufacturing output (1998)	Share of Japan's manufacturing employment (1998)	Number of establishments (1998)	Share of Japan's machinery output (1998)	Share of Japan's machinery employment (1998)
Aichi	30 301	11.4	8.8	13 050	15.3	10.8
Kanagawa	15 115	7.5	5.8	8 940	9.1	7.8
Shizuoka	17 098	5.3	4.9	7 431	5.9	5.5
Tokyo	33 945	6.4	6.6	12 794	5.8	5.6
Osaka	36 045	6.4	7.1	14 944	5.5	6.8
Saitama	20 803	4.8	5.1	9 496	5.0	5.5
Hyogo	15 433	4.7	4.4	5 682	4.4	4.4
Gumma	8 753	2.6	2.5	4 151	3.5	3.2
Nagano	8 902	2.2	2.5	4 652	3.2	3.6
Tochigi	7 664	2.6	2.3	2 905	2.8	2.7
Mie	6 648	2.5	2.1	2 525	2.9	2.4
Hiroshima	8 333	2.4	2.5	3 261	2.7	2.6
Ibaraki	8 904	3.6	3.0	3 468	2.6	3.1
Chiba	9 074	3.8	2.8	3 253	2.4	2.3
Fukuoka	9 308	2.6	2.7	2 687	2.3	2.1
Rest of Japan	137 387	37.0	37.0	38 403	26.8	31.6
Japan	731 765	100	100	137 642	100	100

Notes:
1. The table shows the 15 main Japanese prefectures, where the machinery sector is concentrated.
2. The machinery sector consists of five subsectors: metal products, machinery and equipment, electrical machinery, transport equipment and precision tools.

Source: Japanese Statistical Yearbook (2001).

there are also districts where the main firms are medium-sized firms, who manufacture under their own label, but who combine local contracting out with in-house production (see Whittaker, 1997).

Industrial Structure and Corporate Control

In Japan, approximately 56 per cent of small firms are involved in some form of subcontracting. However, in the machinery sector, over 70 per cent of small firms are subcontractors and this figure is higher than 80 per cent in electrical machinery and transport equipment (Whittaker, 1997). These are the *keiretsu* firms that operate in the company castle towns, where they predominantly supply intermediate goods and services to the larger corporate group firms. The majority of these small *keiretsu* firms are allocated specialised tasks and they rely heavily upon the corporate group firms for new orders (see also Scher, 1997). In effect, the *keiretsu* firms are 'locked in' to a vertical relationship with their main contractor.

The literature emphasises the long-standing close relationships, cooperation and the mutual trust that exist between *keiretsu* firms and their main contractors (see Gerlach, 1992; Scher, 1997). These close relations include the practice of large corporations guaranteeing their subcontractors' income streams, particularly in periods of fluctuating demand. In addition, the corporate group can often obtain low-cost, long-term finance for its suppliers through the banking *keiretsu*. The larger corporations also offer a 'free consultancy' service, providing their subcontractors with advice and information about manufacturing operations, financial matters and foreign markets. In return, some subcontractors are given responsibility for the design and manufacture of complete subassemblies. The 'close ties' are extended through extensive cross-shareholdings, where firms hold reciprocal equity stakes with their trading partners and affiliated firms, which include banks, insurance companies, suppliers and trading companies. It is these arrangements that have led Aoki (1990, 1994) to argue that the Japanese firm and the nature of interfirm relations represent a nexus of treaties, with a non-hierarchical mode of production. This is because all firms recognise their mutual interdependence, their responsibilities and that long-term cooperation can lead to mutual benefit and corporate success.

However, while mutuality and trust may appear as important characteristics of Japanese industrial organisation, when it comes to corporate governance, they should not be equated with equal power in decision-making processes (Sachetti and Sugden, 2002). This is an important distinction, since certain (hierarchical) governance structures are an important mechanism by which a corporate elite can control production activities, in order to pursue their own interests. We would argue, in particular, that (hierarchical) governance structures and their associated control mechanisms allow the elite to pursue their own prosperity, often at the expense of other actors within the industry or locality (see Sugden and Wilson, Chapter 1). In the case of Japan's machinery industries, this is apparent in the pyramidal structure of industrial production where, effectively, a 'formal command structure' exists. The result is that the smaller *keiretsu* firms are often subordinate to the strategic decisions and interests of Japan's large machinery corporations – the dominant firms within the corporate group (Ruigrok and van Tulder, 1995; Cowling and Tomlinson, 2000, 2002).

We can consider this point further, by referring to the example of Japan's automobile industry. The industry has the largest number of interfirm relationships in Japan and close ties are said to exist between the large assemblers and their first, second and lower tier suppliers (Smitka, 1991). However it is the large assemblers that dominate the relationships, through the use of various control mechanisms. These control mechanisms may include an insistence upon their suppliers to comply with a just-in-time (JIT) delivery system and certain quality control measures. Such directives effectively force suppliers to subordinate their production operations entirely to suit their main contractor's requirements, since a failure to comply may lead to a loss of custom. In some cases, just-in-time delivery systems allow the assembler to shift the burden of inventories onto their upstream suppliers, while tightening quality control measures subject the suppliers' production processes to increased monitoring and effectively raise their dependency upon their main contractor (Ruigrok and van Tulder, 1995). A related issue is the practice of open-book accounting, where the price and cost structure of a particular component is analysed by the assemblers in great detail before a price is eventually agreed upon. Usually the 'agreed price' or 'target price' allows the supplier a profit margin, but there is an expectation that the price will fall over time, which forces the supplier to continually reduce costs (Aoki, 1988; Smitka, 1991). The assembler will then accrue most of these productivity gains. Ruigrok and van Tulder (1995, p. 83) have described the system as one where 'the supplier is required to bargain with the assembler literally with all its cards open on the table'.

In addition to these control mechanisms, the large assemblers also use their substantial equity holdings in their core suppliers, to appoint their former executives into key positions within their supply chains. This has the effect of establishing direct lines of communication and allows the assemblers to disseminate and carry out corporate strategy. Reciprocal shareholding arrangements do exist, with some *keiretsu* suppliers even holding stakes in their main contractors. However, firms and subcontractors, lower down the industry's pyramidal structure, have smaller equity stakes in their trading partners and their influence is minimal (see Dodwell Marketing Consultants, 1997). The assemblers can also use personnel exchanges, supplier associations, and technology sharing to exert direct control over their *keiretsu* networks. In this respect, Piore and Sabel (1984) give the example of how Nissan, in the early post-war period, was able to use such channels to control the rationalisation and reorganisation of automobile production.

Finally, it may be argued that institutions, such as the MITI sponsored Public Testing and Research (PTR) centres, could offer smaller suppliers the opportunity to diversify, innovate and become more independent from their main contractors. However, even these institutions – which are exclusively designed to assist Japan's small firms – can be manipulated to suit the larger corporation's interests. Toyota's involvement, at the Aichi PTR centre, is a particular example. Rather than being used as a centre for Toyota's smaller suppliers to advance their own research programmes, the Aichi PTR centre has, in the words of Ruigrok and Tate (1996, p. 397), become 'a tool to help subcontractors meet Toyota's stiff demands'. The authors find that activities at the centre are heavily weighted towards test inspections, with suppliers' processes and components being subject to close scrutiny. Ruigrok and Tate (1996) argue that Toyota has been able to direct the PTR centre's activities to the extent that certification by the PTR centre is now an integral part of the company's domestic production system. They conclude that the Aichi PTR centre has played a major role in sustaining Toyota's ability to exert control over its domestic supply chain.

The pyramidal and formal command structures of Japan's machinery industries, therefore, place the large corporations in a dominant position. Through the utilisation of various control mechanisms, it can be argued that the boundaries of the large Japanese corporation are much wider than its legal frontiers. In effect, the *keiretsu* firms fall under the ambit of the corporate group (see Cowling and Tomlinson, 2000, 2002) and control is exercised from one centre of strategic decision-making (see Cowling and Sugden, 1994, 1998). In the global economy, this has implications for Japan's small machinery firms, who are effectively 'locked in' to their main contractor's supply chain. We will return to this issue in Section 4.

3.   THE GLOBALISATION OF JAPAN'S MACHINERY INDUSTRIES

The Emergence of Japan's Transnational Corporations

The emergence of Japan's large dominant corporations and the structure of production were the result of MITI's industrial policy. Within MITI's policy of targeting strategic industries, Piore and Sabel (1984) note a clear prejudice in favour of promoting the corporate group. Japanese industry was encouraged to adopt a system of mass production based around the large corporations, who were to be supported by networks of *keiretsu* subcontractors. In addition, MITI approved a programme of cartelisation in which failing firms were allowed to merge, which also raised the level of industrial concentration (Piore and Sabel, 1984). MITI's industrial policies effectively enabled Japan to develop its own 'national champions', who were seen as being able to compete, on the global stage, with international rivals from the USA and Europe.

As Japan's large corporations adopted mass production, there were pressures upon MITI to relax the restrictions upon overseas foreign direct investment (FDI) (Mason, 1994). Large-scale production had led to demand deficiencies within Japan, as domestic markets became saturated with consumer durables. Firms sought to overcome falling domestic consumption through the export market. However, this eventually led to large trade surpluses and retaliatory trade barriers, particularly from the USA. With future export growth uncertain, Japan's large corporations began to consider the transnational option.[4] The growing importance of large corporations, within the Japanese economy, placed MITI under strong pressure to liberalise the regulations on FDI. In 1971, MITI removed all the FDI restrictions that applied to Japanese corporations (Mason, 1994).

Since the 1970s, Japanese industry has experienced a significant increase in outward FDI. Between 1981 and 1995, outward Japanese FDI amounted to $470 billion, a fourfold increase in real terms and the highest average growth in overseas investment of any G7 industrial nation (United Nations [UNCTAD], 1997). Japan's machinery sector, in particular, has been most affected by globalisation. By 1998, it accounted for almost 60 per cent of Japan's total outward stock of manufacturing FDI (Organisation for Economic Corporation and Development [OECD], 1999). The dramatic increase in Japanese FDI is a result of many factors. These primarily relate to the growth of regional trading blocs – such as the European Union and the North American Free Trade Area (NAFTA) – which have tried to protect indigenous industries from foreign imports, the yen's appreciation following the 1985 Plaza Accord and higher labour costs in Japan relative to other countries. These have all made it relatively more expensive to export from Japan, and so Japan's transnationals have reacted by increasing their offshore activities to protect and expand their regional and global market shares (Dunning, 1993).

Global Actors

In the modern, global economy, Japan's transnationals have emerged to play a dominant role. Japan is now the home of 17 of the world's top 100 transnational corporations who, collectively, own approximately 16 per cent of the global economy's foreign assets – a position second only to that of the corporate sector of the USA (see UNCTAD, 2000). Table 2.2 provides some details

Table 2.2 Japan's top TNCs ranked by ownership of foreign assets, 1998 (billions of dollars and number of employees)

Corporation	Industrial sector	Assets		Sales		Employment		Global rank by foreign assets	
		Foreign	Total	Foreign	Total	Foreign	Total	All TNCs	By sector
Toyota[1]	*Automotive*	*44.9*	*131.5*	*55.2*	*101.0*	*113 216*	*183 879*	*6*	*3*
Honda Motor	*Automotive*	*26.3*	*41.8*	*29.7*	*51.7*	*–*	*112 200*	*18*	*6*
Sony Corp.[2]	*Electronics*	*–*[3]	*52.5*	*40.7*	*56.6*	*102 468*	*173 000*	*20*	*3*
Mitsubishi Corp.	Diversified	21.7	74.9	43.5	116.1	3 668	11 650	24	2
Nissan Motor	*Automotive*	*21.6*	*57.2*	*25.8*	*54.4*	*–*	*131 260*	*25*	*9*
Mitsui & Co Ltd	Diversified	17.3	56.5	46.5	118.5	–	7 288	37	4
Itochu Corp.	Trading	15.1	55.9	18.4	115.3	–	5 775	45	1
Sumitomo Corp.	*Trading/Machinery*	*15.0*	*45.0*	*17.6*	*95.0*	*–*	*5 591*	*46*	*2*
Nissho Iwai	Trading	14.2	38.5	9.1	71.6	–	4 041	49	3
Matsushita Elect.	*Electronics*	*12.2*	*66.2*	*32.4*	*63.7*	*133 629*	*282 153*	*55*	*7*
Fujitsu Ltd	*Electronics*	*12.2*	*42.3*	*15.9*	*43.3*	*74 000*	*188 000*	*56*	*8*
Hitachi Ltd	*Electronics*	*12.0*	*76.6*	*19.8*	*63.8*	*58 000*	*331 494*	*58*	*9*
Marubeni Corp.	Trading	10.6	53.8	31.4	98.8	–	8 618	68	4
Mitsubishi Motors	*Automotive*	*8.4*	*25.4*	*16.8*	*29.1*	*18 251*	*29 945*	*88*	*14*
Canon Electronics	*Electronics*	*7.4*	*23.4*	*17.8*	*24.4*	*41 834*	*79 799*	*92*	*11*
Bridgestone	*Auto-Parts*	*7.4*	*14.7*	*11.3*	*17.1*	*–*	*97 767*	*93*	*3*
Toshiba Corp.	*Electronics*	*6.8*	*48.8*	*14.5*	*44.6*	*–*	*198 000*	*100*	*12*

Notes:
1. Machinery sector TNCs are in italics.
2. Data on Sony's foreign assets are not published, although the company report that 62 per cent of their 'long-lived' assets (i.e. plant and equipment) is located outside Japan (Sony Corporation, 1999). UNCTAD (2000) have, therefore, ranked Sony accordingly.
3. – Data unavailable.

Source: UNCTAD (2000), *World Investment Report 2000 Cross-Border Mergers and Acquisitions and Development*, New York: UN.

of these 17 transnational corporations, ranking them in terms of their owner-ship of foreign assets. Over two-thirds of these transnationals operate in the machinery sector; the others are Japan's large trading companies (see Table 2.2). Toyota is Japan's largest transnational corporation and, in the global economy, it now rivals the large US automobile manufacturers, Ford and General Motors. However, the degree of transnationality is greater in compa-nies such as Honda, Sony and Bridgestone, which own a greater proportion of their assets outside Japan (see Table 2.2).

Japan's transnationals have used their offshore activities to gain significant market shares in the global economy. In the mid-1960s, Toyota was the only Japanese automobile manufacturer amongst the world's top ten producers. By the mid-1990s, it had quadrupled its market share and was joined in the top ten, by Nissan, Honda and Mitsubishi. Honda is also the world's largest manu-facturer of motorcycles. Within the subcontinental markets of Asia, the large Japanese automotive transnationals have combined market shares in excess of 90 per cent (Dicken, 1998). In the production of rubber tyres, Bridgestone is second only to Michelin. Similarly, in electronics, Sony is now the world's largest company in audio and video equipment while Fujitsu is in the top three of the world's mainframe computer manufacturers (Toyo Keizai, 1999).

To support their overseas activities, Japan's large transnationals have also been strategically establishing a *new* (overseas) *keiretsu* – a transnational network – by actively encouraging their core domestic suppliers to follow them offshore (see also the discussion of technological development and supply chains by Husbands in Chapter 3 of this volume, albeit not focusing on Japanese firms). The rationale behind the new *keiretsu* is that it enables Japan's transnationals to replicate the close domestic interfirm relationships, in overseas locations. These close relations are an important part of Japanese competitiveness, which could be lost when production is shifted offshore. This is particularly the case if Japan's large transnationals have to establish new supply chains with indigenous suppliers, who are generally unfamiliar with Japanese industrial practices (Gittelman and Dunning, 1992). The new *keiretsu*, therefore, reduces the risks associated with international production since it enables Japan's transnationals to continue working with their acknowl-edged suppliers around the globe.

The new *keiretsu* also provides the opportunity for Japanese transnationals to develop industrial linkages across national boundaries. For instance, inter-national personnel exchanges, research and educational linkages are common features of a typical new *keiretsu* network. However, these linkages are totally different to the proposals outlined in Sugden and Wilson's chapter, where it was argued that regions should aim to embrace a more inclusive approach to globalisation, including the possibility of developing multinational linkages. Rather, the linkages created in the new *keiretsu* effectively cross localities, since they are designed and imposed by (Japanese) transnational corporations, to serve the interests of Japan's corporate elite. The new *keiretsu* can, therefore, be regarded as part of the elite globalisation process (see Sugden and Wilson, Chapter 1).

In this respect, the elitist nature of the new *keiretsu* can be seen, by considering the distributional consequences of the transnational network. For instance, the new *keiretsu* allows Japan's transnational corporations greater leverage in their bargaining position with their subsidiaries and enables them to exert direct control over an international division of labour. By using their core Japanese suppliers and employing similar technology as in Japan, Japan's large transnationals can now directly compare international production costs, along the value chain, within a transnational network. In effect, Japan's transnationals have been able to use the threat of relocating production, within the new *keiretsu*, to reduce labour militancy and depress labour costs. This allows the (Japanese) transnational to capture a greater degree of the production surplus – a strategy known as 'divide and rule' (see Cowling and Sugden, 1994; Peoples and Sugden, 2000). James (1989) has also noted that, by locating new production units in areas characterised by high unemployment and low wages, Japanese transnationals have successfully been able to play the international wage game throughout Asia, Europe and North America.

The expansion of overseas affiliates has also led to a significant rise in the proportion of Japan's corporate output produced offshore. Not surprisingly, this is particularly the case in the machinery sector, where the highest overseas production ratios are recorded (see Table 2.3). At the industry level, between 1992 and 1996, Japan's overseas production ratio more than doubled in fabricated metal products, agricultural and industrial machinery and precision tools (see Table 2.3). The most prominent industries were electrical goods (19.7 per cent) and transport equipment (24.9 per cent) and, within these sectors, the level of overseas production has become even higher. For instance, in consumer electronics, offshore production now exceeds domestic output (Electronic Industries Association of Japan [EIAJ], 1997), whilst, in automobiles, the larger manufacturers – notably Toyota, Honda and Nissan – have adapted a similar strategy (Dicken, 1998).

4.   SMALL-FIRM ISOLATION AND THE HOLLOWING OUT OF JAPANESE INDUSTRY

Small-firm Isolation

The continued growth in outsourcing and the increasing involvement of Japan's large corporations in transnational networks threatens the traditional

Table 2.3 Japanese machinery sector overseas production ratios

Industry	1992	1993	1994	1995	1996	1997
Fabricated metal products (ISIC 381) (structural metal products, hand tools, cutlery, foundry products, office furniture)	5	6.3	5.4	9.2	12.1	
Agricultural and industrial machinery (ISIC 382) (machine tools for industry/agriculture, manufacture of engines/turbines, specialist office/ industrial (non-electrical) machinery)	4.1	5.8	8.1	8.1	11.7	
Electric machinery and electric goods (ISIC 383) (electric motors and equipment, semi-conductors, electronics, consumer appliances)	10.8	12.6	15	16.8	19.7	
Transport equipment (ISIC 384) (manufacture of automobiles, motorcycles and bicycles, aircraft, ship building and railroad equipment)	17.5	17.3	20.3	20.6	24.9	
Precision tools (ISIC 385) (professional and scientific instruments, medical equipment optical goods, watches and clocks)	3.6	5.6	6.0	6.6	8.6	
All manufacturing (ISIC 3)	6.2	7.4	8.6	9.1	11.6	12.4
All Japanese transnationals	17.3	18.3	22	25.1	27.5	31.1

Note: Overseas production ratio = sales of Japanese affiliates abroad/total corporate output.

Source: MITI (1998), *The 27th Survey of Overseas Business Activities of Japanese Companies.*

45

close ties between the corporate group and the smaller *keiretsu* firms. Globalisation effectively places Japan's smaller domestic firms in a weaker bargaining position *vis-à-vis* their main contractor, since the latter has access to a global supply chain from which to outsource production. In this respect, procurement rates of intermediate goods, from Japan, fell by a third in the decade between 1986 and 1996, while there was a notable increase in component sourcing from East Asia (MITI, 1998). Furthermore, recent surveys have consistently shown that Japan's smaller firms have experienced a significant fall in order books and have felt under severe pressure to accept lower profit margins because of their main contractor's threat of global sourcing (see for instance, Japanese Small Business Research Institute [JSBRI], 1996). Nissan's recent greater emphasis upon global sourcing and its ultimatum to its smaller *keiretsu* partners to reduce costs or lose future contracts is indicative of the new environment in which Japan's small firms now find themselves (see *Nikkei Weekly*, 25 October 1999 and also 21 May 2001).

For Japan's smaller *keiretsu* firms, the problems posed by global sourcing are particularly acute, given that the majority of them are locked in to vertical relationships with their main contactor. Indeed, MITI (1999) reports that 81.6 per cent of Japan's small firms – the majority from the machinery sector – have never changed their main contractor. In the 1990s, Japan's large corporations have sought to pursue their own global interests, leaving their smaller *keiretsu* partners to face falling order books resulting in an unprecedented rise in the number of small-firm bankruptcy cases (*Nikkei Weekly*, 19 October 1998).

The inability of Japan's small-firm sector to diversify and its over-reliance upon main contractors, in the global economy of the 1990s, has been a key contributor to their faltering financial performance (JSBRI, 1996). As Table 2.4 shows, the profitability of Japan's small firms was significantly lower during the 1990s – when the Japanese economy was more sensitive to transnational activity – than in earlier periods. In this respect, the decline was particularly profound within the machinery industries – Japan's most global sector – where small firms have seen their gross profit margins fall by almost 60 per cent and the return on capital fall by approximately 45 per cent since the mid-1980s (see Table 2.4).

Regional Hollowing Out

The problems experienced by Japan's small firms and the growth in overseas production has raised serious concerns of a hollowing out (*kūdoka*) of Japanese industry. This occurs when the higher profitability of overseas production reduces the relative importance of Japan's core domestic industrial base. This eventually leads to a decline in Japanese international

Table 2.4 The financial performance of Japan's small firms in the machinery sector

	All manufacturing	Fabricated metal products	General machinery	Electrical machinery	Transport equipment	Precision tools
Gross profit margin						
1980–84	2.5	2.9	3.8	2.8	2.3	4.0
1985–89	3.1	4.2	3.6	3.5	2.9	3.7
1990–94	2.4	3.2	2.2	2.2	2.6	2.7
1995–98	1.7	1.8	2.2	2.0	1.3	3.1
Return on capital employed						
1980–84	5.3	5.5	6.4	6.3	5.0	7.5
1985–89	5.4	6.0	5.5	6.1	5.1	5.4
1990–94	4.3	4.9	4.3	4.5	4.5	4.7
1995–98	2.9	2.9	3.3	3.4	2.6	4.1

Notes:
Small firms relate to companies with less than 300 employees. Gross profit margin = ratio of gross profit/sales.
Return on capital employed (ROCE) = ratio of recurring profits to total capital.

Source: Japanese Statistical Yearbook (various issues).

competitiveness, deindustrialisation and the problem of 'structural holes', where once prosperous manufacturing regions experience long-term social and economic decline.

The hollowing out of Japanese manufacturing industry and the machinery sector, in particular, can be seen in Table 2.5. In all prefectures and across industrial sectors, Japan has experienced a significant decline in real output, the number of business establishments and employment during the 1990s. The depression appears to have affected both the machinery and non-machinery sectors with equal magnitude, particularly in terms of lost jobs and factories (see Table 2.5). At the regional level, the large industrial belts of Kanagawa, Tokyo, Osaka and Saitama, in particular, which all rely heavily upon Japan's large (global) machinery corporations, have seen a significant fall in industrial capacity and now experience higher than the national average rate of unemployment.

Interestingly, the decline of the machinery sector in the neighbouring Aichi and Shizuoka prefectures was less marked than in the other major industrial belts – although the non-machinery sector has suffered considerably (see Table 2.4). The relative insulation of Aichi's machinery sector may reflect the fact that it still remains at the core of Toyota's global operations, particularly for research and development and the testing of new products (Ruigrok and Tate, 1996). Similarly, Shizuoka prefecture contains the city of Hamamatsu, which remains at the centre of Honda's global motorcycle business. In addition, Hamamatsu is regarded as a high-tech industrial city that, to some extent, has successfully been able to take advantage of regional assistance through MITI's Technopolis Project (see also Section 5, Whittaker, 1997, pp. 48–9). It could be that, in the machinery sector at least, Toyota's continuing commitments in Aichi and the relative success of Hamamatsu City have, so far, been partial antidotes to the effects of globalisation. However, as the pace of globalisation continues, it is likely that the strategic importance to Toyota and Honda of Toyota City in Aichi and Hamamatsu City in Shizuoka will weaken, as offshore production becomes more attractive. If this occurs, the machinery industries in both Aichi and Shizuoka prefectures will face serious long-term decline.

At this point, we should note that Ozawa (1991, 1992) has argued that the growth in outsourcing is an opportunity for Japanese industry to restructure and upgrade its manufacturing technology by redeploying resources into the development of higher value-added products, while traditional, declining industries are moved offshore. The theory is that this will lead to a 'flying geese formation' of production, where advanced technological work is done in Japan, medium value-added work is done in the newly industrialised economies (NIEs) and so on throughout Asia. The benefits of this pattern are seen as a combination of rising technological standards and the extension of product life-cycles beyond Japanese and Western markets.

Table 2.5   The hollowing out of Japanese manufacturing industry (by prefecture), 1990–98

Prefecture[1]	Unemployment rate % (1995)	Total Machinery Sector			Total Non-machinery Sector		
		% Decline in real output (1990–98)	% Decline in number of establishments (1990–98)	% Decline in employment (1990–98)	% Decline in real output (1990–98)	% Decline in establishments (1990–98)	% Decline in employment (1990–98)
Aichi	3.7	2.9	7.6	7.5	15.5	17.0	14.8
Kanagawa	4.6	3.7	14.6	23.1	11.7	10.8	11.0
Shizuoka	3.5	5.4	6.4	6.7	11.8	10.3	9.6
Tokyo	4.9	16.7	21.0	25.3	13.2	12.5	14.2
Osaka	6.2	4.5	18.7	19.8	23.7	12.6	17.3
Saitama	4.4	10.1	16.0	21.8	11.7	13.3	9.1
Hyogo	5.1	2.1	11.7	12.1	17.1	20.1	18.3
Gumma	3.7	1.3	10.9	10.2	3.7	12.2	7.2
Nagano	2.5	17.6	19.0	14.6	6.7	12.3	11.9
Tochigi[2]	3.7	7.9	9.8	12.2	+1.8*	11.6	9.1
Mie	3.4	1.1	8.3	5.6	14.3	13.8	14.9
Hiroshima	3.7	1.1	6.7	13.0	22.5	17.1	19.1
Ibaraki	3.7	10.1	10.3	13.8	17.0	8.3	5.0
Chiba	4.3	7.4	8.4	15.0	9.0	7.2	9.6
Fukuoka	5.5	2.2	2.5	10.4	14.8	10.1	12.7
Rest of Japan	3.9	7.7	8.5	8.7	9.2	14.4	13.7
Japan	4.2	8.3	12.3	13.1	11.3	13.7	13.4

Notes:
1.   The table shows the 15 main Japanese prefectures, where the machinery sector is concentrated.
2.   *Tochigi actually recorded positive real output growth in non-machinery sector industries over the period.

Source: Japanese Statistical Yearbook (various issues).

However, in the 1990s, Ozawa's arguments would appear to have lost their validity. Japanese offshore affiliates are increasingly being used as a direct substitute for production and, in some cases, for product development (JSBRI, 1996). In this respect, Beamish et al. (1997, p. 26) report a notable change in the strategy of Japanese transnationals, from establishing offshore 'assembly (plants), using parts sourced in Japan, to full manufacturing, to, in some cases, R&D located in the host country'. According to the *Nikkei Weekly* (18 June 2001, p. 4), the rising technological competence of the NIEs has led 'to an increasing number of (Japanese) firms transferring research and development activities, once considered the epitome of Japanese excellence, to (Asian) offshore affiliates'. Whittaker (1997, p. 58) has also noted that, in production, it now only takes a matter of months before the latest Japanese-designed, sophisticated products are able to be manufactured offshore, in East Asia, to serve both the Japanese and Western markets.

These trends have become widely apparent in Japan's machinery industries, raising genuine concerns of a hollowing out of Japanese industry. Deindustrialisation in Japan's industrial belts hampers the country's long-term prospects for economic recovery and a revival in manufacturing employment (Japanese Economic Planning Agency [EPA], 1995). At the regional level, the decline of Japan's small-firm base and the loss of industrial vitality in the industrial districts, weaken the capability for self-regeneration. The contraction of Japan's *keiretsu* networks also reduces the potential for agglomeration economies, which contribute to total factor productivity (TFP) and economic growth. Indeed, in the latter respect, studies have shown that Japan's TFP growth has been declining in all of Japan's major industrial sectors during the 1990s (Jones, 1995; Japanese External Trade Organisation [JETRO], 1997). The decline in Japanese TFP growth appears to correspond with the growth in globalisation and the deterioration in Japan's domestic, manufacturing base.

5. INDUSTRIAL POLICY – SUGGESTIONS FOR RENEWAL

Strategic Failure

In Cowling and Tomlinson (2000), we argued that the hollowing out of the Japanese economy could be seen in terms of a strategic failure. This is a situation that occurs when elite, centralised corporate hierarchies make strategic decisions on key economic variables, such as investment, output and employment, and that these decisions conflict with society's broader interests. There is then no market mechanism available for society to redress the balance and achieve a socially desirable outcome (Cowling and Sugden, 1994). We believe that the concentration of strategic decision-making in corporate Japan and the ever-increasing global interests of Japan's large corporations has precipitated a hollowing out of Japanese manufacturing, raising the spectre of strategic failure.

In order to reverse the current decline, it is necessary for Japan and MITI to engage in a strategic response and, once again, pursue an active industrial policy. However, a prerequisite for such a policy is not only to learn from the experiences and mistakes of previous industrial policies, but also to be fully aware of the dominant role played by transnational corporations. In our view, MITI's apparent post-war favouritism towards the establishment of the corporate group and the promotion of 'national champions' was misplaced, and has not been conducive to sustainable, long-term industrial success. These concerns lead us to offer some of our own proposals for the future direction of industrial policy, with a particular emphasis upon a greater diffusion of strategic decision-making.

Regional Policies and Small Firms

Given the extent of regional hollowing out in Japan (see Table 2.5), it is reasonable to suggest that the main focus of Japanese industrial policy should primarily be towards the regeneration of the prefectures. In this respect, it is perhaps first important to reconsider the Technopolis Project, which was an early attempt by MITI to counteract the effects of outsourcing and avoid problems of hollowing out (see Broadbent, 1989).

The Technopolis Project was launched in 1983, with the aim of establishing a number of high-tech cities throughout Japan's prefectures. In many respects, the Technopolis Project reflected Japan's determination to build and develop 'world cities', each of which could attract and retain major investors and modern industry in the global economy (see also Friedman, 1986, on the world cities concept). The emphasis was upon the creation of science parks, or advanced technological production sites with close linkages with universities and other research centres. By the mid-1990s, approximately 30 projects had begun under the scheme (Whittaker, 1997). At best, the Technopolis Project has been only partially successful. In the early days, some smaller prefectures, such as Oita, were able to use their Technopolis status to regenerate industry within its towns and villages (Broadbent, 1989). We have already noted that Hamamatsu City, in Shizuoka prefecture, is also regarded as being a relatively successful high-tech, Technopolis city (Whittaker, 1997). However, as Table 2.5 illustrates, on the wider scale, the project has not been sufficient to negate the effects of globalisation and the problems of hollowing out.

In this respect, a closer look at the Technopolis Project might provide a reason for its relative failure to avert the hollowing out of industrial Japan.

Under the scheme the main instruments of policy were tax breaks, depreciation allowances and special loan rates (Broadbent, 1989). These types of
subsidy are all policies that generally favour the attraction of large-scale
corporations rather than the development of an independent small-firm base
(Armstrong and Taylor, 2000). In the global economy, this policy bias is
unlikely to encourage long-term investment that is embedded within the local
economy. Large-scale corporations take a global perspective and their regional
operations are likely to be regarded as being nothing more than footloose
investments. Indeed, Broadbent (1989) first recognised this potential problem
during the early stages of the Technopolis Project. Broadbent's (1989, p. 250)
study of Technopolis concluded 'the Japanese State [and the Technopolis
Project] is not very strong in the face of broad world economic trends, [which]
affect the investment logic of individual companies, causing them to respond
in ways similar to that in the West, leading to ever greater international investment' (own additions in brackets).

The inherent bias towards large firms within the Technopolis Project is very
similar to MITI's other post-war industrial policies, which have contributed to
a concentration of strategic decision-making within corporate Japan. In the
light of Japan's strategic failure and the recent experiences of hollowing out,
we would therefore advocate a move towards more non-hierarchical modes of
production, with strategic decision-making becoming more devolved at a local
level. This would lead us to favour policies that strengthen Japan's small-firm
base, with a specific focus upon nurturing independent small-firm entities
rather than subsidising a small-firm base that is subservient to the interests of
the large-scale transnationals. We would particularly welcome policies that
primarily aid the development and extension of those horizontal small-firm
networks within Japan's traditional *sanchi* regions.

In our view, the expansion of Japan's *sanchi* regions offers Japanese manufacturing the best opportunity to arrest the current decline. In particular, the
development of these small horizontal networks may provide the basis for
what Best (1990) has described as 'collective entrepreneurialism'. Here, cooperative clusters of small firms engage in a mode of flexible specialisation,
where they are able to innovate, diversify and eventually emerge to compete
with the large transnational corporations. These small-firm networks are
sometimes referred to as the 'new competition', and are best exemplified in
the Italian industrial districts of Emilia-Romagna. It is, therefore, perhaps
encouraging that MITI has been studying the Italian experience as a way
forward for the revitalisation of Japanese manufacturing (JSBRI, 1996).

It is important to recognise that a wider role for Japan's *sanchi* will require
a significant change of emphasis within Japan. This is particularly the case
within the machinery sector, where transactions are predominantly vertical.
Policies should be geared towards reducing the dependence of small firms

upon their main contractors. They should also favour close cooperation both within and between small-firm networks. At a practical level, the Japanese state could target aid to smaller firms to enable them to upgrade their technological capability. This may provide Japan's small firms with an opportunity to become more independent from their main contractors, since it may allow them to diversify their product range and target niche markets.[5] In addition, MITI could also undertake substantial investment in the upgrading of public infrastructure and expand Japan's public research and development facilities. These facilities should be designed to serve whole networks of small firms and would, therefore, be very different from some of the PTR centres that are currently controlled by Japan's transnational corporations (see Ruigrok and Tate, 1996). Small firms should also be encouraged to foster closer links between themselves, both within and between prefectures. Such linkages could also be allowed to develop at an international level, between Japan's *sanchi* firms and small firms elsewhere, effectively creating multinational webs, which embrace a true sense of multinationalism (Cowling and Sugden, 1999 and also Chapter 1). These webs could be supported with appropriate institutional arrangements at a regional, national and supra-national level, involving industrial and commercial bodies, educational linkages and mutual research centres.

Finally, we should note that our approach to Japanese industrial policy is different from the conventional policy proposals, advocated by Anglo-US commentators. These commentators typically argue that Japan should engage in a further deregulation of its economy and encourage more inward FDI to avoid the problems of hollowing out. However, we would argue that there are no guarantees that such policies would stem or reverse the hollowing out of Japan. Indeed, such measures may even exacerbate the crisis, since they encourage the process of elite globalisation and the concentration of strategic decision-making. In this respect, it is interesting to note that both Renault's purchase of a controlling interest in Nissan and General Motors' increased equity participation in Isuzu have led to automobile plant closures and significant redundancies in Japan's major industrial belts.[6]

Lessons for Wisconsin and Other Regions

We began this chapter with a motivation to learn from Japan's recent experiences to guide the future process of industrial policy-making in Wisconsin and other regions. In South-eastern Wisconsin, for instance, policy-makers are keen to develop both existing and new business clusters, with an emphasis upon attracting high-tech firms to the region. An important facet of South-eastern Wisconsin's approach is the Techstar initiative – a consortium of business, academe and government – which aims to foster technology-related economic development by helping the business community to adopt new technologies (see Mone, Chapter 11 of this volume, and Zimpher et al. in the Appendix to that chapter).

The caveat from Japan's recent experiences is that such initiatives should be fully aware of the types of cluster that South-eastern Wisconsin wishes to develop (see also the chapter by Bellandi in this volume). In this respect, it is important for policy-makers to take full account of the global activities of the larger corporations that South-eastern Wisconsin wishes to attract and the types of industrial linkages that they are likely to build with the state's indigenous firms. The Techstar initiative, for example, shares a number of similarities with the Japanese Technopolis Project, with an emphasis upon the new economy and in attracting and retaining principal investors to the region. These are major considerations since, as we have seen in the case of Japan, clusters that involve networks of small firms subservient to the global interests of a corporate elite are unlikely to provide long-term sustainable economic prosperity.

7.   CONCLUSIONS

This chapter has explored the problems of hollowing out within Japan's machinery industries. We have argued that the current problems of deindustrialisation are linked to the hierarchical nature of Japan's industrial structure and also a misguided industrial policy that appeared to favour the development of large-scale corporations. This has led to a concentration of strategic decisions within corporate Japan. In the global economy, this elite group now regards its future as being increasingly involved in transnational production networks to such an extent that it has precipitated a hollowing out of Japan's industrial base, raising the prospect of strategic failure.

At a fundamental level, it is only through recognising the roots of Japan's strategic failure that we are able to suggest directions for the renewal of Japanese manufacturing and, in particular, the machinery sector. In this respect, we have advocated that Japan move towards a more non-hierarchical mode of production, with a policy emphasis towards the extension of the Japanese *sanchi* and the development of horizontal small-firm networks. It is our view that such a shift in industrial policy-making is more likely to lead to sustainable industrial development and serve the wider public interest.

Finally, this chapter provides an important lesson from the Japanese experience for Wisconsin and other regions and localities that are involved in industrial policy-making. For a long period in Japan's post-war economy, the success of the machinery sector and the cultivation of Japan's large-scale corporations appeared congruent to Japan's industrial development. However, as we have shown, an over-reliance upon transnational corporations is unlikely to provide long-term stability. Industrial policy-makers should be aware of this lesson when considering new policy initiatives.

NOTES

* We are grateful to comments and suggestions from participants at the Second L'institute–Milwaukee Workshop. The usual disclaimer applies. Philip Tomlinson acknowledges financial support from the ESRC grant no. R00429834718 to conduct this project.
1. The machinery sector consists of five industry subsectors: fabricated metal products (ISIC 381), agricultural and industrial machinery (ISIC 382), electrical machinery and electric goods (ISIC 383), transport equipment (ISIC 384) and precision tools (ISIC 385). See Table 2.3 for further details.
2. The economic rationale for the state to encourage industrial development through an institutional style of capitalism and an active industrial policy is associated with the literature on 'development traps' (see Rosenstein-Rodan, 1943; Gerschenkron, 1962; Murphy et al., 1989).
3. The concerns over foreign direct investment were twofold. MITI was concerned that inward flows of FDI would lead to foreign competitors (mainly from the USA) entering and monopolising Japanese markets, at the expense of indigenous industry. There were also fears that outward FDI would lead to 'reverse exports', which would also harm less efficient domestic infant industries (see Bailey et al., 1994).
4. Pitelis (1996, 2000) argues that deficient domestic demand initiates outward FDI.
5. It was suggested to us that the hierarchical nature of Japan's industrial structure might have actually stifled the potential for the Japanese economy to produce sufficient entrepreneurs who would facilitate the promotion of such activities. In this respect, it may therefore be advantageous for MITI to encourage a greater entrepreneurial spirit amongst the wider Japanese small business community perhaps through trade associations and enterprise clubs. For an in-depth review of Japan's small-firm sector, see Whittaker (1997).
6. We are particularly grateful to John Connor, of Purdue University, for this point.

REFERENCES

Aoki, M. (1988), *Information, Incentives, and Bargaining in the Japanese Economy*, New York: Cambridge University Press.

Aoki, M. (1990), 'Toward an economic model of the Japanese firm', *Journal of Economic Literature*, **28**(1), 1–27.

Aoki, M. (1994), 'The Japanese firm as a system of attributes: a survey and research agenda', in M. Aoki and R. Dore (eds), *The Japanese Firm, Sources of Competitive Strength*, Oxford: Oxford University Press, pp. 11–40.

Armstrong, H. and Taylor, J. (2000), *Regional Economics and Policy*, Oxford, UK: Blackwell.

Bailey, D., Harte, G. and Sugden, R. (1994), *Transnationals and Governments, Recent Policies in Japan, France, Germany, the USA and Britain*, London: Routledge.

Beamish, P.W., Delios, A. and Lecraw, D.J. (1997), *Japanese Multinationals in the Global Economy*, Cheltenham, UK and Lyme, US: Edward Elgar.

Best, M.H. (1990), *The New Competition*, London: Polity Press.

Broadbent, J. (1989), 'The technopolis strategy vs. de-industrialisation: high-tech development sites in Japan', in M.P. Smith (ed.), *Pacific Rim Cities in the World*

Economy, Comparative Urban and Community Research Studies Volume 12, London: New Brunswick, pp. 231–53.

Cowling, K. and Sugden, R. (1994), *Beyond Capitalism, Towards a New World Economic Order*, London: Pinter.

Cowling, K. and Sugden, R. (1998), 'The essence of the modern corporation: markets, strategic decision-making and the theory of the firm', *The Manchester School*, **66**(1), 59–86.

Cowling, K. and Sugden, R. (1999), 'The wealth of localities, regions and nations: developing multinational economies', *New Political Economy*, **4**(3), 361–78.

Cowling, K. and Tomlinson, P.R. (2000), 'The Japanese crisis – a case of strategic failure?', *Economic Journal*, **110**(464), 358–81.

Cowling, K. and Tomlinson, P.R. (2002), 'Revisiting the roots of Japan's economic stagnation: the role of the Japanese corporation', *International Review of Applied Economics*, **16**(4), 373–90.

Dicken, P. (1998), *Global Shift, Transforming the World Economy*, Wiltshire, UK: Cromwell Press.

Dodwell Marketing Consultants (1997), *The Structure of the Japanese Auto Parts Industry*, Tokyo: Dodwell.

Dunning, J.H. (1993), *Multinational Enterprises and the Global Economy*, New York: Addison Wesley.

Electronic Industries Association of Japan (EIAJ, 1997), *Facts and Figures on the Japanese Electronics Industry 1997*, Tokyo: Public Affairs Office, EIAJ.

Friedman, J. (1986), 'The world city hypothesis', *Development and Change*, **17**, 69–83.

Gerlach, M.L (1992), *Alliance Capitalism: The Social Organisation of Japanese Business*, California: University of California Press.

Gerschenkron, A. (1962), *Economic Backwardness in Historical Perspective*, Cambridge: Cambridge University Press.

Gittelman, M. and Dunning, J.H. (1992), 'Japanese multinationals in Europe and the United States: some comparisons and contrasts', in M.W. Klein and P.J.J. Welfens (eds), *Multinationals and the New Europe and Global Trade*, Berlin: Springer-Verlag, pp. 237–67.

James, B.G. (1989), *Trojan Horse: The Ultimate Japanese Challenge to Western Industry*, London: Mercury.

Japan Economic Planning Agency (EPA, 1995), *Social and Economic Plan for Structural Reforms – Towards a Vital Economy and Secure Life*, White Paper, Tokyo: EPA.

Japan Small Business Research Institute (JSBRI, 1996), *The Age of Small Business: The Foundation for Reconstruction of the Japanese Economy*, White Paper, Tokyo: JSBRI, MITI.

Japan Statistics Bureau, Management and Coordination Agency (2001), *Japanese Statistical Yearbook 2001*, Tokyo: Japan Statistical Association.

Japanese External Trade Organisation (JETRO, 1997), *White Paper on International Trade*, Tokyo: JETRO Publications.

Japanese Small Business Corporation (JSBC, 1998), *The Position of Japan's SME's* (copies available http://www.jsbc.go.jp/english/esme2.html).

Johnson, C. (1982), *MITI and the Japanese Miracle: The Growth of Industrial Policy 1925–75*, Stanford: Stanford University Press.

Jones, C.I. (1995), 'Time series of endogenous growth models', *Quarterly Journal of Economics*, **110**(2), 495–525.

Marshall, A. (1919), *Industry and Trade*, London: Macmillan.

Mason, M. (1994), 'Historical perspectives on Japanese direct investment in Europe', in M. Mason and D. Encarnation (eds), *Does Ownership Matter? Japanese Multinationals in Europe*, Oxford: Clarendon Press, pp. 1–38.

Ministry of International Trade and Industry (MITI, 1998), *Summary of the 27th Survey of Overseas Business Activities of Japanese Companies (Survey 1997)*, Tokyo: MITI.

Murphy, K.M., Schleifer, A. and Vishny, R.W. (1989), 'Industrialisation and the big push', *Journal of Political Economy*, **97**(5), 1003–26.

Nikkei Weekly (19 October 1998), 'Bankruptcy debt hits 1st half record', New York: Nihon Keizai Shimbun Inc.

Nikkei Weekly (25 October 1999), 'Can Ghosn steer Nissan along the road to recovery?', New York: Nihon Keizai Shimbun Inc.

Nikkei Weekly (21 May 2001), 'Nissan stages swift comeback, but still trails frontrunners', New York: Nihon Keizai Shimbun Inc.

Nikkei Weekly (18 June 2001), 'Japanese R&D trickling overseas: skilled, cheap work forces in other Asian nations attracting Japanese firms', New York: Nihon Keizai Shimbun Inc.

Organisation for Economic Cooperation and Development (OECD, 1999), *International Direct Investment Statistics Yearbook*, Paris: OECD.

Ozawa, T. (1973), 'Technology imports and direct foreign investment in Japan', *Journal of World Trade Law*, **7**(6), 666–79.

Ozawa, T. (1991), 'Japan in a new phase of multinationalism and industrial upgrading: functional integration of trade, growth and FDI', *Journal of World Trade*, **25**, 43–60.

Ozawa, T. (1992), 'Cross investments between Japan and the EC: income similarity, technological congruity and economies of scope', in J. Cantwell (ed.), *Multinational Investment in Modern Europe: Strategic Interaction in the Integrated Community*, Aldershot, UK and Brookfield, US: Edward Elgar, pp. 13–45.

Peoples, J. and Sugden, R. (2000), 'Divide and rule by transnational corporations', in R. Sugden and C.N. Pitelis (eds), *The Nature of the Transnational Firm*, London: Routledge, pp. 174–92.

Piore, M. and Sabel, C. (1984), *The Second Industrial Divide: Possibilities for Prosperity*, New York: Basic Books.

Pitelis, C.N. (1996), 'Effective demand, outward investment and the (theory of the) transnational corporation: an empirical investigation', *Scottish Journal of Political Economy*, **43**(2), 192–206.

Pitelis, C.N. (2000), 'The TNC: an all-weather company', in R. Sugden and C.N. Pitelis (eds), pp. 193–209.

Rosenstein-Rodan, P. (1943), 'The problems of industrialisation of Eastern and South Eastern Europe', *Economic Journal*, **53**, 203–11.

Ruigrok, W. and Tate, J.J. (1996), 'Public testing and research centres in Japan: control and nurturing of small and medium-sized enterprises in the automobile industry', *Technology Analysis & Strategic Management*, **8**(4), 381–401.

Ruigrok, W. and van Tulder, R. (1995), *The Logic of International Restructuring*, London: Routledge.

Sacchetti, S. and Sugden, R. (forthcoming), 'The governance of networks and economic power: the nature and impact of subcontracting relationships', *Journal of Economic Surveys*.

Scher, M.J. (1997), *Japanese Interfirm Networks and their Main Banks*, London: Macmillan.

Smitka, M.J. (1991), *Competitive Ties: Subcontracting in the Japanese Automotive Industry*, New York: Columbia University Press.

Sony Corporation (1999), *Annual Report*, Tokyo: Sony Corp.

Toyo Keizai Inc. (1999), *The Japan Company Handbook*, Tokyo: Toyo Keizai.

United Nations (UNCTAD, 1997), *World Investment Report 1997*, New York: United Nations.

United Nations (UNCTAD, 2000), *World Investment Report 2000: Cross-Border Mergers and Acquisitions and Development*, New York: United Nations.

Whittaker, D.H. (1997), *Small Firms in the Japanese Economy*, Cambridge: Cambridge University Press.

Womack, J.P., Jones, D.T. and Roos, D. (1990), *The Machine that Changed the World*, New York: Rawson Associates.

3. Regional prosperity in a globalised economy: evidence from Mexico

Kaye G. Husbands

1. INTRODUCTION

The impact of trade liberalisation on economic welfare is typically measured by changes in the volume of trade, output, employment, productivity, and the net flow of physical and portfolio capital. While these are adequate static measures of economic activity, they do not capture a country's dynamic capabilities that indicate the potential for long-term growth. Therefore, the assessment of NAFTA's (North American Free Trade Agreement) effect on economic welfare, for example, should take into account the influence of trade liberalisation on technological change, especially in the case of Mexico.

Mexico's road to internationalisation has taken about 20 years. Protectionist policies of the 1960s and early 1970s gave way to export promotion and tariff reduction policies in the late 1970s through to the present. Mexico joined the GATT (General Agreement on Tariffs and Trade) in 1986, NAFTA was initiated in 1994, and Mexico is now poised to be a part of the Free Trade Agreement of the Americas in 2005. The reconfiguration of Mexico's industrial structure accompanied the move to freer trade. Industrial policies that protected infant industries in the 1960s were replaced by government policies in the 1990s, which granted national (Mexican) status to foreign (non-indigenous) firms. As trade liberalises and as most barriers to ownership of capital by foreign companies fall, foreign companies are increasingly becoming the sources of local production and innovation.

The critical question of this chapter is: does economic growth in Mexico depend on the viability of indigenous Mexican firms, or do transplanted production and imports contribute as much or even more to the Mexican economy? More precisely, is there a reduction in indigenous innovation that critically impairs future growth, as foreign firms supplant indigenous firms under liberalised trade and ownership rules?

This question is similar to the 'Who is Us?' question that was posed by Robert Reich over a decade ago. In his 1990 *Harvard Business Review* article, Reich argued that productive capacity is enhanced through the inflow of physical capital. Transplanted firms are a net benefit to domestic productivity and the focus on promoting indigenous firms is misguided. Often, Reich argues, the home-based firms have more productive activity outside the nation than within the home borders. Foreign firms that operate within the home country's geographic borders might contribute more to domestic welfare (through employment and production and technological spillovers) than do indigenous firms. Reich used several industry examples to fortify his point.

Reich's main argument, therefore, is that as advanced economies globalise, their most important competitive asset becomes the skills and cumulative learning of its workforce, not their corporations. Using his example, Corporation A is headquartered in the United States. US investors hold the majority of its shares. The company undertakes much of its research and development (R&D), product design and most of its complex manufacturing outside the borders of the US, while it sells the product mainly in the US. In comparison, there is Corporation B, which is headquartered abroad and citizens of the home country hold the majority of its shares. Its US subsidiary employs mainly US citizens, and the US is the base for much of Corporation B's R&D, product design and manufacturing. Corporation B exports an increasing portion of its US-based production back to its home country.[1]

The capstone of Reich's argument is that foreign subsidiaries in the US improve the productivity of the US worker. For example, the Toyota–General Motors joint venture in California (NUMMI) dramatically improved the productivity of a plant that GM was about to close. Therefore, Reich posits that US ownership of a corporation is much less relevant to domestic economic productivity, than the skills, training and knowledge that are acquired by US workers at transplants. He states that, '[i]f we hope to revitalize the competitive performance of the US economy, we must invest in people, not in nationally defined corporations . . . The American corporation is simply no longer "us". '

Reich's assessment that it is important for a nation to invest in its human capital to boost productivity is strongly supported in both business and economic development literature. For example, Michael Porter's (1990) diamond of competitive advantage includes a node for factor conditions. Investment in the capabilities of local factors of production (including, but not exclusively, labour) creates the basis for future innovation and increased long-term productivity. In Reich's examples, the skill level in the US supports the placement of the full value-added chain of a company in the US, with benefits mutually derived by US workers and the foreign corporations.[2] Following this argument, it is reasonable to expect enhanced social welfare when higher-performing firms replace lower-performing firms, irrespective of the location from which the stronger firms hail. Having the fittest firms survive has clear merit.

Yet consider a scenario that might exist in manufacturing in the developing country context. Suppose that the home country is a latecomer to economic development. In addition, there is a bias by assemblers in the globalised industry to maintain long-term relationships with their traditional suppliers[3] instead of developing new relationships with suppliers in the local manufacturing base. That is, firms that assemble goods in the developing country still rely on their traditional suppliers for inputs (through imports or through local production by transplanted suppliers) rather than sourcing inputs in the developing country. (See also the previous chapter by Cowling and Tomlinson in this volume, discussing supply chains involving Japanese firms.) Furthermore, suppose that strains of technological innovation vary by location, such that technological diversity is reduced as assemblers limit the geographical scope from which they choose suppliers. There are therefore variant strains of technology by geographic location.

One outcome of this scenario, surprisingly, is that static welfare-improving decisions by assemblers might indeed be long-term welfare-impairing. As assemblers continue to utilise and develop products and processes of their traditional suppliers, they are bypassing or supplanting potentially superior technologies of the non-traditional suppliers. But why would assemblers make a non-profit-maximizing decision on their sourcing of technology? The assembler should select the best-available technology, even though it appears that they are blindly wedded to innovations of their traditional suppliers. Indeed, several studies have shown (Helper and Sako, 1995; Dyer, 1996) that strong supplier–customer relationships yield higher profit margins. Such studies recognise the positive net benefits of long-term collaborative relationships between assemblers and suppliers, particularly in the automotive industry. However, those studies do not measure the impact of cooperative vertical relationships on the varieties or strains of innovations that are developed. The focus of those studies is therefore on medium-term tangible outcomes such as the speed of technological development, the number of new products introduced and the number of new processes developed. Issues pertaining to the path dependency of technological innovation and the number of different strains of technology that are cultivated are not discussed in that literature.

In this chapter, it is argued that the fundamentals of indigenous growth – particularly indigenous innovation and entrepreneurship – could create welfare benefits, as seeds of Mexican innovation germinate and contribute to global technological capacity. These benefits, measured dynamically, are enjoyed locally and globally. Therefore, the role of the entrepreneur in Mexico must be factored in as estimates are made of trade liberalisation's impact on domestic economic welfare.

In the specific case of the Mexican automotive industry, assemblers have long been encouraging their traditional suppliers to establish production facilities locally, thereby replacing the productive capacity of competing Mexican suppliers. Only in the case where the product must be augmented and adapted to the Mexican climate, altitude in Mexico City, road conditions, or different utilisation of a product is R&D conducted in Mexico, utilising Mexican ingenuity. Although foreign transplants enhance the domestic capacity to produce goods (typically with lower costs, greater volume, at greater speed and of greater quality and variety), thriving indigenous firms are also essential to Mexico's growth.

The term 'metal ceilings' is introduced here to connote the seemingly impenetrable obstacles that most Mexican autoparts suppliers face as they endeavour to compete in a globalising automobile industry. Few Mexican automotive suppliers – those that either belong to a large enterprise group (*grupo*) or those for which strategic alliances have been successful – are able to push past the prevalent imposing barriers, such as: limited financial resources; dated intellectual and physical capital; imperfect information-sharing and limited communications with customers; and inability to create an adaptable organisation. As the automotive industry globalises, will the role of indigenous Mexican suppliers diminish? If so, then what effect will this have on local (and global) innovation?

This chapter proceeds as follows. Section 2 shows that technological diffusion is, at best, weak through the vehicles of trade and foreign direct investment (FDI). Indigenous innovation is therefore a critical factor in building domestic technological capacity. Section 3 lays the foundational arguments for the positive net benefits of technological diversity. These welfare benefits accrue both locally and globally. Building on this argument, Section 4 examines the case of Mexico, where a national technology policy and fortified industrial clusters are possible solutions to Mexico's lagging technological development. Concluding remarks are made in Section 5.

2.   GLOBALISATION AND TECHNOLOGICAL DEVELOPMENT

Foreign Direct Investment

The terms internationalisation and globalisation are often used interchangeably. However in this chapter the term globalisation goes beyond mere vigorous trade and investment between the countries. Instead, globalisation implies a connection between activities in two or more economies (compare the analysis by Sugden and Wilson in Chapter 1 of this volume). For example, Porter (1990) defines a global firm as one that is highly geographically dispersed and one that has a high coordination of activities that take place in those countries.

A company can thus be a multinational enterprise (MNE), but not a global firm. Such a company might merely have operations in two or more countries but no interconnectedness between any of its dispersed activities. The idea of interconnectedness or linkage of activities between economies around the world that Porter describes is one of the foundational tenets used in this chapter as the effects of globalisation are explored.

Ohmae (1989) argues that newly industrialised countries join the interlinked economies of the United States, the European Community and Japan in creating a 'borderless world', where national differences in corporate production strategies are diminished. Trading blocs, non-government organisations and multinationals are the linkages between countries, 'supra-national institutions' that form synapses between various national systems of production. These synapses allow nations to exchange elements of expertise that are the product of 'subnational institutions'. A firm's access to centres of technological excellence, regional industrial clusters, low wage zones, and export-processing zones is more important to its productivity and profitability, than is the location of its headquarters. Ohmae contends that the importance of national boundaries diminishes in global competition, while the importance of resource accessibility increases.

An alternative view is articulated in Porter (1990), Lundvall (1993), Davies (1996), Hulsink (1996) and Freeman and Soete (1997). These authors argue independently that national systems of technological development and production are quite conspicuous even as supra-national institutions proliferate. Specifically, Porter states that:

> Differences in national economic structure, values, cultures, institutions and histories contribute profoundly to competitive success. The role of the home nation seems to be as strong or stronger than ever. While globalisation or competition might appear to make the national less important, instead it seems to make it more so. With fewer impediments to trade to shelter uncompetitive domestic firms and industries, the home nation takes on growing significance because it is the source of the skills and technology that underpin competitive advantage. (p. 19)

Ohmae's concept of a 'borderless world' is therefore challenged by Porter's characterisation of a national imprimatur on technology and production techniques. Davies (1996) and Hulsink (1996) each take this argument further. They assert that the national brand of technology or a national style of production increases in importance with increased global competition. The nation is still the genesis of research and design, and therefore the foundation for competitive advantage. Diversity of innovation therefore depends on diverse nodes of ingenuity.

Freeman and Soete (1997) utilise research on patent statistics published in Patel and Pavitt (1991) and Patel (1995) to support their hypothesis that multinationals rely primarily on homegrown R&D. The data show that less than 10 per cent of the R&D activities of US companies and less than 2 per cent of R&D activities of Japanese companies is done outside the home country. Product and process design changes that occur outside the home country are made primarily to meet local standards and regulations, to adjust to differences in resource availability, or to learn from local innovative efforts. Most industries are parochial in their adaptation of technological innovation.[4]

Multinational enterprises, therefore, may have a hegemonic influence on local policies and on local innovation. Technological developments in an MNE's home base supplant rather than utilise or fortify local innovation. Stopford and Strange (1991) assert that '[h]owever great the global reach of their operations, the national firm does, psychologically and sociologically, "belong" to its home base'. Host governments are not an even match for the powerful multinational; MNEs can thus shape host-country policies in their favour. Writing in *Economic Geography*, Peter Dicken (1994) reinforces Gertler's assertion that: 'nation-states have produced (and continue to produce) rather distinct national systems of innovation which create particular possibilities for economic change while precluding others' (Gertler, 1992). Dicken argues that the home-base environment of multinationals fundamentally determines the decision-making of the firm, not the local environment in which it establishes a subsidiary or transplant.[5] Thus, the hegemonic reach of multinationals not only shapes a host country's policies, but the intellectual and cultural aspects of the home country implies a deterministic path of innovation that minimises the adaptation of innovation that is generic to the host country. If multinationals significantly dominate or supplant local firms, then the genesis of future innovation will be derived from the dominant (foreign) culture or methodology. The overlay of foreign technology via the MNEs on indigenous technology could eradicate vital strains of innovation that otherwise could be useful to both local and foreign producers. Indeed, the very MNE could reap positive net benefits by integrating traditional methods of production or product development with those that have their genesis in the location of their subsidiary.

Clearly, foreign direct investment can yield positive spillover effects by way of technological upgrading. There is a vast literature documenting the benefits of foreign direct investment to host-country firms and institutions. However, FDI is not a panacea for technological growth, especially in the developing country context. The standard caution is that receptors must be developed in the host country if there is to be a successful transfer of knowledge and know-how. Probing further, Freeman and Soete (1997) poignantly recommend that active policies must exist within the developing country to encourage indigenous entrepreneurship and innovation. Otherwise, technology transfer from MNEs to local firms will meet with limited success. They prescribe the creation in the host countries of institutions that enable local firms to capture and utilise imported technology. Freeman and Soete emphasise the need for active policies that spur local ingenuity. Local improvement of technological capabilities is necessary to enhance the portfolio of innovation that will be useful locally and globally. Thus technology policy must focus not only on developing receptors of new ideas, but also on developing purveyors of innovation.

In the case of Mexico, empirical analysis has shown at least a strong correlation between technology transfer and competitive local conditions. Blomström (1986) uses the 'Mexican Census of Manufactures' for 1970 and 1975, unpublished ownership data segmented by industry and productive efficiency indicators[6] to analyse the effects on the industrial structure and on technology upgrading of FDI. He reports that there is a positive correlation between 'foreign presence' and 'structural efficiency'. On average, the presence of MNEs increases competition in Mexican manufacturing industries. Furthermore, the study shows that production is closer to 'best practice' for the average firms when an MNE is present in a given industry. However, Blomström's study does not find support for a causal relationship between FDI and an increased speed of technology transfer to Mexico. He concludes instead that competitive pressure from MNEs matters more for increased productivity than does explicit technology transfer. The reason is that local input markets are driven to operate more efficiently as suppliers attempt to satisfy global sourcing standards.

Blomström, Kokko and Zejan (1994) report on results based on the same data set to determine which local conditions have a positive influence on technology transfer in Mexico. In addition to pro-competitive market conditions, the level of technology imports is positively correlated with labour skills.[7] Similarly, Grether (1999) finds support for the argument that 'external economies' are generated by MNEs in Mexican manufacturing sectors, with geographic concentration of the labour force as the catalyst for technology diffusion. The empirical analysis supports the conclusion that local conditions must be primed for effective technology transfer. It is not sufficient merely to have an MNE present in a given location for technological diffusion to local firms.

There is clear empirical evidence to support the need for pro-competitive market structures, a skilled or specialised workforce, and the absence of rigid technology transfer controls and oversight. However, these models only capture static relationships. The hegemonic influence of MNEs on local innovation can diminish the long-term or dynamic benefits of innovation. Therefore, the need for the development of local subsystems of innovation is at least twofold: first, it is necessary for the capture and appropriate utilisation of foreign technology; and second, it is necessary for the creation of new technologies, which might at least be orthogonal and hopefully complementary to the borrowed technology. Increased technological diversity, whether it is in the form of machines, processes or know-how, is theoretically shown to be globally welfare-improving (see Section 3 below). Freeman and Soete argue that the synergy of subnational systems of innovation and imported technology is necessary for 'sustaining a global regime favorable to catching up and development'. This argument suggests a role for local industrial clusters – an existing and developing subnational system of innovation in Mexico. This solution is discussed in Section 4.

Trade

Globalisation may promote technology sharing, not just through the movement of physical capital, but also through the freer movement of goods across borders. Hence, the effectiveness of technology transfer through trade is well surveyed in the literature. Using several Monte Carlo simulation experiments, Keller (1998) tests whether actual trade patterns are necessary for international spillovers in research and development. Interestingly, he gets simulations with counterfactual trade patterns to generate similar or larger positive R&D spillovers compared to models with 'true' patterns of trade. Furthermore, some of the specifications where distinct patterns of trade were undetectable also yielded positive R&D spillovers. Keller, therefore, concludes that, '[t]rade-unrelated technology diffusion' matters more than just establishing a trade link.

In a subsequent paper, Keller (2000) uses data from eight countries in the Organisation for Economic Cooperation and Development (OECD) to determine the effect of trade on the technological capacity of the importing firm. It is hypothesised that firms can benefit from the technology efforts of their trading partner, particularly when imported intermediate inputs embody technologies that differ significantly from homegrown technologies. Keller has made three important findings:

1. There is evidence that countries benefit more from domestic R&D than from R&D of the average foreign country.
2. Conditional on technology diffusion from domestic R&D, the import composition of a country matters, but only if it is strongly biased toward or away from technological leaders.
3. Differences in technology inflows related to the patterns of imports explain about 20 per cent of the total variation in countries' productivity growth rates. (p. 35)

Latecomer developers might therefore gain by importing from technology leaders, provided that they are severely lagging in technology. However, if they import from countries similar to themselves, then local development of technology trumps access to foreign technology through trade. Since Keller finds that technology inflows related to trade only explain one-fifth of the total variation in productivity, then there is arguably a significant role for local development of technology independent of external markets.

Technology upgrading could also result from the desire to become competitive in foreign markets. For example, the technical sophistication of foreign buyers could challenge local firms to invest in world-class technology. In addition, buyers might specify and even provide the leading-edge technology that is required to make their product first rate. Competition in export markets could also have positive spillover effects to local non-exporters that are in the industry cluster. Using data on Colombia and Morocco,[8] Clerides, Lach and Tybout (1998) empirically test the hypothesis that export-led growth improves technical efficiency. The hypothesis could not be rejected for Colombian firms. These firms did see improvements in labour productivity and in skill intensity as a result of exporting. Non-exporters also reaped efficiency gains generated by the exporters. For Morocco, exporting activities increased costs in some sectors and decreased costs in others. Only for apparel and leather goods was the phenomenon of 'learning by exporting' observed in Morocco. The authors admit that the association (not causal relationship) between exporting and economic efficiency could have been the result of selection bias: firms that could more easily jump the technology hurdle were more likely to compete in export markets.

In sum, globalisation may foster technology upgrading by facilitating freer trade and linkages between trading partners. However, latecomer developers – such as Mexico – are better primed to reap the benefits of such linkages if local technology development systems exist. The literature on foreign direct investment and trade supports the view that indigenous innovation is a necessary, though not sufficient, element for technological development in developing countries. This is not a new idea.

The important extension in this chapter is that indigenous innovation in developing countries could have positive spillover effects on the developed nations. For example, firms in the US, Japan and Europe might find that access to very distinct technology processes spurs the development of new products and processes that are not only utilised in the country of origin – in this case a developing country – but also in global markets. Specific case studies for Mexico that exemplify such synergy are presented in the next subsection.

Indigenous Innovation and 'Metal Ceilings'

An established and effective national system of innovation is critical for the international exchange of knowledge, even though each country may have its own ethos in learning. Strassmann (1968) perceives 'tacit knowledge' as strategic, while difficult to communicate across borders. Nevertheless, his research shows that '[o]ne can borrow most effectively if one also has the capacity to be original. Still, countries can develop, though at a slower rate, on the basis of passive, even haphazard, borrowing'. A corollary to this proposition is that true integration in global technological development requires that developing countries become sources – not just receptors – of innovation as well.

Strassmann uses case studies on Mexican industries to illustrate how local characteristics shape the type and style of newly developed products or processes. Though not intentioned, these case studies also demonstrate the positive spillover effects of innovations in Mexico to foreign producers. For example, Strassmann describes how the Mexican patented process of making stabilised tortilla flour evolved. A specific process that has its genesis in Mexican craft-styled mills in the nineteenth century was further developed in the early twentieth century by trial and error experimentation. Subsequently, more formal directed research in the 1950s was conducted to fine-tune and patent the process. Banco de Mexico sponsored the research at the Instituto Mexicano de Investigaciones Technologicas. The patented process was then purchased by the Quaker Oats Company, which established plants in Texas and California.

In another case, Strassmann describes the innovative contribution to steel production by HYLSA (Hojalata y Lámina), the still-existing steel monopoly in Monterrey, Nueva Leon. Several US companies, including Standard Oil, US Steel, Republic Steel, National Lead and Allis-Chalmers, raced to develop a direct reduction process for iron using natural gas. However, HYLSA's continuous process was found to be superior because of the scientific and financial resources dedicated to the project. It is worth noting that HYLSA's expertise was not reliant only on Mexican ingenuity: their chief engineer was trained at the Massachusetts Institute of Technology and there was cross-fertilisation of ideas from different nations over a couple of decades. Nevertheless, the contribution of Mexican ingenuity was critical to the forward leap in the continuous-process technique for steel production.

Although Strassmann's study clearly shows the global utility of research spawned in Mexico, other researchers have uncovered the more prevalent practice of foreign technology supplanting local inventiveness. Buitelaar, Padilla and Urrutia (1999) look at the role of *maquiladora*[9] plants in technological development. The authors administered a questionnaire to 75 firms in six countries, including Mexico, Guatemala, El Salvador, Honduras, Costa Rica and the Dominican Republic. For the most part, local technology development was limited to creating prototypes or conducting product testing for local markets. In Mexico, only four of the *maquila* plants surveyed had product design departments, with foreign and local engineers; the only case where all of the design took place in Mexico was a furniture factory that sold products locally. The other three indigenous plants contributed minimally to product design, creating the appearance that satisfied local tastes. Since the ultimate decisions on technological innovation were made at the headquarters of the *maquila* and not at the local plant, the entrepreneurial spirit of local engineers was diminished. Capture by the MNE meant that autonomous design and fabrication work would not yield a just reward.

In the case of the Mexican automotive industry, there is yet another aspect of the relationship between MNE and local producer that imposes a metal ceiling on local innovation. All of the assemblers of cars and light trucks are foreign companies. Therefore, local companies are in the position of producing autoparts according to the blueprints or specifications that flow down from the assemblers. Companies that supply the original equipment manufacturers (OEMs) and those that produce aftermarket parts have little choice but to accept predetermined plans for products. Based on materials gathered during site visits to auto assemblers and suppliers during the early 1990s, Husbands (1994) describes the standard practice for assemblers to certify the production processes of local suppliers without granting the latitude to suppliers to do product innovation.[10] One particular assembler's list of certified suppliers revealed that none was certified for product development. Interviews with suppliers corroborated these findings, as they rehearsed the difficulties in getting assemblers to review or test prototypes of newly developed products.[11]

Such decisions by the assemblers could purely reflect short-run profit maximisation decisions. Even if certified Mexican suppliers satisfy cost, reliability, delivery and other performance metrics, their technology might not be deemed satisfactory by the assemblers. Products that are independently developed by local suppliers might not fit the product development strategies of the assemblers. The technology lag between the Mexican suppliers and the traditional suppliers utilised by the assemblers could pose an insurmountable hurdle. Uncertainty among assemblers about the technological capabilities of Mexican suppliers could have the same effect as an actual technology lag of Mexican suppliers relative to traditional suppliers. If any of these conditions held for Mexican suppliers, then it would be logical for traditional suppliers to be the technology leaders and for the Mexican suppliers to follow.

Buitelaar, Padilla and Urrutia (1999) find ample evidence that technology is transferred 'ready-made' by MNEs to firms in host countries. They state that:

> . . . transnational corporations do not stimulate procurement of local inputs, either
> because the corporation is vertically integrated, or because they have an established
> network of suppliers . . . it is difficult for local firms to enter, because of the certi-
> fication process for suppliers that requires time, money and technological capabili-
> ties those firms lack.

Yet, performance and perceptual obstacles can be overcome through market
signals. The certification and competition procedures that are utilised by
assemblers should be the very vehicles that allow indigenous suppliers to
signal their competitive advantages if any exist. If the financial, performance
and technology hurdles are overcome, then the local suppliers should be on the
same playing field as the traditional suppliers.

One such case was discovered during a discussion with product development engineers at an auto parts plant. The supplier is a subsidiary of a
Mexican *grupo*; it benefits from the shared financial, marketing and technological assets of the conglomerate. This firm was interviewed precisely
because it had world-class manufacturing and technological capabilities. In
the mid-1990s, this firm submitted what was determined to be the 'winning
bid' by the potential customer, a foreign automobile assembler. However,
the business was awarded to a supplier from the assembler's home country
that had not previously made the product. The product was the specific
expertise of the Mexican supplier. In other words, the Mexican supplier
did not get the business, even though it had superior technology, delivery
capabilities, quality, marketing expertise, as well as the lowest cost. This
case drives home the legitimacy of the term metal ceiling. The Mexican
supplier faced an obstacle that was insurmountable at the time: long-term
relationship-building between the assembler and one of its component
producers.[12]

The assembler's decision could have been optimal; relationship-building
between assemblers and their suppliers has been shown to yield higher profits
and shorter lead-times in product development. However, it is also possible
that the assembler forfeited even higher long-term profits, that could have
resulted from sampling a new source of ingenuity.[13]

In summary, local benefits from FDI can be illustrated by an inverted U-
shaped curve: increasing benefits up to a threshold where too many transplants reduce the social benefit of multiple strains of innovation.
Indigenous innovation is a necessary component of local development,
particularly in a globalising world. Furthermore, diversification of sources
of innovation can yield a global public good. In the case of the Mexican
auto industry, the melding of production paradigms from the US, Japan,
Germany and Mexico can be beneficial to local firms, to the MNEs and to
the industry at large.

3. THE CASE FOR TECHNOLOGICAL DIVERSITY

The case for technological diversity is well supported by three articles written by Martin Weitzman: 'On diversity' (1992); 'Hybridizing growth theory' (1996); and 'The Noah's Ark problem' (1998). Taken together, these articles establish that there are positive welfare effects from preserving a diverse canonical set, and that there is an optimal method for choosing the elements that should comprise the canon, even if resource constraints exist. Weitzman's (1992) dynamic programming equation can be used to generate an optimal classification scheme and an optimal conservation strategy in several disciplines from ecology to economics. His basic unit of analysis, a 'species', is defined in the traditional biological sense, or as 'an individual, a subspecies, a specimen, an object, or almost anything else depending on the context'. Weitzman's diversity taxonomy may take the form of differences in aesthetic value or information content. The literature on strategic groups can also be informed by his paradigm. In the context of this chapter, a species is interpreted as a vane of knowledge or know-how.

Take, for example, a case where the production processes for the same automotive product differ between two countries. The difference could be generated by input cost differences (statics), or by differences in the evolution of production techniques (dynamics). Although the latter might be influenced partly by the former, there remains a genuine uniqueness to the evolutionary process of technological development between the two countries. There are observable differences in process and product innovation across geographical borders for the same product.

Weitzman creates a theoretical construct that is pictured by an evolutionary tree. His biodiversity-styled model generates three key findings:

1. Diversity function: a 'network' is the best representation of the diversity function, which is 'some unrooted spanning tree'.
2. Loss of diversity valuation: estimated loss is pictorially calculated as if an 'evolutionary branch were snapped off the rest of the tree and discarded'.
3. Optimal conservation strategy: eliminate the 'least valuable' species. If the budget constraint is binding and, say, one species must be eliminated, then choose the one to eliminate from the two most closely related species in the set.

Consider the case of the constrained optimisation problem for technological diversity. Here Weitzman's model implies that social welfare increases when dissimilar or complementary strains of technology are combined. If objects are complementary, then there are increasing returns to added species and the joint utility is superadditive. When objects are very similar, then there are diminishing returns to added species and the joint utility is subadditive. Weitzman's proof of the welfare loss of diminished diversity combined with Dicken's (1994) evidence that multinationals do forestall local product and process technological development initiatives presents a powerful recipe suggesting that the recent attrition of Mexican autoparts suppliers could have negative long-term repercussions on manufacturing particularly in Mexico but also globally.

Taking the metaphor a step further, Weitzman (1996) argues that there is a branching or path dependency of innovation: '. . . there is a rigorous sense in which the state of present technology depends increasingly over time on the random history that determined which parent technologies happened to have been chosen in the past'. Technological diversity therefore enhances innovation and innovation is necessary for growth. This link between diversity and growth through innovation is critical. Preserving a diverse set of technologies could dominate the cultivation of ideas through long-term technology development agreements. Technological diversity promotes combinatoric growth, which dominates exponential growth. Weitzman's argument reinforces the assertion by Henri Poincaré that: 'Among chosen combinations the most fertile will often be those formed of elements drawn from domains which are far apart' (Weitzman, 1996).

Like Strassmann, Weitzman (1998) invokes the role of the social planner in the process of promoting growth through technological diversity. Strassmann briefly mentions the social planner, who 'must possess a willingness to wait and to defend a few failures and delays; they must understand the difficult maneuvers that lie between laboratory proof and first commercial sales'. In Weitzman's case, the social planner is Noah, who must foster the preservation of as many different species on earth, with limited space in the ark. Although Weitzman does not give a formulaic solution to which species are 'favoured' or why they are favoured, he does give a ranking formula that assists the social planner in prioritising the species (or innovation) to include in the canon:

1. Distinctiveness – How different is one innovation from another?
2. Utility – How much does society value a given innovation directly and indirectly?
3. Survivability – How much can the survivability of an innovation be improved?
4. Cost – How much does it cost to improve the survivability of a node of innovation?

These four elements can be combined to form an index that could be used by governments or firms as they establish a portfolio of innovation. This theory does not imply an invasive role of government in entrepreneurial activities. It does imply, however, that a government should develop a technology policy that provides for the generation and preservation of unique and diverse technologies. The government does not have to be the provider of such research directly. Given the public good characteristics of innovation, government may provide funds for research using the diversity index as a guide for the distribution of funds. In addition, it may establish and enforce laws that protect the property rights of inventors. Such policies are not in place or enforced globally. A more in-depth discussion of policy implications occurs in Section 4 below.

An individual firm could use a technology diversity index to isolate the pools of technological innovation from which to draw as they develop new products. As was discussed earlier, auto assemblers have a tendency to collaborate with their traditional suppliers on product development. In the case of Mexico, local suppliers were left out of the product development process and only relied on for the manufacturing of parts and possibly for minor adjustments to the process used to produce the parts. Even these process innovations involved strong oversight by the foreign assembler. Employing the diversity index could give assemblers an indication of missed opportunities from bypassing the raw input of indigenous innovation. Since the assemblers do source various inputs from Mexico, one of the local inputs that could be profitably utilised is indigenous innovation.

It is likely that auto assemblers in Mexico restrict sourcing of new products from indigenous suppliers because of the adverse selection problem. It could be cheaper for Ford, say, to develop a product in-house or collaboratively with a traditional supplier, because the market for innovation is inefficient in Mexico. Innovation is a public good; once a new idea is developed, the marginal cost of transferring the information from one firm to another is negligible. Therefore, an MNE might expect local suppliers to offer inferior innovations, since the going price offered will bring 'lemons' to the market instead of 'plums'. Any plum idea would bring higher returns to indigenous firms if such firms were to develop and sell the product themselves, rather than selling the innovation to an MNE. A rational assembler would therefore shun innovation from the fringe (local suppliers), thereby reducing incentives for local companies to innovate. A rational local supplier would also reduce its product development activities, particularly if it produces high-quality inventions. The nature of the vertical relationship between the assembler and supplier implies that the superior local inventor will not be able to sell their idea at a fair price. Based on Weitzman's theoretical models, this outcome is welfare reducing.

At the firm level, one solution to this problem could be that assemblers offer 'prizes' for best new idea to keep innovation going at the indigenous level. The ultimate prize would be the utilisation of the new idea in the production of existing or prototype vehicles. This idea might run foul of the long-term agreements that assemblers have with their traditional suppliers for product and technology development. The portfolio approach to innovation therefore requires careful valuation of returns to technological diversity. The diversity index described earlier could assist assemblers as they negotiate technology agreements with traditional and local parts suppliers.

4.   THE ROLE OF INDUSTRIAL CLUSTERS AND TECHNOLOGY POLICY

In a globalising world, subnational institutions such as industrial clusters contain the nucleus from which different varieties of innovation germinate (see also the discussions of clusters in many other chapters in this volume, including those by Schweitzer and Di Tommaso, and by Bellandi). This section discusses the role that industrial clusters play in creating cells of entrepreneurship. The discussion then focuses on the evolution of technology clusters in Mexico and their link to the local educational system.

The Role of Clusters

From an economic efficiency standpoint, innovation should take place in clusters, but not necessarily where production occurs. Ellison and Glaeser (1997) show empirically that various factor endowments and network externalities cause production to cluster in certain geographic areas. Those factors are different from those that cause innovative activities to cluster in other areas. Kelly and Hageman (1999) utilise patent data for US industries at the two-digit level and get similar findings.[14] Their empirical model reveals that innovation and production have different patterns of geographical distribution. Firms locate their R&D centres where other firms are conducting similar research and not necessarily where they are producing.[15]

There is empirical support for the hypothesis that agglomeration economies exist for innovation. Furthermore, there is evidence to support the proposition that regional networks of innovation are critical for growth. Using patent and location data from the US semiconductor industry, Almeida and Kogut (1999) find that regional networks provide a nurturing environment for start-ups and small firms. Large firms also benefit from the density of innovative activity in regional clusters, but they also rely on linkages to entrepreneurial and production activities in other countries. Thus, regional technology clusters – which may vary geographically from regional industrial clusters – reduce the costs of innovation and increase the communication of ideas among engineers.

Other researches find that a fertile technology cluster is a necessary organism for the generation of innovative ideas and for economic growth. Jaffe,

Trajtenberg and Henderson (1993) find that nascent firms are closely linked to regional networks. Furthermore, controlling for the density of innovative activity, they find that patent citations tend to cluster in the SMSAs where the patent was originally developed. There is also evidence that entrepreneurs rely on venture capitalists and on local suppliers as they develop new products and grow their businesses (see Rogers and Larsen, 1984); Eisenhardt and Schoonhoven, 1990; and Willner, Chapter 4 of this volume). Almeida and Kogut summarise their findings from interviews with 76 start-up semiconductor firms in the US as follows: 'Over 88 per cent of the founders were employed in the same region prior to the formation of the start-up. As can be seen, previous local experience of entrepreneurs influences the location of start-up activity and therefore the firm's networking potential.'

The Specific Case of Mexico

Resource constraints, including financial bottlenecks and the paucity of venture capital plague Mexico's economic development. Relative to developed countries, Mexico has a limited pool of inventors. Ramírez and Unger (1998) published several metrics for science and technology in Mexico. One of the stunning comparisons is the proportion of engineers and scientists in 1991. For Mexico, 9.4 of every 10 000 individuals in the labour force are engineers or scientists. The same statistic for the UK is 35.9/10 000 and that for Japan is 68.8/10 000. Large conglomerates (or *grupos*) monopolise these scientific resources, and they have the internal financing necessary for R&D. Therefore, the location of innovative activity is centred around the *grupos*, and there is therefore little dispersion of innovative activity.

Rabellotti and Schmitz (1999a), study the shoe industry in Italy, Brazil and Mexico (Guadalajara and Nuevo Leon). Using factor analysis to identify relationships between several variables and the performance of a given cluster, they find that firm size, quality of product and collective efficiency have a positive influence on firm performance, in that order. Collective efficiency is only positively linked to performance in two of the six clusters that they observed in Mexico. There is no case among the Mexican clusters where there is poor collective efficiency and high performance. Their finding supports the proposition that industrial clusters are necessary but not sufficient for improved economic performance of Mexican firms.

The importance of the *grupo*'s resources and the evidence that industrial or technology clusters are a critical component for economic development suggest that a hub-spoke configuration of indigenous innovation is likely to evolve in Mexico. This configuration has clear benefits, but one particular drawback: the regional concentration of a limited number of conglomerates reduces the diversity or sampling of entrepreneurial talents. There are only 10 to 12 conglomerates (see Ramírez and Unger, 1998) and they are geographically concentrated in pockets in northern and central Mexico. Furthermore, the market concentration of these few firms creates inefficiencies in input and output markets. There must therefore be a solution to the technology lag in Mexico that utilises local technology clusters, while distributing the sampling of innovation and reducing the inefficiencies that come with market power. One such remedy is the development of linkages between industry and educational resources. Ramírez and Unger find that such linkages are underdeveloped, creating a gulf between demand conditions and technological initiatives.

Education and the Brain Drain

Buitelaar, Padilla and Urrutia (1999) describe the tangible benefits to *maquiladoras* in northern Mexico from a strong education base there. CONALEPs, CECATIs, CETIS, state universities and various campuses of the Monterrey Institute of Technology (ITESM) integrate the needs of local industry into their curricula. Buitelaar et al. describe the activities of a 'liaison committee', which is comprised of plant workers, as well as students and professors from local academic institutions. Husbands (1994) similarly found that the engineering, manufacturing and business schools of ITESM in Monterrey and local firms jointly develop prototypes and solutions to problems with existing products. These firms compensate ITESM by providing some of the latest robots or computers in addition to members of their staff, who lecture students on the practical applications of their respective programmes. Workers from local plants also receive training at the university. These collaborative agreements between universities and industry benefit both large and small firms. Indeed, Feldman (1994) finds that small firms are twice as 'sensitive' to research performed in neighbouring universities than large firms.

A technology policy that is comingled with a dynamic educational policy can create both short-term and long-term benefits for Mexico (see also Mone in Chapter 11 of this volume, discussing the role of universities in regional economic development). However, these benefits will be diminished or short-lived, if there is no enforceable protection of property rights. Technological innovations will be under-produced if local competitors or MNEs appropriate rents due to inventors. Strassmann (1968) prescribes that a national educational policy that breeds scientists and engineers be accompanied by a national science policy that stimulates and protects intellectual capital.

There are two caveats to what seems to be a logical and efficient solution to Mexico's technology lag. First, there is the looming problem of the 'brain drain'. Talented Mexican students or entrepreneurs might find that they can earn higher rents across the border in the US than in Mexico. Proximity to the US creates a vertical dynamic that limits growth, much as the vertical relationship between assembler and supplier limits innovation. Over time, if the 'leavers' return to Mexico with capital and know-how, then Mexico could still benefit from its initial educational investment, and the cross-pollination of ideas could be welfare-improving for both Mexico and the US.

Secondly, Mexico's latecomer status will place it in direct competition with countries like South Korea or Taiwan (see Lowe and Kenney, 1999). The argument follows that as globalisation continues, Mexico will find its place cemented in the global value-added chain primarily as a manufacturing base. However, even if Mexico is not able to leapfrog other countries in terms of technological capacity, its absorptive capacity for innovation will be enhanced, contributing to greater growth for Mexico. Furthermore, a stronger base of indigenous innovation in Mexico will also have positive welfare effects globally: technological diversity spurs innovation that leads to growth.

5. CONCLUSIONS

The spatial mismatch of raw, untapped indigenous innovation, financial bottlenecks and other infrastructural limitations must be remedied for Mexico to develop productive and attractive technology hubs. If Mexico continues to play the role of low-cost manufacturing base and does not develop its technological capabilities in this globalising world, the benefits of globalisation will be diminished. Although Mexico has the most to gain from its investment in technological capacity, it is shown in this chapter that other countries can benefit from new and diverse sources of ideas and know-how.

Mexican automotive parts suppliers have been scrambling for more than one decade to appear competitive in their globalising industry. Not only did trade and investment liberalisation remove the false sense of security that they were price competitive, but the diffusion of lean production techniques worldwide forced indigenous suppliers to recognise a widening gap in capabilities. Although Mexican suppliers sought to maintain or establish new technology and equity alliances with foreign, world-class partners, they came upon at least two hindrances. First, given the vertical nature of relationships in the automotive industry, assemblers determine which suppliers will play a collaborative role in the value chain. Traditional suppliers – that is, suppliers with which the assemblers have long-term relationships irrespective of market – had long ago captured these plum positions. It was very difficult, therefore, for a Mexican supplier to ascend the hierarchy of the supply chain.

The second hindrance faced by indigenous Mexican autoparts suppliers is that, for the most part, they have been relegated to second-tier or third-tier status. Therefore, Mexican suppliers are not encouraged to engage in product development. Assemblers invest heavily in supplier development programmes to improve the production processes of the suppliers. Local suppliers might even contribute to some process innovation techniques. But the high-value-added business of product development is typically not obtained by indigenous suppliers. In their subtier position, Mexican suppliers have little control over their business, and they are easily replaced by competing (typically) foreign suppliers. Such suppliers are seeking evasive alliances with foreign producers as a stopgap strategy before exit. However, since NAFTA reduces the incentives for foreign companies to form partnerships with Mexican suppliers, the absolute number of partnerships will be significantly reduced.

In the wake of NAFTA and changes in the rules that designate enterprises as 100 per cent Mexican, the eagerness of foreign companies to partner with Mexican companies is waning. Assemblers have already begun to increase sourcing from their traditional suppliers. The pressure is on some traditional suppliers to relocate to Mexico to create a more efficient just-in-time supplier network in Mexico. Mexican suppliers are finding it much more difficult to improve their core factors through alliances. This strongly implies that small and medium-sized Mexican suppliers will continue to exit the market or be absorbed by more viable Mexican or foreign firms (see again Chapter 2 on the Japanese experience). The effect of such consolidation and rationalisation of production is positive in the sense that inefficient firms are removed from the market. However, if the diversity in technological innovation is diminished, the cost of these exiting firms could weigh critically in the overall welfare of the local (and possibly global) marketplace.

Emerging markets are enticing to auto assemblers because of the potential high growth rate of sales and long-term profits. As assemblers broaden their sales scope, they are also attempting to rationalise their global supplier base. Because of this broadening marketing focus of assemblers and the relaxation of import substitution rules in emerging economies, indigenous suppliers are increasingly facing world-class competition on price, quality, delivery, service, market flexibility, global organisational structure and ecology. Because of their latecomer status in the global supply chain, most of these suppliers are currently encountering a metal ceiling that they must push hard against to overcome. Only those suppliers that have the core capabilities of sound financial margins, strong intellectual capital, efficient mechanisms for internal and external communications and a well-tooled learning organisation will be equipped to push past this repelling ceiling.

The main solution that evolves from this discussion is a national technology-cum-educational policy, which builds and strengthens local industrial or technology clusters. This is a grand solution in an environment that is resource constrained. Nevertheless, a bootstrap method that first recognises the location of vibrant clusters and then begins to develop linkages between those clusters and local educational resources is a robust and viable beginning. Because of its vertical and horizontal linkages, the automotive industry is one that could be taped initially. However, there are no limitations, and it might just be the case that other industries yield greater economic benefits from the development and diffusion of diverse technologies. The process of globalisation could disperse these benefits beyond Mexico's borders.

NOTES

1. At the time when Reich published his article, an example of Corporation A could have been IBM where 40 per cent of world employees in 1989 were foreign, or Texas Instruments, which had many of its activities (including R&D) in East Asia. Toshiba and Honda could have been examples of Corporation B. In the late 1980s, these companies exported significant proportions of their production from US transplants to Japan. In fact, Reich states that, 'American subsidiaries of Hitachi, Matsushita, Siemens, Thomson, and many other foreign-owned companies lose no opportunity to contribute funds to American charities, sponsor community events, and support public libraries, universities, schools and other institutions'.
2. More supporting evidence is found in Birdsall, Ross and Sabot's (1995) study on the East Asian 'miracle'. Human capital investment joined by increased demand for the products made by countries such as Korea, Japan, Singapore and others, were key contributors to dynamic economic growth in that region from the 1960s through the latter part of the 1980s. For that time period, the educational base of these countries is statistically linked to growth rates of gross domestic product of between 5 and 8 per cent per year. Surely the accumulation and full utilisation of human capital is one of the cornerstones of economic development – no argument there.
3. These are the suppliers with which a given assembler has a long-term relationship that could involve codevelopment of products and technology.
4. For pharmaceutical and even electronics firms, Freeman and Soete find that the tentacles of technological learning must reach beyond national borders. In addition, the pharmaceutical industry must conform to local government regulations on the production and distribution of products.
5. One manager of a US subsidiary in Mexico stated that he had strict rules regarding problem-solving on the plant floor: 'dont fix anything, ask first'. Another manager of a transplanted US supplier claimed that he wanted to see problems solved through confrontation and argument, rather than through mild discussions, as was the custom among the Mexican workers at his plant.
6. Productive efficiency is measured by the following variables: Herfindahl index, market growth, foreign share and the rate of technical progress (relative changes in labour productivity in best practice plants).
7. The level of technology imports is measured as the average payments per employee for imported patents, trademarks and technical assistance, while the ratio of white-collar workers to blue-collar workers is the proxy for the availability of skilled labour. Utilising data on US subsidiaries in 33 countries, Kokko and Blomström (1995) show support for the hypothesis that competition, investment and education policies promote technology transfer to the host country, while government regulations on technology transfer can be counterproductive.
8. Data limitations lead to Mexico's omission from most of the analysis.
9. A Mexican company which operates under a maquila program approved for it by the Mexican Secretariat of Commerce and Industrial Development (SECOFI). (www.udel.edu/leipzig/texts2/vox128.htm, 16 May, 2003).
10. Process innovation was encouraged, only if it did not diminish product quality or delivery times, and the assembler typically captured the rents from the resulting cost reductions.
11. Owing to confidentiality agreements, it is not possible to reveal the names of the companies that were interviewed, nor the products that the companies produced.

12. Today, that Mexican company is nevertheless thriving. Over time, it has been able to establish its capabilities with the Big-Five assemblers, and it sells its product worldwide. Furthermore, that supplier has become a multinational, with design and production facilities in a few countries.

13. Ramírez and Unger (1998) point out only one association between an auto assembler and a few local suppliers, where 'simultaneous engineering' took place. In the 1990s, there was a joint venture between Chrysler and six Mexican suppliers to design an engine. The venture was deemed to be a success.

14. Kelly and Hageman (1999) admit that patent applications are not a pure proxy for innovative activity. However, they rely on those data since previous studies show a positive and significant relationship between R&D expenditure and patenting (see Bound, Cummins, Griliches, Hall and Jaffe, 1984 and Pakes and Griliches, 1984). Carpenter, Narin and Woolf (1981), Narin, Noma and Perry (1987), Trajtenberg (1990) and Albert, Avery, Narin and McAllister (1991), show that the number of patent citations is a good indicator of the social, economic and technological importance of innovation.

15. These studies could be used to support the claim that MNEs should not colocate R&D and manufacturing activities. Instead they should conduct research close to home or in another R&D centre (typically in another developed nation), rather than locate in a developing country. However, this ignores the potential benefits to the MNEs from diversifying sources of innovation.

REFERENCES

Albert, M.B., Avery, D., Narin, F. and McAllister, P. (1991), 'Direct validation of citation counts as indicators of industrially important patents', *Research Policy*, **20**, 251–9.

Almeida, P. and Kogut, B. (1999), 'The exploration of technological diversity and geographic location in innovation', in Z.J. Acs and B. Yeung (eds), *Small and Medium-Sized Enterprises in the Global Economy*, Ann Arbor, MI: University of Michigan Press, pp. 103–20.

Berry, S., Grilli, V. and Lopez de Silanes, F. (1993), 'The automobile industry and the Mexico–US Free Trade Agreement', in P.M. Garber (ed.), *The Mexico–US Free Trade Agreement*, Cambridge, MA: MIT Press.

Birdsall, N., Ross, D. and Sabot, R. (1995), 'Inequality and growth reconsidered: lessons from East Asia', *World Bank Economic Review*, **9**(3), 477–508.

Blomström, M. (1986), 'Foreign investment and productive efficiency: the case of Mexico', *Journal of Industrial Economics*, **35**(1), 97–110.

Blomström, M., Kokko, A. and Zejan, M. (1994), 'Host country competition, labor skills, and technology transfer by multinationals', *Weltwirtschaftliches-Archiv*, **130**(3), 521–33.

Bound, J., Cummins, C., Griliches, Z., Hall, B.H. and Jaffe, A. (1984), 'Who does R&D and who patents', in Z. Griliches (ed.), *R&D Patents, and Productivity*, Chicago: University of Chicago Press, pp. 21–54.

Buitelaar, R.M., Padilla, R. and Urrutia, R. (1999), 'The in-bond assembly industry and technical change', *Cepal Review*, **67** (April), 137–55.

Carpenter, M.P., Narin, F. and Woolf, P. (1981), 'Citation rates to technologically important patents', *World Patent Information*, **3**(4), 160–63.

Clerides, S.K., Lach, S. and Tybout, J.R. (1998), 'Is learning by exporting important? Micro-dynamic evidence from Colombia, Mexico, and Morocco', *Quarterly Journal of Economics*, **113**(3), August, 903–47.

Davies, S. (1996), 'Innovation in large technical systems: the case of telecommunications', *Industrial and Corporate Change*, **5**(4), 1143–80.

Dicken, P. (1994), 'Global–local tensions: firms and states in the gobal space-economy', *Economic Geography*, **70**(2), 101–28.

Dyer, J. (1996), 'Specialized supplier networks as a source of competitive advantage: evidence from the auto industry', *Strategic Management Journal*, **17**, 271–91.

Eden, L. (ed.) (1994), *Multinationals in North America*, Calgary: University of Calgary Press.

Eden, L. and Appel Molot, M. (1993), 'The NAFTA's automotive provisions: the next stage of managed trade', *The NAFTA Papers: C.D. Howe Commentary*, **53**, Ontario Canada: C.D. Howe Institute.

Eisenhardt, K. and Schoonhoven, C. (1990), 'Organizational growth: linking founding team, strategy, environment, and growth among U.S. semiconductor ventures, 1978–1988', *Administrative Science Quarterly*, **35**, 504–29.

Ellison, G. and Glaeser, E.L. (1997), 'Geographic concentration in US manufacturing industries: a dartboard approach', *Journal of Political Economy*, **105**(5), 889–927.

Feldman, M. (1994), *The Geography of Innovation*, Economics of Science, Technology and Innovation Series Vol. 2, Dordrecht and London: Kluwer Academic Publishers.

Freeman, C. and Soete, L. (1997), 'National systems of innovation', in *The Economics of Industrial Innovation*, Third Edition, Cambridge, MA: MIT Press, pp. 295–315.

Gertler, M.S. (1992), 'Flexibility revisited: districts, nation-states and the forces of production', *Transactions of the Institute of British Geographers*, **17**, 259–78.

Grether, J.-M. (1999), 'Determinants of technological diffusion in Mexican manufacturing: a plant-level analysis', *World Development*, **27**(7), 1287–98.

Helper, S. and Sako, M. (1995), 'Supplier relations in Japan and the United States – are they converging?', *Sloan Management Review*, Spring.

Hoffman, K. and Kaplinsky, R. (1988), *Driving Force: The Global Restructuring of Technology, Labor and Investment in the Automobile and Components Industries*, Boulder: Westview Press.

Hulsink, W. (1996), 'The new telecommunications in the Netherlands: strategy, policy and regulation', *Telecommunications Policy*, **20**(4), 273–89.

Husbands, K. (1994), 'Strategic alliances in the Mexican auto parts industry', International Motor Vehicle Program Working Paper.

Jaffe, A., Trajtenberg, M. and Henderson, R. (1993), 'Geographic localization of knowledge spillovers as evidenced by patent citations', *Quarterly Journal of Economics*, **108**(3), 577–98.

Keller, W. (1998), 'Are international R&D spillovers trade-related? Analyzing spillovers among randomly matched trade partners', *European Economic Review*, **42**, 1469–81.

Keller, W. (2000), 'Do trade patterns and technology flows affect productivity growth?', *The World Bank Economic Review*, **14**(1), 17–47.

Kelly, M. and Hageman, A. (1999), 'Marshallian externalities in innovation', *Journal of Economic Growth*, **4** (March), 39–54.

Kokko, A. and Blomström, M. (1995), 'Policies to encourage inflows of technology through foreign multinationals', *World Development*, **23**(3), 459–68.

Lowe, N. and Kenney, M. (1999), 'Foreign investment and the global geography of production: why the Mexican consumer electronics industry failed', *World Development*, **27**(8), 1427–43.

Lundvall, B. (1993), 'Comparing the Danish and Swedish systems of innovation', in R. Nelson (ed.), *National Innovation Systems: A Comparative Analysis*, Oxford: Oxford University Press, pp. 265–98.

Narin, F., Noma, E. and Perry, R. (1987), 'Patents and indicators of corporate technological strength', *Research Policy*, **16**(2), 143–55.

Nichols, N.A. (1993), 'From complacency to competitiveness: an interview with Vitro's Ernesto Martens', *Harvard Business Review*, September–October, 163–71.

Ohmae, K. (1989), 'Managing in a borderless world', *Harvard Business Review*, May–June, 152–61.

Pakes, A. and Griliches, Z. (1984), 'Patents and R&D at the firm level: a first look', in Z. Griliches (ed.), *R&D Patents, and Productivity*, Chicago: University of Chicago Press, pp. 55–72.

Patel, P. (1995), 'Localised production of technology for global markets', *Cambridge Journal of Economics*, **19**(1), 141–53.

Patel, P. and Pavitt, K. (1991), 'Large firms in the production of the world's technology: an important case of "non-globalisation"', *Journal of International Business Studies*, 1–21.

Porter, M.E. (1990), *The Competitive Advantage of Nations*, New York: Free Press, pp. 543–73.

Rabellotti, R. and Schmitz, H. (1999a), 'The internal heterogeneity of industrial districts in Italy, Brazil and Mexico', *Regional Studies*, **33**(2), 97–108.

Rabellotti, R. and Schmitz, H. (1999b), 'Recovery of a Mexican cluster: devaluation bonanza or collective efficiency?', *World Development*, **27**(9), 1571–85.

Ramírez, J.C. and Unger, K. (1998), 'Mexico's national innovation system in the 1990s: overview and sectoral effects', in R. Anderson, T. Cohn, C. Day, M. Howlett and C. Murray (eds), *Innovation Systems in a Global Context: The North American Experience*, Montreal: McGill-Queen's University Press.

Reich, R. (1990), 'Who is Us?', *Harvard Business Review*, January–February.

Rogers, E. and Larsen, J. (1984), *Silicon Valley Fever*, New York: Basic Books.

Rugman, A. and Gestrin, M. (1993), 'The strategic response of multinational enterprises to NAFTA', *Columbia Journal of World Business*, **28**(3) (Winter), 318–29.

Salas-Porras, A. (1998), 'The strategies pursued by Mexican firms in their efforts to become global players', *Cepal Review*, **65** (August), 133–53.

Stopford, J.M. and Strange, S. (1991), 'Rival states, rival firms: competition for world market shares', in *Cambridge Studies in International Relations*, **18**, Cambridge: Cambridge University Press.

Strassmann, W.P. (1968), 'Innovation, technology, and economic development', in *Technological Change and Economic Development: The Manufacturing Experience of Mexico and Puerto Rico*, New York: Cornell University Press, pp. 221–65.

Trajtenberg, M. (1990), 'A penny for your quotes: patent citations and the value of innovations', *The Rand Journal of Economics*, **21**(1), 172–87.

Vernon, R. (1994a), 'Multinationals and nation states: key actors in NAFTA', in L. Eden (ed.), *Multinationals in North America*, Calgary: University of Calgary Press, pp. 25–52.

Vernon, R. (1994b), 'The North American auto industry under NAFTA: making the positive sum solution happen', *North American Outlook*, **5**(1) (November).

Weitzman, M. (1992), 'On diversity', *Quarterly Journal of Economics*, **107**(2), 363–405.

Weitzman, M. (1996), 'Hybridizing growth theory', *American Economic Review*, **86**(2) (May), 297–12.

Weitzman, M. (1998), 'The Noah's Ark problem', *Econometrica*, **66**(6) (November), 1279–98.

Womack, J.P., Jones, D.T. and Roos, D. (1990), *The Machine that Changed the World*, The MIT International Motor Vehicle Program, New York: Harper Perennial.

4. Economic activity, market structure and public policy

Johan Willner[*]

1. INTRODUCTION

This chapter deals with the relationship between important dimensions of social welfare and economic activity, when higher welfare for some groups means lower profits. I shall argue that the view that there is always a trade-off between, for example, enterprise formation and equality or job security is oversimplified. Consequently, there is at least some scope for an industrial policy that promotes economic activity without dismantling what is usually understood as the welfare state.

High direct and indirect labour costs, regulation and a large public sector have often been blamed for lower growth and higher unemployment in Europe than in the US. For example, Stan Siebert argues in Chapter 5 in this volume that higher economic activity requires greater labour market flexibility, and that the so-called new economy reinforces the stark choice between wages and labour standards on the one hand and employment on the other.

However, a brief overview of recent research and a model, which incorporates some important aspects of the debate, will suggest that this view is too simplistic. Many authors have emphasised access to credit as a barrier to entry, and this will be included in the formal analysis, which also deals with the impact of wages (and indirectly taxes) and job security. When a trade-off exists at all, it can be shifted, for example through the presence of public and/or cooperative ownership. This not only increases the number of competitors but also affects the behaviour of private firms.

It will turn out that the presence of a firm with wider objectives can lead to increased output and employment for a given wage rate and level of job security, or it can increase the wage rate if there is full employment. Moreover, the wage rate among employees with short-term contracts does not reduce output and employment if there is credit rationing, even if there is no public production. Public production can compensate for harmful effects of job security, if there are such effects at all. In addition, a conventional dynamic model of enterprise formation would suggest that the market might never become competitive even if there are no barriers to entry.

This is the first contribution to include entry, exit and credit rationing (albeit as a first approximation) in a mixed oligopoly. If the number of firms is fixed, public production increases output and employment, and will increase the number of firms as well if credit rationing is a barrier to entry. The public firm can affect output also under free entry, although to a more limited extent unless it becomes a public monopoly.

We proceed as follows. Section 2 presents an overview of conflicting views on employment and enterprise formation, while Section 3 analyses the role of public ownership as a complement to a sector of small and innovative firms. Section 4 presents an oligopoly with and without free entry and credit rationing, suggesting that the trade-off between different desirable objectives is more complex than usually believed even in such a simple setting. Section 5 illustrates why there may be a scope for public intervention despite free entry, using a dynamic model of enterprise formation, which grinds to a halt under reasonable circumstances. Section 6 introduces a public firm into the model of Section 4, analysing its effect on enterprise formation and showing how a possible trade-off can be shifted through public production. A final section provides concluding remarks, including a discussion of policy choices.

2.   ECONOMIC ACTIVITY AND ENTERPRISE FORMATION IN THE EARLIER LITERATURE

The so-called 'eurosclerosis' hypothesis explains higher unemployment and/or lower growth in Europe as caused by a combination of labour market rigidities, union density, an excessive social safety net, and high public consumption and hence taxes (see, for example, Siebert, 1997). Eurosclerosis implies high direct and indirect labour costs, which reduce entry among potential innovators and make existing firms reluctant to expand. Also, the willingness to become self-employed is believed to be low, not least because paid employment is too attractive.

However, labour economists have pointed out that 30 per cent of Europeans lived in countries with lower unemployment than in the US in the mid-1990s. Within Europe there was no obvious connection between flexibility and growth and employment. Unemployment benefits and union density may increase unemployment, but only if there is no active labour market policy and centralised bargaining. Moreover, all skill groups in Europe are affected by slower employment growth, and not only low-skill groups as eurosclerosis would imply. By contrast, employment in the US has increased despite no real wage reduction. This suggests that differences in employment can at least partly be blamed on demand-side factors, such as credit constraints or product market imperfections (Nickell, 1997; Krueger and Pischke, 1997).

Fiscal redistribution and expenditures on public consumption and investments are often seen as expensive luxuries, given their alleged harmful effects on the enterprise sector. But while expenditures on infrastructure, research and education increase the equality of both opportunity and outcome if the rich are net contributors, they also increase private sector productivity (Sinn, 1996; Mamatzakis, 1997). For example, university research seems to be more important for US high-tech companies than research within the companies themselves, in particular in biotechnology (McMillan et al., 2000). The social safety net does not only redistribute incomes but makes it possible to insure those who are not yet born against unfortunate circumstances, before their capabilities and opportunities are known. Like other forms of insurance, this causes moral hazard. But moral hazard is beneficial in this context, because it means an increased willingness to take entrepreneurial risk. As the market cannot provide such an insurance, the welfare state therefore increases efficiency as well as equity (Sinn, 1996).[1]

It is often argued that Sweden illustrates how the welfare state reduces economic growth (see Henreksson, 1996; Lindbeck, 1997), but the observation that Sweden is lagging behind is disputed (see Korpi, 1996; Dowrick, 1996). While the literature as a whole is inconclusive, it is notable that a number of cross-country studies fail to support the view that growth is negatively related to public sector size or equality (Agell et al., 1994; Persson and Tabellini, 1994; Atkinson, 1999).

Conventional theory explains entry in terms of profit opportunities (Audretsch and Mata, 1995). For example, high direct and indirect labour costs and opportunity costs (if it is too attractive to be an employee) are believed to reduce entry, like high union density (Gentry and Hubbard, 2000; Ilmakunnas and Kanniainen, 2001). Higher inequality would on the other hand have the opposite effect (Evans and Leighton, 1989; Blanchflower and Oswald, 1998; Lindh and Ohlsson, 1998; Ilmakunnas and Kanniainen, 2001). If such views are correct, the best way to promote enterprise formation would be to make labour cheap and flexible, to reduce social security, and to cut back public services. But this would exclude large segments of the population from the prosperity that such reforms are supposed to generate.

But studies of the impact of price–cost margins on entry suggest that lower costs would have a slow and limited effect and that other factors dominate (see Geroski, 1995). For example, the non-pecuniary benefits of being independent seem to be more important than profitability for the decision to become self-employed (Hamilton, 2000). Also, the observation that a significant proportion of those who are in paid employment would prefer to become self-employed (see Blanchflower et al., 2001) is inconsistent with the notion that it is too attractive to be an employee.

Problems with access to credit can explain why many of those who would prefer to become self-employed do not become entrepreneurs (see for example Lechner and Pfeiffer, 1993; Brito and Mello, 1995; Link and Scott, 1995; Audretsch and Elston, 2002).[2] This would also explain why small firms, which are seen as more risky, more often run into difficulties in an economic downturn. Credit rationing is also consistent with the observation that family wealth (often in the form of an inheritance) increases the probability of becoming self-employed (Lindh and Ohlsson, 1998; Blanchflower et al., 2001), and can explain why higher income inequality increases entry.[3]

An improved access to credit for the SME sector can stimulate enterprise formation without necessarily causing increased inequality, contrary to the recommendations that are based on the eurosclerosis hypothesis.[4] But credit for start-ups has in Europe been organised mainly through formal venture capital funds based on institutional investors and run by investment bankers. The venture capital market in the US (and to some extent the UK) is less formal and largely based on networks of wealthy and often retired so-called business angels. These have an industrialist's know-how rather than expertise in financial asset management. While formal venture capital funds are useful at later stages of a firm's life-cycle, the informal market provides an important initial screening device that can help to eliminate non-serious entrants. This also suggests that the public sector can be helpful in creating networks of experts (Mason and Harrison, 1998; Cowling, 1998).

The structure of the banking sector may also matter. Small firms in Germany have been less constrained than elsewhere, because they have mainly been financed by savings banks and cooperative banks, which have been kept informed through board membership. Medium-sized German firms have, by contrast, been affected negatively by the internationalisation of the commercial banking sector (Audretsch and Elston, 2002).[5]

While some monitoring of entrants by public authorities and banks may be necessary, there are large variations between countries in the amount of bureaucracy associated with entry. Fonesca et al. (2001) have compared start-up cost in the major OECD economies using an index in terms of time consumption and the number of procedures. Not surprisingly, high start-up costs have a negative impact on both employment and entry. Start-up costs are high in Spain (23.5 weeks and 17 procedures), followed by Italy and Germany. Finland and Sweden are in an intermediate position, while the least bureaucratic country (one week and two procedures) is Denmark (like Finland and Sweden associated with Scandinavian style), followed by the UK and the US.

However, to encourage the SME sector through better access to credit and reduced start-up costs might not have a significant effect on employment, which must therefore be addressed by other means as well. The SME sector's share of total output/employment is moderate in most industrial countries

(Geroski, 1995; Baldwin, 1998; Audretsch et al., 2001; Almus, 2001). Also, its effect on the degree of competition in the market is insignificant (Audretsch and Mata, 1995). On the other hand, entry and exit can affect the composition of an industry and may hence increase or reduce its share of innovative firms (Audretsch and Mata, 1995; Audretsch et al., 2001).

While there has recently been a moderate increase in the SME sector's share of employment, there is no similar increase in its share of output. The beneficial effects may show up later, but this increase may also be caused by outsourcing rather than new activities. Also, entry sometimes means that an incumbent establishes a competing firm in order to deter genuine competitors (Schultz, 2001). An increase in the number of small firms may even indicate industrial decline (Baldwin, 1998; Spilling, 1998).[6] Instead of just focusing on entry and survival, policy-makers should therefore encourage innovative groupings of small enterprises, such as the industrial districts in Emilia-Romagna in Italy, which may be extended to multinational networks (Cowling and Sugden, 1999). (See also Bellandi in Chapter 9 of this volume on the Italian case, and Schweitzer and Di Tommaso in Chapter 8 on biotechnology clusters.)

A policy that supports innovation and not just entry can promote R&D cooperation between small firms that cannot afford research laboratories of their own. As Oughton and Whittam (1994) point out, there is then a lower risk for collusion in prices or quantities than among larger firms. But competition may also be desirable at the R&D stage as well, insofar as parallel research increases the probability that an innovation is made. Public/private partnerships can then provide access to research laboratories and thus increase the number of potential innovators (see Link and Scott, 1995). Business parks provide access to university research but also benefits of agglomeration, and so-called business incubators can offer access to additional services such as accountancy or credit advice.[7]

This discussion suggests an industrial policy, which encourages technically progressive entrants without featherbedding the business community as a whole, at the expense of the rest of society. Where there is a lack of private venture capital, public sector funds with the right kind of know-how can step in, and can also work in partnership with the informal venture capital market. Excessive administrative procedures can be reduced in many countries without the increased inequality that is often what 'flexibility' is meant to achieve. Publicly funded research expenditures should increase, because its results are freely available, unlike the research output in big corporations. There might be benefits also for the business community associated with research, education, a public infrastructure, and a social security system that prevents social exclusion (see also Husbands in the previous chapter). Research joint ventures and networking between the SME sector and universities should be encouraged.

Start-ups, which are organised as profit-sharing cooperatives, can achieve a flexibility that does not require the dismantling of industry-wide standards for paid employees.[8]

3.   THE SIGNIFICANCE OF PUBLIC PRODUCTION

The previous section has emphasised methods to stimulate entry without generating inequality, but it has also highlighted the limitations of an approach that is focused on enterprise formation only. An increased number of small firms is not always a sign of industrial development, and SMEs are not in general efficient employment creators. To reduce wages and deregulate the labour market in the hope of entry or expansion would not have a significant impact on employment (see Krueger and Pischke, 1997), and would contradict other social objectives. On the other hand, a targeted policy can enhance diversity, long-run growth, and development through a thriving sector of small firms. This suggests a twofold approach, which supports innovative small firms but also ensures a desirable level of economic activity outside this sector.

Traditionally, the welfare state meant more than just a social safety net. It meant an expansionary macroeconomic policy but also publicly funded research and education, which also benefited the corporate sector. US results have highlighted the importance of university research for advanced sectors such as biotechnology (see McMillan et al., 2000). While Europe has a number of successful universities, it remains a challenge to develop an interaction with the business sector, which does not threaten the autonomy that is necessary for the research community (see Grande and Peschke, 1999).

But the welfare state also meant a mixed economy with a public enterprise sector (and often a cooperative sector as well), implying that economic activity was not dependent on profit opportunities alone. Private firms were supposed to flourish through innovations rather than cheap labour, while public ownership filled the gap where other producers were too few or nonexistent.

It is worth pointing out that some extent of public ownership has also been supported by non-socialist governments in many countries. State enterprises have been tools for an anti-inflationary and/or expansionary policy or to ensure a consumer-friendly pricing policy in a number of countries, such as France, Germany, Italy and the UK. But more often they were established because of a lack of private venture capital, or as a way to accelerate post-war restructuring, when private firms did not emerge spontaneously. Cases in point are Austria, Finland, Germany, Italy, Ireland and Sweden (see contributions in Parker, 1998).[9]

Sweden and Finland have experienced a rapid transformation from agricultural backwardness, and public production of private goods has played a prominent role in both cases.[10] Finland's first manufacturing state-owned companies emerged soon after independence to ensure domestic ownership in the forest and basic metal industries, followed by producers of fertilisers and electric power in the 1930s and by companies contributing to post-war reconstruction, including the need to pay damages to the Soviet Union, in the 1940s.[11] Later state-owned companies were established in oil refinery, electric power generation and steel.

Like in Finland, early state-owned manufacturers in Sweden were established in the paper and pulp industry and in mining in order to exploit natural resources under domestic ownership. The scale of the investments needed has also called for public activity in recent times, as in the case of nuclear power. Companies have also been established in order to ensure the supply of certain products like X-ray films or pharmaceuticals. While the public enterprise sector was smaller than in Finland, the state has also been involved in for example railway rolling stock, trucks and similar equipment, and hotels and restaurants.

State enterprises have often, as in Finland and Sweden, been established in regions, which private owners would not have chosen, but otherwise they have been encouraged to behave as private firms, albeit under restrictions on layoffs etc., which have now been removed. But public enterprises can have a role also by not behaving according to private sector standards. Product market concentration may lead to a suboptimal level of output, and this may affect employment as well (see Krueger and Pischke, 1997). Public ownership can then improve economic activity and allocative efficiency by forcing profit-maximising firms to reduce their profit margins and hence to increase output and employment (on such a mixed oligopoly, see, for example, Cremer et al., 1989; De Fraja and Delbono, 1990; Willner, 1994).

Public ownership may also be part of an R&D policy. It is well known that market provision of R&D can mean both over- and underprovision. The presence of public ownership may improve performance then as well. As Dasgupta and Stiglitz (1980) point out, competition between private firms can generate excessive R&D in the form of duplication despite too slow technical progress. A mixed duopoly can then lead to higher welfare than if both firms are private, and will reduce duplication (Delbono and Denicolò, 1993). But if an innovation is easy to imitate once it is made, other firms can be free riders, which reduces the incentive to spend on R&D. The public firm in a mixed duopoly would then spend relatively more and the private firms less than if both firms were private, with positive effects on welfare for certain kinds of innovations (Poyago-Theotoky, 1998).

Public ownership is now unfashionable. To combine private and public ownership is believed to be too expensive, and existing state enterprises are therefore privatised. However, empirical findings such as Martin and Parker (1997), surveys of earlier findings by Millward (1982), Boyd (1986), or Willner (2001), and theoretical studies such as Pint (1991) and De Fraja (1993), suggest that this negative view on public ownership is prejudiced.[12] It should therefore come as no surprise that the size of the public enterprise sector is positively rather than negatively related to economic growth in the OECD countries (Fowler and Richards, 1995).

The role of public ownership therefore has to be reconsidered if it is untrue that it always makes a firm significantly less efficient. It is then meaningful to ask how public production can correct for market failures, and how a trade-off between economic activity and other desirable objectives can be shifted. While an explicit analysis of how public production can affect R&D is outside our scope, we shall also consider the impact of public production on the number of firms, thus revealing some surprising mechanisms.

Moreover, if entry into the private enterprise sector brings about economic progress as intended, the future standard of living would be higher. Some evidence suggests that this might reduce the willingness to become self-employed (Ilmakunnas and Kanniainen, 2001). This suggests a need for other ways to stimulate economic activity and dynamism than by relying on people willing to become self-employed. Public and cooperative enterprises may then have to play a more prominent part in the future, even in countries where they have not been favoured at present.

4.   THE CONVENTIONAL OLIGOPOLY

This section provides a basic model of a conventional oligopoly, which approaches perfect competition if technology permits a large number of firms. It also highlights the assumptions behind the popular view of a trade-off between economic activity and employee welfare, and illustrates how the presence of credit rationing may partly change the way in which the market is affected by direct and indirect labour costs.

In each firm $i, i = 1, 2, \ldots n$, variable costs cx_i are proportional to output and consist of unit wage costs and components such as raw material and depreciation. A wage increase among employees with short-term contracts would then be reflected in an increase in c if other things are equal. There are also costs F_i that are fixed when firms decide on output. However, they are related to capacity, and assumed to be proportional to expected output x^E with the coefficient f. Fixed costs may also include wages, as when some employees have long-term contracts. A wage increase is then reflected in f as well. There will be no explicit analysis of public services and social security, but it will be assumed that an improvement increases c and possibly also f because of higher taxes.

We focus on an equilibrium in which expectations are fulfilled. It will therefore be convenient to use the following abbreviation:

$$q = \frac{f}{c + f}.$$ (4.1)

This expresses the proportion of fixed costs of total costs. An increase in the proportions of workers, which cannot be laid off in the short run, is therefore reflected in an increase in q.

Let p and x denote price and quantity and consider a general inverse demand schedule $p = D(x)$. The demand schedule should be consistent with the existence of a Cournot equilibrium, which is also well-behaved in the sense that the price is increasing in marginal costs and decreasing in the number of firms.[13]

Profit maximisation will therefore under normal conditions lead to an equilibrium price $p^c(n,c)$ and an equilibrium output $x^c(n,c)$. Higher wages among those on short-term contracts then increase the price and reduce output. It is obvious that lower output also means lower employment with this kind of technology. But it also follows that better job security, as for example reflected in a higher q when $c + f$ is unchanged, increases output and employment, because this reduces marginal costs. It also follows that a higher wage rate among workers with long-term contracts does not reduce employment.

We can include entry and exit in the model by introducing a zero-profit condition.[14] Suppose that firms have to borrow so as to be able to pay the fixed cost F_i before the output is sold, but ignore for the moment the possibility of credit rationing. The conventional view of entry then means that new firms are established until no genuine profits can be earned:[15]

$$(p^c - c)x_i^c - (1 + r)F_i = 0.$$ (4.2)

Use the definition of F_i and rearrange:

$$p^c(n,c) - c - (1 + r)f = 0.$$ (4.3)

We can now use implicit differentiation of (4.3) to analyse the impact of changes in c and f on the number of firms when entry depends on profit opportunities:[16]

$$\frac{\partial n}{\partial c} = \frac{1 - \partial p^c / \partial c}{\partial p^c \partial n},$$ (4.4)

$$\frac{\partial n}{\partial f} = \frac{1 + r}{\partial p^c / \partial n}.$$

(4.5)

Rewrite c as $(1 - q)(c + f)$ and suppose that there is a change in q for a given $c + f$, as for example when there is a *ceteris paribus* increase in the proportion of employees with long-term contracts. Implicit differentiation with respect to n and q then yields:

$$\frac{\partial n}{\partial q} = \frac{(c + f)(r + \partial p^c / \partial c)}{\partial p^c / \partial n}.$$

(4.6)

In the normal case on which we focus, where $\partial p^c / \partial n$ is negative, (4.5) and (4.6) are negative, but (4.4) is ambiguous. For example, such popular explicit functional forms as linearity and isoelasticity yield opposite signs. Let n_1 be associated with the demand function $p = a - x$, where a is a positive parameter, and let n_2 be associated with an isoelastic demand function where η denotes the absolute value of the price elasticity of demand. We then get the following expressions for the number of firms:

$$n_1 \approx \frac{a - c}{f(1 + r)} - 1,$$

(4.7)

$$n_2 \approx \frac{c + (1 + r)f}{\eta(1 + r)f}.$$

(4.8)

It can now easily be verified that the former is decreasing and the latter increasing in c. Higher wages among workers on short-term contracts can both increase and reduce the number of firms, depending on the shape of the demand schedule, but higher job security reduces the number of firms.

Suppose now that there is a limit for how much the firms in the industry can borrow at the rate of interest r, for reasons mentioned in Section 2 but not modelled explicitly. Let this limit be K. Each firm borrows an amount F_i, which means that $\sum_i F_i = K$ must hold true. In equilibrium this means:

$$x^c(n,c)f = K.$$

(4.9)

It follows from implicit differentiation that an increase in c, and hence a wage increase among workers with short-term contracts, will increase the number of firms if $\partial x^c / \partial n$ is positive:

$$\frac{\partial n}{\partial c} = - \frac{\partial x^c / \partial c}{\partial x^c / \partial n}. \tag{4.10}$$

The intuition is based on the fact that higher c makes each firm smaller, and hence more firms will get access to credit.

It is obvious that an increase in f reduces the number of firms. To see that an increase in q has the same effect, write c as $(1 - q)(c + f)$ and differentiate (4.9). This yields:

$$\frac{\partial n}{\partial q} = - \frac{x - f \partial x^c / \partial c}{q \partial x^c / \partial n}. \tag{4.11}$$

This expression is negative, because of the signs of the partial derivatives in the numerator and the denominator. Output and employment will on the other hand not depend on c, because output must equal K/f according to (4.9). But an increase in f or q will have a negative effect.

We can sum up the discussion of the effects of an increase in c, f and q on economic activity and the number of firms in Table 4.1.

Note that we might also assume that the firm must borrow in order to cover not only F_i in advance but also the wages. The price would then be $(1 + r)(c + f)$ under completely free entry and exit. This would imply that output and employment depend on $c + f$ but not on its composition. In other words, higher job security as reflected in a higher f at the expense of c would not reduce employment. If there are adverse effects of q, as in the model version on which the table is based, they are implied by the rate of interest and presumably weaker than the effects of c and f.

It follows that the conventional view of how direct and indirect labour costs affect output, employment and the number of firms is too simplistic even in the light of this admittedly simple model. Where there seems to exist a trade-off, economic activity can be improved through the rate of interest and improved access to credit. Sections 5 and 6 below will highlight other factors that affect the market structure, namely the dynamics of entry and the para-doxical consequences of public production.

5. THE LIMITS OF FREE ENTRY

There are other reasons than in the previous sections for why there may still be a role for public policy when there is free entry and exit. A dynamic process of enterprise formation may stop before we reach the

Table 4.1 The impact of labour costs and job security under different entry conditions

	A fixed number of firms	Free entry and exit	Credit rationing
Higher wages among workers with short-term contracts	Output and employment decreases	Lower output and employment; ambiguous effects on the number of firms	No effect on output and employment; more firms
Higher wages among workers with long-term contracts	No effect on output and employment	Lower output and employment; fewer firms	Lower output and employment; fewer firms
Higher proportion of workers with long-term contracts	Higher output and employment	Lower output and employment; fewer firms	Lower output and employment; fewer firms

theoretical maximum number of firms that was analysed in the previous section. The analysis also highlights why it is still meaningful to analyse not only changes in the number of firms but also the implications of a given market structure.

In a dynamic setting, the model would imply that the entry occurs until no genuine profits can be earned. When applied on, for example, regional economic development, such an approach rules out the fundamental problem that business enterprises do not necessarily emerge even if there are opportunities to earn profits and no credit rationing. This can be a problem even when q is not high enough to imply a natural oligopoly.

Most models of enterprise formation assume that the change in the number of firms is proportional to the size of the profits. For example, let β be a positive parameter, and let π_i represent the profits of a typical private firm in the market. If potential entrepreneurs observe that incumbents are able to earn profits, there will be entry. However, it makes sense to assume that there is a more rapid adaptation process if firms make losses, because some of them would then go bankrupt. Suppose that β is a positive parameter and μ a term, which reflects other factors than profits. Negative values of μ would reinforce the problem of a halted convergency, and vice versa. We focus on cases where there are too few firms, in which case we apply the following equation, which is similar to Geroski (1995):

$$m_t - m_{t-1} = \beta \pi_{t-1}^i + \mu. \tag{4.12}$$

The model is otherwise similar as in the linear version in the previous section, but fixed costs are now proportional to the output level of the previous period, so that $F_i = f x_{t-1}^i$.[17] Derive the profits under linear demand, insert in (4.12), and ignore other factors than profits:

$$m_t - m_{t-1} = \beta \left[\left(\frac{a-c}{m_{t-1}+2} \right)^2 - f \frac{a-c}{m_{t-2}+2} \right]. \tag{4.13}$$

This is a non-linear second-degree difference equation, and its time-path is difficult to characterise in detail, also because of the fact that m can take only integer values. Simulation with reasonable values of the parameters reveals that there is indeed a tendency towards convergence in the direction of the predicted equilibrium number of firms. But the model also suggests that the existence of profit opportunities (a positive square bracket in (4.13)) may not be sufficient to support entry, because new enterprises are established only as long as $m_t - m_{t-1}$ is greater than one. In other words, the process may grind to a halt. For example, let m^* denote the number of firms, which implies that $m_t - m_{t-1}$ becomes too small. It can be solved from the following equation:

$$1 = \beta\left[\left(\frac{a-c}{m^* + 2}\right)^2 - f\,\frac{a-c}{m^* + 2}\right]. \tag{4.14}$$

We get the following solution:

$$m^* = 2\left(\frac{a-c}{\sqrt{f^2 + 4/\beta} + f} - 1\right). \tag{4.15}$$

An infinite value of β would yield $m^{**} = [(a - c)/f] - 2$ as when there is no delay in enterprise formation, in which case industry output would be $x^{**} = a - c - f$, but a low value can mean that the difference between the theoretical equilibrium values and the values associated with halted enterprise formation is significant. Let M and X denote $100(m^{**} - m^*)/m^*$ and $100(x^{**} - x^*)/x^*$ respectively:

$$M = 100\,\frac{a-c}{a-c-f}\,\frac{\sqrt{f^2 + 4/\beta} - f}{\sqrt{f^2 + 4/\beta} - f}, \tag{4.16}$$

$$X = 100\,\frac{\sqrt{f^2 + 4/\beta} - f}{2(a-c-f)}. \tag{4.17}$$

Four examples may indicate the potential importance of this finding. First, suppose that $a = 100$, $c = 2$, $f = 2$ and $\beta = 0.2$. This would yield $M = -42.90$ per cent and $X = -1.51$ per cent. Second, change f to 5 so as to get $M = -14.89$ per cent and $X = -0.91$ per cent. Third, let f remain at 2 but set $\beta = 0.1$. This yields $M = -54.79$ per cent and $X = -2.41$ per cent. Finally, if $f = 5$ and $\beta = 0.1$, we get $M = -23.93$ per cent and $X = -1.64$ per cent.

The fact that the process of enterprise formation is halted at m^* implies a potential role for public policy. The relative difference in the number of firms may be more dramatic than in industry output, but an output distortion of nearly 2 per cent is not negligible. Also, the phenomenon should be a matter of concern if the number of enterprises today has favourable effects that are not captured by the model.

6. ECONOMIC ACTIVITY AND ENTREPRENEURSHIP IN A MIXED OLIGOPOLY

This section focuses on public production of private goods as a way to increase production given the labour costs or vice versa. Public and commercial enterprises have sometimes been created without intention to affect the allocation in other ways than by increasing the number of producers, in extreme cases from zero to one. But a mixed oligopoly usually means that the public firm has a different objective function as well, and this may affect private sector decisions on entry and output. The previous mixed oligopoly literature has focused on distortions in price, output, or R&D among big corporations, but this analysis will show that public production can affect the entry decision as well.

Both normative and positive models of public ownership tend to emphasise other than purely commercial objectives, which either reflect a genuine ambition to increase welfare or a pressure from special interest groups such as consumers and/or employees. More sophisticated models of a mixed oligopoly have been explored elsewhere (see, for example, Willner, 1994, and Willner, 1999b), but here we ignore an explicit analysis of the objective function. Instead, we assume that the public firm chooses a given level of output x_1. Values that are larger than under profit maximisation are seen as reflecting welfare maximisation or other non-commercial objectives, such as a bias in favour of consumers/voters for opportunistic reasons.[18]

Consider first how the presence of public ownership affects output and employment when there is a given number m of private firms, so that the total number of firms is $n = m + 1$. Suppose that demand is linear. Take the first-order condition for a private firm, add and solve for the private sector output x^p as a function of x_1, m and c:

$$x^p = \frac{m(a - c - x_1)}{m + 1}.$$
(4.18)

Add to x_1 to get industry output:

$$x^m = \frac{m(a - c) + x_1}{m + 1}.$$
(4.19)

If m is fixed, the effects of changes in c, f and q are the same as in the conventional oligopoly. But public policy can now affect output and employment through the output of firm 1 and thus shift the trade-off between x^p and c. If firm 1 just maximises profits, it would produce $(a - c)/(m + 2)$, but higher levels would lead to higher industry output and employment. If x_1 equals its welfare maximising level, no private firm would be active. We shall assume that x_1 is in the interval between its profit and welfare maximising values.[19] Welfare is increasing in x_1 in this interval and therefore always higher than if firm 1 is privatised.[20]

Next, consider the case of completely free entry and exit. Set the profit margin of a private firm equal to zero:

$$\frac{a - c - x_1}{m + 1} - (1 + r)f = 0. \tag{4.20}$$

This yields:

$$m = \frac{a - c - x_1 - (1 + r)f}{(1 + r)f}. \tag{4.21}$$

The number of firms is now decreasing in both c and f. Note also that public production reduces the number of firms. Inserting in (4.19) yields:

$$x^m = a - c - (1 + r)f. \tag{4.22}$$

This means that the output of firm 1 has no impact on output and employment as long as the private firms are not completely crowded out. Firm 1 then becomes a public monopoly, which can increase output to its welfare maximising level and beyond. But a market where firms always enter until we reach perfect competition would not be an obvious candidate for public intervention in the first place. To assume that such conditions always prevail would all but rule out the possibility that countries and regions may have low economic activity despite an abundance of cheap and flexible labour.

On the other hand, if n firms can make significant profits while there would be losses if their number was $n + 1$, as can happen if n is small, the public firm may have a significant impact on output despite free entry. It can increase output until the profits of the n firms are nearly zero. The public firm can also affect output if the process of enterprise formation grinds to a halt, as described in the previous section.

Next, consider the impact of public production when (only) private firms are subject to credit rationing. Set $\sum_i^m F_i$ equal to K:

$$f \frac{m(a - c - x_1)}{m + 1} = K. \tag{4.23}$$

The number of firms is therefore:

$$m = \frac{K}{f(a - c - x_1) - K}.$$ (4.24)

It follows that higher wages among those on short-term contracts will increase the number of firms. But an increase in the output of firm 1 has the same effect, and suggests that there are some unexpected ways to support enterprise formation in the presence of credit rationing. The intuition is that an increase in both c and x_1 makes each firm smaller, and this allows new firms to enter. But an increase in f and to some extent q has the opposite effect, because they create economies of scale. If both job security and a large number of firms are seen as desirable, the trade-off can be shifted through higher c and x_1.

Inserting into (4.19) so as to get industry output yields:

$$x^m = \frac{K}{f} + x_1 = \frac{K}{q(c + f)} + x_1.$$ (4.25)

The wages among those on short-term contracts do not affect output. There are adverse effects of f and/or q, but these can be offset through higher public production, which also reduces the size of the private firms. The favourable effects on output and the number of firms of public production under credit rationing may also highlight the success of establishing state enterprises in the lack of private venture capital during early stages of Scandinavian industrialisation (see Willner, 1998).

The impact of the mixed oligopoly can now be summarised in Table 4.2. Note also that the case where firms have to borrow in order to cover wage costs as well would imply that job security (the composition of a constant sum $c + f$) has no adverse effects, by a similar argument as in Section 4.

7. CONCLUSIONS

The formal analysis has focused on output, employment and the reduction of market power as main reasons for why a large number of firms is beneficial. However, economic activity can then be increased also through reduced profit margins caused by competition from a non-profit-maximising public firm, which forces private firms to reduce their prices. The overview of the literature also emphasises smaller firms as sources of

Table 4.2 The impact of labour costs, job security and public production in a mixed oligopoly

	A fixed number of private firms	Free entry and exit	Credit rationing
Higher wages among workers with short-term contracts	Lower output and employment	Lower output and employment; fewer private firms	No effect on output and employment; more private firms
Higher wages among workers with long-term contracts	No effect on output and employment	Lower output and employment; fewer private firms	Lower output and employment; fewer private firms
Higher job security	Higher output and employment	Lower output and employment; fewer private firms	Lower output and employment; fewer private firms
Higher output in the public firms	Higher output and employment	Fewer private firms; limited effects on output and employment unless the market becomes a public monopoly	Higher output and employment; more private firms

dynamism and diversity. It remains to include these aspects in the analysis. For example, the presence of credit rationing could be explained by firms being heterogeneous firms and/or by a risky behaviour that may be socially beneficial. Public policies that affect entry may then also have consequences for future growth.

The model and the overview of the empirical literature suggest that it is not always true that high wages and job security have adverse effects on economic activity. It therefore seems that industrial policy can achieve higher economic activity and more entry, without just promoting profits at the expense of the rest of society. The earlier literature mentions a number of ways to encourage innovative small firms, such as to provide incentives for R&D cooperation and to support networks that provide access to publicly funded research. Credit rationing also appears as an important barrier to entry both in the literature and in the model. The model suggests that there are better approaches to public ownership than to privatise, because an increase in public production can then paradoxically increase entry and thus offset possible negative effects of for example, job security on the number of firms.

A dual strategy, which emphasises both public production and a thriving SME sector, may be needed not least against the background of globalisation and the threat of so-called social dumping. This reinforces the need of producers that would not play governments against each other in the pursuit of profits through cheap labour and bad working conditions.

NOTES

* This contribution belongs to a series of papers developed from a first draft which was written during visits to the University of Warwick and the University of Wisconsin-Milwaukee, and presented at the Second L'institute–Milwaukee Workshop, and in revised form at the 5th Annual EUNIP Conference, Vienna, December 2001. Comments by participants are gratefully acknowledged.

1. However, Ilmakunnas and Kanniainen (2001) argue that this kind of social insurance cannot eliminate genuine entrepreneurial risk completely.
2. On the other hand, Acemoglu (2001) suggests that the proportion of those industries where credit constraints matter grew more slowly in Europe than in the US, but does not otherwise find strong evidence in favour of the credit-rationing hypothesis.
3. Credit rationing also causes a proportionately greater shake-out among small firms during an economic downturn. This may explain why survival is more important than entry for the size of the SME sector (see Audretsch and Mata, 1995; Geroski, 1995).
4. For example, evidence from Austria suggests that risk guarantees can help small firms to reach minimum efficient scale and venture capital can reduce the exposure to demand fluctuations (Deutsch, 2001).
5. The fact that the crisis of the 1990s eliminated most of the savings bank sector in, for example Finland, suggests a need for alternative sources of credit. By contrast, a similar banking crisis in Norway was solved through temporary state ownership.
6. The main entry threat in high-tech industries consists of a firm's own employees, whose salaries should therefore be high enough to induce them not to become competitors.

Reduced start-up costs can therefore cause firms to pay even more to prevent entry, which would increase prices and reduce output and employment (Burke and To, 2001). At least if there is vertical product differentiation, higher entry costs can on the other hand induce incumbents to produce close substitutes, so that the total surplus becomes higher (Peitz, 2002).

7. While their success has been mixed so far, evidence from Italy suggests that business incubators make it easier to adopt advanced technologies and to establish research collaboration, at least if innovation systems are weak (Colombo and Delmastro, 2001).

8. It is also possible to allow potential innovators, which can provide high future wages, to deviate from standard industry-wide labour market practices (Audretsch et al., 2001). This may not however always be beneficial, because central bargaining eliminates or reduces the adverse effect of unionisation on employment (Nickell, 1997).

9. There have been islands of public ownership even in the US, where for example the Tennessee Valley Authority was established because of the risk and high costs associated with hydroelectric power (Monsen and Walters, 1983; Hausman and Neufeld, 1999).

10. See Willner (1998), for a more detailed presentation on privatisation and public ownership in the Nordic EU countries

11. A case in point is Valmet, which made aeroplanes, ships and tractors and which is now world leader in paper and board machines.

12. The World Bank report *Bureaucrats in Business* (1995) provides an overview in favour of privatisation on efficiency grounds. A recent survey by Megginson and Netter (2001) also interprets the empirical literature as favouring privatisation, but the choice of sources is in both cases described biased and to some extent focused on Third World or transition economies.

13. As among others Seade (1980) has pointed out, entry can in theory increase the price. While this would have interesting policy consequences, such an outcome nevertheless seems to be a curiosity that is outside the scope of this contribution. It can be shown that it requires a steeply decreasing price elasticity of demand (as a function of the price), in which case higher marginal costs can also reduce the price. Note however that demand functions derived from Stone-Geary utility functions are associated with decreasing demand elasticity if goods are complements, in which case there may exist a Cournot equilibrium that is associated with a price that is increasing in n.

14. Note however that Section 2 suggests that a model version in terms of a zero-profit condition offers a poor prediction of the actual number of firms. The analysis should rather be interpreted in terms of a theoretical maximum number of firms.

15. With an alternative interpretation, capital is borrowed from owners that earn a rate of profit r under completely free entry and exit.

16. Strictly speaking, differentiating requires n to belong to R^+. Only integer values of n make sense, but if the derivative f_n a function $f(n)$ is positive, $f(n^*+1) > f(n^*)$ normally holds true. For a more detailed justification of this procedure, see Seade (1980).

17. This causes no problems when entry occurs, because each firm then reduces its output, and no bottlenecks will occur. To apply the model in the opposite case would require the use of more expensive hired capacity, or an assumption that it is possible to produce more than planned for one period but that a subsequent increase in capacity is then necessary.

18. Some arguments for privatisation, like in Boycko et al. (1996), are based on an assumption that public sector decisions are biased in this way, but I have shown elsewhere that public ownership can be superior to privatisation in a bargaining model under such conditions (see Willner, 2001).

19. A firm that gives some weight to welfare may in fact get higher profits (see, for example, Fehrstman, 1990 or Willner, 1994). It is obvious in this model as well that firm 1 gets higher profit if it produces more than the private firms and thus increases welfare.

20. It also follows that firm 1 can affect income distribution. Suppose that the demand for labour is proportional to output, and consider the market-clearing wage rate. Output is then constrained by the availability of labour. An increase in x_1 will then have no effect on output but will shift the demand for labour so that wages are higher and profits lower.

REFERENCES

Acemoglu, D. (2001), 'Credit market imperfections and persistent unemployment', *European Economic Review*, **45**(4–6), 665–79.

Agell, J., Lindh, T. and Ohlsson, H. (1994), 'Tillväxt och offentlig sektor', *Ekonomisk Debatt*, **22**(4), 373–85.

Almus, M. (2001), 'What characterizes a fast growing firm?', Mimeo, Centre for European Economic Research.

Atkinson, A.B. (1999), *The Economic Consequences of Rolling Back the Welfare State*, Cambridge, MA and London: CES and MIT Press.

Audretsch, D.B. and Elston, J.A. (2002), 'Does firm size matter? Evidence on the impact of liquidity constraints on firm investment behavior in Germany', *International Journal of Industrial Organization*, **20**(1), 1–17.

Audretsch, D.B. and Mata, J. (1995), 'The post-entry performance of firms: an introduction', *International Journal of Industrial Organization*, **13**(4), 413–20.

Audretsch, D.B., van Leeuwen, G., Menkveld, B. and Thurik, R. (2001), 'Market dynamics in the Netherlands: competition policy and the role of small firms', *International Journal of Industrial Organization*, **19**(5), 795–821.

Baldwin, J.R. (1998), 'Were small producers the engines of growth in the Canadian manufacturing sector in the 1980s?', *Small Business Economics*, **10**(4), 349–64.

Blanchflower, D.G. and Oswald, A.J. (1998), 'What makes an entrepreneur?', *Journal of Labor Economics*, **16**(1), 26–60.

Blanchflower, D.G., Oswald, A.J. and Stutzer, A. (2001), 'Latent entrepreneurship across nations', *European Economic Review*, **45**(4–6), 680–91.

Boycko, M., Schleifer, A. and Vishny, R.W. (1996), 'A theory of privatisation', *Economic Journal*, **106** (March), 309–19.

Boyd, C.W. (1986), 'The comparative efficiency of state owned enterprises', in A.R. Negandhi (ed.), *Multinational Corporations and State-Owned Enterprises: A New Challenge in International Business*, Greenwich, CT and London: Research in International Business and International Relations, JAI Press, pp. 178–94.

Brito, P. and Mello, A.S. (1995) 'Financial constraints and post-entry performance', *International Journal of Industrial Organization*, **13**(4), 543–65.

Burke, A.B. and To, T. (2001), 'Can reduced entry barriers worsen market performance? A model of employee entry', *International Journal of Industrial Organization*, **19**(5), 695–704.

Colombo, M.G. and Delmastro, M. (2001), 'How effective are technology incubators? Evidence from Italy', Mimeo, Università di Pavia and CIRET-Politecnico di Milano.

Cowling, M. (1998), 'The entrepreneurial society in practice', in K. Cowling (ed.), *Industrial Policy in Europe. Theoretical Perspectives and Practical Proposals*, London and New York: Routledge and L'institute, pp. 133–51.

Cowling, K. and Sugden, R. (1999), 'The wealth of localities, regions and nations; developing multinational economies', *New Political Economy*, **4**(3), 361–78.

Cremer, H., Marchand, M. and Thisse, J.F. (1989), 'The public firm as an instrument for regulating an oligopolistic market', *Oxford Economic Papers*, **41** (April), 283–301.

Dasgupta, P. and Stiglitz, J. (1980), 'Industrial structure and the nature of innovative activity', *Economic Journal*, **90** (June), 266–93.

De Fraja, G. (1993), 'Productive efficiency in public and private firms', *Journal of Public Economics*, **50**(1), 15–30.

De Fraja, G. and Delbono, F. (1989), 'Alternative strategies of a public enterprise in oligopoly', *Oxford Economic Papers*, **41** (April), 302–11.

De Fraja, G. and Delbono, F. (1990), 'Game theoretic models of mixed oligopoly', *Journal of Economic Surveys*, **4**(1), 1–18.

Delbono, F. and Denicolò, V. (1993), 'Regulating innovative activity. The role of a public firm', *International Journal of Industrial Organization*, **11**(1), 35–48.

Deutsch, E. (2001), 'Survival of SME's under risk guarantee schemes', Mimeo, Vienna: University of Technology.

Dowrick, S. (1996), 'Swedish economic performance and Swedish debate: a view from outside', *Economic Journal*, **106**(493), 1772–9.

Evans, D.S. and Leighton, L.S. (1989), 'Some empirical aspects of entrepreneurship', *American Economic Review*, **79**, 519–35.

Fehrstman, C. (1990), 'The interdependence between ownership and market structure: the case of privatization', *Economica*, **57**(227), 219–38.

Fonesca, R., Lopez-Garcia, P. and Pissarides, C.A. (2001), 'Entrepreneurship, start-up costs and employment', *European Economic Review*, **45**(4–6), 692–705.

Fowler, P.C. and Richards, D.G. (1995), 'Test evidence in the OECD-countries, 1965–85: the relationship between the size of the public enterprise sector and economic growth', *International Journal of Social Economics*, **22**(3), 11–23.

Gentry, W.M. and Hubbard, R.G. (2000), 'Tax policy and entrepreneurial entry', *American Economic Review*, **90** (May) (Papers and Proceedings), 283–7.

Geroski, P. (1995), 'What do we know about entry?', *International Journal of Industrial Organization*, **13**(4), 421–40.

Grande, E. and Peschke, A. (1999), 'Transnational cooperation and policy networks in European science policy-making', *Research Policy*, **28**(1), 43–61.

Hamilton, B. (2000), 'Does entrepreneurship pay? An empirical analysis of patterns of self-employment', *Journal of Political Economy*, **108**(3), 604–31.

Hausman, W.J. and Neufeld, J.L. (1999), 'Falling water: the origins of direct federal participation in the U.S. electric utility industry 1902–1933', *Annals of Public and Cooperative Economics*, **76**(1), 49–74.

Henreksson, M.L. (1996), 'Sweden's relative performance: lagging behind or staying on top?', *Economic Journal*, **106**(439), 1749–59.

Ilmakunnas, P. and Kanniainen, V. (2001), 'Entrepreneurship, economic risks, and risk insurance in the welfare state: results with OECD data 1978–93', *German Economic Review*, **2**(3), 195–218.

Korpi, W. (1996), 'Eurosclerosis and the sclerosis of objectivity: on the role of values among economic policy experts', *Economic Journal*, **106**(439), 1727–46.

Krueger, A.B. and Pischke, J.-S. (1997), 'Observations and conjectures on the U.S. employment miracle', National Bureau of Economic Research, Working Paper 6146.

Lechner, M. and Pfeiffer, F. (1993), 'Planning for self-employment at the beginning of a market economy: evidence from individual data of East German workers', *Small Business Economics*, **5**(2), 111–28.

Lindbeck, A. (1997), 'The Swedish experiment', *Journal of Economic Literature*, **35** (September), 1273–319.

Lindh, T. and Ohlsson, H. (1998), 'Self-employment and wealth inequality', *Review of Income and Wealth*, **44**(1), 25–42.

Link, A.N. and Scott, J.T. (1995), 'Public/private partnerships: stimulating competition in a dynamic market', *International Journal of Industrial Organization*, **19**(5), 763–94.

Mamatzakis, E.C. (1997), 'The role of public sector infrastructure on private sector productivity in a long run perspective', Working Paper.

Martin, S. and Parker, D. (1997), *The Impact of Privatisation. Ownership and Corporate Performance in the UK*, London and New York: Routledge.

Mason, C. and Harrison, R. (1998), 'Public policy and the development of the informal venture capital market: UK experience and lessons for Europe', in K. Cowling (ed.), *Industrial Policy in Europe. Theoretical Perspectives and Practical Proposals*, London and New York: Routledge, pp. 199–223.

McMillan, G.S., Narin, F. and Deeds, D.L. (2000), 'An analysis of the critical role of public science in innovation: the case of biotechnology', *Research Policy*, **29**(1), 1–8.

Megginson, W.L. and Netter, J.M. (2001), 'From state to market: a survey of empirical studies on privatization', *Journal of Economic Literature*, **XXXIX**(2), 321–89.

Millward, R. (1982), 'The comparative performance of public and private ownership', in Lord E. Roll (ed.), *The Mixed Economy*, London: Macmillan.

Monsen, R.J. and Walters, K.D. (1983), *Nationalized Companies: A Threat to American Business*, New York: McGraw-Hill.

Nickell, S. (1997), 'Unemployment and labor market rigidities: Europe versus North America', *Journal of Economic Perspectives*, **11**(3), 55–74.

Oughton, C. and Whittam, G. (1994), 'Competition and cooperation in the small firm sector', Discussion Papers in Economics No. 9401, University of Glasgow.

Parker, D. (ed.) (1998), *Privatisation in the European Union. Theory and Policy Perspectives*, London and New York: Routledge.

Peitz, M. (2002), 'The pro-competitive effect of higher entry costs', *International Journal of Industrial Organization*, **20**(3), 353–64.

Persson, T. and Tabellini, G. (1994), 'Is inequality harmful for growth? Theory and evidence', *American Economic Review*, **84** (June), 600–621.

Pint, E.M. (1991), 'Nationalization vs. regulation of monopolies: the effects of ownership on efficiency', *Journal of Public Economics*, **44**(2), 131–64.

Poyago-Theotoky, J. (1998), 'R&D competition in a mixed duopoly under uncertainty and easy imitation', *Journal of Comparative Economics*, **26**, 415–28.

Schultz, N. (2001), 'Profitable cannibalization', Mimeo, Universität Würzburg.

Seade, J. (1980), 'On the effects of entry', *Econometrica*, **48** (March), 479–89.

Siebert, H. (1997), 'Labor market rigidities: at the root of unemployment in Europe', *Journal of Economic Perspectives*, **11**(3), 37–54.

Sinn, H.-W. (1996), 'Social insurance and risk-taking', *International Tax and Public Finance*, **3**, 259–80.

Spilling, O.R. (1998), 'On the re-emergence of small scale production. The Norwegian case in international comparison', *Small Business Economics*, **10**(4), 401–17.

Willner, J. (1994), 'Welfare maximisation with endogeneous average costs', *International Journal of Industrial Organization*, **12**(3), 373–386.

Willner, J. (1996), 'A comment on Bradburd: privatisation of natural monopolies', *Review of Industrial Organization*, **11**(6), 869–82.

Willner, J. (1998), 'Privatisation in Finland, Sweden and Denmark – fashion or necessity?', in D. Parker (ed.), *Privatisation in the European Union. Theory and Policy Perspectives*, London and New York: Routledge, pp. 172–90.

Willner, J. (1999a), 'Market structure, corporate objectives and cost efficiency', in K. Cowling (ed.), *Industrial Policy in Europe. Theoretical Perspectives and Practical Proposals*, London and New York: Routledge, pp. 290–310.

Willner, J. (1999b), 'Policy objectives and performance in a mixed market with bargaining', *International Journal of Industrial Organization*, **17**(1), 137–45.

Willner, J. (2001), 'Ownership, efficiency, and political interference', *European Journal of Political Economy*, **17**(4), pp. 723–48.

World Bank (1995), *Bureaucrats in Business. The Economics and Politics of Government Ownership*, Oxford: Oxford University Press.

5. Notes on labour market flexibility: questions for the new economy[*]

Stanley Siebert

Italy's three main trade unions declared last night that nearly all their 11m members had supported a one-day general strike in protest at labour market reforms proposed by Silvio Berlusconi's centre-right government . . . The government plans to reform Article 18 of the Workers' Statute which gives judges the right to reinstate a sacked worker if he or she is found to have been dismissed without just cause. (James Blitz and Fred Kapner, *Financial Times*, 17 April, 2002)

1. INTRODUCTION

This chapter is concerned with labour market institutions and earnings/income inequality. It is clear that institutions such as strong trade unions with extended collective agreements coupled with minimum wage legislation have reduced earnings inequality amongst OECD states (Lucifora, 2000). Strong unions also passionately support employment protection laws underpinning job security – as the quotation above shows. The conclusion here is seemingly optimistic (Lucifora, p. 10): 'Governments can have a role in supporting those institutions which have proved effective in dealing with the problem of growing earnings inequalities and low wage employment'.

Yet many rich countries with low earnings inequality at the same time present a picture of high and concentrated unemployment, plus low and declining labourforce participation. Italy – where earnings inequalities on some measures have even declined – is a case in point (Dell' Aringa and Lucifora, 2001, Figure 10). Unemployment and low labourforce participation may be attributable to the very unions and minimum wage laws – together with high social security taxes and employment protection laws – that we praise for raising standards in the labour market. A contradiction thus appears to emerge. Policies, that cut the bottom off the earnings distribution, might merely cause unemployment, and push people into the bottom of the income distribution. This is the controversial 'eurosclerosis' hypothesis (see Johan Willner in this volume), which we will examine first.

We also need to assess what weight to place on movements into and out of the bottom of the earnings distribution. If people need to search somewhat longer for jobs whose pay and conditions have been improved – or decide to take early retirement – is this such a bad thing, so long as welfare and retirement payments are sufficiently generous? Richard Freeman (1994, p. 20) has asked: 'America creates more jobs than Europe, but are they worth having?'. He accepts the eurosclerosis hypothesis ('the collapse of earnings for low-skilled Americans must be a major contributing factor to low US unemployment'). But, at the same time, he believes (1994, p. 24) that this widening of the US earnings distribution has created 'a polarised society ... with half a million homeless in the street and millions living in urban slums'. In this case, unemployment might be no bad thing since the alternative is low-paid, insecure jobs, with no union representation. If the eurosclerosis hypothesis is correct, then the improved conditions of those who have a job are bought at the expense of the worsened – or at least changed – conditions of those who are on welfare. Nevertheless, in the Freeman view, the unemployed are better off than they would have been in low-paid jobs. Eurosclerosis, if it occurs, therefore does not matter.

The proposition that low-paid jobs are not worth having is testable, using results from the new studies on happiness. In fact, as we shall see, happiness appears to be linked closely to having a job, while the pay in that job matters little. The implication is that 'bad' jobs are worth having, and are better than the life of European-style unemployed welfare recipients.

The 'new economy' is conventionally taken as the rise of skilled-labour-using technologies, coupled with increasing global competition (compare Chapter 1 of this volume). Both these factors reduce the demand for unskilled labour in the developed world. For these reasons, we would expect the lower tail of the earnings distribution in developed (e.g. OECD) countries to become longer. In other words, increased global competition means unskilled workers in, say, the UK, need to earn somewhat less so as to be able to compete in the world market. In these circumstances, labour market institutions, by preventing a widening of earnings differentials, may have even more of a displacement effect on unskilled workers. The rise of the new economy, therefore, makes investigation of our two questions on eurosclerosis and the worth of 'bad' jobs more urgent.

2.   THE LINK BETWEEN INCOME AND EARNINGS DISTRIBUTIONS

It is important to get the link between the income and earnings distributions right. Conventionally, the income distribution is taken to link closely with the earnings distribution, because, after all, earnings make up on average about 70 per cent of pre-tax and transfer income (Gottschalk and Smeeding, 1997, p. 671). However, at the bottom end of the income distribution, earnings are unimportant because most income is made up of transfers. People here are unemployed. One approach to testing the eurosclerosis hypothesis, therefore, is to investigate whether pushing up unskilled pay, and so reducing numbers on low pay, is matched by increasing numbers on low income. In other words, countries with few low paid, at least in an absolute sense (though we consider both absolute and relative definitions), should have many on low incomes. Let us see whether there is any evidence for this proposition.

Table 5.1 gives various measures of incomes and earnings, on both an absolute and relative basis. Taking earnings first, column (1) gives relative low pay, the proportion earning less than 2/3 of the median. Column (2) then gives an absolute measure of low pay. The figure here provides a comparison of hourly labour costs of the bottom 10 per cent of workers in manufacturing across countries. Countries such as West Germany have high costs for the bottom 10 per cent, US$16.3, both because of having high labour costs relative to the US, and because of having a compressed earnings distribution. It is interesting to note how, according to these estimates, labour costs of the bottom 10 per cent in US manufacturing, $7.8, are lower than most of the other countries in the table. The bottom correlations panel of Table 5.1 shows columns (1) and (2) are well correlated, −0.775. Hence, countries in our sample that have high relative earnings for the unskilled also have high absolute labour costs. (Remember that much of these high labour costs represent taxes, so differences in take-home pay are less.) Unskilled workers therefore cost less in the US than in most other developed countries, despite the fact that the US is the richest country.

Let us now turn to the income distributions. Column (3) gives an absolute measure of low incomes, and column (4) a relative measure, the bottom decile relative to the median. The bottom correlations panel shows that these measures are hardly correlated, 0.266, so it makes a difference which one we choose to use. In fact, the pattern is that relative incomes correlate well with relative earnings (−0.838), and absolute incomes with absolute earnings (0.696), but mixing relative with absolute works less well, as might be expected. The link between relative incomes and earnings is graphed in Figure 5.1, and that between absolute incomes and labour costs in Figure 5.2. As can be seen, both relationships are quite tight, and there is no sign of any of the countries with high unskilled earnings or labour costs having many on low incomes. Hence it seems that we can accept that the prevalence of low earnings and of low incomes – whether relative or absolute – goes together. (It is interesting to note, however, that *changes* in earnings inequality, column (5), are not well correlated with any of the other measures – see below.) In

Table 5.1 Earnings and income distributions, Western Europe, the US and Japan

	(1) % earning < 2/3 median (%)	(2) Labour costs per hour, mfg, bottom 10%	(3) Log av. incomes, bottom quintile	(4) Bottom decile income/ median income (%)	(5) Change in earnings gini over 1980–90	(6) Bargaining coordination index
Australia	13.8	8.7	8.71	45	1	3
Austria	13.2	9.5	–	56	–	6
Belgium	7.2	14.2	8.61	58	1	4
Canada	23.7	7.7	8.77	47	1	2
Denmark	–	13.9	8.49	54	1	6
Finland	5.9	16.2	8.81	58	3	5
France	13.3	9.9	8.50	55	0	4
Ireland	–	–	7.53	50	1	2
Italy	12.5	10.9	8.54	56	–1	4
Japan	15.7	8.3	8.86	–	1	4
N. Zealand	16.9	5.1	8.31	–	1	3
Netherlands	11.9	12.8	8.43	57	1	4
Norway	–	17.5	9.02	56	1	6
Portugal	–	2.4	7.97	–	0	4
Spain	–	–	8.55	49	–	3
Sweden	5.2	16.7	8.84	57	3	6
Switzerland	13	13.8	–	54	–	4
UK	19.6	7.6	8.50	44	3	2

Table 5.1 continued

	(1) % earning < 2/3 median (%)	(2) Labour costs per hour, mfg, bottom 10%	(3) Log av. incomes, bottom quintile	(4) Bottom decile income/ median income (%)	(5) Change in earnings gini over 1980–90	(6) Bargaining coordination index
US	25	7.8	8.39	36	3	2
W. Germany	13.3	16.3	8.78	57	1	5

Notes:
(1) Figures are for full-timers, early 1990s: OECD (1996), Tables 3.1, 3.2.
(2) Figure is in US$, 1990 prices. It is derived by applying the OECD (1996, Table 3.1) bottom decile/median earnings ratio to the United States (1995, Table 1394) international hourly labour cost figures, and taking $16 as the benchmark US 1990 median hourly labour cost.
(3) Figure is in US$ at PPP, 1985 prices: Dollar and Kray (2001a), data appendix.
(4) Figures are for various dates 1984–91: Gottschalk and Smeeding (1997), Figure 2.
(5) The figure relates to change in market income inequality (earnings plus dividends and other market sources), generally around 1980–90, with –1 denoting a small decline, 0 approximate stability, and 1, 2, 3 small, moderate and large (over 15%) increases: Gottschalk and Smeeding (1997), Table 4.
(6) Figure is the sum of union coordination and employer coordination indices, going from 1 = low to 6 = high (Nickell and Layard, 1999, p. 3041). See Flanagan (1999, p. 1153) for a different index, which rates Japan more, and Sweden less, coordinated than this one.

Correlations between the variables are as follows, with ***, **, * denoting significance at the 1%, 5% and 10% levels:

	(1)	(2)	(3)	(4)	(5)
(2)	-0.775***				
(3)	-0.376	0.696***			
(4)	-0.838***	0.737***	0.266		
(5)	0.025	0.231	0.213	-0.354	
(6)	-0.800***	0.654***	0.479**	0.778***	-0.059

110

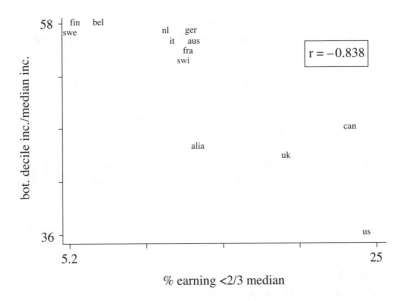

Figure 5.1   The link between relative incomes (bottom decile to median) and relative earnings (% paid less than 2/3 median)

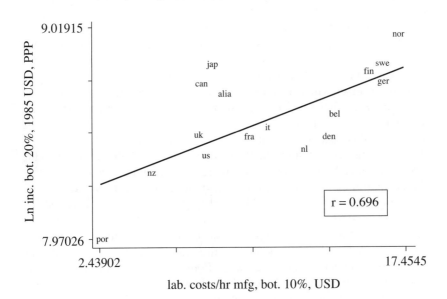

Figure 5.2   The link between absolute incomes (bottom quintile) and absolute labour costs (bottom decile)

particular, there is no sign here that countries with high unskilled labour costs, which have 'cut off the bottom' of the earnings distribution via unions and extended collective agreements, are paying for this by pushing many onto low welfare incomes.

At the same time, it must be acknowledged that many countries coordinate their wage and income interventions. Minimum wages and state income support levels are formally linked, for example, in the Netherlands. In such countries, workers displaced by the minimum wage/extended collective agreement system might suffer little immediate income loss. ('Immediate', because in the long run they will suffer by losing on-the-job training, and becoming dependent – see below.) Since the income distribution is controlled, it is therefore fruitless to look for changes in its lower tail. Yet, the process of switching low wages for low incomes might still be the consequence of minimum wages/extended collective agreements, as in the eurosclerosis hypothesis.

Furthermore, there are 'good' and 'bad' reasons for increases in unskilled labour earnings (see Siebert, 2001). A good reason is where there is an increase in the demand for unskilled labour relative to its supply, so that the increase in earnings is an equilibrium outcome. A bad reason is where extended collective agreements, for example, push up unskilled wages irrespective of the state of the market. Our analysis in Figures 5.1 and 5.2 cannot test for these distinctions.

To investigate the eurosclerosis hypothesis, therefore, alternative tests are worth considering. Most analysts have concentrated on testing for whether labour market opportunities, for example unemployment, diminish as the extended collective agreement/employment protection system widens. We would expect unskilled employment/population ratios to be smaller, and unemployment higher under such systems. The evidence here, at first glance, seems mixed. Nickell and Bell (1996, p. 303), for example, argue that the UK's unskilled unemployment record is just as bad as West Germany's despite the fact that the unskilled/skilled pay ratio has fallen far more in the UK. Krueger and Pischke (1997, p. 16) agree, stating that 'the evidence that the decline in employment in France and Germany is concentrated among the unskilled is surprisingly shallow'. They prefer to emphasise restrictions on business start-ups, which are more difficult in Germany, rather than labour regulation in explaining Germany's poor performance. However, Krueger and Pischke do not dismiss the labour side (1997, p. 26): they believe both the labour side (e.g., wage floors) and restrictions on entrepreneurs are important. The difficulty here, however, as they admit, is to find empirical counterparts for these entrepreneurship restrictions, and subject the argument to test.

3. UNSKILLED EMPLOYMENT OPPORTUNITIES

Theory

Keeping to the labour side, and concentrating on employment opportunities, we have the benefit of several multivariate cross-country panel studies (see Addison and Texeira, 2002, for a recent review). Let us now consider this approach.

According to the eurosclerosis hypothesis, unskilled employment and unemployment react negatively to laws raising wages and working conditions. However, the impact of laws raising working conditions is a relatively new object of study. Thus, some clarification particularly of the possible effects of employment protection laws (EPL) is necessary (for more detail, see Addison and Siebert, 1999, pp. 35ff).

EPL was first analysed as an implicit tax on labour demand, counterbalanced by a rightward shift of labour supply (Summers, 1989). Such an analysis captures the fact that EPL is disliked by employers, but liked by workers. Whether there are any displacement effects for employment cannot be predicted in advance, since these depend on whether the costs to employers are outweighed by benefits to workers. Employment effects are in any case likely to be minor, so long as wages fall to reflect the better working conditions. This argument has been borne out in the US, where wages are flexible. For example, the requirement that company insurance plans be extended to include maternity expenditures has been found both to raise company insurance premiums, and to reduce the wages of women in the 20–40 age group (Gruber, 1994).

Nevertheless, more recently it has been argued that displacement effects are likely to predominate for unskilled workers. One reason, advanced by Saint-Paul (1996, p. 136) is that EPL prevents firms replacing unskilled workers with skilled, should they want to. With EPL it becomes sensible for firms to preserve the 'option value' of a job vacancy, that is, to wait until a skilled worker is found for a vacancy rather than filling it immediately with an unskilled worker. A second reason is that unskilled workers are more likely to 'take advantage' of EPL, for example, to take time off sick. EPL then causes firms to become more 'choosy' about filling vacancies, which works against unskilled workers. Third, unskilled workers are more likely to be employed in small firms. In general, it seems the small firms are most affected by labour regulation, perhaps because of their less sophisticated personnel policies. Finally, unskilled workers might have less flexible wages, since unskilled wages are more constrained by minimum wage and unemployment benefit 'floors'. For all these reasons, unskilled workers are in the firing line.

EPL may also slow the reallocation of labour from declining to new sectors.

However, this effect only matters when there is much change. When times are reasonably certain, layoffs are a problem of the future, and can be well discounted. In any case, as Nickell and Layard (1999, p. 3063) have stressed, EPL need not slow labour reallocation much in practice because there is so much voluntary turnover – firms can rely on natural wastage. For example, job tenures of 5–10 years would imply turnover rates of 10 to 20 per cent – arguably, quite enough room for manoeuvre. Moreover, OECD research (1996, Table 5.1) has shown that in fact there seems to be as many job gains (firms expanding and opening) and job losses (firms closing and/or contracting) in the supposedly sclerotic economies as in the US. On the other hand, it must be remembered that quit rates among permanent workers in protected European firms are very low, less than 1 per cent a year (Morton and Siebert, 2001, Table 1). Average turnover rates are driven up by high turnover among a minority of workers in peripheral jobs.

Furthermore, the job gains and job losses argument also seems to disappear on closer examination. The case of Portugal is instructive, given its high ranking on the EPL scale (see Table 5.2). Contrasting Portugal with the US, we see that the US's job changes tend to be transitory – existing firms expanding or contracting – rather than permanent – firms opening and closing (Blanchard and Portugal, 2001, p. 190). The pattern is the opposite in Portugal, which fits in with EPL preventing transitory changes, but at the expense of causing permanent closures. Also, when using quarterly rather than annual rates of job gains/losses, Portugal's quarterly figure is lower than that for the US, again because Portugal has fewer transitory job changes (a difference that is less likely to show up on an annual measure). Blanchard and Portugal (2001, p. 205) conclude: 'Employment protection (may) eliminate three out of every four desirable job separations in Portugal'. Therefore, it seems that EPL can very well act as a barrier to labour reallocation.

Results

Let us turn now to the impact of EPL on unskilled employment and unemployment opportunities. A first issue to be solved is how to measure unskilled opportunities. Table 5.2 presents some measures, together with the OECD's EPL ranking across countries. Columns (1) and (2) relate to the youth, taking the 20–24 group rather than the wider 15–24 group, so as to get around complications caused by school choice. (By the time people are 20, their employment/unemployment outcomes are not much influenced by differences in national school and youth training systems.) Youth workers are a typical outsider group, and have been the subject of other studies (for example, Scarpetta, 1996). Column (1) gives the youth unemployment rate, but the employment/population ratio (column 2) is less likely to be influenced by special training measures that governments tend to

Table 5.2 Unskilled employment opportunities, Western Europe, the US and Japan

	(1) Unemployment rate, 20–24 (%)	(2) Employment/ population rate, 20–24 (%)	(3) Long-term unemployment rate (%)	(4) Employment/ population rate, 55–64 (%)	(5) Employment protection score rank
Australia	13.3	71.3	2.7	40	5
Austria	7.1	71.1	–	28	12
Belgium	15.2	51.1	5.1	22	10
Canada	13.7	68.2	0.9	45	3
Denmark	14.6	68.8	3	52	8
Finland	18.3	55.2	1.7	39	9
France	21.6	45.4	3.9	35	17
Ireland	18.9	61	9.4	39	4
Italy	28.8	45.1	5.3	40	19
Japan	4.2	71	0.4	64	14
N. Zealand	13.8	68	2.3	43	7
Netherlands	8.7	69.5	3.5	22	10
Norway	10.9	63.1	1.2	61	16
Portugal	10.3	64.6	2	47	20
Spain	37.1	44.6	9.7	35	18
Sweden	12.1	68.6	0.4	67	12
Switzerland	–	–	0.5	70	6

Table 5.2   continued

	(1) Unemployment rate, 20–24 (%)	(2) Employment/ population rate, 20–24 (%)	(3) Long-term unemployment rate (%)	(4) Employment/ population rate, 55–64 (%)	(5) Employment protection score rank
UK	13.1	70	3.4	48	2
US	10	69.7	0.6	54	1
W. Germany	5.2	69.7	2.2	39	15

Notes:
(1), (2), (4).   Figures are averages over 1989–94; OECD (2001), CD-ROM.
(3)   Figure is average over 1989–94: Nickell and Layard (1999), data appendix.
(5)   The measure relates to the late 1990s. It is based on an assessment of the employment protection laws in each country, for example months of severance pay required, and procedural inconveniences for dismissal (scored 0 = simple written notice, up to 3 = government permission required). Countries are then ranked from 1 = least strict, up to 20, OECD (1999), Table 2.5.

Correlations between the variables are as follows, with ***, **, * denoting significance at the 1%, 5% and 10% levels:

	(1)	(2)	(3)	(4)
(2)	−0.841***			
(3)	0.741***	−0.611***		
(4)	−0.257	0.365	−0.590**	
(5)	0.260	−0.504**	0.167	−0.107

use to massage unemployment figures. Hence, we emphasise the employment/ population ratio: you hold a job or you don't.

Table 5.2 (column 3) also presents data on the long-term unemployment rate. This rate is important as an indicator of the concentration of unemployment. Also, EPL and long-term unemployment are well linked in theory. EPL might drive the overall unemployment rate either way, depending upon its effects in reducing outflows into unemployment versus reducing inflows into employment (as firms become more choosy about hiring). However, the long-term unemployment rate is unambiguously driven up by strict EPL. Strict EPL means job security, which means low outflows from jobs. Such low outflows are likely to be counterbalanced by low inflows into jobs, and hence higher unemployment duration. Of course, there is more to unemployment duration than EPL. Column (3) shows the US to have low long-term unemployment, 0.6 per cent, but this is because welfare benefits are low and of short duration. We can control for these factors. Again, if wages are flexible enough downwards, employers need not become more choosy in selecting workers – particularly if the economy is doing well. We can control for these factors as well. The question is whether EPL drives up long-term unemployment, *ceteris paribus*.

Table 5.2 also presents figures on the employment/population ratio for older workers, 55–64 (column 4). This category, of course, is by no means solely composed of unskilled groups. However, movements in the ratio are likely to be driven by those doing less well in the labour market, who will be less skilled, or at least inappropriately skilled. It seems sad to see Belgium, for example, with only 22 per cent of its 55–64 category working. France and Germany are not much better. Norway, Sweden, Switzerland show what can be done. But, on the face of it, eurosclerosis can hardly be blamed for the low over-55 employment/population ratio since highly regulated countries such as Sweden are doing well. Indeed, the simple correlation between EPL and the over-55 employment/population variable is low, –0.107, as shown in the bottom table. Nevertheless, our studies (Morton and Siebert, 2001) of large manufacturing plants in France and Germany show almost no production workers over 55 in these plants, a stark contrast with the UK. Managers, it seems, are using early retirement programmes to 'encourage' older workers to leave (few older workers being hired in any case[1]). Hence it seems worth continuing the search for determinants of older workers' employment population behaviour.

The next issue to tackle is modelling the determinants of unskilled employment/unemployment. Here we have the benefit of several multivariate cross-country panel studies (see Addison and Texeira, 2002). To minimise controversy, I shall follow the specification set out by Nickell and Layard (1999), and even use their data where possible. The data are for 20 OECD countries, using averages for variables for two time periods 1983–88, and 1989–94. The results are summarised in Table 5.3.

Table 5.3 Determinants of unskilled worker job opportunities

Independent variables (means)	Young workers (20–24)[a] Emp./pop. rate[a] (4.15)		Unemp. rate[a] (2.53)	Long-term unemp. rate (0.63)	Older worker emp./pop. rate (55–64)[a] (3.75)
Union density (42%)	-0.00	-0.00	0.012**	0.023*	0.00
Collective agreement coverage[b] (70)	-0.004***	-0.003*	0.006	0.005	-0.007***
Tax wedge (48%)	-0.006**	-0.007***	0.032***	0.032*	0.006
EPL ranking, late 80s and 90s (larger = more strict)[c] (10)	-0.010***	-0.009**	0.005	0.060	0.004
Unemployment benefit replacement rate (57%)	-0.002*	-0.00	0.009	0.020	-0.004
Benefit duration (2.4 years)	0.00	0.00	0.00	0.331**	0.00
Act. lab. exps./unemp. person as % of GDP/cap. (12%)	0.002	0.002			
Change pay inequ. in 80s[d] (1.2)		0.037	-0.012*	-0.028*	0.008**
Public pension expenditure as % of GDP[e] (9.7%)			-0.177**	-0.328*	-0.083***
Bargaining coordination index (larger = more coord.) (4)	0.083***	0.079**	-0.423***	-0.734***	0.100**
R^2, observations	0.77, 37	0.77, 34	0.80, 34	0.78, 34	0.75, 39

Dependent variables, in logs.

Note: Equations are fitted to data for 20 OECD countries, using GLS random effects, for averages of two time periods 1983–88 and 1989–94. Controls are, in addition to the listed variables: fixed effects for countries, change in inflation, a dummy for 1989–94, and house owner-occupation rate. ***, **, * denotes significance at the 1%, 5% and 10% levels.

Sources:
Data were kindly provided by Nickell and Layard (1999), except for:
a OECD (2001) CD-ROM.
b OECD (1997), Table 3.3), with Ireland assigned the same collective agreement coverage as the UK.
c OECD (1999, Table 2.5) and (1994, Table 6.7).
d See text Table 5.1, column (6).
e ILO (2000, Table 14). Since an ageing population will itself drive up social security expenditure via pensions, the pension variable is endogenous (dependent upon employment–population choices of older workers). Hence it needs to be instrumented, which is done by regressing the 1990 and 1995 values on the 1985 value. This procedure is similar to the instrumenting for expenditure on active labour market policies (carried out by Nickell and Layard, 1999, pp. 3053).

Beginning with the youth employment/population rate, the first two rows measure the impact of unionisation, taken both in terms of union density, and collective bargaining coverage. Both variables are necessary here, since union membership cannot alone hope to capture possible impacts of union power in raising wages, given that extension of collective agreements to third parties (with no part in negotiating the agreement) is common in some countries. France in particular has low density (only about 10 per cent), but extensive collective bargaining coverage (about 90 per cent) due to extensions (OECD, 1997, p. 71). These extensions are akin to setting legally binding minimum wages for a set of jobs rather than just the jobs at the very bottom of the earnings distribution, and are consequently more intrusive than minimum wage legislation alone. Indeed, Germany does not even have a national minimum wage, but instead uses extended collective agreements to achieve the same end.

The estimated coefficients (×100) give the change in percentage points of the dependent variable. To illustrate, taking the collective agreement coverage coefficient, –0.004, a decrease in collective agreement coverage from the average (70 per cent) to the current UK level (about 40 per cent) gives a boost to youth employment/population of about 12 per cent (= –30 · –0.004 · 100). This effect is slightly reduced, –0.003, in the second column, which incorporates the change in pay inequality variable (listed in Table 5.1). The pay inequality variable attempts explicitly to account for changes in the earnings distribution, and so will naturally take over some of the effects of collective agreement coverage. (The pay inequality variable does not reach significance in the youth employment/population regression, but it is significant in the youth unemployment regression.) The important point is that increases in collective agreement coverage, or the tax wedge, or EPL, and reduction in pay inequality all have adverse effects on youth employment. Generally, these variables drive up youth unemployment as well. The eurosclerosis hypothesis predicts precisely such effects.

Can corporatism come to the rescue, by helping employers and unions to form 'encompassing' coalitions (Mancur Olsen's term, used in Summers et al., 1993, p. 386)? Encompassing coalitions lead to the more responsible exertion of union power. In Table 5.3's regressions, to avoid controversy, we use the Nickell–Layard bargaining coordination index as a measure of corporatism. The values of this index are given in column (6) of Table 5.1. Clearly there are strong assumptions involved in its construction (see Summers et al., 1993, pp. 387ff for discussion). As Table 5.3 shows (penultimate row), the increased bargaining coordination index brings a strong improvement to the youth employment/population ratio, 0.083. Nickell and Layard (1999, p. 3067) point out that a 100 per cent unionised and collective agreement-covered country, which is also fully corporatist, has no different an unemployment rate from a non-corporatist, zero-union and zero-coverage country. This argument holds well for all our variables, because the positive effects of bargaining coordination are strong in all cases.[2] Since the corporatist countries are also the well-regulated 'sclerotic' countries, it seems therefore that the eurosclerosis hypothesis can be countered.

Corporatism as a means of taming union power is undoubtedly important, but there are problems here. At the outset, there is the problem of measurement: the use of Flanagan's (1999, p. 1153) index would give less clear-cut results. But, for the sake of argument, let us skirt this problem (it applies to the EPL index, too). The main difficulty then revolves around the fact that, taxes, EPL and benefit replacement, in practice, vary in parallel with corporatism. In our dataset there are good correlations between these variables.[3] Summers et al. (1993) have advanced the argument that, at least as regards labour taxation, there is a causal link with corporatism. The reason for the link is that in a corporatist environment, the union bargainers can more certainly ensure that taxes are spent to the benefit of their members. Wages can be set to reflect this 'social wage'. Therefore taxes on labour need not have such a distortional effect on labour supply decisions within a corporatist framework, and the labour tax burden can be allowed to rise. (This argument is related to corporatism reducing the 'holdup' problem, as stressed by Teulings and Hartog [1998, p. 85].) Interestingly, Summers et al. point (1993, pp. 404ff) to the way in which the labour tax burden in Sweden only began rising after 1956 when Sweden's national union confederation (the LO) started centralised bargaining with the employers' federation (the SAF). Thus the possibility arises that high labour taxes – and, by extension, EPL, benefit replacement levels, and obviously collective agreement coverage and earnings differentials – are set better within a corporatist framework.[4]

But the point remains that corporatist countries generate poor job performance if we link high taxes and labour regulation to corporatism. For example, let us suppose that a 10 per cent increase in corporatism brings also a 10 per cent increase in collective agreement coverage, in the tax wedge, in EPL and in the unemployment benefit replacement rate. Applying these changes to the youth employment/population ratio using the coefficients in Table 5.2 results in the adverse effects overwhelming the positive.[5] To put the argument in another way, suppose we gave Italian values of the above variables to the UK, offsetting this with the Italian level of bargaining coordination. The UK would be far worse off. Its youth employment/population ratio would fall by 24 per cent. The position would be worse still if we allow for the effect of corporatism in reducing earnings differentials (by incorporating the change in pay inequality coefficient, 0.037). In practice, therefore, a high value of corporatism, while good in itself, is accompanied by high values of other variables such as EPL, which cancel out these effects.

In addition to the youth employment/population rate, Table 5.3 contains results for other variables, which we take up briefly. Looking first at the youth unemployment rate column, the results are broadly similar to the youth employment/population column. The EPL variable is positive but not significant, which is surprising. However, the significant negative coefficients on the active labour market expenditures, and change in pay inequality variables are soaking up this effect. The union density and tax wedge variables act in the usual way to increase unemployment, and the bargaining coordination variable reduces it. The long-term unemployment rate column has a similar pattern, with EPL again being insignificant (in Nickel and Layard's formulation, EPL is in fact significant). The duration of unemployment benefits is also significant, as might be expected. For both youth and long-term unemployment the change in pay inequality variable is large and significant. Finally, the older worker employment/population equation results bear a lot of similarity to the young worker result, in particular the collective agreement coverage and bargaining coordination variables have opposing effects. However, the EPL variable is not significant for the older group, while the public pension expenditure variable is highly significant (the change in pay inequality variable, when included, is insignificant here).

In sum, the results for Table 5.3 indicate that the collective agreement coverage, tax, EPL and change in pay inequality variables all behave in accordance with the eurosclerosis hypothesis. The bargaining coordination variable does not – but its countervailing effect is only partial. In particular, it is important to note how a reduction in pay inequality increases both youth and older worker unemployment. This finding is in line with the proposition advanced above: cutting the bottom off the earnings distribution tends to shift workers – particularly the unskilled – from low paying jobs onto welfare. Bover et al. (2000, p. 411), in their detailed examination of why Spanish unemployment is so much higher than Portuguese (see Table 5.2) come to the same conclusion: 'By preventing wage dispersion from adjusting in the face of changing demand for skills, the Spanish labour market bought lower wage inequality at the price of a much greater incidence of unemployment'. But are these low-paying jobs really 'worth having', in any case? We now turn to happiness studies.

4.   UNEMPLOYMENT AND LIFE SATISFACTION

Table 5.4 summarises the results of five recent life satisfaction studies ('life satisfaction' to distinguish from job satisfaction, which of course cannot be

Table 5.4 Unemployment and life satisfaction

Study	Happiness measure	Remarks
(a) 1984–90 waves of German Socioeconomic Panel	How satisfied are you at present with your life as a whole these days? 10pt scale	Longitudinal study, males only. Only 5% of employed are in lowest categories 1–4 (mean 7.4), but 14% of out-of-workforce (mean 6.8), and 29% of unemployed (mean 5.6). Moving into (out of) unemployment causes a 1.2pt fall (1.1pt rise) in the index
(b) 1992–99 waves of British Household Panel	12 questions on general psychological health, aggregated into a 12pt index	Mean score for employed is 10.3, for unemployed is 9.3. Yearly individual income is insignificant. Moving into (out of) unemployment causes a 1pt fall (1.4pt rise) in the index. Unemployment effect halved if all others in household also unemployed
(c) 1992 British Household Panel	Have you recently been feeling reasonably happy, all things considered? Reduced to 2pt scale	Unemployed have a 2.56 greater chance of reporting unhappiness compared with the low paid (earning < 1/3 median). No significant difference between high and low paid
(d) US General Social Survey, 1972–98	Taken all together, how would you say things are these days – would you say you are very happy, pretty happy or not too happy?	In an OLS equation, the coefficient on unemployment is −0.24, that on annual income is 0.000004
(e) Survey of 6000 men in Switzerland	As in (a). 8pt scale	Unemployment has a large negative effect, income situation of the household a small positive effect

Note: It is possible to calculate a 'compensating variation' for the amount of income that is needed to compensate an individual for the drop in happiness due to unemployment. For example, using the coefficients in (d), to make good the fall in happiness of −0.24, an unemployed individual would have to receive an annual income increase of $60,000 (= 0.24/0.000004).

Sources: (a) Winkelman and Winkelman (1968); (b) Clark (2002); (c) Theodossiou (1998); (d) Blanchflower and Oswald (2000); (e) Frey and Stutzer (2000).

assessed for people without jobs). Subjective happiness data can be faulted because its interpretation requires interpersonal comparisons of utility, and assumes that happiness is cardinally measurable (for problems associated with subjective data, see Bertrand and Mullainathan, 2001). However, panel data help, because then the issue of whether individuals anchor their scales at different levels does not arise. We track individuals over time, and only require that their internal metric be time-invariant. Panel studies also help address the issue of causality: it might be that unemployed individuals are unhappy for unobserved reasons, and this is why they are unemployed. Hence, rows (a) and (b) of Table 5.4 give results from panel studies. The study in row (c) compares unemployed with low-paid people. Here, the question of whether low-paid workers feel themselves worse off than unemployed is addressed directly. The final rows, for completeness, give the results from ordinary cross-section studies using US and Swiss data.

The fundamental point is that all the studies give a high negative impact for unemployment on happiness. The longitudinal studies show that, tracking a given individual, a move from employment to unemployment causes a fall in life satisfaction. A move from unemployment into employment causes an equal and opposite increase in life satisfaction. The implication is that it is not something intrinsic to the unemployed individual that is causing the low satisfaction, but unemployment itself. As for income, this has a small, often insignificant effect. The cross-section studies in the last three rows all agree with these findings. The direct comparison in row (c) between the unemployed and the low paid, finds the unemployed far more unhappy.

Being out of the labourforce also has a negative impact (row (a)). This result indicates that we should also worry about the low European labourforce participation of the over-55s, and their high early retirement rates. Evidently, early retirement is a mixed blessing.

There is a little evidence, but not much, for the view that low-paid jobs are 'not worth having'. The study reported in row (a) finds that employed workers with past unemployment experience are less satisfied than those without such experience. A possible reason for this difference is that individuals with past unemployment experience currently have insecure jobs. Job insecurity lowers life satisfaction, too. There is also the finding in Clark's (2002) study reported in row (b), that the unemployed suffer less if others in the family or region are unemployed. A trouble shared is a trouble halved. But it is a big step from these observations to say that a state-provided income, even if secure and high, is a substitute for a job.

In sum, we can see that the immediate loss of income due to being unemployed makes a minor contribution to the loss of life satisfaction. The non-pecuniary aspects are much more important. This result follows from the fact that people (men certainly) place much more weight on jobs than money as a source of happiness.

5. CONCLUSIONS

Our findings on eurosclerosis (Table 5.3) indicate that labour regulation imposing good working conditions eliminates 'bad' jobs. Moreover, strict labour regulation and strong trade unions are closely linked. At the same time, the findings of happiness research above indicate that the average unemployed person would much rather have a job, even a 'bad' job, than remain on welfare. Such labour regulation, therefore, causes unskilled workers (without the skills to compete for good jobs) to suffer.

Perhaps it would be possible to construct corporatist institutions, which permitted the worker representation benefits of a strong trade union movement without such costs as strict EPL? The quote at the beginning of this chapter is pessimistic. Yet the question is important because freedom of association, like freedom of the press, is part of a democratic society. Trade unions have been in the forefront of the fight for democracy in many countries – South Africa and Poland are cases in point (see Siebert, 2001). Simply wishing trade unions away is neither possible nor desirable. Searching for the happy medium for union power is a central political issue, as the UK's history over the past 20 years demonstrates. This chapter demonstrates how important this search continues to be.

NOTES

*   I am grateful to Clive Belfield for many discussions, and for comments from participants at the L'institute–Milwaukee Workshop, 2001, and the Friedrich-Naumann Foundation Colloquium, Potsdam 2002, but retain responsibility for errors.
1.   In general, the age distribution of new hires does not match the age distribution of those already employed. Both US and Hong Kong data (see Hutchens, 1986 and Heywood et al., 1999) show that the share of older workers among new hires is less than the share of older workers in the workforce for the majority of firms. Because this index is less than unity, firms that employ older workers evidently do not, in general hire older workers. However, the opportunity index is higher than unity for some firms – perhaps as many as 30 per cent of firms – indicating a preference for older workers here. So far, it seems there has been no UK analysis of hiring older workers.
2.   For example, for the youth employment/population variable, the first column gives the combined effects of 100 per cent coverage and full coordination (= level 6) as $-100 \times 0.004 + 6 \times 0.083 = 9.8$ per cent improvement in youth employment/population.
3.   The simple cross-country correlation of the coordination variable with EPL is 0.514**, with the tax wedge 0.527**, with union density 0.536**, and with coverage 0.617***. Table 5.1's lower panel also shows that the coordination variable is well correlated with lower earnings and income dispersion.

4. However, Summers et al. (1993, p. 407) warn: 'Part of the logic of socialism was that a wise government could internalize everything and so generate efficient economic outcomes. This has proved wrong, and should give pause about excessively benign views of negotiated alternatives to market solutions'.
5. Increasing all the independent variables by 10 per cent gives: collective agreement coverage (–7 · 0.4), the tax wedge (–4.8 · 0.6), bargaining coordination (+0.4 · 8.3), EPL (–1.0 · 1.0), and the replacement rate (–5.7 · 0.2). Adding these gives total = –4.5. Hence the result is to reduce the youth employment/population ratio by 4.5 per cent.

REFERENCES

Addison, J. and Siebert, S. (1999), 'Regulating European labour markets: more costs than benefits?', Institute of Economic Affairs Hobart Paper 138.

Addison, J. and Texeira, P. (2002), 'The economics of employment protection', Unpub. paper, Department of Economics, University of South Carolina.

Bertrand, M. and Mullainathan, S. (2001), 'Do people mean what they say? Implications for subjective survey data', *American Economic Review*, **91**(2), May, 62–72.

Blanchard, O. and Portugal, P. (2001), 'What hides behind an unemployment rate: comparing Portuguese and U.S. labor markets', *American Economic Review*, **91**(1), March, 187–207.

Blanchflower, D. and Oswald, A. (2000), 'Well-being over time in Britain and the USA', Unpub., July.

Blitz, J. and Kapner, F. (2002), 'Millions of Italians join protest against labour reform', *Financial Times*, 17 April.

Bover, O., Garcia-Perea, P. and Portugal, P. (2000), 'Labour market outlines: lessons from Portugal and Spain', *Economic Policy*, **15**, 381–427.

Clark, A. (2002), 'Unemployment as a social norm: psychological evidence from panel data', Unpub. paper.

Dell' Aringa, C. and Lucifora, C. (2001), 'Inside the black box: labour market institutions, wage formation and unemployment in Italy', Unpub. paper.

Dollar, D. and Kray, A. (2001a), 'Growth is good for the poor', World Bank Research Working Paper 2587, April.

Dollar, D. and Kray, A. (2001b), 'Trade, growth and poverty', World Bank Research Working Paper, June.

Flanagan, R. (1999), 'Macroeconomic performance and collective bargaining: an international perspective', *Journal of Economic Literature*, **37**, 1150–95.

Freeman, R. (1994), 'Jobs in the USA', *New Economy*, **1** (Spring), 20–25.

Frey, B. and Stutzer, A. (2000), 'Happiness, economy and institutions', *Economic Journal*, **110** (October) 918–38.

Gottschalk, P. and Smeeding, T. (1997), 'Cross national comparisons of earnings and income inequality', *Journal of Economic Literature*, **35** (June), 633–87.

Gruber, J. (1994), 'The incidence of mandated maternity benefits', *American Economic Review*, **84** (3), June, 622–41.

Heywood, J., Ho, L. and Wei, X. (1999), 'The determinants of hiring older workers: evidence from Hong Kong', *Industrial and Labor Relations Review*, **52**, 444–59.

Hutchens, R. (1986), 'Delayed payment contracts and a firm's propensity to hire older workers', *Journal of Labor Economics*, **4**, 439–57.

ILO (2000) (International Labour Office), *World Labour Report 2000*, Geneva: ILO.

Krueger, A. and Pischke, J.-S. (1997), 'Observations and conjectures on the US employment miracle', NBER Working Paper 6146, August.

Lucifora, C. (2000), 'Wage inequalities and low pay: the role of labour market institutions', in M. Gregory, W. Salverda and S. Bazen, *Labour Market Inequalities: Problems and Policies in International Perspective*, Oxford: Oxford University Press.

Morton, J. and Siebert, S. (2001), 'Labour market regimes and worker recruitment and retention in the European Union: plant comparisons', *British Journal of Industrial Relations*, **39**(4), December, 505–28.

Nickell, S. and Bell, B. (1996), 'Changes in the distribution of wages and unemployment in OECD countries', *American Economic Review*, **86** (May), 302–8.

Nickell, S. and Layard, R. (1999), 'Labor market institutions and economic performance', in O. Ashenfelter (ed.), *Handbook of Labor Economics*, Vol. 3c, Amsterdam: Elsevier, pp. 3029–84.

OECD (1994), *Employment Outlook*, Paris: Organisation for Economic Cooperation and Development.

OECD (1996), *Employment Outlook*, Paris: Organisation for Economic Cooperation and Development.

OECD (1997), *Employment Outlook*, Paris: Organisation for Economic Cooperation and Development.

OECD (1999), *Employment Outlook*, Paris: Organisation for Economic Cooperation and Development.

OECD (2001), *Labour Market Statistics CD-ROM*, Paris: Organisation for Economic Cooperation and Development.

Saint-Paul, G. (1996), *Dual Labor Markets: A Macroeconomic Perspective*, Cambridge, MA: MIT Press.

Scarpetta, S. (1996), 'Assessing the role of labour market policies and institutional settings on unemployment: a cross-country study', *OECD Economic Studies*, No. 26, 43–98.

Siebert, S. (2001), 'Investment, employment and South African labour laws: an international comparison', *Free Market Foundation Monograph No. 30*, Johannesburg, September.

Summers, L. (1989), 'Some simple economics of mandated benefits', *American Economic Review*, **79**(2), May, 177–83.

Summers, L., Gruber, J. and Vergara, R. (1993), 'Taxation and the structure of labour markets', *Quarterly Journal of Economics*, **108**(2), May, 385–411.

Teulings, C. and Hartog, J. (1998), *Corporatism or Competition?*, Cambridge: Cambridge University Press.

Theodossiou, I. (1998), 'The effects of low-pay and unemployment on psychological well-being: a logistic regression approach', *Journal of Health Economics*, **17**, 85–104.

United States (1995), *Statistical Abstract of the United States*, Washington: US Department of Commerce.

Winkelman, L. and Winkelman, R. (1998), 'Why are the unemployed so unhappy? Evidence from panel data', *Economica*, **65**, 1–15.

6. Antitrust issues: global cartels, competition law and the new economy

John M. Connor

1. INTRODUCTION

Joel Klein, at the time the Assistant Attorney General in charge of the Antitrust Division of the US Department of Justice, gave a speech in May 2000 on the topic of antitrust policies that made the following unvarnished claim:

> the core principles of antitrust reflected in the Sherman Act ... should not be changed in this [new economy] era ... The legitimate ways of acquiring and maintaining market power are essentially the same today as they were a hundred years ago; and the illegitimate ways are fundamentally the same as well. (Klein, 2000, pp. 1–2)

Klein then goes on to enumerate the principal methods of monopolising markets, using illustrations from the DOJ's case against Microsoft, an avatar of the new economy (see Box 1).[1]

BOX 1.   THE MICROSOFT CASE

In a unanimous and forceful opinion, the federal Court of Appeals in Washington, DC on 28 June, 2001 ruled that Microsoft had abused its monopoly position in the market for PC operating systems (Labaton, 2001a). This decision opens the company to years of private antitrust litigation by rivals that it injured and possibly by consumers or the state attorneys general. The appeals court rejected the government's claim that Microsoft had attempted to monopolise the market for Internet browsers and remanded the question of whether Microsoft had illegally tied its own browser to its Windows operating system to a lower court for retrial.

'Every so often hard cases made good law', said one antitrust expert (Elhauge, 2001). Because the appeals court contains

---

several antitrust sceptics and because it is 'one of the best antitrust opinions in years', it is unlikely to be further appealed to the Supreme Court (ibid.). However, a break-up of Microsoft now seems remote (Krugman, 2001). Besides treble damages awards in private antitrust suits, Microsoft will probably face some sort of conduct restrictions from a negotiated settlement with the government or attorneys general. The ruling will likely '. . . guide business practices in the shifting technology markets . . .' (Elhauge, 2001).

Much of the discussion of the role of competition policies in the new economy has focused on the inevitability of market power as a goal and driver of business behaviour in the new era (Summers, 2000). High-tech, knowledge-based industries are often viewed as embodying characteristics that make them 'breeding grounds for monopolies' (Schwartz, 2001). Economies of scale and scope, lock-in effects, and network effects typically create barriers to entry that convert the first-mover advantages of innovators into durable monopoly positions.[2]

The initial dilemma facing antitrust enforcers is to distinguish market power earned by 'skill, foresight, and industry' from market power gained by collusion, predation, exclusionary practices, or other forms of monopolisation. If structural conditions permit it, all businesses seek market power because it benefits employees, shareholders and other stakeholders. However, if market power verges into monopoly power, then it is likely that consumers will be harmed; moreover, if the monopoly is acquired through monopolisation, the competitive process itself may be harmed.[3]

Having determined that there is probable cause for an antitrust violation, antitrust officials are faced with a second dilemma: fashioning a workable remedy. In many cases, new economy markets contain innate antidotes for monopoly power. '[I]n the absence of illegal practices, technology will be able to erode almost any barrier to entry' (Klein, 2000, p. 7). In other cases, new economy markets have features that appear to bestow natural monopolies on the industry's dominant firm(s). Barring a return to direct regulation, designing remedies that will enhance consumer welfare is particularly difficult. Either they are imposed too slowly to accommodate rapidly changing conditions, or they may severely reduce consumer benefits. As two supporters for Microsoft put it '. . . the application of antitrust principles should take account of the important ways new economy industries differ from traditional ones' (Evans and Schmalensee, 2001).

In discussing the relationship of antitrust enforcement to the new economy,

Klein (2000) and others have almost exclusively focused on monopolisation (i.e., unilateral market power). My purpose in this chapter is to redress this imbalance in the literature by exploring certain effects of the new economy on collusive international business schemes and describing the responses of competition-law agencies to the growing threat of global cartels (multilateral market power). The nexus between the new economy and cartel formation is perhaps more subtle and speculative than is the case for monopolisation, yet I believe the connections are real. Moreover, while trustbusters are somewhat on the defensive when prosecuting national technological champions, they continue to enjoy widespread political and popular support in pursuing global price fixers (e.g., Labaton, 2001b).

It need hardly be mentioned that economists universally condemn illegal cartels because of their unfavourable impacts on efficiency and income redistribution.[4] Sellers' cartels invariably damage the direct buyers of their products and by means of pass-on effects reduce the effective incomes of intermediate distributors and final consumers; buyers' cartels harm their suppliers. The deadweight losses generated by cartels may be regional, national, or multinational, depending on the geographic extent of the affected markets. While, since the late 1990s, the principal focus of attention has been directed at global cartels and enforcement by the US, EU, and other large jurisdictions, it is a curious fact that the focus of antitrust enforcement has shifted somewhat toward smaller units of government and toward smaller countries with nascent antitrust traditions. This trend points to the continuing need for regional policy solutions to problems affecting regional prosperity (Sugden and Wilson in this volume).

This chapter will illustrate these points by reference to a number of global cartels discovered and prosecuted since 1995, focusing particularly on the best-documented case of lysine. After a description of demand and supply conditions in the global market for lysine, I will recount the major events in the cartel's formation, operation and prosecution. The next sections explain why cartel investigations and prosecutions have become more effective in the last five years or so. Finally, the concluding section attempts to delineate hypotheses about how the emergence of the new economy has contributed to the resurgence of global cartels that began in the 1980s.

2. THE LYSINE MARKET[5]

Origins of the Industry

The world lysine industry is one of the first and most successful biotechnology industries that have emerged since World War II. Building upon scientific discoveries made in the late 1950s, the industry has experienced rapid growth and changes in market structure. Patents and production secrecy restricted the number of companies to three food manufacturers until 1990. Since then at least seven new companies have entered the lysine industry. As technological barriers have fallen, backward vertical integration into starch manufacturing and firm-specific assets in marketing bulk animal-feed ingredients have given advantages to experienced agribusiness firms. Despite the increase in sellers, five companies continue to dominate global production.

Lysine is an amino acid, a naturally occurring protein essential for the growth of muscle tissue in humans and animals. There are about 20 amino acids manufactured in commercial quantities worldwide. Lysine is one of three amino acids that dominate sales of these types of organic chemicals.

More than 90 per cent of the volume of lysine manufactured in the 1990s was purchased by producers of mixed animal feeds. Lysine is one of the major ingredients included in concentrates that are added to rough grains and oilseed meals to make balanced feeds for farm animals. The amino acids in balanced feeds help to stimulate the rate of growth and lean muscle development of poultry, swine, fish, and other monogastric animals. Animal breeders have been developing varieties of swine and poultry that can absorb higher levels of lysine, which allows for shorter growing cycles and brings to market leaner animals. Consumer desires for low-fat meats and farm-raised seafood in high-income countries, coupled with the increased demand for high-protein foods generally, are ultimately responsible for the rapid growth in demand for lysine and other feed additives.

Before 1960, lysine was extracted from vegetable proteins by means of chemical hydrolysis. This process yielded natural lysine that organic chemical companies now sell for $3 to $5 per pound. Extraction is still the method employed to make most pharmaceutical-grade lysine, but the selling price makes such lysine too costly to be used by food manufacturers on a regular basis. In 1956, a Japanese biochemist discovered that the metabolic processes of certain strains of bacteria produced an amino acid (glutamic acid). Within two or three years, the Japanese food and drug manufacturer Kyowa Hakko was selling commercial quantities of monosodium glutamate (MSG) using this new fermentation process. By 1958, Kyowa Hakko had developed a related technology to make lysine from fermentation.

Working on a parallel scientific track, the larger Japanese food processing company Ajinomoto also exploited the newly discovered fermentation technique. Ajinomoto had become the world's first manufacturer of MSG soon after the compound was discovered by a scientist at the University of Tokyo in 1908. By the late 1950s, Ajinomoto was manufacturing both MSG and pharmaceutical-grade lysine with a process that used dextrose as the feedstock for bacterial fermentation. Because the new technology yielded amino acids at considerably lower costs than the traditional chemical-extraction method, sales of lysine for animal feeds became economical. By 1960, Ajinomoto had begun selling feed-grade lysine in the domestic market. Japanese exports of feed-grade lysine grew rapidly from the late 1960s.

Market Structure 1970–90

Both Kyowa Hakko and Ajinomoto have continued to be leaders in basic and applied research in fermentation processes, genetic engineering and other biotechnologies that have led to improved methods of manufacturing amino acids. Both companies benefited from substantial research and development (R&D) subsidies for biotech companies organised by Japan's Ministry of International Trade and Industry in the early 1980s. They both own patents on the most efficient microbial strains, and many of the exact details of their lysine production processes continue to be protected by company secrecy. The formulation of the sweet soup that is fed to the microorganisms is a balanced mixture of 20 or more ingredients. Moreover, several of the best microbial strains are now zealously protected by patents.

Both companies began to invest abroad in the late 1970s. First, Ajinomoto established a joint venture in France named Eurolysine in 1974. Eurolysine's plant near Amiens came on stream a few years later. This plant was expanded at least four times in the 1980s, making it the largest lysine plant in the world. Second, Kyowa Hakko set up a lysine joint venture in Mexico in the late 1970s with Mexican government participation called Fermentaciones Mexicanos (or Fermex). Fermex began production at the Veracruz-area plant on a very small scale in 1980, probably utilising molasses from the local cane-sugar industry. The Fermex plant was expanded three times in the 1980s.

Thus, until 1980, the world lysine industry was a duopoly consisting of two Japanese firms, each with two plants. Both companies were recognised as leaders in Japan's highly advanced biotechnology industry. Indeed, both subsequently claimed to have first commercialised the production of lysine via fermentation of sugars.

The lysine duopoly became a triopoly in 1980 with the entry of the Miwon Group of South Korea. Miwon was an industrial–financial conglomerate of several operating companies with minority interests in each other but under the ultimate control of one family. These are called *chaebols*. Miwon's assets devoted to animal feeds and starch processing operated under the Sewon name. In the late 1970s, Sewon believed itself to be the third largest Asian manufacturer of animal feeds, starch and related products.

Sewon built a moderate-size lysine plant in Busan, South Korea in the late 1970s which came on stream in early 1980. It is apparent from its subsequent behaviour that Sewon was implementing a marketing strategy fairly common among South Korean manufacturers. Sewon would aim to steadily increase its global market share by exporting from a single plant in Korea that would be relentlessly expanded through massive borrowing. By 1990, Sewon's plant had been significantly expanded on three occasions to six times its original capacity, and all but a tiny portion of its production would be exported, mostly within Asia.

In 1980, Ajinomoto's two production units gave it about 60 per cent of the global production potential. Large capital expenditures for expansions of its Japanese and French plants as well as new plants in Thailand and the United States, allowed Ajinomoto to hold on to its dominant global position throughout the 1980s, yet heavy investment by its rivals caused Ajinomoto's share to slip to 50 per cent by 1990. Kyowa built the first plants in North America, beginning with the Fermex plant in Mexico that opened in 1980. Kyowa's US plant was located in Missouri on the Mississippi River, allowing the plant inexpensive access to molasses made in the sugar-cane areas near the Gulf of Mexico. This plant, operated by Kyowa's wholly owned US subsidiary Biokyowa, came on stream in 1984. Ajinomoto's similarly sized plant in Iowa began production two years later; this plant used dextrose piped to it from an adjacent corn refinery operated by Cargill, a major corn refiner. Ajinomoto's global capacity increased from 44 million pounds in 1980 to 170 million in 1990, yet the other producers were building so quickly that Ajinomoto's share peaked in the late 1980s, slipping to just below 50 per cent by 1990. Kyowa Hakko's production capacity rose from about 11 million pounds to more than 90 million during the same period; its share rose from 15 to 27 per cent. Finally, Sewon's impressive expansions in South Korea raised its global share from 15 per cent in 1980 to 19 per cent by 1990.

Technical barriers to entry seem to be high, because two large European chemical manufacturers attempted to enter the lysine industry before 1990, but neither was successful. In 1975, chemical-industry magazines carried the announcement that France's largest chemical company, Rhône-Poulenc, was going to build a 10-kilotonne lysine factory in Lyon, France. Kyowa Hakko was to be a minority partner. For reasons that are not clear, this plant was never built. It is likely that Ajinomoto's plans for Eurolysine were well enough advanced that the Rhône–Kyowa joint venture was pre-empted.

The second firm to plan on manufacturing lysine was the German metals and chemicals company Degussa. Sometime around 1988, Degussa developed a plan to build a lysine plant in the United States. Degussa had significant expertise in manufacturing some other amino acids (it was the world leader in methionine) and had a good R&D base to exploit. Degussa approached Archer Daniels Midland Co. (ADM) to get a bid on a long-term supply contract for dextrose, the intended feedstock for Degussa's new venture. On the surface, ADM would have appeared to be a prime candidate as a joint venture partner for Degussa. In addition to leading positions in grain trading and soybean processing, ADM was the world's largest starch manufacturer, producing large volumes of dextrose and other corn-fermentation products. ADM was keen on diversifying into high-priced feed ingredients like lysine, but lacked the technological expertise in manufacturing amino acids that was Degussa's forte. However, Degussa's overture turned out to be a major strategic blunder, because its request simply alerted ADM to an opportunity for itself. ADM decided to take a look at the lysine market itself, liked the high prices and rapid growth it saw, and launched its own feasibility study.

ADM made a firm commitment to enter lysine manufacturing in July 1989. Besides Degussa's expression of interest, ADM had figured out why Japan was importing such large amounts of dextrose. It was the feedstock being purchased by Ajinomoto to make lysine, which was then re-exported from Japan back to the United States.[6]

Global demand for lysine in 1980 was just below 70 million pounds (Figure 6.1). During the decade of the 1980s the volume of purchased lysine grew at an annual average of nearly 17 per cent, reaching about 320 million pounds by 1990.

North American consumption accounted for as much as 40 per cent of global consumption in the early 1980s, but drifted down to about one-third by the end of the decade (Figure 6.1). Western Europe also accounted for about one-third of global sales volume in the mid-to-late 1980s. Both areas

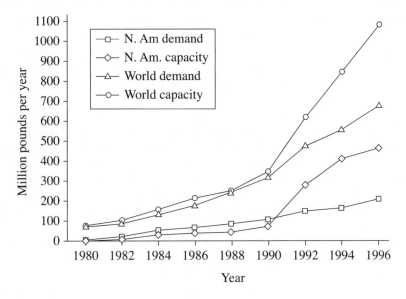

Figure 6.1   Lysine production capacity and consumption, 1980–96

contained highly industrialised poultry and pork subsectors, large-scale farm producers who could appreciate the small boosts in productivity that attended the optimisation of feed rations, and high-income populations with huge appetites for meat in their diets. Demand for lysine was growing by about 10 to 12 per cent per year in North America, driven mainly by shifts in consumer preferences for poultry over beef and for lower fat pork products. Similar trends in Japan and Europe were responsible for volume growth averaging 8 to 10 per cent per year.

Agricultural producers in both high-income regions were early adopters of scientific animal nutrition practices. However, poultry and hog producers were just catching on to the benefits of balanced feeds in the 1980s. Moreover, the urban consumers of the many newly industrialised countries of Asia and Latin America were expanding their purchases of meat products far faster than consumers in the industrialised countries. As a result, Asia and Latin America saw demand for lysine grow at far faster rates than Western Europe and North America. In the 1980s, rates of volume growth of lysine in Asia (excluding Japan) and Latin America were in the 12 to 16 per cent per year range.

Market Structure in the 1990s

The rate of growth of global demand slowed somewhat in the 1990s. During 1990–96, it averaged about 13 to 14 per cent per year. Although North America and Western Europe had growth slightly below the global rate, the gap between these richer areas and Asia/South America was not as great as formerly. However, the rate of expansion in production capacity far outpaced increases in consumption in the 1990s. Consequently, global utilisation rates fell to the low 60 per cent range during the mid-1990s. With significant excess capacity developing and plants opening in lower-cost areas, the two Japanese lysine manufacturers were placed in the painful position of having to close their first manufacturing facilities in Japan.

The years 1989–91 were a major transition period for the global lysine industry. Throughout the 1980s, production had been dominated by Ajinomoto (50 to 65 per cent of global capacity) and the other Japanese pioneer, Kyowa Hakko (20 to 30 per cent). The South Korean upstart, Sewon, borrowed mightily to achieve its goal of controlling about 20 per cent of world supply, but never quite got there. As recounted above, two new players decided to enter the lysine industry in 1989, and by early 1991 the industry supported five suppliers instead of three. Because ADM's new plant was so huge, it had by far the greatest effect on prices and seller behaviour.

ADM's huge plant in Decatur began selling its production in February 1991. Small at first, volume sold by ADM rose exponentially to about 4 million pounds per month in the last quarter of 1991. At that rate, ADM's annual *production* had already surpassed Kyowa's total US *capacity* in 1990 and was double Ajinomoto's US capacity (Figure 6.2).

Ajinomoto and Kyowa's positions slipped badly as a result of ADM's aggressive expansion. Both companies added new capacity at its North American plants. Ajinomoto's plant in Iowa was expanded by 50 per cent in 1991, 167 per cent in 1993, and another 50 per cent in 1996. Despite these heroic investments, Ajinomoto's share of North American lysine capacity fell from 35 per cent in 1990 to 14 per cent in 1992; it would continue to have about 20 to 25 per cent of the region's capacity through 1998. Kyowa also made substantial investments to expand its plants in Mexico and Missouri almost every year in the decade. However, Kyowa's share also declined from 65 per cent the year before ADM entered to 23 per cent two years later. By 2000, Kyowa held about 15 to 20 per cent of the Continent's lysine capacity.

In the 1990s, a couple of small lysine plants managed to begin production under ownership of new companies. By the end of the 1990s these plants, located in Slovakia, South Africa and China, still accounted for less than 3 per cent of global production. However, a much larger plant in Nebraska was due to begin production in 2000–01. This plant is a joint venture between Degussa, the would-be partner spurned by ADM in the late 1980s, and ADM's archrival Cargill. In late 1997, the Asian financial crisis forced Sewon to sell its lysine business to the leading German chemical company BASF.

Until 1990, the majority of lysine production took place in Asia. However,

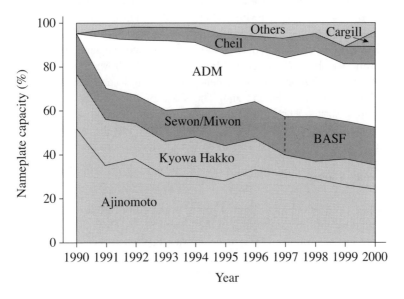

Figure 6.2   Global capacity of leading lysine producers, 1980–2000

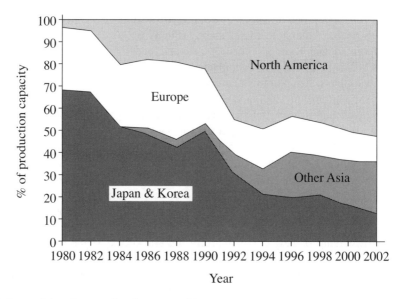

Figure 6.3   Geographic location of lysine production capacity, 1980–2002

the location of production has become more diverse over time (Figure 6.3). In the early 1980s, about two-thirds of lysine capacity was located in Japan and most of the rest in France. From 1984 to 1990, about half of global capacity was in Asia, of which a small but growing portion was located outside of Japan and Korea; Europe contained 25 to 30 per cent; and the Japanese plants in North America about 20 per cent. After 1990, the North American (and especially US) share jumped to 40 per cent early in the decade and increased to more than 50 per cent by the end. The share of Europe, Japan and Korea continued to shrink. The biggest change was the increase in other Asian locations since 1990; Thailand, Indonesia and China are the major countries getting more lysine capacity. This trend is expected to continue.

The Lysine Cartel

The lysine cartel is one of a score of global commodity cartels discovered and prosecuted by antitrust authorities in the United States, Canada, the European Union and other countries. However, it was the first to be exposed by US authorities, the first to be successfully prosecuted in nearly 50 years, and the first of several other global-cartel investigations.[7]

In common with several other global cartels, the lysine cartel was initiated after a period of low prices caused by the opening of ADM's large plant that

resulted in widespread industry overcapacity. The low prices were purpose-
fully generated by ADM as a way of forcing the three established Asian
producers to meet and to begin discussing about forming a cartel. A few
unprofitable months were sufficient to persuade the long-time industry leaders
(Ajinomoto and Kyowa Hakko) who yielded market share to the brash
American company ADM, that a cartel would restore long-term profits.
Although the oligopolistic consensus on prices and volume shares broke down
on one occasion, for the most part the conspirators were able to negotiate a
series of quarterly price agreements that were implemented for all areas of the
world with a fair degree of cooperation for three years, 1992–95. The pattern
of transaction prices of lysine in the US and EU clearly demonstrates how
effective the conspiracy was in raising prices (Figure 6.4). The graph shows
that ADM's entry in February 1991 caused prices to fall precipitously for 18
months. Then, after a lag of two months, the cartel's June 1992 price-fixing
agreement took hold. Except for a brief price war in early 1993, lysine prices
remained well above the long-run marginal costs of production of the cartel's
low cost manufacturer.[8]

As the cartel matured, the agreements became more detailed and elaborate.

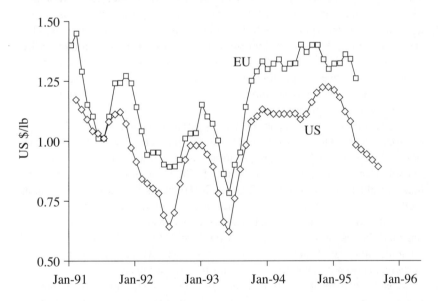

Note: US prices from sales by the four largest manufacturers (see Appendix A of Connor, 2000
for details). EU prices from a European Commission notice published on the *RAPID* website in
2001, in euros, translated into US dollars at the prevailing monthly interbank exchange rate.

Figure 6.4   Lysine transaction prices, US and EU markets, 1991–96

Cheating was held in check by monthly reporting of the participants' lysine production that was analysed by an ersatz industry trade association. At its peak of effectiveness, the cartel was able to raise global prices of lysine by about 50 per cent; on average over the life of the lysine conspiracy, prices were elevated about 20 per cent above competitive (and preconspiracy) levels. Several other cartels were able to overcharge their customers by even larger rates.

The conspiracy ended in June 1995 because the FBI had the cooperation of a disaffected ADM Vice President. With ample evidence of the crime, including audio and video tapes, ADM paid a $100 million fine. Three of its officers were sentenced to a collective 99 months in prison.

3.   THE CUSTOMERS' COSTS OF GLOBAL CARTELS

Customers of effective sellers' cartels are negatively affected in two ways. First, and quantitatively larger, purchasers of cartelised products overpay for the goods they continue to buy during the conspiracy period. A customer overcharge is a transfer of income from buyers as a group to the sellers as a group. That is, as a cartel's collusive behaviour begins to raise prices above competitive levels, the joint profits of the cartel members rise roughly by the same amount that buyers' purchases fall. If a cartel is able to operate at peak efficacy, the sum of its members' profits will be almost as high as a monopolist would be able to extract in the same market. In equilibrium, the monopoly profits going to the conspirators will be equal to the sum of the lost revenues of direct and indirect buyers and the effective reduction in purchasing power by the ultimate consumers.

The second negative impact on buyers is the so-called 'dead-weight loss' or 'social loss'. This injury to buyers is an indirect consequence of higher prices. Under normal demand conditions, as a cartel is effective in raising market price, the quantity of sales will fall. The value of these lost sales is the dead-weight loss to customers. Because it represents both lost production as well as lost consumption, all social groups are injured: owners of the productive units, workers, intermediate buyers and consumers. Consumers either must use the disposable income they would have spent on the overpriced good on some other good they regard as inferior or do without. Of course, cartel participants do not make profits on sales they do not make.

Table 6.1 gathers information on the dollar losses to customers (direct buyers, indirect commercial buyers and consumers) from three cartels. Unlike previous calculations, this table attempts to estimate the customer injuries worldwide by extrapolating comparable US losses to a global scale. The total losses incurred by buyers of lysine, citric acid, vitamins and goods made from these ingredients amounted to $8.8 billion during the various conspiracy periods.

Table 6.1   Summary of customer losses due to global price fixing, 1989–99

Affected market			Losses to customer[a]		
Product	Period	Global sales	Overcharge	Dead-weight loss	Total
			Million US dollars		
Lysine	1992–95	1660	330	33	363
Citric acid	1991–95	3950	690	60	750
Bulk vitamins:					
A	1990–99	5740	1473	189	1662
C	1991–95	4000	460	26	486
E	1990–99	10 840	3822	674	4496
B group[b]	1989–98	3483	668	64	732
Carotenoids	1991–98	1004	267	36	303
Premixes	1990–98	9 094[c]	NA	NA	NA
Total	1989–99	39 771	7710	1082	8792

Notes:

NA = not available.

[a]   The overcharge is the increase in the cost of the product to buyers, both direct and indirect, due to the increase in the market price caused by the cartel. The consumer portion of the dead-weight loss is the reduction in purchases caused by the decrease in the quantity produced by the cartel during the affected period. In the absence of precise information, I assume that the own-price elasticity of demand is -1 when the price was at or close to the monopoly level; for the formula used, see Peterson and Connor (1996). The overcharge rate calculated for the United States was applied to global sales.

[b]   The B complex of vitamins that were cartelised includes B1, B2, B3 (niacin), B4 (choline chloride), B5, B6, B12, and folic acid. The conspiracy period varies by vitamin: 1990–99 (B3, B12), 1991–95 (B2), 1991–98 (B5), 1991–94 (B1, B6, folic), and 1989–98 (B4).

[c]   As no reliable estimates of global sales are available, I simply doubled the US sales estimates. Actual global sales could be 50 per cent higher.

Source: Connor (2001b, Table 19.5).

4.   ANTICARTEL ENFORCEMENT

Legal sanctions for price fixing may result from criminal prosecutions of corporations or individuals by government agencies, from civil penalties after administrative hearings, or from civil suits launched by injured parties.[9] There are not as yet any multilateral organisations with antitrust-enforcement authority, but such federated structures as the United States, Canada and the European Union; their member states and provinces; and about 100 other national units have antitrust statutes and agencies to enforce them (Connor,

1997; ICPAC, 2000). However, the rigour of actual enforcement falls across a wide spectrum, with the United States typically acknowledged as occupying one end of the range, and with Japan and most low-income countries at the other end. Historically, the priority accorded to prosecuting cartel activity has varied considerably across the decades. In the United States, three periods of intense anticartel enforcement may be discerned: 1905–17, 1939–49, and 1995 to the present. Variation in the degree of enforcement is partly a matter of political forces, but seems more forcefully determined by episodes of cartel formation and discovery.

Historical Background

Soon after they first appeared in the US economy around the 1870s, popular books were written about the 'trusts' that were organised in the sugar, railroad, petroleum, tobacco and many other industries. Richard Ely's classic book *Monopolies and Trusts*, published in 1900, was one of the first serious economic analyses of the phenomenon. 'Trusts' was the turn-of-the-century term for large economic combinations, often forged by mergers, for creating and sustaining market power. Today these organisations would be called holding companies, syndicates, pools, joint sales agencies, or simply monopolies.

Cartels, in the modern business meaning of that term, also first appeared in Europe in the 1870s. These new business organisations seem to have been particularly sophisticated, effective and enduring in Germany. Indeed, the word 'cartel', first used in British newspapers in 1902, was borrowed directly from the German word *kartell* (see Box 2). Cartels in Europe came to dominate many branches of the mining, manufacturing, and transportation sectors (Webb, 1997). Nearly all of them disbanded during World War I. Trusts in the United States mostly ceased to operate during 1912–14, not because of the War (US entry began in 1917) but because of the federal government's legal victories under the Sherman Act.

BOX 2.   CARTEL

A cartel is an association of two or more legally independent firms that explicitly agree to coordinate their prices or output for the purpose of increasing their collective profits. Cartels can use various subtle techniques to communicate, monitor and enforce agreements, but those conspiracies that engage in overt agreements about market price and quantity are called 'naked' cartels.

The word cartel came into English in the sixteenth century to mean a written agreement between opposing armies for the exchange of prisoners. This meaning was extended by German writers in the 1880s to describe a government coalition that brought together normally antagonistic political parties. Shortly thereafter, the word *kartell* was applied to a combination of two or more business rivals for the purpose of regulating prices or output of an industry. The word cartel was first used in English in 1902 in the business sense in three British publications to refer to what were formerly called 'producers' syndicates' or 'trusts' in the sugar and steel industries (*Oxford English Dictionary*).

Ultimately, more than 100 of the turn-of-the-century cartels operated across national borders. Most of the cartels originally established in the German chemical industries incorporated international partners. Of these, the dyestuffs cartel is perhaps the best documented. This German–Swiss creation successfully predated on smaller producers in France, Britain and the United States (Stocking and Watkins, 1946).

Many private commodity cartels were re-established during the interwar period in Europe. During the 1920s and 1930s, at least 180 of the formerly 'domestic' cartels (some controlled exports) took on an international character. By one estimate, international cartels came to control about 40 per cent of world merchandise trade (Edwards, 1976). Stocking and Watkins (1946) wrote about several international cartels that were active in the interwar period in magnesium, aluminium, incandescent electric bulbs and several chemicals. One example was the second dyestuffs cartel. The original dyestuffs cartel was reborn in 1927 when a French dyes syndicate joined with an already operating German cartel. In 1929, the four Swiss dye manufacturers became members, and in 1931 the UK's Imperial Chemical Industries (ICI) joined. During the 1930s this dyestuffs cartel controlled 60 to 70 per cent of world production capacity and well over 80 per cent of global exports. Japanese dye manufacturers were not full members of the cartel, but some had brief bilateral agreements with some of the cartel's members. At the time, US dye manufacturers had a tacitly collusive group that affected prices and technology, but they did not join the global cartel.

Some of the interwar cartels operated without the direct participation of US companies. However, several US companies collaborated with members of German cartels in other ways that ultimately aided the Axis war effort. By the late 1930s, it had become clear that industrial cartels in Germany and Japan had become essential instruments of national conquest and war planning.

The embarrassing role of international cartels in contributing to World War II led to a highly active programme of prosecutions by the US Department of

Justice in the late 1940s. Most of these cases successfully prosecuted US companies for having made market-allocation agreements with European companies that covered Europe and the Americas.[10] Some of the cases involved criminal charges, particularly when major manufacturers engaged in naked price fixing (ICPAC, 2000).

The US convictions of the 1940s seem to have deterred the formation of all but a handful of international cartels for nearly 40 years. In any case, the first successful US conviction of any consequence was the lysine cartel in 1996.[11] Such prosecutions were also rare in other jurisdictions. Since 1996, scores of international cartels that affected global markets have been sanctioned by the European Commission or courts in the United States, Canada and other countries.

Price Fixing Penalties

The severity and absolute size of both US government fines and private treble damages awards have increased throughout the 1990s to unprecedented levels. Although nearly all global price fixers were granted significant discounts from the maximum possible fines, the US fines imposed on cartel participants steadily increased as a proportion of the economic injuries generated by cartel activities. From a maximum on a single company fine of only $2 million at the beginning of the decade, the record fine by 1999 had reached $500 million. The upward trend can be traced in part to an increase in the statutory fine from $1 million per count in 1989 to $10 million in 1990 and in part to the imposition of federal felony sentences that permit fines of up to twice the harm (double the overcharges and perhaps the dead-weight loss as well). The huge fines on ADM ($100 million), UCAR ($110 million), BASF ($225 million), and Hoffmann-La Roche ($500 million) have certainly created enormous publicity that can only add to the deterrence effect of US antitrust enforcement. Yet, the fines so far have fallen well short of the twice-the-harm upper limit. Moreover, by charging smaller subsidiaries of parent multinationals and by offering multiyear instalment payments, the DOJ has signalled its reluctance to impose fines akin to corporate capital punishment. That is, the government has not imposed fines in excess of a defendant's ability to pay out of fear of creating a bankruptcy, a fear probably shared by the federal judiciary. While such reluctance may be understandable from the point of view of anticipated popular reactions to perceived excessive judicial reach, there is little legal or economic support for bankruptcy avoidance as a criterion for fines. Nor have multiple counts been filed against defendants in the 1990s, though they were common in antitrust cases before the 1990s.

The Antitrust Division has, since 1996, relied almost exclusively on large fines as the sole sanctions on corporations in criminal price fixing cases. There is no doubt that fines are among the most concrete sanctions that can be applied; also, once having been paid, they require no further government oversight. Yet, there are several cases of corporate recidivism in price fixing, which suggests that the earlier fines were too small or short-lived (see Connor, 2001b for details). There is a wide panoply of additional corporate sanctions that the government has the power to request from the courts or could require in guilty plea agreements. Specific managers could be required to be fired or banned from the industry. Boards of directors could be restructured to include more independent members on key committees. Tougher antitrust compliance programmes could be required for convicted firms. In lieu of fines, assets can be seized. 'Structural relief', i.e., the dissolution of corporate units, could be mandated for those businesses that are located in the United States.

US law, unlike that of all but a few other jurisdictions, treats price fixing as a *personal* criminal matter for managers of a conspiracy.[12] The US government has been increasing the severity of the fines and prison sentences for executives directly involved in global price fixing. There is considerable scope for increasing the fines on convicted felons, and there will doubtless be higher amounts seen in the future. However, it is probably prison sentences that will ultimately make more of an impression on the individuals themselves and future potential violators. The two-year sentences placed on ADM's Michael Andreas and Terrance Wilson were clearly seminal events. The seven German and Swiss executives so far facing a prison sentence in the vitamins cartel case is further evidence of the DOJ's intentions to seek tough penalties. EU fines have risen to as high as €1600 million in 2001, but EU rules do not permit prison sentences on managers for price fixing violations, though some of the member states do have such laws.

In the United States and a few other countries, private parties can add considerably to the woes of publicly prosecuted cartel participants. Combined with the double-the-harm fines, treble damages raise the potential legal liability to a theoretical level of *five times affected US sales*. In fact, *parens patriae* suits by the states' attorneys general and indirect purchaser suits in 16 or so states raises the potential monetary liability for corporate price fixers to nearly *eight* times affected sales. In practice, no cartel has been assessed fines or private payments as high as three times the relevant sales, but the potential is there.

In the EU, private antitrust suits are theoretically possible in most of the member states' national courts. Indeed, both the European Commission and the European Courts have urged such suits, but injured parties have been reluctant to file because the size of the awards has been so small in the past and because European law firms are reluctant to represent these parties on a contingency basis.

In the European Union, Canada and several other countries, the example of the United States seems to have encouraged a significant stiffening of antitrust penalties for cartels. US fines, prison sentences and private settlements for price fixing escalated impressively in the 1990s as a result of changes in US laws, the expansion of cartel injuries, and newfound vigour among both public and private prosecutors. In the next section, the issue of the adequacy of the new penalty structures is addressed. Are they sufficient, too low, or too high? Most importantly, are the harsher penalties imposed on global price fixers in the 1990s likely to deter further future violations?

Deterrence

The two main purposes of monetary penalties for economic crimes are to *compensate* injured victims of the crime and to *punish* the perpetrators so as to prevent them from repeating the same crime in the future. In addition, penalties can serve to compensate professionals to detect, to investigate, or to provide legal advice concerning antitrust violations. The treble-damages provision for private plaintiffs in Sherman Act cases in the United States was designed specifically for all three purposes. Perhaps the goals could have been achieved with only double damages, but that would require that a high share of all conspiracies are discovered and punished. If on the other hand only one-tenth of all conspiracies (more accurately one-tenth of the compensable harm created by all such conspiracies are uncovered), then settlements of even ten times the damages are inadequate to deter repetitive crimes. On the assumption that civil plaintiffs actually receive amounts close to what the law permits, most legal scholars defend the treble-damages rule as a reasonable compromise (White, 2001). However, if settlements fall well below treble damages or the chances of discovering a clandestine cartel are low, then the treble-damages rule is too lenient because it has no deterrence effect (that is, settlement costs for perpetrators are less than the expected monopoly profits).

When the ability to extract monopoly profits through civil suits is inadequate, then public prosecutors should be able to demand larger fines. The increases in financial penalties for price fixing violations in the United States that became law in 1987 and 1990 were partly in response to the perceived inadequacy of civil penalties. The toughening of the fine structure for cartel violations in the European Union in the late 1990s was partially a response to the lack of civil suits in national courts and to the absence of personal penalties for price fixing in most European jurisdictions. Indeed, the evolving standard for EU fines seem to be 'US plus'.

The competition-law prosecutors are quite proud of their enhanced fine levels. US prosecutors assert that in general their fines force firms to disgorge more than their illicit US profits. The Canadian federal prosecutor, referring to the fines for vitamin cartel members stated that they '. . . were big enough to eliminate most illicit profit' and that the defendants '. . . still face huge legal fees and civil liability. . .' (*Toronto Star*, 23 September 1999). Class counsel is quoted as being quite pleased at the size of the civil settlements. Counsel for the federal class of lysine plaintiffs defended the settlement of 7.2 per cent of affected sales by asserting that it was among the highest percentage recoveries ever made in a civil price fixing case (*National Law Journal*, 12 October 1998). Yet, despite the higher fines, in 1998, DOJ officials stated that they would like to have greater powers to extract higher price fixing fines (Klein, 1998).

Clearly, government fines and civil penalties (where they are permitted) are jointly determined. Yet, some legal commentators have argued that the penalties are too high, while others believe that they are too low. Even US prosecutors realise that record-setting fines may be insufficient to deter. When announcing the plea bargains for the major vitamin manufacturers, Joel Klein noted that the $14 million fine paid by Hoffmann-La Roche in 1997 was insufficient to keep the company from continuing to fix prices in vitamins for another year.

Criticism that antitrust penalties are too low is much easier to find in the press. The $100 million fine on ADM was described as too generous, a 'sweetheart deed' and a 'bargain'. However, the reasons for these descriptions are obscure or unexamined assumptions. The incompetence of government lawyers faced with attorneys that were the best that money could buy; political largesse; reluctance to hobble a national business champion; and ADM's huge cash reserves were all cited as support. The positive reaction of the stock market to the announcement of ADM's fine does indicate that investors had speculated that it would be higher. In the case of private settlements there is abundant evidence that the smaller buyers of cartelised products received significantly lower payout rates than did the opt-outs that settled later. However, none of these reasons seems to prove that the penalties were ineffective.

More trenchant are assertions that monetary sanctions extracted from cartel participants in the 1990s were lower than the monopoly profits earned (Barboza, 1999). According to some critics, crime pays, and one of the main reasons it pays is that antitrust agencies only calculate harm to buyers within their jurisdiction when deciding on appropriate fines (Adams and Bell, 1999). It is true that in the case of about 20 global cartels convicted by the US government, only two rather small cartels were assessed fines on the basis of their affected global sales rather than the normal US sales. Moreover, US courts (among the few in the world that assess large civil penalties) do not generally permit overseas buyers to join local buyers as plaintiffs in treble-damages suits. Thus, in the era of global cartels that make large shares of their monopoly profits outside a given jurisdiction the chances that price fixing pays is quite large. Added to that is the fact that the secretiveness of cartels makes them difficult to discover. Deterrence can work only if the *probable* costs of prosecution exceed the *expected* monopoly profits. For example, assume that a cartel has two-thirds of its business outside the United States and that the chances of being caught are 20 per cent. Then to deter cartel formation, the potential conspirators must guess that the probable US criminal and civil penalties will be at least *15 times* their legal profits. Such high penalties are impossible under current US law even as a theoretical proposition; in practice, the cartels of the 1990s only paid about double their illegal profits.

Therefore, as impressive as the total dollar penalties imposed on global cartels may appear, by some yardsticks they are not particularly large. Three objective standards of severity suggest themselves: the actual penalties compared to the maximum legal liability, compared to the economic harm caused to customers, and compared to the monopoly profits generated by the cartel.

Among the companies involved in global price fixing in the 1990s, the best-documented example of financial and reputational losses is the Archer Daniels Midland Company (ADM). During the fiscal years ending 30 June 1992 to 30 June 1996, ADM's pretax profits were between 6.5 and 9.3 per cent of sales. However, beginning in fiscal 1996, ADM's profit rate plunged each year as it incurred antitrust costs. During 1997–2000, pretax profits averaged only 3.5 per cent of sales, or less than half the 1992–96 period. After-tax profits fell even more precipitously because companies are not permitted to offset part of the costs of fines and civil settlements by income tax reductions; that is, ADM's effective tax rate rose by as much as ten percentage points in 1997–99 because antitrust payments are not tax deductible. While other factors such as the 1997–98 East Asian financial crisis and falling agricultural commodity prices have contributed to ADM's poor profit performance, direct antitrust costs accounted for 55 to 63 per cent of ADM's profit declines in 1995–96 and 1996–97. Falling sales revenues from lysine and citric acid attributable to the break-up of the two cartels further added to ADM's poor financial performance in 1996 and 1997. These impacts on ADM's bottom line are all the more impressive in light of the fact that the two products accounted for less than 5 per cent of the company's sales.

Abundant information on ADM's illegal profits from the lysine and citric acid cartels, together with fairly reliable information on the financial costs incurred for these infractions, permits one to develop an answer to the age-old question about crime: does it pay?

The answer seems to be that ADM clearly bore more US financial costs from antitrust legal actions against it than it earned in the form of monopoly profits from the lysine cartel. US antitrust costs exceeded the extra profits from collusion by about $70 million. However, ADM earned small positive returns from lysine price fixing on a non-US accounting basis. In other words, because government fines were smaller and civil suits uncommon outside the United States, ADM has so far profited from its lysine price fixing outside the United States. On a global basis, ADM did not make its crime pay, but the loss in net revenues was relatively small, about $43 million (Connor, 2001b, Table 19.4).

An important lesson from this analysis is that the full force of the law could have vastly increased ADM's antitrust liabilities. Had the maximum legal sanctions been imposed, ADM's net losses from its participation in the lysine cartel could have reached $490 million in the United States or $1.6 billion worldwide. Note that this analysis of the costs and returns to price fixing does not include ADM's role in the citric acid cartel, which had global sales and monopoly overcharges twice the size of the lysine cartel. Given its market share, ADM's net legal exposure from citric acid price fixing probably approached another $2 billion.

ADM is probably exceptional because it was a special target of the DOJ's ire. Preliminary calculations of the fines and penalties paid by Hoffmann-La Roche (well over $1500 million) indicate that Roche still profited handsomely from its vitamins and citric acid collusion.

Corporate Recidivism

The sad truth is that many corporate price fixers that have been prosecuted and punished seem ready to take the risk again. The cases studied in Connor (2001b) point to a downside of firm diversification. When corporations with multiple lines of business enjoy the financial success that flows from a cartel in one line of business, they are likely to form or enter a cartel for another line of business.

Most of the companies convicted for global price fixing in the 1990s are diversified firms. Frequently, the cartelised product comprises only a tiny share of the company's total sales. At least 13 multinational chemical or agribusiness companies engaged in multiple conspiracies. ADM, for example, was convicted for price fixing in two markets, but engaged in from two to five more conspiracies. The list of corporate 'repeat offenders' suggests the need for fine guidelines that explicitly raise fines in such cases.

Antitrust Prosecutors: Elevated Reputations

The worldwide convictions of global cartels elevated the reputations of pros-ecutors among nearly all groups of society. The widespread revelations of the cartels' insidious methods and the scope of their damage to global markets has reinforced the educated public's appreciation of the social benefits of the antitrust laws. Except for a minority ideologically opposed to the laws themselves, business leaders and their legal advisors have a renewed conviction about the importance of avoiding price fixing behaviour. In the United States especially, markedly tougher investigatory techniques and a string of courtroom victories have deepened the image of the antitrust agencies as organisations armed with formidable legal powers. At the same time, the legal community has a heightened realisation of the expanded powers of the enforcement agencies to dispense valuable concessions for clients under investigation. Finally, rapidly escalating international cooperation among the world's competition-law authorities has convinced multinational businesses and their executives that locations outside North America no longer provide shelter from criminal antitrust charges.

The 1998 courtroom victory in Chicago against three ADM executives has had an especially strong impact. The convictions and harsh sentences meted out in *US* v. *Michael Andreas et al.* had the effect of reversing the DOJ's image of incompetence (or at least being out-gunned) earned because of two embarrassing trial losses in the early 1990s (*US* v. *General Electric and De Beers Consolidated*, *US* v. *Appleton Papers*). The trial victory was also important because it eased fears that someone so politically important as ADM Chairman Dwayne Andreas could not prevent the wheels of justice from grinding to a halt. As *The New York Times* put it, the 1998 verdict '. . . marks a sweeping victory for Federal prosecutors . . .' and shows that Dwayne Andreas could not prevent '. . . the weight of the judicial system from falling on his son and one-time heir apparent . . .' (18 September 1998). Antitrust lawyers interviewed by the *Chicago Tribune* just after the trial's conclusion said that the lysine and citric acid cartel convictions showed that the antitrust law 'has teeth again' (20 September 1998).

Perhaps the major reason for the renewed respect accorded antitrust prosecutors are the huge, newsworthy fines and settlements made in the late 1990s. The $100 million fine paid by ADM for its role in fixing the prices of lysine and citric acid was probably the seminal event among many. Canada has similarly extracted record antitrust fines from members of the global food-and-feed-ingredient cartels. The EU's fines for lysine price fixing, while not quite the largest ever seen, were given extensive coverage in the European press. The punishments on individuals for global price fixing by North American courts have been if anything more shocking to multinational businesspeople. Besides the lengthy prison sentences imposed by US courts on dozens of violators, one German CEO paid a fine of $10 million for his role in fixing the global prices of graphite electrodes. Canadian courts for the first time imposed a prison sentence for price fixing in the case of a vitamin manufacturer.

Almost equally important in raising the public's consciousness about the

seriousness of antitrust enforcers is the marked transformation in US investigatory tactics. Prior to 1990, violations of the Sherman Act were misde-
meanours. In common with other less serious white-collar crimes, the FBI
employed a limited range of relatively gentle investigatory methods. However,
since 1990, FBI probes into global price fixing have used the full range of
'blue-collar' tools of the trade, methods long employed against drug dealers,
kidnappers and in counterintelligence: audio and video tapes, tapping tele-
phones, undercover informants, and 'flipping' small fish to get the big fish
(Eichenwald, 2000).

The third factor responsible for the perception of prosecutorial power in
antitrust matters is the enhanced range of sentencing discretion available to
public prosecutors. To obtain the cooperation of credible witnesses, prosecutors have long made deals for reduced sentences, but now that the potential
fines and prison sentences are so much greater than before, the degree of
downward departure is also ever so much greater. Judges rarely fail to approve
reductions recommended by the DOJ. Moreover, to gain a company's cooperation, all but one or two of many potentially liable conspirators in the company
are granted complete immunity from prosecution. For example, in the case of
Ajinomoto, only two officers were fined, nine were granted immunity, and one
remains a fugitive. In economic terms, perhaps the greatest grant of leniency
was made to ADM in return for the company's rather spotty cooperation in the
DOJ's citric acid prosecution. Among the most valuable of many favours
showered on ADM was the DOJ's promise that it would not prosecute ADM
for alleged price fixing in the market for corn fructose. Federal antitrust prosecutors also have great discretion in awarding leniency or amnesty to
confessed corporate or individual price fixers (see Box 3). The latest leniency
guidelines appear to be quite precise in print, but in practice prosecutors have
a great deal of discretion in applying them to specific cases. The EU recently
implemented its own leniency programme for price fixing cases. A related
concession of great interest to most businesspeople in global industries is the
power of the DOJ to grant free entry to the United States to convicted price
fixing conspirators, even those guilty of felonies.

The prosecutions of global cartels in the late 1990s also revealed some limitations in the powers of federal prosecutors. First, it is apparent that one reason
for the successes in the lysine and citric acid cases was the active involvement
of the highest-level officials during the investigation and plea-bargaining
phases. Involvement of so many high officials was indicative of the high priority and extreme caution accorded to these cases, but it also demonstrated how
thinly stretched were its human resources. At the same time, the demands on
the Division for merger clearances and other cases escalated.

Second, the antitrust agencies may have been hampered by other resource
constraints. During the prosecution of the global conspiracies, the DOJ's

---

BOX 3. THE US ANTITRUST LENIENCY PROGRAMME

The present programme was developed and put in place by the Antitrust Division in August 1993 under the leadership of Anne Bingaman. Amnesty will be granted to a company and all its employees if the company meets five conditions. The firm must (1) approach the DOJ before the agency has opened an investigation, (2) have stopped colluding, (3) confess to corporate guilt (rather than blame a rogue employee), (4) show that it was not the originator of the conspiracy and not the 'enforcer' of cartel discipline, and (5) agree to full cooperation from all its employees. If condition (1) is not met, the firm may still be offered leniency but full amnesty is unlikely and a guilty plea will be necessary.

Automatic leniency is a powerful temptation for guilty price fixers to accept because it practically guarantees no fines. However, the DOJ cannot insulate an amnestied firm from civil damages or prosecution by overseas antitrust agencies. The DOJ programme is unique in the federal government but is being imitated for cartel prosecution in the EU and other jurisdictions.

---

antitrust resources were lower than in the 1980s. The Antitrust Division's annual budget in 1998 was only $98 million; it employed 363 attorneys, down from 456 in 1980. A record number of mergers required that large resources be devoted to monitoring corporate acquisitions. Moreover, the Division was pursuing the largest monopoly case in 20 years. Resources available to the EU's DG-IV are even more modest. Brussels has less than 100 competition-law professionals. EU investigations require the cooperation of national courts and police agencies, and the scope of the questioning allowed is far narrower than under US or Canadian laws. The EU Competition Commissioner is requesting expanded powers and staff.

International Antitrust Cooperation

Many governments have made substantial progress in signing protocols, cooperation agreements, and formal treaties that can facilitate international cooperation in antitrust matters between the DOJ and its sister organisations abroad. These new instruments supplement traditional international law mechanisms such as diplomatic channels. For example, by January 2000, the United States had signed 30 Mutual Legal Assistance Treaties (MLATs) that can be used for antitrust purposes. There have been several instances in which MLATs have been used to conduct simultaneous executions of subpoenas, search warrants, or witness interviews in international cartel matters. In addition, bilateral antitrust cooperation protocols have been signed by the DOJ with sister agencies in Canada, Brazil, Japan, Israel, Germany and the EU that permit limited forms of enforcement cooperation. The biggest limitation to international antitrust cooperation has been in sharing confidential business information, particularly when such information has been obtained through compulsory legal processes. In late 2001, the world's 12 major antitrust agencies joined to form an informal coalition called the International Competition Network (BRW (*Business Review Weekly*), 2001).

On balance, these new instruments have helped DOJ investigations of global cartels in precious few instances, and they rarely prove crucial to the outcome. However, there is a very positive interaction between leniency programmes and obtaining relevant overseas evidence. When a target of a global cartel investigation *voluntarily* agrees to cooperate, then the legal barriers to obtaining relevant information abroad appear to melt away. Officials in foreign jurisdictions can and do cooperate without any offence to their sovereign rights. In sum, it is mostly the unilateral efforts of antitrust authorities that are succeeding in overcoming traditional barriers to international antitrust-law enforcement.

The Localisation of Antitrust

Running counter to the trend of international convergence and cooperation among the world's top-level antitrust agencies is a renewed interest in enforcement by smaller units of government, for example state governments in the United States or member states of the EU. Each of the 50 US states has its own antitrust statutes, most of them resembling federal law quite closely.[13] In the case of markets that do not spill across state lines, federal law cannot be applied for constitutional reasons. In some areas, state antitrust laws diverge in substantive ways from federal laws. For example, in about one-third of the states, indirect purchasers of cartelised products may seek damages, whereas such buyers have no standing to sue in federal courts. The rigour with which states enforce their antitrust statutes varies considerably because of long-standing local political preferences or turnover in elected state attorneys general.

A more important trend has been the development of multistate coalitions of state attorneys general, acting through their citizens in federal court. This centuries-old power was formalised by amending the Sherman Act in 1976. One of the largest actions of its type was announced in October 2000. Forty-three states settled out of court with the six largest vitamin manufacturers that fixed vitamins prices during 1989–99. The states received $335 million, most of it for compensating consumers and local businesses that purchased vitamins indirectly.

In Europe also, the member states of the EU are being encouraged to take on more enforcement responsibility for competition laws. In part, this represents an attempt by the European Commission to increase overall enforcement effort in the EU. More important, the member nations have generally increased the ability of their national regulatory commissions to issue heavier sanctions on cartels. In the UK, for example, the 1998 Competition Act permits the Office for Fair Trading (OFT) to apply higher fines for infringements of price fixing laws. A new bill proposed by the government in 2001 will facilitate damages suits by buyers in cartelised markets, actions repeatedly encouraged by decisions of the European Court of Justice. Unlike all but a few other countries, the bill will also authorise damages to be recouped by consumers as indirect buyers. Finally, the bill will permit the OFT to assess personal fines and prison sentences on businesspeople who carry out price fixing (Peretz, 2000). Although the UK and other countries are moving toward US-style legal rules for antitrust, there seems to be no mechanisms for cross-national legal actions within the EU.

5. POLITICAL SUPPORT FOR THE ANTITRUST LAWS

The United States' antitrust laws have generally received bipartisan support from the US Congress. While the support of presidential administrations for antitrust enforcement has ebbed and waned over time, neither political party nor ideological orientation can explain such cycles. This comment is especially true for the Sherman Act prohibition of conspiracies in restraint of trade. With respect to antimonopoly enforcement, there appears to be some tendency for major cases to be brought during the last year or two of a presidential administration.

The revelations about the global cartels in the late 1990s have reinforced political commitment to anticartel enforcement, and the relevant agencies have responded by shifting resources toward investigating and indicting international price fixing conspiracies. The US shift has been further justified by a US appeals court ruling in 1997 that clarified the law on extraterritorial violations for the Sherman Act. At the state level, large monetary settlements involved in the global vitamins case prompted no less than 44 attorneys general to band together in 1999 to sue to recover price fixing injuries. In the European Union, the commissioners in charge of the competition laws have sometimes come from political traditions antithetical to the antitrust philosophy of preserving the competitive process in markets, yet they have developed a zeal for their work typical of converts. In late 1999, the European Commission's DG-IV formed a new unit specifically focused on anticartel investigations.

The global cartels were also responsible for accelerating the trend evident since 1945 for countries outside North America to adopt new or more stringent anticartel legislation. Since 1996, countries as diverse as New Zealand, the United Kingdom, South Africa, Sweden and the Netherlands have revised and strengthened their antitrust laws governing price fixing. The ADM case was cited as one reason for raising the maximum fine for cartel behaviour in New Zealand in 1998. In 1999, South African legislation brought its fine structure in line with EU standards and permitted civil suits to seek private damage awards. Following the adoption of a set of recommendations on hard-core cartels by the Organisation of Economic Cooperation and Development in 1999, at least four of its member states – Denmark, Sweden, the Netherlands and the UK – significantly strengthened their competition laws in the area of price fixing (*European Report*, 7 June 2000).

A more recent set of OECD recommendations urges greater international cooperation in fighting global cartels, but the statement merely blesses a trend that has been strong since 1990. New bilateral agreements are being signed almost every month that make information-sharing and coordinated investigations possible. Cooperation among the US, EU, Canadian and Australian antitrust agencies is already intense. A rather extraordinary example of such partnerships was the simultaneous raids by police agencies in Europe, the US and Japan on the corporate offices of manufacturers of graphite electrodes. Whether enhanced international investigation might evolve into the establishment of a multilateral antitrust agency is uncertain. However, even though a distinguished advisory panel set up by the DOJ's Antitrust Division was split on the idea, public opinion in the United States seems to be shifting toward such an arrangement for limited areas of antitrust enforcement. Smaller countries and the EU seem to favour centralisation of antitrust authority in a body like the World Trade Organisation.

6. THOUGHTS ON THE GLOBAL CARTEL PANDEMIC AND THE NEW ECONOMY

The lysine industry may not be everyone's idea of the prototypical new economy exemplar, but it is typical of the markets that were cartelised in the 1980s and 1990s. Lysine is a tradeable homogenous organic chemical. Like most of the other industries that spawned global price fixing, sales were highly concentrated on a worldwide basis, production was relatively high-tech, growth was rapid, and barriers to entry were created by scale economies, vertical integration economies, and asymmetry of access to biotechnologies. Although the product is not knowledge-intensive, the production process is.

The outbreak of global cartels that were discovered beginning in 1995, and continue to be investigated in large numbers, came after a hiatus of more than 50 years.[14] Most of the prosecuted global cartels began operating between 1985 and 1992, but the reasons for this timing remain puzzling. But there is no question that these new economy cartels are the first to operate with truly global planning horizons. Unlike the international cartels of the 1930s, price setting and the allocation of market shares were implemented for the four largest continents: North and South America, Europe and Asia.[15] The private cartels formed prior to 1940 involved at most Western Europe and North America, and often only one of those. Moreover, these earlier cartels rarely if ever involved Japanese or other Asian conspirators. The new economy global cartels almost always had Japanese members or any Asian producers among the top five or so in global market shares.

Most of the new economy cartels were careful not to allocate individual customers among themselves. By doing so, cartel members did not tip off their customers because of inexplicable refusals to deal, behaviour that might well have alerted antitrust officials that illegal collusion was afoot. Customers were also generally disadvantaged in their dealings with the conspirators because they were numerous and ill-informed about price or about the competitive factors that might cause price increases. Prices were not reported by government agencies or other third parties because they were negotiated as private treaties between buyers and sellers. Secrecy about costs of production and what caused costs to vary put buyers at a further disadvantage in understanding price movements. Lysine and other cartelised products typically comprised such a small share of costs for the buyers' products that, like consumers in a grocery store, the industrial buyers had little or no incentive to train procurement specialists for these minor ingredients.

The lower costs of modern means of transportation and communication also facilitated the formation of the new economy cartels. The ease and frequency with which marketing managers travel helped lower the administrative costs of collusion and may have induced a false sense of security about the possibility of being discovered and prosecuted. Most of the recent global cartels used existing industry trade associations as covers for many of their illegal meetings; where they did not exist, such associations were created to explain the frequent (usually quarterly) international meetings that were necessary to hammer out the details of the collusive agreements. Indeed, it appears that the Commission of the European Communities played an unwitting role in easing the transaction costs of colluding by positive encouragement of global industry task forces as adjuncts to the EU's many groupings of national industry federations.[16] Finally, the increasingly global scope of everyday business seems to have made overt price agreements relatively straightforward. Ethnic, language, or business-practices differences among the global conspirators were no impediments to negotiating price deals nor to the monitoring of the ongoing agreement.

Many of these same features of the new economy are also responsible for an increasing convergence among national jurisdictions with respect to the content and execution of competition laws (Connor, 1997), especially anticartel laws.[17] Officials of the major antitrust agencies meet at least annually, and large multilateral conferences are becoming more common. As mentioned above, treaties and protocols have made sharing investigatory facts and documents easier. Even simultaneous raids of suspected cartel's members' headquarters have become more frequent (Canada, Australia, Germany, Japan and the EU have joined with US agencies in such joint operations). Spurred on by policy statements of the United Nations and the OECD, governments have increased the penalties for price fixing convictions, in many cases following the lead of the United States by making the violations serious criminal matters. The size and powers of many antitrust agencies have been expanded since the early 1990s, partly because the revenues from fines levied on guilty conspirators can easily exceed agency costs of investigation and prosecution. Indeed, the new economy may be seen as responsible for spreading the capitalist notion that antitrust enforcement can become a profit centre for governments: price fixing fines not only punish violators but also may be seen as user fees that offset the costs of prosecution.[18]

While government prosecution of price fixing is converging globally, the same cannot be said for private civil actions. Treble-damages suits by injured parties have been authorised in the United States since 1890, and since at least the 1970s have become quantitatively more important in the federal courts than government-prosecuted antitrust cases. Christening injured citizens and their lawyers to become private prosecutors of the antitrust laws is a market-type solution for market failure that is heartily endorsed by both the mainstream and the Chicago School of economics. The liberalisation of the rules for forming class actions has greatly increased the effectiveness of private price fixing cases, and in the sense that lawyers' fees are a declining share of recoveries by the victims, more efficient as well.[19] However, private price fixing actions have been slow to spread outside a few Anglophone countries with English Common Law traditions (e.g., Canada and Australia, but curiously not the UK itself). Either the courts are unwilling to make the injury awards large enough or the entrepreneurial spirit needed by law firms is wanting.

Regional economic development programmes often involve the creation or stimulation of geographic clusters of putatively synergistic firms (see Bellandi in this volume, and Schweitzer and Di Tommaso). In some cases, the synergies are expected to arise from economies generated by input markets or distribution facilities common to the cluster. In other cases the synergies may arise from more formal joint ventures among the firms in the cluster. Recent antitrust exemptions for R&D joint ventures in the United States make these ventures easier to operate; EU competition law has long permitted enterprises that generate innovations to escape some of the usual restrictions on oligopolistic conduct.

While most of the vertical and horizontal R&D arrangements are innocent sources of market power, this chapter may be seen as a caution about other horizontal forms of intra-cluster cooperation. The benefits from such cooperation may vanish if national or local antitrust rules are not observed. When horizontal contacts result in attempts to prevent entry into the cluster (monopolisation), cause exit of cluster rivals (attempts to monopolise), or facilitate agreements on prices, the social costs of otherwise desirable development could easily escalate.

NOTES

1. The four main examples are intimidation of distributors that need the monopolised product, coercing rivals in various equipment or software markets to drop innovative product marketing plans, tying products to induce customers to drop purchases of substitute products, and predatory techniques to raise rivals' costs.
2. Lock-in effects arise from the costs incurred by consumers or businesses when they switch from an old system with a significant learning-by-doing sunk investment to a new system. Network effects cause the value of technology to increase exponentially with the growth of interconnectedness.
3. Monopoly power is a high degree of market power (Hovenkamp, 1999, p. 269). The former is long run, usually because of barriers to entry or exit, whereas the latter may be short run.
4. Some cartels are legal in the sense that their members are state enterprises protected from legal action by national sovereignty. Other cartels engage in commodity storage activities with government support and arguably positive effects on dynamic price stabilisation (Scherer and Ross, 1990). However, the case for net efficiency benefits from *private*, *extralegal* cartels has yet to be made.
5. For sources of information and more details about the industry, see Connor (2001a).
6. Almost simultaneously with ADM, a small lysine plant came into production on the island of Java, Indonesia. The plant was owned by a joint venture formally named Cheil Samsung Astra (CSA), which was mostly controlled by South Korea's Samsung *chaebol*. Although Cheil would expand its plant five times in the 1990s, it remained the smallest of the five leading producers in that decade.
7. The story of the 1992–95 lysine cartel can be found in Connor (2001c) and in greatest detail in Connor (2001b). At least two other cartels were formed by lysine manufactures in the 1970s and 1980s, but these were confined to Asia in one case and North America in the other. A few members of two international cartels operating in North America (plastic dinnerware, thermal fax paper) were prosecuted in the early 1990s by US authorities, but not all the members were successfully prosecuted.
8. See Connor (2001b) wherein ADM's internal processing and marketing costs are shown to be nearly constant at $0.78 per pound, including a normal return on investment.
9. The vast majority of private civil suits are settled out of court prior to the conclusion of a trial. Many administrative fines are appealed to courts. In some countries, corporate boards or managers may be subject to collateral shareholders' suits.

10. Roughly 60 per cent of the interwar international cartels had US companies as members. Some of the other cartels were prosecuted because the non-US parent companies had involved their US subsidiaries.
11. The uranium cartel case of 1975 is an exception. Also, 1994–95 cases involving diamonds and thermal fax paper were lost by the US DOJ (Connor, 2001b, pp. 66–9).
12. The exceptions include Canada, Japan, South Korea and a few member states of the EU. However, only the US Department of Justice routinely seeks fines and prison sentences for a few managers in each corporate cartel member.
13. Several states adopted these laws several years before the 1890 Sherman Act. Rules of evidence and other court procedures tend to be very similar as well.
14. Prosecution of the interwar cartels ended in the late 1940s. Although three or four alleged international cartels were indicted between 1950 and 1995, with one exception (industrial diamonds), the geographic scope of the collusion was confined to one continent (Connor, 2001b). During 1999–2000, the US DOJ had at least 30 grand juries investigating alleged global cartels.
15. Australia and New Zealand were often treated as separate collusive zones, but usually African sales were managed along with West Asian territories as part of collusive deals for Western Europe.
16. The European Citric Acid Manufacturers' Association is under investigation for having aided years of collusion.
17. As the Boeing–McDonald Douglas and GE–Honeywell cases illustrate, the same may not be true for merger enforcement.
18. The idea that antitrust fines are hidden taxes on business infuriates the radical conservatives who write editorials for the *Wall Street Journal*. Since 1995, the Antitrust Division of the US DOJ has generated almost $2 billion in price fixing fines. However, a wise and popular law directs these monies to funds that compensate the victims of violent crimes through state-run programmes.
19. Legal fees averaged more than 40 per cent of recoveries before the 1970s, but now average less than 20 per cent for the larger price fixing cases (and as low as 5 per cent in the Christies case).

REFERENCES

Adams, K. and Bell, A. (1999), 'Overseas victims of price fishing should be welcomed into US courts', *Legal Times* (25 October), 36–9.
Barboza, D. (1999), 'Teasing down the façade of "Vitimins, Inc." ', *The New York Times* (10 October), section 3, p. 1.
BRW (2001), Let's hear it for competitive harmony', *Business Review Weekly*, 13 December, 22.
Connor, J.M. (1997), 'International convergence of antitrust laws and enforcement', *Antitrust Law and Economics Review*, **28**,17–30 and 73–94.
Connor, J.M. (2000), *Archer Daniels Midland: Price Fixer to The World*, Staff Paper 00–11, West Lafayette, IN: Department of Agricultural Economics, Purdue University (December) (http://agecon.lib.umu.edu/cgi-bin/pdf_vies.pl?paperid=2871).
Connor, J.M. (2001a), 'Evolution of the global lysine industry', *Review of Agricultural Economics*.
Connor, J.M. (2001b), *Global Price Fixing*, Boston/Dordrecht/London: Kluwer Academic Publishers.
Connor, J.M. (2001c), ' "Our customers are our enemies": the lysine cartel of 1992–95', *Review of Industrial Organization*, **18**(February), 5–21.
Edwards, C.D. (1976), *Economic and Political Aspects of International Cartels*, New York: Arno Press.

Eichenwald, K. (2000), *The Informant*, New York: Broadway Books.

Elhauge, E. (2001), 'Competition wins in court', *The New York Times* (1 June).

Ely, R.T. (1900), *Monopolies and Trusts*, New York: Macmillan.

Evans, D.S. and Schmalensee, R. (2001), 'Some economic aspects of antitrust analysis in dynamically competitive industries', Working Paper No. W8268, Cambridge: National Bureau of Economic Research (May).

Guerrera, F. (2001), 'Hectic year for monti in his crusade against "Cancers" ', *Financial Times* (28 December), 4.

Hovenkamp, H. (1999), *Federal Antitrust Policy*, Second Edition, St Paul, MN: West Group.

ICPAC (2000), *Final Report of the International Competition Policy Advisory Committee to the Attorney General*, Washington, DC: US Department of Justice.

Klein, J.I. (1998), 'Testimony before the US Senate Committee on the Judiciary, subcommittee on antitrust', Washington, DC (26 February).

Klein, J.I. (2000), 'Rethinking antitrust policies for the new economy', Speech at the Haas/Berkeley New Economy Forum, Portola Valley, California (9 May).

Krugman, P. (2001), 'The smell test', *The New York Times* (1 July).

Labaton, S. (2001a) 'Appeals court voids order for breaking up microsoft', *The New York Times* (29 June).

Labaton, S. (2001b), 'The world gets tough on price fixers', *The New York Times* (3 June).

Peretz, G. (2000), 'Opinion', *The Lawyer* (4 February), 19.

Peterson, E.B. and Connor, J.M. (1996), 'Consumer welfare loss estimates in differentiated food product markets', *Review of Agricultural Economics*, **18**, 233–46.

Scherer, F.M. and Ross, D. (1990), *Industrial Market Structure and Economic Performance*, Third Edition, Boston: Houghton Mifflin.

Schwartz, J. (2001), 'The land of monopolies', *The New York Times* (1 July).

Soon, J. (2001), 'Let's all club together to tackle cartels', *Australian Financial Review* (19 December), 47.

Stocking, G.W. and Watkins, M.R. (1946), *Cartels in Action: Case Studies in International Business Diplomacy*, New York: The Twentieth Century Fund.

Summers, L.H. (2000), 'The new wealth of nations', Speech at the Hambrecht & Quist Technology Conference, San Francisco, California (10 May).

Webb, S.B. (1997), *Cartels and Business Cycles in Germany, 1880 to 1914*, Cheltenham, UK and Lyme, US: Edward Elgar.

White, L.J. (2001), 'Lysine price fixing: how long? how severe?', *Review of Industrial Organization*, **18**, 23–31.

7. Economic gains from regional concentration of business operations

James Peoples[*]

1. INTRODUCTION

Theory suggests that regional concentration of business operations can enhance production efficiency (Marshall, 1879). However, there has been a trend of growing geographical dispersion of business operations in the US. For example, major companies in brewing and automobile manufacturing have become much less centrally located. The rationale for such business trends, in part, is the ability to quickly service local markets, to reduce the company's reliance on any one local labour market, to avoid high transportation costs, and to minimise potential harm from declining local economic conditions.[1] The dispersion of business operations, though, is not limited to large multiplant corporations. Smaller fringe firms might avoid local competition over resources and instead choose to set up operations in locations with low industrial concentration.

Given the rationale for dispersing operations regionally, this study examines whether it is still advantageous for US companies to operate mainly in a few localities. It is possible that regional concentration of operations presents business with a competitive advantage by enhancing productivity. Enhanced productivity occurs in part, because regionally concentrated business activity facilitates the development of expertise centres. These centres are most likely to be located in metropolitan areas given that large pools of skilled workers reside in these locations. This study tests the hypothesis on regional industrial concentration and industry performance in the US by estimating a productivity equation that includes regional concentration of industry operations as an explanatory variable. In contrast, past research on agglomeration and US productivity considers local population density and industry density as a determinant of productivity. Such research does not indicate whether enhanced industry performance is associated with industries manufacturing their goods primarily in a few of these metropolitan areas. Examining the performance effect of regional concentration of business activity allows for testing if companies risk low productivity by locating their operations across several cities. Furthermore, focusing on regional industrial concentration more closely resembles the research approach on the

159

performance effect of industrial clusters in other countries (Pinch et al., 1999; Malmberg et al., 2000, and Becchetti et al., 2000).

The remainder of this chapter is organised as follows. Section 2 examines why production economies might be associated with regional concentration of business activity. Section 3 presents the data set and estimation approach used to examine industry performance and regional industry concentration. Section 4 presents the estimation results on industry productivity levels. Section 5 provides further analysis by comparing education attainment levels by regional industry concentration. Findings from this analysis help provide insight on the mechanism by which regional concentration of business operations can enhance industry performance. Last, concluding comments on the benefits that metropolitan areas derive from regional concentration of business operations are presented in Section 6.

2. PRODUCTION ECONOMIES DERIVED FROM REGIONAL CONCENTRATION OF BUSINESS OPERATIONS

Several studies indicate that in US manufacturing, firm size is associated with economies of scale (Baumol, 1977; Panzar and Willig, 1977). The cost advantage large firms derive from these economies helped facilitate the development of highly concentrated industries.[2] Historically, in the US, large dominant firms concentrated their manufacturing operations across a small number of metropolitan areas. For instance, automobile, textile and railroad equipment manufacturing were primarily manufactured in Detroit, New York and Chicago, respectively. Past research argues that geographic concentration of business activity enhances industry productivity regardless of relative firm size (Bellandi, 1989). Bellandi identifies benefits from production specialisation, accumulation of industry-specific skills and innovation contribution as productivity enhancements associated with regional concentration of business (see also Bellandi in this volume, Chapter 9).

Access to a large pool of local workers allows firms to assign groups of individuals to very specific production tasks. Proficiency gains are accelerated when workers are allowed to focus on a small set of job responsibilities. Regional concentration of business operations can further enhance proficiency gains since workers residing in close proximity are more likely to engage in mutual training (Bellandi, 1989). Such informal methods of training can easily lead to the development of formal education systems teaching industry-specific skills. Bellandi notes that this accumulation of industry-specific skills fostered by regional business concentration contributes to a fertile environment for innovative production techniques (see also the contribution by

Husbands in this volume, and that by Schweitzer and Di Tommaso). The close proximity of several industry specialists promotes the exchange of ideas needed to promote the development of new inventions and better production processes (Bellandi, 1989, pp. 145–6).

The concentration of high-technology firms in Silicon Valley is a prime example of the key role that skilled labour plays in the development of a regional centre of expertise. Rosenfeld (1996) reports that the need for skilled workers was so great in this region that institutions of higher learning such as Stanford University, the University of California, and San Jose State University expanded their graduate-level engineering programmes to meet this demand (see also Mone in Chapter 11 of this volume). In addition, several two-year colleges in the area developed technical training programmes tailored to match the technical needs of this industry. The regional benefits from supporting the development of this centre of expertise is highlighted by the substantial prosperity associated with this industry. As Rosenfeld reports, in 1990, the high-technology firms in Silicon Valley exported $11 billion of electronic equipment. These sales represented nearly one-third of the nation's total.

The enhancement of productivity resulting from the regional concentration of business, however, might diminish with greater volume. For instance, at high output levels, learning curves tend to flatten, and gains from specialisation are offset from inefficiencies associated with high volume (Asher, 1956 and Brock, 1975). The prospect of declining productivity could provide greater impetus for regional dispersion of production. Hence, it is not clear, *a priori*, if industries enjoy better production performance from concentrating most manufacturing activity at a few metropolitan locations. Further examination of this issue, then, requires the use of empirical analysis.

Past work indicates that regional concentration of business operations at major metropolitan areas in the US is associated with greater productivity. For instance, Sveikauskas (1975) finds that labour productivity increases 6.39 per cent each time a city doubles in size. This result supports the notion that access to a large pool of workers enhances industry performance. More recent research by Ciccone and Hall (1996) finds that doubling employment density increases average labour productivity by 6 per cent. Access to a large supply of skilled workers might have contributed to the positive productivity–employment density association as Ciccone and Hall also report that labour productivity increases by 0.8 per cent for each 1 per cent increase in schooling. These authors, however, do not examine whether educational attainment of workers is associated with regional concentration of business operations. Furthermore, past research does not examine whether US manufacturers set up operations in a few metropolitan areas, and if this geographic concentration of business activity is associated with greater productivity.

Information in Table 7.1 suggests that US manufacturing is concentrated

Table 7.1 Largest metropolitan employment shares of US workforce for individual manufacturing industries

Manufacturing industry	Metropolitan area	Employment share of workforce (four largest employment shares)	Manufacturing industry	Metropolitan area	Employment share of workforce (four largest employment shares)
Meat products	Chicago	0.1675	Not specified food industries	Chicago	0.125
	Dallas	0.0369		Los Angeles	0.0937
	Detroit	0.0985		New York	0.125
	Los Angeles	0.1379		Wilmington	0.0625
Dairy products	Boston	0.0637	Tobacco manufacturers	New York	0.2968
	Buffalo	0.0711		Nassau	0.0937
	Chicago	0.0931		Los Angeles	0.0625
	Los Angeles	0.0931		Miami	0.0468
Canned fruits and vegetables	Bergen, NJ	0.0389	Knitting mills	Jersey City	0.1267
	Chicago	0.0732		Miami	0.0892
	Los Angeles	0.0846		New York	0.3803
	San Jose	0.0366		Nassau	0.0610
Grain mill products	Aurora	0.0526	Dyeing and finishing textiles	Bergen, NJ	0.2152
	Cincinnati	0.0736		Los Angeles	0.1265
	Los Angeles	0.1421		Pawtuckett, RI	0.0633
	St Louis	0.0526		Miami	0.0379

Industry	City	Value		City	Value
Bakery products	Los Angeles	0.0925	Floor coverings	Los Angeles	0.3766
	Chicago	0.1419		Providence	0.0909
	Philadelphia	0.0963		Philadelphia	0.0779
	New York	0.0722		New York	0.0648
Sugar and confectionery products	Los Angeles	0.0649	Yarn, thread and fabric mills	New York	0.1475
	Milwaukee	0.0259		Los Angeles	0.0819
	New York	0.0844		Providence	0.0773
	Philadelphia	0.0671		Lowell	0.0632
Beverage industries	Chicago	0.0671	Miscellaneous textile mill products	New York	0.1315
	Denver	0.0711		Pawtuckett, RI	0.1403
	Milwaukee	0.0711		Providence	0.0877
	New York	0.0577		Wilmington	0.0877
Miscellaneous food preparations	Chicago	0.125	Apparel and other finished textile products	Bergen, NJ	0.0349
	Los Angeles	0.138		Jersey City	0.0425
	Bergen, NJ	0.0629		Miami	0.0495
	New York	0.074		Philadelphia	0.0428
Miscellaneous fabricated textile products	Los Angeles	0.1612	Industrial and miscellaneous chemicals	Chicago	0.0523
	New York	0.0794		Houston	0.0699
	Jersey City	0.0864		Philadelphia	0.0755
	Detroit	0.0771		Wilmington	0.2119
Pulp, paper, and paperboard mills	Chicago	0.0602	Petroleum refining	Houston	0.1219
	Cincinnati	0.0446		Los Angeles	0.1285
	Los Angeles	0.0660		Philadelphia	0.1285
	Hamilton, OH	0.0504		Wilmington	0.0873

Table 7.1   continued

Manufacturing industry	Metropolitan area	Employment share of workforce (four largest employment shares)	Manufacturing industry	Metropolitan area	Employment share of workforce (four largest employment shares)
Miscellaneous paper and pulp products	Chicago	0.0878	Miscellaneous petroleum and coal products	Boston	0.0673
	Los Angeles	0.0814		Dallas	0.0961
	New York	0.0751		Somerset	0.0961
	Philadelphia	0.0702		Philadelphia	0.0673
Paperboard containers and boxes	Chicago	0.1568	Tyres and inner tubes	Akron	0.5470
	Los Angeles	0.0691		Chicago	0.0854
	Philadelphia	0.0503		Denver	0.0342
	Bergen, NJ	0.0417		Los Angeles	0.0598
Newspaper publishing and printing	New York	0.0758	Other rubber products	Akron	0.1191
	Philadelphia	0.0579		Chicago	0.0968
	Los Angeles	0.0873		Los Angeles	0.1017
	Boston	0.0686		Philadelphia	0.0397
Printing, and publishing except newspapers	Chicago	0.1023	Miscellaneous plastic products	Chicago	0.0975
	New York	0.1195		Detroit	0.1200
	Philadelphia	0.0622		Los Angeles	0.1065
	Los Angeles	0.0774		Philadelphia	0.0410

Industry	City	Value
Plastics, synthetics, and resins	Wilmington	0.1258
	Chicago	0.0758
	Detroit	0.0465
	Philadelphia	0.0672
Drugs	Somerset	0.1170
	Philadelphia	0.1388
	Wilmington	0.0571
	Chicago	0.0631
Soaps and cosmetics	Cincinnati	0.1179
	Los Angeles	0.0889
	Somerset	0.0789
	New York	0.0739
Paints, varnishes and related products	Detroit	0.1501
	Los Angeles	0.1118
	Somerset	0.0351
	Philadelphia	0.0511
Agricultural chemicals	Chicago	0.0804
	Houston	0.0919
	Los Angeles	0.0804
	Wilmington	0.2299
Wood building and mobile homes	Fort Worth	0.1111
	Portland, OR	0.0667
	Riverside, CA	0.1778
	Seattle	0.2000

Industry	City	Value
Leather tanning and finishing	Philadelphia	0.1111
	Boston	0.0741
	Milwaukee	0.3333
	New York	0.1111
Footwear, except rubber and plastic	Boston	0.1558
	Miami	0.1306
	Pittsburgh	0.0050
	Portland, OR	0.0653
Leather products except footwear	Chicago	0.0777
	Miami	0.0825
	New York	0.1116
	Providence	0.0922
Logging	Houston	0.1290
	Seattle	0.1613
	Tacoma	0.1935
	Vancouver	0.0645
Sawmills, panning mills and millwork	Dallas	0.0335
	Los Angeles	0.0698
	Portland, OR	0.0949
	Seattle	0.0754
Other primary metal industries	Detroit	0.0740
	Los Angeles	0.0679
	Pawtuckett, RI	0.0377
	Providence	0.0589

Table 7.1 continued

Manufacturing industry	Metropolitan area	Employment share of workforce (four largest employment shares)	Manufacturing industry	Metropolitan area	Employment share of workforce (four largest employment shares)
Miscellaneous wood products	Chicago	0.0844	Cutlery, handtools and other hardware	Boston	0.0776
	Houston	0.0507		Detroit	0.0588
	Los Angeles	0.1554		Los Angeles	0.1176
	Seattle	0.0405		Milwaukee	0.0612
Furniture and fixtures	Chicago	0.0741	Fabricated structural metal products	Chicago	0.0620
	Los Angeles	0.2061		Dallas	0.0340
	New York	0.0547		Detroit	0.0660
	Philadelphia	0.0451		Philadelphia	0.0593
Glass and glass products	Detroit	0.0656	Screw machine products	Chicago	0.1742
	Los Angeles	0.1182		Cleveland	0.0968
	Philadelphia	0.0788		Detroit	0.1387
	Pittsburgh	0.1125		Los Angeles	0.1129
Cement concrete, gypsum and plaster products	Chicago	0.0604	Metal forgings and stampings	Chicago	0.0986
	Detroit	0.0627		Detroit	0.2532
	Philadelphia	0.0697		Milwaukee	0.0641
	Riverside, CA	0.0511		Cleveland	0.0756

Industry	City	Value	Industry	City	Value
Structural clay products	Cleveland	0.0568	Ordnance	Cincinnati	0.0633
	Dallas	0.0795		Denver	0.1202
	Houston	0.0455		Los Angeles	0.1013
	Los Angeles	0.0909		San Jose	0.0379
Pottery and related products	Denver	0.0409	Miscellaneous fabricated metal products	Chicago	0.1464
	Los Angeles	0.1393		Cleveland	0.0648
	Philadelphia	0.0492		Detroit	0.0867
	Trenton	0.1475		Los Angeles	0.1194
Miscellaneous non-metallic mineral and stone products	Chicago	0.0930	Not specified metal	Chicago	0.2272
	Detroit	0.0668		Fort Worth	0.0909
	Los Angeles	0.0930		Los Angeles	0.1818
	Philadelphia	0.0959		Philadelphia	0.1818
Blast furnaces, steelworks rolling and finishing mills	Chicago	0.1169	Engines and turbines	Bridgeport	0.0630
	Detroit	0.1454		Chicago	0.0462
	Gary	0.1073		Detroit	0.1848
	Pittsburgh	0.10299		Milwaukee	0.3361
Iron and steel foundries	Chicago	0.1000	Farm machinery and equipment	Chicago	0.0842
	Cleveland	0.1000		Detroit	0.0947
	Milwaukee	0.0815		Milwaukee	0.1579
	Portland, OR	0.1000		Racine	0.2210
Primary aluminium industries	Chicago	0.1036	Construction and material handling machines	Chicago	0.0656
	Cleveland	0.0836		Cleveland	0.0619
	Los Angeles	0.1593		Houston	0.2040
	Pittsburgh	0.05577		Milwaukee	0.0655

Table 7.1 continued

Manufacturing industry	Metropolitan area	Employment share of workforce (four largest employment shares)	Manufacturing industry	Metropolitan area	Employment share of workforce (four largest employment shares)
Metal working machinery	Chicago	0.1078	Ship and boat building and repairing	Los Angeles	0.0602
	Detroit	0.2840		Philadelphia	0.1277
	Los Angeles	0.0527		Providence	0.1687
	Pittsburgh	0.0417		Vallejo, CA	0.0749
Office and accounting machines	Detroit	0.0405	Railroad locomotives and equipment	Chicago	0.2763
	Los Angeles	0.0540		Joliet	0.1052
	New York	0.0641		Pittsburgh	0.1052
	Stamford	0.0844		Portland, OR	0.0921
Electronic computing equipment	Boston	0.1679	Guided missiles, space vehicles, and parts	Anaheim	0.0625
	Los Angeles	0.0433		Denver	0.0732
	New York	0.0351		Los Angeles	0.3667
	San Jose	0.1268		Seattle	0.0498
Machinery, except electrical, N.E.C.	Chicago	0.0911	Cycles and miscellaneous transportation equipment	Detroit	0.3489
	Cleveland	0.0502		Los Angeles	0.0671
	Detroit	0.0724		San Jose	0.1007
	Philadelphia	0.0568		Riverside, CA	0.0738
Not specified machinery	Chicago	0.1250	Scientific and controlling instruments	Boston	0.1212
	Detroit	0.2083		Chicago	0.0485
	Nassau	0.1250		Los Angeles	0.0744

Industry	City	Value	Industry	City	Value
Household appliances	New York	0.0833	Optical and health services supplies	Philadelphia	0.0719
	Chicago	0.1562		Boston	0.0710
	Cleveland	0.0976		Chicago	0.0600
	Los Angeles	0.1133		Los Angeles	0.0833
	New York	0.0976		Somerset	0.0416
Radio, TV and communication equipment	Boston	0.0758	Photographic equipment and supplies	Bergen, NJ	0.0689
	Chicago	0.1321		Boston	0.2252
	Dallas	0.0707		Chicago	0.0689
	Los Angeles	0.0824		Los Angeles	0.0804
Electrical machinery, equipment and supplies, N.E.C.	Boston	0.0736	Watches, clocks, and clockwork devices	Bergen, NJ	0.1000
	Chicago	0.0859		Chicago	0.6667
	Los Angeles	0.0697		Los Angeles	0.1833
	San Jose	0.0775		New York	0.1500
Not specified electrical machinery	Chicago	0.0667	Toys, amusement, and sporting goods	Chicago	0.0953
	Los Angeles	0.0762		Los Angeles	0.1511
	Nassau	0.1047		New York	0.0349
	San Jose	0.1047		Providence	0.0442
Motor vehicles and motor vehicle equipment	Chicago	0.0405	Miscellaneous manufacturing industries	Chicago	0.0662
	Detroit	0.5567		Los Angeles	0.1079
	Los Angeles	0.0319		New York	0.1058
	Wilmington	0.0307		Providence	0.1720
Aircraft and parts	Fort Worth	0.0746	Not specified manufacturing industries	Boston	0.4482
	Hartford	0.0599		Chicago	0.1448
	Los Angeles	0.2168		Los Angeles	0.0896
	Seattle	0.1386		New York	0.1586

Note: N.E.C. = not elsewhere specified.

Source: 1991–93 Annual Current Population Survey OutGoing-Rotation-Group files.

regionally. The four-city regional concentration ratio of the manufacturing industries reported in Table 7.1 is on average 40 per cent. While this mean value of regional concentration of industry operations is relatively large, it is not large enough to dismiss the possibility of some industries dispersing their operations to take advantage of possible cost savings. Evidence in Table 7.1 shows the type of industry that benefits from locating business operations across several regions. For instance, the smallest four-city regional concentration ratio occurs in fabricated structural metal products. In this industry, 22.13 per cent of the workers reside in Chicago, Dallas, Detroit and Philadelphia. The high transportation cost of shipping this material and the geographic dispersion of purchasing companies such as construction firms presents weak incentive for regional concentration of business operations in the fabricated structural metal industry. Table 7.1 also shows the type of industry that benefits from regional concentration of business operations. Tyre and inner tube manufacturing has the largest regional concentration ratio, with 72.69 per cent of the workforce employed in Akron, Chicago, Denver and Los Angeles[3] and 54.7 per cent of the domestic workforce in tyre manufacturing reside in Akron, Ohio. The advantage of manufacturing a disproportionate share of tyres in this city is its close proximity to Detroit, Michigan, which is the centre of US automobile production.

Findings in Table 7.1 also indicate that the location of domestic US manufacturing is most prevalent in five major metropolitan areas: Boston, Chicago, Los Angeles, New York and Philadelphia.[4] These locations represent all but the southern US region. The historical emphasis on agriculture in the US south contributes to the relative absence of industrial concentration in this region. Nonetheless, the access to low-wage non-union workers has created an incentive for industrial migration from the north to the south.[5]

Table 7.1 additionally reveals high regional production concentration ratios where metropolitan areas possess some physical advantages for producing certain industrial products. For instance, major shipbuilding centres are located at cities with major ports.[6] Workers in logging primarily reside in heavily forested locations in the north-west US, such as Seattle, and Tacoma, Washington. A large share of workers employed in the petroleum refinery industry reside in oil-producing areas such as Houston and Los Angeles. Some metropolitan areas that are not one of the major five employing cities have a large share of workers in industries that have historically manufactured specific products. Milwaukee, Pittsburgh and Detroit are examples of smaller cities with a tradition of producing beer, glass and automobiles, respectively. Evidence in Table 7.1 shows that these cities still employ a large share of workers in their traditional areas of expertise.[7]

Last, Table 7.1 shows a non-trivial amount of horizontal and vertically related industries located in the same metropolitan areas. Some examples of vertical concentration are depicted by large industry shares of logging and sawmill manufacturing workers residing in Seattle, and engines and farm equipment manufacturing in Milwaukee. Horizontal concentration of business activity is depicted by large industry shares of aircraft and guided missile manufacturing workers residing in Los Angeles, and optical health supplies and scientific instruments in Boston and in New York.[8]

In sum, business activity in US manufacturing depicts companies producing goods in a few metropolitan areas. At issue is whether this regional concentration of business activity is associated with greater productivity.

3. DATA AND ESTIMATION APPROACH

Three separate data sources are used to examine industrial productivity and regional concentration of business activities. Industry information on 1992 total factor productivity levels is taken from the National Bureau of Economic Research–Center of Economic Studies (NBER–CES 1958–96) Database.[9] Additional industry information on 1992 industry capital/labour ratios, average plant size, industry four-firm ratios and industry fifty-firm Herfindahl indices are taken from the 1992 Census of Manufactures. This data source uses the four-digit standard industrial classification to identify industries. These industry measures are converted to three-digit classifications since the three-digit standard industrial classification code is used to identify industries' labour productivity. A weighted average procedure is used for this conversion. Last, individual information on workers' residency, and industry of employment from the 1991–93 annual Current Population Survey (CPS) OutGoing-Rotation-Group files are used to construct four-city concentration ratios and four-city Herfindahl indices by industry. These measures are depicted by the following equations:[10]

$$(\text{C4-city})_j = \sum_{k=1}^{4} s_k \quad \text{and} \quad (\text{H4-city})_j = \sum_{k=1}^{4} (s_k)^2$$

where (C4-city) and (H4-city) are the respective four-city regional concentration and four-city Herfindahl indices, 'j' indexes industry, 'k' indexes standard metropolitan statistical area (SMSA), and 's' depicts an SMSA's share of the national industry employment for the jth industry.[11] Since the CPS uses the three-digit census industry classification, individual workers' industries of employment are reclassified to match the standard industrial classification code. Matching these industry measures at the three-digit level allows for constructing a sample of 77 industries in US manufacturing.

The industry sample population is used to estimate the following industrial productivity equation:

$$\ln(\text{prod}_j) = \alpha + \beta_1 (regional\ concentration)_j + \beta_2 \ln(plant\ size)_j \atop + \beta_3 \ln(K/L)_j + \beta_4 \ln(industry\ concentration)_j \quad (7.1)$$

where prod depicts total factor productivity levels for 1992, regional concentration is a dummy variable that depicts the critical four-city regional concentration level. The variable plant size is the mean plant size for the jth industry. The variable K/L is the industry capital/labour ratio, and the variable industry concentration depicts the four-firm census concentration ratio or the fifty-firm Herfindahl index. The estimated coefficient of primary interest is β_1. This coefficient measures the log difference in industry productivity levels associated with the level of regional industry concentration.[12] The coefficient β_1 is also used to determine the critical city concentration level. After using different values of the regional concentration ratio to estimate equation (7.1), the ratio associated with the largest estimate of β_1 is the critical concentration level. Identifying the critical regional concentration level provides a benchmark for analysing whether regional concentration of business operations are near optimal levels needed to enhance productivity.

The specification of equation (7.1) models productivity as dependent on economies of specialisation and technology investment. It is hypothesised that industries with high regional concentration ratios and those investing in large plants are more productive because such industries are ideally suited to promoting employee specialisation. Industries with high capital/labour ratios take advantage of labour-saving technology to boost industry productivity. Last, high profits associated with industry concentration provides dominant firms with the resources needed to invest in productivity-enhancing technology (Schumpeter, 1943).[13] On the other hand, the lack of competition in these industries does not present strong incentive to invest in new technology. Hence, the association between industry concentration and productivity is not certain, *a priori*.

4.   PRODUCTIVITY RESULTS

Productivity results from estimating equation (7.1) for US manufacturing industries are presented in Table 7.2. The signs of the estimated coefficients on the control variables are consistent with economic theory. Higher productivity occurs in capital-intensive industries and in industries that make use of large plants. For instance, a 1 per cent increase in the capital/labour ratio is associated with a 0.29 per cent increase in productivity. A 1 per cent increase in plant

Table 7.2   *Industrial productivity results from estimating equation (7.1) (log of industrial total factor productivity is the dependent variable)*

Explanatory variables	Estimated coefficients				Mean	Standard deviation
	(1)	(2)	(3)	(4)		
Intercept	−0.373 (−1.257)	−0.3735 (−1.250)	−0.343 (−1.031)	−0.342 (−1.028)	1.000	0.000
Cities with highly concentrated industrial employment (critical four-city concentration	0.1129* (1.695)	–	0.1100* (1.645)	–	0.4025	0.1229
Cities with highly concentrated industrial employment (critical four-city Herfindahl)	–	0.096* (1.646)	–	0.093* (1.688)	0.0637	0.0619
Four-firm concentration ratio (logs)	0.0496 (0.649)	0.0477 (0.616)	–	–	39.73	16.716
Fifty-firm Herfindahl index (logs)	–	–	0.022 (0.457)	0.0201 (0.427)	710.225	470.10
Capital/labour ratio(log)	0.2957* (1.740)	0.2842* (1.669)	0.2993* (1.751)	0.2884* (1.684)	64.449	53.21
Average plant size (log)	0.3234* (1.743)	0.3061* (1.650)	0.3258* (1.744)	0.309* (1.657)	56.6	44.7
R-Squared	0.0763	0.0666	0.0715	0.0625		
F-Score	2.507	2.303	2.386	2.200		
Number of observations	77	77	76	76		

Note: * Significant at the 10% level.

Source: Census of Manufactures and Bureau of Labor Statistics.

size is associated with a 0.32 per cent increase in productivity. Productivity levels in manufacturing are not closely linked with industry concentration. This result comports well with the notion that productivity is retarded in non-competitive markets given the likelihood that firms in these industries do not engage in competitive pricing.

After estimating equation (7.1) when using different regional concentration ratios, this study finds that the critical regional concentration level equals 0.40.

Interestingly, this critical level matches the mean regional concentration level for US manufacturing. At this level of business concentration productivity is statistically significant, and 11.9 per cent higher than in less regionally concentrated industry. The productivity advantage derived from concentrating business operations in a few localities does not differ markedly when using the four-city Herfindahl measure. The Herfindahl measure of concentration indicates a 10.0 per cent productivity advantage for companies regionally concentrating business operations above the critical level of 0.065. This critical level nearly matches the 0.0637 mean Herfindahl level of regional concentration. Apparently, then, the mean geographic dispersion of business operations is at the critical level needed to enhance industry productivity.

In sum, finding a significantly higher productivity level for industries that concentrate their business operation in a few metropolitan areas supports the notion that these business centres contribute to a firm's competitive advantage. Regional prosperity is a likely externality flowing from the improved business performance. Job security and high salaries associated with successful business operations are key factors that support a vibrant regional economy.[14]

5.   EDUCATIONAL ATTAINMENT AND REGIONAL CONCENTRATION

While evidence on productivity and industrial concentration suggests that locating business operations at a few metropolitan areas is conducive to greater productivity, an explanation of this association has not been tested. Past research indicates that metropolitan areas provide the critical mass of skilled workers needed to enhance productivity (Callejon and Costa, 1997).[15] To examine if city concentration is associated with greater skill attainment, this study uses individual information from CPS files to estimate the following educational attainment equation:

$$\text{Prob } (college\ degree = 1)_j = \Phi[\gamma_0 + \gamma_1 \mathbf{X} \qquad (7.2)$$
$$+ \gamma_2 (critical\ regional\ concentration)_j]$$

where 'j' indexes industry, and Φ is a normal probability function. College degree is a binary variable with a value of one if the individual has earned a college degree, and zero otherwise. Increasing demand for college educated workers due to greater use of technology in manufacturing dictates using the college degree binary variable to identify high-skilled workers. The control vector $\mathbf{X}$ includes variables representing individual workers' age, and dummies depicting whether these individuals reside in the north-east, north central or southern region of the US (as opposed to residing in the western region of the country). Dummies also depict whether individual workers are union members, married, black, white, female, employed as technicians, managers, sales representatives, clerical workers, craft workers, non-transportation operatives, transportation operatives, labourers and service workers (as opposed to professionals). The variable critical regional concentration is a dummy variable equalling one if an individual works at one of the four major employment cities for industries with regional concentration ratios greater than 0.40. Using the critical regional concentration ratio as a determinant allows for testing if workers employed in industries' major production centres are more likely to attain greater formal schooling. The estimated coefficient on the optimal regional concentration variable depicts the difference in education attainment associated with the regional concentration of business activity.

The education attainment results from estimating equation (7.2) are reported in Table 7.3. The results of the estimated coefficient on the control variables depict the expected signs and statistical significance. Education attainment for workers employed in manufacturing industries is found to decrease with age. This result is indicative of the US trend of easier access to a college education for members of the younger generations. Higher educational attainment is also associated with workers who reside in the north-east region of the US who are married, male, non-black minorities, employed as professionals or non-union workers.[16]

The findings in Table 7.3 also suggest that regional concentration of business activity is associated with higher educational attainment. For example, the estimated coefficient on the four-city regional concentration dummy is statistically significant and positive. The significance of the estimated coefficients on these regional concentration dummies permits estimation of the association between regional business concentration and educational attainment. For a worker with mean characteristics, the predicted probability of attaining a college degree increases by 5.96 percentage points if he or she is employed in one of the four cities of business concentration for a given industry. This differential is nearly 24 per cent greater than the 24.96 percentage probability of other workers attaining a college degree.[17]

To test if the employment of highly educated workers explains the high productivity levels associated with industries concentrating the operations in a few key locations, production equation (7.1) is now specified to include the estimated difference of workers' educational levels across manufacturing industries. This variable is derived by initially estimating equation (7.2) except it excludes the regional concentration dummy and includes dummies for the industries listed in Table 7.1.[18] The estimated coefficients on the industry dummies are then used to depict educational attainment differences.

Table 7.4 lists the results from estimating the new specification of the productivity equation. The value of the estimated coefficients on the control

Figure 7.3   *Education attainment results from estimating equation (7.2)*
              (probit procedure with the binary variable equalling one if
              individual attains a college or graduate degree)

Explanatory variables	Estimated coefficient	Chi-squared
Intercept	1.202***	133.21
Individual works in one of the four high employment cities for a given industry (dummy = 1 if yes)	0.149***	14.95
Age	–0.005***	9.104
US residency		
North-east	0.1839***	14.420
North central	0.00067	0.0002
South	0.0475	0.6007
Married	0.0322	0.6373
Union member	–0.4334***	39.505
Black	–0.5479***	30.982
White	–0.4692***	48.648
Female	–0.2928***	48.5826
Occupations		
Technician	–1.158**	173.137
Manager	–0.349***	41.079
Sales	–0.365***	21.0433
Clerical	–1.588***	495.828
Craft	–1.957***	872.8107
Operatives	–2.259***	1114.095
Transportation operatives	–2.0379***	185.5385
Labourer	–2.550***	178.311
Services	–1.816***	86.6916
Log-likelihood score	–3086.426	
Number of observations	7,863	

Note: *** Significant at the 1% level.

Source: 1992 Annual Current Population Survey file.

variables are not appreciably different from the results presented in Table 7.2.
Capital intensity and plant size are still positively associated with productivity
levels, and large firms' share of industry output does not have a significant
effect on productivity. The findings in Table 7.4 also shows that a workforce
with high educational attainment is associated with greater productivity. The
estimated coefficient on the interindustry educational attainment differential

Table 7.4   *Industrial productivity results when including educational*
attainment as an explanatory variable (log of industrial total
factor productivity is the dependent variable)

Explanatory variables	Estimated coefficients			
	(1)	(2)	(3)	(4)
Intercept	−0.469 (−1.479)	−0.434 (−1.221)	−0.447 (−1.491)	−0.444 (−1.240)
Cities with highly concentrated industrial employment (critical four-city concentration	0.0880 (1.390)	0.0819 (1.261)	–	–
Cities with highly concentrated industrial employment (critical four-city Herfindahl)	–	–	0.0765 (1.078)	0.0697 (0.959)
Estimated industry Educational attainment differential	0.169 (1.693)	0.1782 (1.726)	0.169 (1.693)	0.1782 (1.726)
Four-firm concentration ratio (logs)	0.064 (0.793)	–	0.0656 (0.791)	–
Fifty-firm Herfindahl index (logs)	–	0.0287 (0.557)	–	0.0456 (0.0913)
Capital/labour ratio (log)	0.3344* (1.919)	0.342* (1.956)	0.332* (1.844)	0.317* (1.814)
Average plant size (log)	0.355* (1.919)	0.362* (1.904)	0.338* (1.786)	0.327* (1.732)
R-squared	0.0995	0.0989	0.0897	0.0902
F-score	2.547	2.514	2.360	2.369
Number-of obs.	77	77	76	76

Note: * Significant at the 10% level.

Source: Census of Manufactures and Bureau of Labor Statistics.

variable is positive and statistically significant. High levels of educational attainment helps explain the high productivity levels of industries with a critical share of business operations concentrated at a few locations. Now the estimated coefficient on the critical regional concentration ratio is not statistically significant. At the critical four-city regional concentration ratio industry productivity is now 9.2 per cent higher than in less concentrated industries. This contrasts to the 11.9 per cent productivity advantage reported in Table 7.2. A similar reduction of the productivity advantage arises when using the Herfindahl index to measure regional concentration. At the critical regional concentration level productivity is 7.2 per cent higher than in less concentrated industries. This productivity advantage compares less favourably to the 10 per cent advantage reported in Table 7.2.

In sum, while the results on educational attainment cannot be used to reveal whether a region's large pool of skilled workers attracts business or whether the development of successful business attracts skilled workers, these results do show how vital an educated workforce is to the economic success of domestic firms in a globally competitive economy. (On education and economic development, see also the chapters by Husbands and by Willner in this volume, as well as the following chapter by Schweitzer and Di Tommaso.)

6.   CONCLUSIONS

This study was motivated by the notion that it may no longer be advantageous for US companies to locate their business mainly at a few industry-specific centres of operations. While a critical mass of skilled employees working in close proximity should promote relatively high productivity gains, such gains may diminish as industry volume increases. If that is the case, there is less incentive for large US firms locating most of their operations at a few metropolitan areas. The results from this study, however, suggest that concentrating business activity at a few centres of industry-specific activity does enhance productivity. Such a finding is consistent with product market outcomes in other countries such as Italy and Sweden. Evidence from this study also suggests that higher educational attainment is associated with greater regional concentration of business activity. The employment of workers with substantial formal education helps explain the productivity advantage derived from the regional concentration of business operations.

While these results identify performance gains derived from regional concentration of business operations, some caution is warranted when interpreting such findings. This study's information is limited to US industrial centres. US multinationals, however, are increasingly producing more of their goods abroad. Hence, using measures of domestic employment shares to depict regional concentration of business activity may be misleading. Including the share of foreign employment of US industries, though, may not necessarily weaken the results presented in this study. Foreign operations are likely to also develop within regional centres of expertise and further enhance industry performance. Such analysis presents a path for future research on regional concentration and industrial productivity. Nonetheless, findings from this study indicate that regional economies can prosper by working with institutions of higher education and with industries to develop centres of business expertise.

NOTES

*   The author thanks Marco Bellandi, Maria Callejon, Cecilia Conrad, Lisa De Propris, Kaye Husbands, Harold Rose, participants at the L'Institute–Milwaukee Workshop, and NEA/AEA Joint Summer Program Conference for their valuable suggestions and comments. The author is also grateful for the research assistance provided by Angelina Ordinez and Saif Sallam Alhakimi.
1.   See Berry et al. (1976) for a more in-depth analysis on the cost advantages of regional dispersion of business operations.
2.   The mean four-firm industry concentration for US manufacturing was 39.735 for 1992. *Source: Census of Manufacturing.*
3.   Fabricated structural metal products and tyre manufacturing, respectively, have the highest and lowest regional business concentration when using the Herfindahl index as a measure.
4.   Los Angeles is one of the four major manufacturing employers for nearly two-thirds of the industries reported in Table 7.1.
5.   General Motors' decision to build production facilities in the state of Tennessee is an example of north–south manufacturing migration.
6.   The four major shipbuilding locations listed in Table 7.1 are ranked in the top 35 ports by cargo volume, *Source*: US Army Corps of Engineers, Navigation Data Centre (1998).
7.   Milwaukee's large employment share of brewery workers is depicted in its ranking in beverage employment on Table 7.1. Data used to compile employment share information classifies beer brewing in the more aggregate category of beverage production. Milwaukee's high ranking in the beverage industry is also attributable to it being a major milk producer.
8.   The mean value of regional concentration might understate regional concentration of business activity given the propensity for industries with horizontal relationships to produce goods in the same metropolitan areas.
9.   Industry information from 1992 is used in this since this is the most recent date when data are available for all the industry measures used in this study.
10.   CPS files covering the years from 1991 to 1993 are pooled together to construct a data set that is large enough to calculate city concentration measures.
11.   252 US metropolitan areas are included in this study's data set.
12.   Percentage differentials are calculated as $(\varepsilon^{\alpha} - 1) \times 100$.
13.   High industry concentration ratios depict non-competitive market structure.
14.   Data taken from this study indicate that workers receive substantially higher earnings in industries that locate their business operation at a few localities. For example, in 1993 workers employed in such industries receive a mean earnings of \$693.86 a week, compared to \$619.01 per week received by their counterparts in other industries.
15.   Callejon and Costa (1997) observe that regional concentration of business operations generates a pool of workers with industry-specific skills. They also maintain that both employers and workers benefit from the development of such a pool. Employers face a more elastic

supply of labour, which allows them to adjust firm employment to business cycles, while workers enjoy greater job security because they are not dependent on the employment of a monopsonistic employer.

16. The higher educational attainment reported for male workers compared to women might reflect the absence of information on less aggregate measures of workers' occupations. For instance, the low education attainment for women might reflect their disproportionate employment share in occupations that require less schooling, however, these occupations cannot be identified using this study's highly aggregate occupation classification.

17. The association between regional concentration of business operations and educational attainment is also positive and statistically significant when using the city concentration dummy that depicts individuals working at one of the four major employment cities for any industry.

18. Meat products is the industry of comparison when estimating the education attainment differentials.

REFERENCES

Asher, H. (1956), 'Cost–quantity relationships in the airframe industry', R-291 (Santa Monica RAND Corporation).

Baumol, W. (1977), 'On the proper tests for natural monopoly in a multiproduct industry', *American Economic Review*, **67** (December), 809–22.

Becchetti, L. and Rossi, S. (2000), 'The positive effect of industrial districts on the export performance of Italian firms', *Review of Industrial Organization*, **16** (February), 53–68.

Bellandi, M. (1989), 'The industrial district in Marshall', in E. Goodman and J. Bamford (eds), *Small Firms and Industrial Districts in Italy*, London: Routledge, pp. 137–53.

Berry, B., Conkling, E. and Ray, M. (1976), *The Geography of Economic Systems*, Engelwood Cliffs, NJ: Prentice-Hall.

Brock, G. (1975), *The US Computer Industry*, Cambridge, MA: Ballinger.

Callejon, M. and Costa, M.T. (1997), 'Agglomeration economies and the location of industry', Working paper presented at the International Conference on Industrial Policy for Europe, London: Royal Institute of International Affairs, Chatham House.

Ciccone, A. and Hall, R. (1996), 'Productivity and the density of economic activity', *American Economic Review*, **86** (March), 54–70.

Malmberg, A., Malmberg, B. and Lundequist, P. (2000), 'Agglomeration and firm performance: economies of scale, localisation, and urbanisation among Swedish export firms', *Environment and Planning*, **32** (February), 305–21.

Marshall, A. (1879), *The Economics of Industry*, London: Macmillan.

Panzar, J. and Willig, R. (1977), 'Economies of scale in multi-output production', *Quarterly Journal of Economics*, **91** (August), 481–93.

Pinch, S. (1999), 'Paul Krugman's geographical economics, industrial clustering and the British motor sport industry', *Regional Studies*, **33** (December), 815–27.

Rosenfeld, S. (1996), 'United States: business clusters', in *Networks of Enterprises and Local Development*, Paris, France: OECD.

Schumpeter, J. (1943), *Capitalism, Socialism and Democracy*, London: Allen & Unwin.

Sveikauskas, L. (1975), 'The productivity of cities', *Quarterly Journal of Economics*, **89** (August), 393–413.

8. Why do biotechnology firms cluster? Some possible explanations

Stuart O. Schweitzer and Marco R. Di Tommaso[*]

1. INTRODUCTION

Industrial history shows us how firms have always been unequally distributed geographically. In all industrial periods, firms have been sensitive to specific factors that have favoured one location instead of another. In other words, firms are not indifferent to geography and have always had their set of preferences in this strategic field. The aggregate result of single firm localisation choices is that, if firms are attracted by similar factors that can be found in one location and not in another, they will tend to cluster in those specific geographic areas. The focus of this chapter is to study the reasons for clustering in the relatively new high-technology sectors, including biotechnology.

Cities like Manchester, Lyon and Detroit in the last centuries, or more recently areas like Shanghai, Dublin, or San Francisco, have shown superior capacity, both to attract existing firms and to 'incubate' new ones. It was in those places, and not in other locations, that particular industrialisation processes occurred. Geography clearly matters because each place has always been associated with special abilities to attract new firms and start new ones.

The earliest industrial agglomerations typically could be understood in terms of location of natural resources. Some firms located close to the water, as it represented one of the first sources of energy. Steel refineries tended to cluster near sources of raw materials, such as coal or iron ore. In other cases, firms decided to build their plants in areas where climate favoured particular production processes, or in areas that were centres of political activity.

Other firm agglomerations can be explained by transport costs. In many cases, plants have tended to be located in port cities or, according to the nature of the goods, close to rail lines and, more recently, in proximity to airports or highway junctions. Here agglomerations occur because transport costs of raw materials, intermediate goods, or final products are high and firms choose those localities that offer particular advantages because of their easier access to transport.[1]

Other agglomerations of firms, such as the British 'manufacturing belts', the Italian 'industrial districts' or the American industrial metropolises have grown because of another centripetal force. In these areas too, firms have shown a propensity to locate near natural resources, urban infrastructures and services. But they also have been shown to be attracted by other firms: firms seek out one another (Marshall, 1890; Becattini, 1989; Krugman, 1991 and 1995).

All these 'old economy' dynamics are evidently relevant today, as we consider the 'new economy'. Of course we have to update some traditional considerations, but at the end of the story, even high-technology firms continue to cluster, seemingly for similar reasons as they have always clustered. These firms, too, look for economies that typically can be found in urban areas; basically traditional and innovative physical infrastructures, and in many cases they are also interested in staying close to large concentrations of demand (Camagni, 1992; Walsh, 1993; Feldman, 1994).

Both in the old and in the new economy today firms continue to seek out economies of particular areas as well as economies derived from the proximity of other specialised and complementary firms (and institutions). This is one of the lessons we learn from the experiences of the American Silicon Valley (Saxenian, 1994) or of the Italian industrial districts (Becattini, 1989; see also Bellandi in the next chapter of this volume). Both in the traditional and in the new industries, firms seem to locate close to strategic resources. However, in the new economy new key resources join the old ones. 'Intangible resources' such as knowledge, know-how, skills and relations enter the decision process (see also Husbands in Chapter 3).[2]

Of course, in these general introductory considerations it is implicit that all the above-mentioned centripetal forces can occur together and in many cases they overlap, making the weight of each single factor difficult to understand and quantify. Also, distinctions among industries cannot be ignored, as the mix of centripetal and centrifugal forces changes dramatically sector by sector and probably also country by country.

The policy perspective of our exercise is that governments will be better able to take measures to encourage firms to locate in particular areas if they are armed with better information on how firms locate. This information will be useful to all levels of policy-making, from localities, to regions, and to national governments.

2.   THE CASE OF HIGH-TECHNOLOGY FIRMS IN THE HEALTH INDUSTRY

Because of the strong government role in all industrialised countries, the traditional policy perspectives on health care are strongly influenced by the dilemma of how to provide an acceptable level of care within budget constraints. Governments, especially in democracies, are sensitive to demands for health care, but at the same time they recognise that national resources are limited.

Another way of looking at the health sector suggests that providing an acceptable level of care at minimal cost is not a sufficient guide to appropriate policy intervention. This alternative view recognises the strategic value of health-related industries, such as pharmaceuticals or biotechnology. In an earlier study, we called this perspective the Health Industry Model (Di Tommaso and Schweitzer, 2000). This model points out economic advantages that health industries bring to countries. Advantages exist in terms of scientific spillovers from one industry to another, creating wealth through expansion of high-wage and high-profit firms, and participating in the increasingly interconnected world open economy in which health services, medical technology, and even patients themselves, become part of international trade.

These attractions have led many industrialised countries to try to develop policies that will encourage growth of high-technology industrial sectors including health manufacturing industries, such as biotechnology, bioengineering, and medical equipment and services. In this context, many countries are trying to create their own 'Hi-Tech Valley', modelled after America's Silicon Valley or other similar successful international experiences, including Sophia Antipolis (France), the Silicon Fen (Cambridge, UK), Bio-Gen-Tec-NRW (North Rhine-Westphalia, Germany), or Tsukuba (Japan).

This chapter sets out a framework to test various hypotheses concerning where high-technology firms locate and we will focus on the case of biotech companies.[3] In doing so, policy considerations are formulated that might be useful for countries (and subnational units such as regions) to use to attract new firms or encourage the growth of existing firms in these industries.

3. DISTRICTS, CLUSTERS AND 'VALLEYS'. WHY DO FIRMS AGGLOMERATE?

The extensive literature on clustering of firms follows two main themes. The first is that there are specific factors that draw particular firms to a particular locality (see Table 8.1 at the end of this section). In the old economy these factors were ease of transportation, location of either supply or product markets, or natural resources (Weber, 1909; Lösch, 1940; see also Peoples, Chapter 7 of this volume). In the new economy, with output so high in terms of value per unit of size or weight, transportation costs have largely been eliminated as an important consideration. Moreover, the inputs, as the outputs, may not be physical at all, but rather intellectual in nature, so that 'commerce' consists more of transmission of digitised information over the Internet than of sending actual physical outputs.[4] Over the last three centuries, the main source of wealth in market economies has switched from natural assets (land, raw materials and relatively unskilled labour), through tangible created assets (buildings, machinery and equipment, and finance) to intangible assets (knowledge, information, intellectual properties and brands) (Dunning, 2000). Furthermore, Zoltan Acs (1998) shows that not only transportation costs, but also 'tariff walls' tumbled because of the enhanced importance of information and intangible assets in productive processes. Therefore, when we think about the role that natural resources may play today when firms choose where to locate their plants, it is clear that there is little that is similar to the role of coal in earlier centuries that determines the location of firms today (Breschi, 2000).[5]

The second theme in the literature focuses on synergies among firms, and it describes the process by which firms cluster together because of the benefits they perceive they obtain within a cluster. Firm agglomeration per se offers advantages because of physical proximity. In general, to be close to other firms is important, but the proximity to other similar, specialised and complementary firms can offer even greater benefits. Growing firms clustered together have access to a local market for skills that reduce specialised labour search costs, a local specialised supply of raw materials (ready to be used and less expensive), equipment and services, and technical and market flows of specific knowledge (Marshall, 1890; Becattini, 1989; Krugman, 1991). Basically, firms choose a particular location because it is there that they can exploit the positive externalities produced by other firms. Firms wish to exploit unwanted, unpaid and outside-the-market side effects of other firms' activity. These spontaneous by-products of economic activities tend to be characterised by non-rivalry and non-excludability: these economies are part of a common pool from which any actor can freely draw (Feldman 1994; Audretsch and Feldman, 1996; Audretsch, 1998; Cooke, 2001).

Several theoretical contributions – from Alfred Marshall to Paul Krugman – and much international experience – like Italy's industrial districts – offer confirmation of the crucial role of spatial proximity. However, should physical proximity among firms in industries like biotech, still be considered relevant? In other words do the above issues still apply? Learning from the experiences of places like the Silicon Valley we may assume that the existence of a local market for skills should be considered as one of the most important competitive factors. And probably the existence of a local specialised supply of labour and technical services is also a central consideration. Finally, without any doubt, in industries such as biotech, physical proximity offers the possibility of freely drawing from a common pool of knowledge (Kenney, 1986; Swann et al., 1998).

Agglomeration, however, may offer advantages that go beyond the ones linked to the 'passive' exploitation of other firms' proximity. At least in principle, a cluster of firms is the right environment for the development of strategic relations among firms. In other words, the assumption is that firms, inspired by what and who they see close to them, show a greater propensity to cooperate (Cooke, 2001). Cooperation – either vertical or horizontal – may concern aspects such as process and product development, quality control, training, lobbying, or marketing. In this case, the strategy of the firm suggests location choice based upon the wish to establish durable relations with other firms. In contrast to passively acquired external economies linked merely to proximity, the wish of establishing collective actions with other firms involves active and consciously pursued interfirm relations. Collective actions are the result of explicit and voluntary cooperative behaviours able to offer to the firms involved economies that differ from the normal economies of proximity because of excludability and compensation mechanisms (Di Tommaso and Rabellotti, 1999).

Economies associated with collective actions are the competitive factors of more complex arrangements such as the Italian industrial districts, where small and medium-size firms clustered together have clearly developed the capacity to compete at the global level (Bianchi, 1995).

Table 8.1   Localisation and agglomeration dynamics. What do firms look for?

	Advantages
1. Place-specific geographic endowments	• availability of natural resources; • availability of raw materials; • urban facilities; • infrastructures (ports, railways, etc.); • knowledge (universities, research centres).
2. Other firms (proximity and interaction)	• local specialised labour market; • specialised suppliers of goods and services; • knowledge spillovers; • collective action.

4.   BIOTECH CLUSTERS

In the case of biotech, are place-specific geographic endowments still relevant? Is spatial proximity a central aspect? Are collective actions important in the case of biotech? If so, will physical proximity either result from or encourage greater interfirm relationships? In other words, is it also true that biotech firms tend to cluster because they need to establish cooperative relations with other similar or complementary firms? The answer is not so intuitive because in principle, given the intangible nature of biotech inputs and outputs, and given the new way in which people can interact, one might hypothesise that these firms might function just as well if they were located at opposite ends of the earth from one another! To try to answer these questions we look first at the life-cycle of firms in this particular industry.

The Life-cycle of Biotechnology Firms

One can make useful inferences about the location of biotechnology firms by understanding how these firms are first created. Biotechnology firms are frequently started as spin-offs from universities. Biotech start-ups represent the combined talents of a scientist, a source of capital and management expertise. It is common, especially in the US, that a venture capitalist will act as a catalyst, searching for academic scientists who have ideas that are ready for product development. If some are found, negotiations are held that may result in the creation of a new enterprise. With this scenario, it is not unusual for the newly created firm to be located close to the university where the scientist continues his or her faculty association[6] (Kenney, 1986; Prevezer, 1995; Audretsch and Stephan, 1996; Zucker, Darby and Armstrong, 1998; Breschi, 2000; McMillan et al., 2000).

   Thus, spatial proximity is still a relevant concept. However, the most relevant object of proximity in the case of biotech is universities as sources of knowledge. Firms are often born close to universities as a result of spin-off processes. The aggregate result is that one would expect firms to cluster together around universities and research centres (Senker, 1998; Swann et al., 1998; Zucker, Darby and Armstrong, 1998; European Commission, 2001). But one may also suggest that this is just one of the issues that explain the biotech clustering process. Entrepreneurs may look also for advantages linked to the proximity of other similar and complementary firms: a local market for skills (i.e. students and professors), a local specialised supply of goods and services (i.e. venture capital, telecommunication), and a common pool of knowledge. Moreover, one may also suggest that clusters offer further advantages thanks to the potential development of collective actions (among universities, firms, and other relevant actors such as hospitals and laboratories) and that these advantages are clearly perceived by entrepreneurs.

The experience of hi-tech clusters has also demonstrated the importance of capital. Frequently the principals in the firm are paid little in cash, but are paid mainly in equity interest in the venture. Other costs, however, are real and must be met by actual cash. Venture capital is a useful mechanism for raising this initial capital, because it tends to be non-bureaucratic and geographically mobile (Florida and Kenney, 1988). As the start-up firm matures, its need for capital continues to grow, and the likelihood of scientific success increases. As the needs for capital continue, the type of funding often shifts from highly speculative venture capital to more public funding, sometimes through an Initial Public Offering, in which the firm 'goes public' by selling shares on a recognised stock exchange (Smith and Florida, 1998).

It could be argued that clusters of knowledge-based firms may constitute a context that is especially well-suited to the venture capital market. The hypothesis is intuitive: as Marshall noted a long time ago, in an agglomeration of specialised firms, knowledge is in the air. This Marshallian atmosphere may reduce information asymmetries among the actors offering and demanding credit. A venture capitalist located within (or anyway familiar with) the cluster has preferential access to specific information, such as the reputation of the entrepreneurs. Moreover, venture capitalists looking for the best projects, at the national and international levels, may save search costs because they know that they will find top-ranking projects in a particular locality where specialised firms have clustered together (see for example the Silicon Valley case). When they focus on a particular cluster they have the chance to compare, at lower cost, alternative projects because of the proximity of a plurality of similar firms operating in the same field.

However, it has to be noted that different models of biotechnology clusters exist. The existence of different modalities of firms' origins suggests that localisation dynamics may follow different paths and that factors underlying biotechnology clusters may not be identical everywhere (CENSIS, 2000). While in the US and to some extent in the UK, biotechnology start-ups have been founded by the private conjoint initiative of 'entrepreneurs–scientists' and venture capitalists as a spin-off from academic research, in other countries new biotech firms have been founded as spin-offs from large pharmaceutical and chemical corporations (i.e. in Italy)[7] or as publicly supported initiatives in particular areas (i.e. in French technopoles).[8] Therefore, in trying to build a framework to test different hypotheses on biotech firm location, several localisation factors must be taken into account.

5.   HYPOTHESES ON WHERE BIOTECH FIRMS LOCATE

According to traditional theories of firm location, one could hypothesise that biotech firms would locate near population centres, where the labour force is most abundant and hiring the easiest. This is a sort of null-hypothesis because it says little about the particular nature of high-tech industries and firms. It merely suggests that biotech firms locate where workers are, just as other firms tend to do, at least where there are no particular natural factors (ports, highways, natural resources, etc.) altering the picture.

It is possible to identify more specific hypotheses on localisation of biotech firms. Firstly, rather than being distributed randomly, according to the population, biotech firms might be localised near urban centres. Urban areas are often cited as a preferred location for high-technology firms. An urban location offers small high-tech start-ups the presence of several types of both public and private services, and the possibility to be in close contact with their final market (Camagni, 1992).

In addition, firms may be spin-offs, or derivatives, of existing firms. An example is the pharmaceutical industry, which derives from the chemical industry. In fact, prior to World War II, pharmaceuticals were little more than purified chemicals produced and sold to pharmacists who compounded them and packaged them into forms that could be taken conveniently by patients, according to physicians' orders. If one looks at pharmaceutical firms in the US today, one sees that many of them are located in the mid-Atlantic states, especially New Jersey and Delaware, where the chemical industry first grew in the nineteenth century. Taking this as a model, one might hypothesise that biotechnology firms are spin-offs from pharmaceutical firms, and would therefore tend to be located near them. But this model of biotech firm development fails to capture the essential differences in scientific basis and paradigm between pharmaceuticals and biotechnology. A closer observation of biotech firms shows that they grew independent of pharmaceutical firms, though a welter of mergers in recent years has brought them together (Ernst & Young, 2001). These linkages illustrate another fact in the development of biotech firms, and they also illustrate the needs of pharmaceutical firms. Biotech firms need scientific expertise, capital, and management skills to grow. But once products are nearing the end of the research and testing phases, a new set of expertise is needed: marketing. Marketing is more than advertising, it is working with a network of sales personnel who are connected to medical decision-makers: physicians and health plans. This infrastructure capability has, of necessity, been assembled over decades by traditional pharmaceutical companies, but is unlikely to be in place in biotechnology firms. In addition, major pharmaceutical firms are eager to stock their product 'pipeline' with new products. The way to accomplish firm objectives in both industries is, of course, to forge relationships between pharmaceutical firms and biotechnology companies. These relationships take many forms, ranging from the simple exchange of marketing services in return for royalty payments, to outright mergers.[9] But the observation that biotechnology and pharmaceutical firms are often linked together does not imply that the former is a spin-off of the latter.[10]

Another hypothesis can be identified taking into account health care structures, such as hospitals, in which many research efforts are usually conducted, especially with respect to applied research and product testing. It is possible to consider hospitals and similar institutions as factors affecting location decisions of biotech firms.

An important consideration in the biotech industry is that it relies on information and uniquely skilled personnel – not a typical cross-section of worker skills. If so, then one might expect the biotech firm to locate near sources of scientifically-skilled personnel, perhaps near colleges or universities. This hypothesis might not be specific enough, however. Our life-cycle scenario suggests that the firm's initial key employer comes from a university or research institute, and the firm is likely to retain ties to that institution. At the beginning, the need is simple – that the person must retain the academic appointment in order to continue the line of basic research and to retain a salary while other compensation from the start-up firm is merely speculative ownership shares (Audretsch and Feldman, 1998; Zuker, Darby and Armstrong, 1998). But a university also provides other key scientific workers in the form of graduates or even graduate students. Thus a useful modification would be that biotech firms would locate near research-oriented universities and institutions, not near educational institutions in general.

6. TWO PERSPECTIVES ON BIOTECH FIRM LOCATION

To better understand the factors determining the location of high-technology firms, there are two perspectives that can be employed. We call the first the 'County Manager' view. This is the view used by regions as they attempt to attract high-technology firms. There are various policy instruments at the disposal of a regional government. Examples include property tax concessions, subsidies for construction costs, relaxation of planning or environmental regulations, and construction of highways, rail lines, Internet links, and other utility services. All of these have been used in the past to attract firms to particular cities, counties, or regions.

A second perspective on the location decision is called the 'Entrepreneurial View'. This is the perspective of the scientist–entrepreneur who feels ready to begin a start-up company and is deciding where to locate the firm. The

Entrepreneurial View focuses on things that are key to the decision-maker, including the intellectual, legal and bureaucratic environment for a start-up. The two views overlap, of course, as the entrepreneur certainly needs to consider the cost of establishing a firm in a particular area and proximity to other factors (including proximity to other firms). But the entrepreneur is also likely to consider his or her present employment situation, including the faculty appointment at a research-oriented university or institute. A major consideration for the scientist–entrepreneur is the ease with which the university allows off-campus initiatives.

Tests of location can employ multiple regression analyses, with the local area the unit of observation. The dependent variable will be the number of firms within each given area, and the independent variables will be the existence of various factors outlined above: highways, Internet facilities, colleges and universities, and so forth. Some of these variables will be dichotomous variables, and others, like tax rates, may be expressed as continuous variables. The results of this analysis will be the extent to which each included independent variable determines the number of firms located within an area.

A complementary analytical approach is a statistical simulation study. A simulation is done in which biotech firms are allocated geographically according to the strength of each variable (or a set of variables) in question: population for example. One then compares the distance between each *actual* biotech firm and a matching *simulated* firm. The aggregate distance for *all* firms is a measure of how well the simulation hypothesis describes the location of biotech firms. The simulation is then redone for another hypothesis, according to the location of colleges and universities, for example. The simulation model that produces the lower aggregate distance between the simulated and the actual firms is the best.

7.   CONCLUSIONS

The purpose of this chapter is to present an analytical approach to identifying policy instruments that will encourage development of high-technology industries in areas or countries. It appears that understanding the origins of high-tech firms is important in developing policies that promote their location. And if our hypotheses on the evolution of the biotech clustering process are correct, specific policy considerations are indicated. Clustering is an evolutionary phenomenon where centripetal and centrifugal forces may emerge. In this scenario, policies able to manage the evolution of the process might become necessary. Proximity advantages may encourage cluster development but free rider problems may also cause a delocalisation process. Proximity economies are important but what matters is the development of collective actions among the different actors involved in the production processes. Collective actions are very fragile mechanisms and policy intervention may prevent or correct undesirable failures.

If our depiction of the life-cycle of biotech firms is accurate, and is consistent with the model by which firms cluster together in proximity to research universities and institutes, an important policy instrument is strongly suggested: the creation of a network of strong research-oriented universities that are structured so as to support and even promote spin-off high-tech firms.

Better analysis of the origins of high-technology firms in various industries is needed, because these considerations are important from both a macro and a micro perspective. The macro view considers national or regional policies that governments can undertake to promote development of high-tech industries, including biotechnology. Usually, however, these macro policies are insufficient, in themselves, especially if one sees as crucial decisions by individual scientist–entrepreneurs to begin firms whose intellectual origins lie within universities and research institutes. Lessons must be learned from universities with particularly successful histories of encouraging spin-off activities.

Not only will policy instruments and considerations discussed in this chapter be applicable for biotechnology firms, but they are undoubtedly useful for other high-technology industries as well, including aerospace, computer chips, software and telecoms. All of these industries are knowledge-intensive and are likely to experience the same life-cycle as that described for biotech firms. In fact, one can observe that many high-tech industrial clusters, including many of the most prominent ones in Europe and the US, are clusters of firms in many different industries. There appear to be common factors linking firms together and forming clusters, even in different industries. We have suggested that one common feature is the need to be close to sources of knowledge.

NOTES

*   This chapter has benefited from the discussion with a number of colleagues from the Ferrara Health Industry Policy Project, including Patrizio Bianchi, Lauretta Rubini, Daniele Paci and Sandrine Laboury. We would like also to acknowledge the helpful comments from participants to the Fourth L'institute–Ferrara Graduate School in Industrial Development Policy (September 2001) and to the Second L'institute–Milwaukee Workshop (July 2001) where preliminary versions of this chapter were presented. Although this chapter is the result of a long-run collaboration among the two authors, Di Tommaso has primarily contributed to Sections 2, 3 and 4 while Schweitzer has primarily worked on Sections 5 and 6.

1.   Minimisation of transportation costs related to the distance from markets or from raw materials represents the core of traditional location theories, such as in Weber (1909) and in Von Thünen (1910).

2.   The literature on 'intangible resources' is extensive and rapidly growing. See, among others, Lundvall (1992); Von Hippel (1994); Hodgson (1999); Nooteboom (2000); OECD (2000; 2001); Malmberg and Maskell (2001).

3. Myriad definitions of biotechnology exist. For a comprehensive analysis of this aspect see Kenney (1986), Zucker, Darby and Armstrong (1998) and Buiatti (2001). We use a narrow definition of biotechnology as the industrial use of recombinant DNA and cell fusion and novel bioprocessing techniques to obtain products with applications for human health care. In doing so biotechnology can be considered as an industry, rather than a mere 'enabling set of technologies' (DTI, 1999), composed of specialised firms known as 'dedicated biotechnology firms' or DBFs (European Commission, 2000), which have entered the sector with the explicit aim of exploiting the new technologies of life sciences. In Ernst & Young's biotechnology annual report, this industry is called the 'entrepreneurial life science sector' (Ernst & Young, 2000 and 2001).

4. The 'dematerialization of productive processes' (Hodgson, 1999) and the pervasive role of knowledge in the modern system of production has led many economists to use the term 'knowledge-based economy' to describe the current state of the economy (Dunning, 2000; Cooke, 2001; OECD, 2001; Malmberg and Maskell, 2001).

5. In the new system of knowledge-intensive capitalism, intelligence and intellectual labour replace physical labour as the fundamental source of value and profit (Hodgson, 1999). Furthermore, the bases of industrial competitiveness have been shifted from static price competition to dynamic improvement, benefiting firms that are more able to innovate and create knowledge rather than their competitors (Malmberg and Maskell, 2001). Therefore the key resources in the new economy are the capacity to innovate, to create, to absorb and to manage new knowledge (Lundvall, 1992; Feldman, 1994; Nonaka, 1995; Nooteboom, 2000; Cooke, 2001).

6. The linkages between companies and scientists require a deeper analysis. In fact, the geographical dimension of the links between a scientist and a biotech firm should be shaped by the role played by the scientists: they can facilitate knowledge transfer, or signal the quality of the firm's research to both capital and resource markets, but they can also help to create the scientific direction of the company (Audretsch and Stephan, 1996; Stephan and Everhart, 1998). In addition it is possible to note that younger scientists are more likely to be involved with a local rather than a non-local firm (Audretsch and Stephan, 1996; Audretsch, 1999). Finally Audretsch and Stephan (1996) provided evidence that well-known scientists (i.e. authors of numerous publications and Nobel Prize winners) are more likely to be involved in non-local linkages with biotech firms.

7. Orsenigo (2001) has described the unsuccessful case of Lombardy in creating a competitive area for the development of biotechnology firms.

8. The French approach to the development of high-tech industries has been traditionally characterised by a strong presence of the public sector and it is sometimes termed 'high-tech Colbertism' (CENSIS, 2000). On French technopoles see also France Biotech (2000).

9. In the literature it has been widely stressed that biotechnology firms and pharmaceutical companies have complementary assets. In fact, new biotech firms lack competence and experience in clinical testing and in other procedures related to product approval, as well as marketing competencies and financial resources. Such competencies and resources are available to large established pharmaceutical companies, which nevertheless lack flexibility and specialisation to adopt the new technological paradigm quickly (Senker, 1998; Pammolli and Riccaboni, 2000; Malerba and Orsenigo, 2001; Mytelka and Pellegrin, 2001).

10. However, as Breschi et al. (2001) have observed, Italian biotechnology firms have been founded mainly as spin-offs from large chemical and pharmaceutical companies, rather than from research institutions. Therefore it can be relevant to include this hypothesis among the possible factors underlying biotech clusters.

REFERENCES

Acs, Z.J. (ed.) (1998), *Regional Innovation, Knowledge and Global Change*, London and New York: Pinter.

Audretsch, D.B. (1998), 'Agglomeration and the location of innovation activity', *Oxford Review of Economic Policy*, **XIV**(2), 18–29.

Audretsch, D.B. (1999), 'Knowledge spillovers and the role of small firms', Paper presented at the International Conference 'Knowledge Spillovers and the Geography of Innovation: A Comparison of National Systems of Innovation', Saint-Etienne, 1–2 July.

Audretsch, D.B. and Feldman, M. (1996), 'R&D spillovers and the geography of innovation and production', *American Economic Review*, **86**(3), 630–40.

Audretsch, D.B. and Stephan, P.E. (1996), 'Company–scientist locational links: the case of biotechnology, *American Economic Review*, **86**(3), 641–52.

Becattini, G. (1989) 'Sectors and/or districts: some remarks on the conceptual foundations of industrial economics', in E. Goodman and J. Bamford (eds), *Small Firms and Industrial Districts in Italy*, London: Routledge.

Bianchi, P. (1995), 'Industrial districts and industrial policy: the new European perspective', *Journal of Industry Studies*, **3**, 16–29.

Breschi, S. (2000), 'La geografia delle innovazioni tecnologiche', in F. Malerba (ed.), *Economia dell'Innovazione*, Rome: Carocci, pp. 343–72.

Breschi, S., Lisson, F. and Orsenigo, L. (2001), 'Success and failure in the department of biotechnology clusters: the case of Lombardy', in G. Fuchs (ed.), *Comparing the Development of Biotechnology Clusters*, New York: Harwood Academic Publishers.

Buiatti, M. (2001), *Le biotecnologie*, Bologna: Il Mulino.

Camagni, R. (1992), *Economia urbana*, Rome: Carocci.

CENSIS – Forum per la Ricerca Biomedica (2000), *Cultura scientifica e ricerca biotecnologica*, http://www.censis.it/censis/ricerche/2000/frbiomedica/, July 2001.

Cooke, P. (2001), 'Regional innovation systems, clusters, and the knowledge economy', *Industrial and Corporate Change*, **10**(4), 945–74.

Di Tommaso, M.R. and Rabellotti, R. (1999), *Efficienza collettiva e cluster di imprese: oltre l'esperienza italiana*, Bologna: Il Mulino.

Di Tommaso, M.R. and Rubini, L. (2002), *Policies for the Development of Health Industry*, Proceedings of the Second Edition of the Ferrara Health Industry Policy Forum, Ferrara: Gabriele Corbo Editore.

Di Tommaso, M.R. and Schweitzer, S.O. (2000), 'The health industry. More than just containing costs', Paper presented at the Health Industry Policy Forum, Ferrara, 21–22 May.

DTI (Department of Trade and Industry UK) (1999), 'Biotechnology clusters', Report no.1888, http://biotechknowledge.com/showlibsp.php3?uid=1.

Dunning, J.H. (ed.) (2000), *Regions, Globalization and the Knowledge-based Economy*, New York: Oxford University Press.

Ernst & Young (2000), *Convergence: Ernst & Young's Biotechnology Industry Report, Millennium Edition*, New York: Ernst & Young LLP.

Ernst & Young (2001), *Integration: Ernst & Young's Eighth Annual European Life Science Report*, http://www.ey.com/global/gcr.nfs/international/life_science_-_Library.

European Commission (2000), *European Bio-Entrepreneurs. Examples of Start-up Companies in the Biotech Sector*, Luxembourg: Office for Official Publications of the European Communities.

European Commission (2001), *European Competiveness Report 2001*, Luxembourg: Office for Official Publications of the European Communities.

Feldman, M.P. (1994), *The Geography of Innovation*, Boston: Kluwer Academic Publishers.

Florida, R. and Kenney, M. (1988), 'Venture capital, high technology and regional development', *Regional Studies*, **22**(1), 33–48.

France Biotech (2000), *Biotechnologies in France*, http://www.france-biotech.org.

Hodgson, G.M. (1999), *Economics and Utopia*, New York: Oxford University Press.

Kenney, M. (1986), *Biotechnology: The University–Industrial Complex*, Yale: Yale University Press.

Krugman, P. (1991), *Geography and Trade*, Cambridge, MA: MIT Press.

Krugman, P. (1995), *Development, Geography and Economic Theory*, Cambridge, MA: MIT Press.

Lösch, A. (1940), *The Economics of Location*, Jena: Fisher.

Lundvall, B.A. (1992), *National Systems of Innovation. Towards a Theory of Innovation and Interactive Learning*, London: Pinter Publishers.

Malerba, F. and Orsenigo, L. (2001), 'Innovation and market structure in the dynamics of the phyarmaceutical industry and biotechnology: towards a history friendly model', Paper presented at the DRUID Nelson and Winter Conference, Aalborg, 12–15 June.

Malmberg, A. and Maskell, P. (2001), 'The elusive concept of localization economies – towards a knowledge-based theory of spatial clustering', Paper presented at the AAG Annual Conference 'Industrial clusters revisited: innovative places or uncharted spaces?', New York, 27 Febuary–3 March.

Marshall, A. (1890), *Principles of Economics*, London: Macmillan; Italian version (1977), *Principi di Economia*, Torino: UTET.

McMillan, G.S., Narin, F. and Deeds, D.L. (2000), 'An analysis of the critical role of public science in innovation: the case of biotechnology', *Research Policy*, **29**(1), 1–8.

Mytelka, L.K. and Pellegrin, J. (2001), 'Can SMEs survive? Static vs dynamic externalities in the French biotechnology industry', Paper presented at the DRUID Conference, Aalborg, 12–15 June.

Nonaka, H. Takeuci (1995), *The Knowledge Creating Company*, New York: Oxford University Press.

Nooteboom, B. (2000), *Learning and Innovation in Organizations and Economies*, Oxford: Oxford University Press.

OECD (2000), 'Science, technology and innovation in the new economy', Policy brief, September, http://www.oecd.org.

OECD (2001), *OECD Science, Technology and Industry Scoreboard. Towards a Knowledge-based Economy*, Paris: OECD Publications.

Orsenigo, L. (2001), 'The (failed) development of a biotechnology cluster: the case of Lombardy', *Small Business Economics*, **XVII**, 77–92.

Pammolli, F. and Riccaboni, M. (2000), 'Technological competencies in networks of innovators. The case of biopharmaceuticals', mimeo.

Prevezer, M. (1995), 'The dynamics of industrial clustering in biotechnology', *Small Business Economics* (9), 255–71.

Saxenian, A.L. (1994), *Regional Advantage: Cultural and Competition in Silicon Valley and Route 128*, Cambridge, MA: Harvard University Press.

Senker, J. (ed.) (1998), *Biotechnology and Competitive Advantage. Europe's Firms and the US Challenge*, Cheltenham, UK and Northampton, MA, USA: Edward Elgar.

Smith, D.F. and Florida, R. (1998), 'Venture capital's role in regional innovation systems: historical perspective and recent evidence', in Z.J. Acs (ed.), *Regional Innovation, Knowledge and Global Change*, London and New York: Pinter.

Stephan, P.E. and Everhart, S.S. (1998), 'The changing rewards to science: the case of biotechnology', *Small Business Economics*, **X**, 141–51.

Swann, G.M., Prevezer, M. and Stout, D. (1998), *The Dynamics of Industrial Clustering: International Comparisons in Computing and Biotechnology*, Oxford and New York: Oxford University Press.

Von Hippel, E. (1994), 'Sticky information and the locus of problem solving: implications for innovation', *Management Science* (40), 429–39.

Von Thünen, J.H. (1910), *Der Isolierte Staat in Beziehung auf Landwirtschaft und Nationaloekonomie*, Jena: Fisher; English Version, *Isolated State* (1966), Oxford and New York: Pergamon Press.

Walsh, V. (1993), 'Demand, public policy and innovation in biotechnology', *Science and Public Policy* (June), 138–56.

Weber, A. (1909), *Theory of the Location of Industries*, Chicago: University of Chicago Press.

Zucker, L.G., Darby, M.R. and Armstrong, J. (1998), 'Geographically localized knowledge: spillovers or markets?', *Economic Inquiry*, **XXXVI** (January), 65–86.

9. Industrial clusters and districts in the new economy: some perspectives and cases

Marco Bellandi[*]

1. INTRODUCTION

'Industrial clusters' and 'industrial districts' seem to offer an interesting model for local and regional development in many parts of the developed and less developed world. They prosper where international markets are open to trade. However, the progress of globalisation and of the connected diffusion of new information and communication technologies seems to raise important problems. This chapter presents a condensed summary of concepts and questions related to (territorial) clusters of specialised production activities (more briefly, what might be called 'industrial clusters' or simply 'clusters'). It also addresses local development in this context.

Section 2 recalls some general issues illustrated by specific types of cluster, namely those centred in Italian industrial districts in the last half-century. Section 3 goes into the details of some preliminary definitions concerning clusters and local development. Section 4 tries to expand on the problems raised by the new economy. Section 5 applies the previous remarks to some aspects of debates concerning cluster development in a particular case; it concentrates on South-eastern Wisconsin.

2. SOME SUGGESTIONS FROM ITALIAN EXPERIENCE

Large Companies and Industrial Districts

Among most industrial, development and business economists, the starting-point for interpretation is the reference to a rational economic organisation and to a path for industrialisation defined in the leading capitalist economies, which must be imitated by backward or laggard economies. The growing role and visibility of large firms in the first half of the twentieth century had a pivotal importance in defining this point. The large firms are seen as the engine of the combination of capital and science. The scientific organisation of the production and distribution processes is defined in the R&D laboratories and in the marketing divisions, generally resulting in new opportunities for internal economies of scale and scope. Followers can then imitate the technological frontier, since science creates models easy to reproduce. Some other intuitions are connected to this first one, for example: a) the working of the economic system in general, and particularly its development models and its forms of industrial organisation, may be defined in a first approximation without explicit geographical qualifications; b) the small firm in a modern industrial economy may have either an interstitial role or a role dependent upon the strategies of the large companies. It is a 'top-down' approach to economic and regional development.

In the 1970s these views were also dominant among the studies of Italian economy and society. However, in those same years several 'surprises' appeared in the macroeconomic evidence, pointing to several cases of successful development of populations of small- to medium-sized specialised firms. Such populations often appeared to be largely independent from the activities of large companies, while embedded in a local context allowing a rich reproduction of trust relations, entrepreneurial attitudes and complementary specialised competencies.

Industrial Districts and External Economies

Prosperity in populations of relatively small and specialised firms is not exclusive to Italian experience. Indeed, see for example, the discussion of Japan by Cowling and Tomlinson in this volume, and also Schweitzer and Di Tommaso in the previous chapter. Nor is such prosperity new in the history of contemporary industry. However, within Italian experience, the most discussed are the cases in which:

- a set of connected industrial and tertiary (private and public) activities is the main core of economic and social life of a local system, that is, of an area where a community of people lives and works, with a great deal of persistently overlapping experiences;
- within such a set, several specialised firms, largely local, small- to medium-sized, and independent, realise complementary and substitute products and services; some products are largely sold on external markets, and define the industrial image and the economic standing of the area;
- the local firms are largely connected by way of both market and non-market[1] mechanisms.

A local system that complies with such inner, intermediate structural characteristics is an 'industrial district'.

Granted an apparatus of modern civil and commercial law, given an open
space of mobility for persons and tangible and intangible goods, then the space
of competitive advantage for district-like forms of organisation is connected to
worlds of flexible specialisation and worlds of diffused innovation. According
to current understanding, in flexible specialisation worlds, markets are characterised by a demand for diffused and variable customisation. The extension
of the demand does not depend only upon low prices or advertising games, but
also upon the capacity of the producers to explore and promote differences
between consumers, and to adapt to them with timely customisation.
Technologies have increasing returns for processes of production, which,
however, can be broken down into a multiplicity of specialised activities, operated by a population of interacting specialised companies. In the worlds of
innovation, the market demand for single types of innovative products is by
definition more generic, less rooted in a well-specified set of preferences; the
single processes of production are less articulated in specialised activities.
However, what matters is that the development of innovation asks for merging
sets of different productive knowledge that rarely can be controlled and
managed by any single company.

The combination of the inner intermediate conditions and of the basic
external ones defines a space of competitive advantages that manifest themselves in terms of economies of scale and scope, partially external to the single
firms but internal to the local system. Such economies are defined by two
levels of performance. The first is the firm level, where value, that is, differential economies on costs or in access to market, are realised. The second is
the system level, whereby the elements of the inner intermediate structure are
confirmed by economic choices. Economies of specialisation are clearly relevant at the firm level. The sources of such economies are the well-known principles of industrial efficiency and increasing returns, which can be potentially
active for a decentralised system in certain conditions, for example in the presence of the exterior basic characteristics of global context recalled before.
They are the principle of multiples, the principle of pooled reserves, and the
economy of large machines and large transactions.[2]

Other types of external economies, the economies of learning and creativity,
are directly relevant both at the first and at the second level of performance. They
help the reproduction of appropriate sets of skills and business capacities, their
matching in the local organisations, and the emergence of novelties in products,
capacities and technology (Becattini, 1990). Innovations, especially incremental
innovations, spring from the interaction of a rich set of original approaches to a
delimited field of business and production activities – approaches that are embedded into the life (educational, working, etc.) experiences of large groups of

producers and traders. Decentralised industrial creativity can be fruitfully applied to enlarging the capacity of adaptation and customisation of teams of companies, in markets such as those referred to before. Some successful innovations may also have indirect positive effects. For example, when new nuclei of productive knowledge are inserted within the district, consequently enlarging its inner structural multiplicity, and opening new fields of market activity for local specialised firms.

The realisation of district economies needs the solution of incentive and coordination problems. A coherent integration of the complementary specialised activities of independent firms and teams of firms demands many informational and normative goods that are complementary to the workings of markets for intermediate products. They are goods such as technical standards and jargon, assessment of reputation capitals and types of sanctions for incorrect behaviour, basic professional formation and training for locally specialised skills, diffusion of general information about technology and world markets, environmental safeguards, etc. As far as the population of specialised firms is concerned, they are local public goods (or local multilateral external effects). If they are not governed, externalities in the markets of labour, of intermediate products and of production services arise.

A type of solution, possibly consistent with a high degree of realisation of the external economies, lies in the supply of these goods not by markets, but through the collective action of the district's agents. Organisations of different types may operate jointly, with tiers that also include focused types of public intervention: such as when public bodies for formal training sustain the production of new competencies inside the system according to some standard. A similar solution can be envisaged for the supply of a specific industrial infrastructure.

Some progressive features of the inner social structure help an effective supply of local public goods. The importance of a set of basic structural conditions in the local context is confirmed by some suggestions taken from the 'Italian laboratory'. They are common conditions in the most dynamic areas, like the importance of the accumulated reserves of complementary technical and transaction competencies, the redundancy of savings and time for productive purposes, and the diffusion of entrepreneurial aptitudes and market rules of trust. Conversely, the strong embeddedness of the principal industrial activities pulls the reproduction processes of such 'local factors' and activates their reserves to a high degree. However, the endogenous process can be interrupted by radical challenges, from the global side, or from the emergence of local faults or deviations. The role of strategic conduct or of random events for the long-run vitality of the local system comes under a clearer light at this point. When they are reproduced by the consistent economic behaviour of local (economic and political) agents, such local factors constitute a 'local social capital'.[3]

The Two Engines of Italian Industrial Strength in the 1990s

According to a recent synthesis proposed by G. Becattini (2000), Italian economic growth in the last decades has been pulled by 'two types of industrial engine', each with its own logic. One engine is centred on large companies; the other engine is the industrial district, characterised by a population of small- to medium-sized specialised firms (see also Becattini and Rullani, 1996; Brusco, 1996; Russo, 1996).

The clearest examples of large companies' pulling development are found in areas where a large part of the employment is concentrated in one or a few big branches or headquarters, and where the branches or headquarters are the focus of the local social and economic life ('company towns'; in this volume, see also Cowling and Tomlinson on the Japanese case). Here, processes of local change depend heavily on the strategies of the large companies' decision-makers.[4] Hidden cases are represented by local systems whose economy depends strictly on the demand, the supply, or the network organisation of one or a few large companies that have no big plants in the area, if any plants at all. Large companies also have 'arenas', that is, areas in which they do not have a clearly dominant role, but where they play market and innovation games with other players, private and public, more or less embedded in the area. Examples of such arenas may be the great dynamic cities and the strong industrial districts.

A rough way to assess the diffusion of different types of areas of industrial activity follows a multiple step methodology. The first step is the empirical identification of proxies of the local systems in which the country can be divided. The second step is the classification of the local systems according to the relative importance of manufacturing industries in terms of employees. A third step is the classification according to the relative employment importance of plants of different sizes. Other steps follow, which are not introduced here (see Sforzi, 1989; Brusco and Paba, 1997; De Propris, 2000).

Concerning the first step, I would only recall that in Italy the identification of 'local systems' has been adopted by the Italian National Institute of Statistics, Istat (see Sforzi, 1997). It is based on data concerning daily commuting from home to job location. The data are collected at the municipality (*comune*) level within the national Census, every ten years. An algorithm, working on these data, looks for sets of contiguous municipalities. Each set has to show a high degree of self-containment of the (sum of the) commuting inflows and outflows based on the municipalities of the same set (more than 75 per cent). The attribution of each municipality to one set or the other, among the contiguous ones, is regulated by the maximisation of the inclusion degree. These 'local systems of labour' (the Istat – Sforzi terminology) belong to the family of the travel-to-job areas and of the daily urban systems.

After some early experimentation, the local system of labour approach has been extensively applied in assessing the role of industrial districts over recent decades (Brusco and Paba, 1997; Signorini, 2001). Another recent application concerns the comparison among the district areas and the large companies' areas. Data collected in the 1991 Census and in the 1996 Intermediate Census have been elaborated to give a picture of these types of local system.[5] The result is the partition of the Italian local systems in different classes. The main distinction is between manufacturing (MLS) and non-manufacturing local systems (NMLS): the first ones show a proportion of manufacturing employment in total (non-agricultural) employment higher than the national average; the opposite sign characterises the second systems.

An important classification among manufacturing local systems is based on the relative weight of employment in small, medium and large plants. The definition of the size changes according to different authors. In Sforzi (1997), manufacturing local systems of small firms are those in which the proportion of employment in manufacturing plants with 1–49 employees is higher than the national average (and locally prevalent, in the case of comparison with other classes). In manufacturing local systems of small- to medium-sized firms, the plant size is in the 50–249 range. In manufacturing local systems of large firms, the plant size is 250 employees and over. In Solinas and Baroni (2001) the small firm system (MLSSF) corresponds to a range of 1–99 employees in manufacturing plants; the medium firm one (MLSMF) corresponds to the range 100–499; the large firm system (MLSLF) corresponds to plants of 500 employees and over.[6]

Large plants are the field of large companies. Medium-sized plants are frequently, but not always, the expression of production decentralisation by larger firms. The manufacturing local systems of small firms (and those of small- to medium-sized firms, in Sforzi's classification) have a large but not perfect nor fixed overlapping with the identification of Italian industrial districts adopted in various case studies. Table 9.1, excerpted from the work of Solinas and Baroni, gives a few quantitative measures.

Such figures do not give, per se, an interpretation of what is the relative weight of the different industrial engines in Italy. Nor do we have an interpretation of the way in which the two engines combine positively or interfere negatively. However, considering the figures, the suggestion that in Italy large companies now have very few areas, and perhaps an increasing number of arenas, is quite clear. The relationship can also run the other way round. What is the meaning of a reduction of the central role of big plants in an area that maintains a strong manufacturing specialisation? It may be a case of concealing power, that is, of decentralising productive activity while keeping a decisive role in the area. But it could also be a case in which a decreasing local strength of the big firm gives way to the other engine of industrial development. Both cases have been reported and also observed in the past decades.

Table 9.1   Manufacturing employment by type of local system in Italy, 1991 and 1996

Type	1991				1996			Var.%
	Number of employees	Number of local systems	% of employment		Number of employees	Number of local systems	% of employment	Number of employees
MLSSF	1 840 638	187	35.2		1 743 807	193	35.9	−5.3
MLSMF	779 383	65	14.9		802 509	78	16.5	3.0
MLSLF	544 286	27	10.4		425 695	21	8.8	−21.8
NMLS	2 063 242	505	39.5		1 883 748	492	38.8	−8.7
Total	5 227 549	784	100.0		4 855 759	784	100.0	−7.1

Note: See text for the types of local systems.

Source: Elaboration by Solinas and Baroni (1997) from Census 1991, and Intermediate Census 1996, Istat.

A third case, that a deeper comparison between 1991 and 1996 suggests (Solinas and Baroni, 2001), is signalled by some local systems transiting from the 'small firm' status to the 'medium-sized firm' status. These may be the result either of an increasing local presence of external large companies, or of the increasing size of plants run by local firms, or both. Some case studies report the greater importance of such a phenomenon, and its association with an increasing extent of ownership ties among groups of firms, within the district and outside it, perhaps internationally (Dei Ottati, 1997; Corò and Rullani, 1998; Tessieri, 2000).

International Perspectives

The coexistence of the two types of industrial engine is not exclusive to Italy, even if Italy, among industrialised countries, is the case in which the 'district motor' has had in the last 30 years a role more clearly comparable to that of the 'large company motor'. The idea that district-like conditions may be associated with important opportunities for economic growth and local development has won the attention of many social scientists and policy-makers around the world. Debates on flexible specialisation and worlds of possibilities (Piore, 1990; Sabel and Zeitlin, 1997), regional worlds of production (Scott, 1988; Salais and Storper, 1997), post-Fordism (Amin and Thrift, 1994), innovative milieux (Maillat, 1998; Crevoisier, 1999), regional systems of innovation and regional governance (Braczyk, Cooke and Heidenreich, 1996) have expanded the 'Italian lesson' and have had a quite large resonance. In recent years, in particular, the contribution by Porter (1998) on clusters has had an important effect of diffusing the idea among business economists and practitioners in the USA and many other countries. Finally, research on the identification of local systems on conceptual grounds similar to those applied in Italy has developed in other countries, for example in Spain (Callejon and Costa-Campi, 1996; Costa-Campi and Viladecans-Marsal, 1998) and the UK (De Propris, 2000). See also Peoples in Chapter 7 of this volume, discussing the US.

3. INDUSTRIAL CLUSTERS AND LOCAL DEVELOPMENT

The productive core of an industrial district is represented, as we have recalled before, by a set of connected industrial and tertiary (private and public) activities, largely localised within the district, and run by different, more or less specialised, firms. Such a set is what nowadays is called a 'cluster' (or an 'industrial cluster').[7] Clusters have attracted the attention of industrial and business economists, since they represent an object for the application and development of concepts in the realms of the economics of industrial organisation and of business studies. Furthermore, clusters are easily found in many regional contexts, also outside the social and territorial conditions that have characterised Italian industrial districts in the last decades. Like in the Italian experiences, clusters in different contexts are often associated with the opportunity for pursuing paths of local development. In this section we try to make more explicit the main characteristics connected to the concept of cluster. Let us consider a set of related questions.

Why Talk of Clusters Instead of Firms Connected by Markets? Why Look for Clusters and Not for Industries or Sectors in a Region?

The cluster is made up of a network of economically independent agents, also connected by market exchanges, but fundamentally sharing non-market mechanisms of governance. These mechanisms are represented by trust within bilateral or team exchanges, and by collective action supporting the availability of specific public goods. Such goods are specific to the needs of the cluster and to the variable teams of agents operating in its context. The type of action here envisaged also seems to be fundamental in cyberspace, according to Shapiro and Varian (1999, p. 228):

> Many commentators have likened cyberspace to the Wild West, where old patterns of behavior no longer apply and everything is up for grabs. Perhaps, but the lone cowboy approach rarely works in the information age. Network economics and positive feedback make cooperation more important than ever. Most companies need to cooperate with others to establish standards and create a single network of compatible users. But as soon as the ink is dry on the standards agreement, these same companies shift gears and compete head to head for their share of the network. The term *coopetition* captures the tension between cooperation and competition prevalent in network industries.

The terms 'industry' and, especially, 'sector' are associated commonly with the idea of firms producing a set of similar products, using a set of similar inputs, and with a set of similar technological solutions. This idea is necessarily used in the statistical classifications of economic activities. However, when statistical sectors (or industries) are given a substantive meaning in empirical research (units of economic discourse and analysis), they imply a very rigid and static representation of the world of production. The term 'cluster' is instead attached to the idea of an evolving set of private and public activities, more or less specialised, complementary and substitutive, realising different but connected products and services. Each cluster generally has some vertical extension (input–output relations), but it also hosts horizontal relations (among activities realising similar products) and diagonal relations (different activities supplied by a common upstream activity, or supplying a common downstream activity). This set may constitute a rich field for different but interconnected entrepreneurial projects.

The sector representation takes the mass production world, with homogeneous products and vertical integrated companies, as a polar model; companies are castles of industrial rationality enacting their plans upon territories and the human beings. The cluster representation is connected to worlds of production where the division of labour develops rapidly and in differentiated, unexpected ways. Sets of economic and social projects evolve together, taking different and changing organisational forms. Note that a set of activities led by the strategy of a large company, perhaps owning a big plant and managing the life of a set of nearby subcontracting firms, is not a cluster in the sense here suggested. It is just a business network, or a part of such a network.

Why do we Associate Industrial Cluster with Territorial Closeness or Embeddedness?

The economic space of single companies has no definite territorial boundaries. But industrial districts suggest that the sources of collective action and effects, defining a cluster, are more easily found when the human constituencies also share a common territory. Why? The answer has two levels, at least.

The industrial bases of territorial clustering
Considering the industrial organisation of the cluster, it is usual to point to the agglomeration effects connected with the territorial characteristics of some specific public goods (infrastructure, standards), and to the easy face-to-face contacts. On the basis of shared public goods, the exchange of complex or tacit information for innovative projects within teams of complementary producers, and the working of bandwagon effects among competitors, is made easier by face-to-face contacts. Of course, you also have to explain why and when these effects are important. We will come back to this point later.

The social bases
A large stream of literature on clusters, innovative milieux, industrial districts and regional innovation systems, is concerned with the sources of collective action and of innovative team action. There is a quite large agreement that those sources are to be identified with common attitudes towards trust and entrepreneurship, and by 'cognitive proximity', that is, shared knowledge on individual preferences and skills in production processes and organisation (see Dei Ottati, 1994; Johannisson et al., 1994; Dupuy and Gilly, 1999). Such conditions are more easily reproduced when the economic relations overlap with a dense network of social relations. The sharing of job, family, civic,

shopping and recreational experiences within a delimited territory by a delim-ited group of people is what defines a locality, taking Sugden and Wilson's terminology (in Chapter 1 of this volume). Such common life experiences make the emergence and reproduction of common attitudes easier. In some cases, the economic, social and political traditions of the locality and its productive structures guide the process towards trust, entrepreneurship and cognitive proximity in some fields of business activity: here the locality is an 'innovative milieu' (Maillat, 1998). The industrial district is a clear model of an innovative milieu.

How is Cluster Development Consistent with Local Development?

You could think of local development as a process of economic growth that happens in a locality as a consequence of convergence in the investment choices of footloose firms. The convergence may be explained by usual loca-tion theory: low transportation costs, cheap or skilled labour, low environ-mental costs, incentives by local authorities, etc. The experience of industrial districts suggests a richer significance: it is envisaged as a process of economic and social change, where cumulative investments in technical, human and social capital are led by the decisions of people living and work-ing in the locality. Local development in this richer sense may have windows of opportunity if it can employ some peculiar factor of long-term productivity. The overlapping of life experiences in the community represents precisely such a peculiar factor, when it takes the form of social relations supporting diffused trust, entrepreneurship and cognitive proximity in some fields of busi-ness activity. Furthermore, the reproduction of such an orientation on commu-nity experiences also demands an appropriate industrial organisation, giving appropriate rewards to trust and entrepreneurship, and supporting the evolving fabric of complementary nuclei of productive knowledge. The cluster structure is consistent, at least in general terms, with such requirements.

Various types of combination between locality and cluster structure can be considered. The classical one is the industrial district, where the locality is dominated by just one industrial cluster led by teams of small- to medium-sized companies, largely but not completely specialised in manufacturing goods. Two other types are the great city and the rural locality, hosting a vari-ety of more or less interconnected clusters. In the case of the cities, the clus-ters usually have a greater proportion of tertiary functions. In the case of the rural localities, the presence of activities connected to natural resource management is relatively more prominent. In all three cases, the clusters have a peculiar strength if the locality is an innovative milieu; and, vice versa, the locality may prosper as an innovative milieu if its clusters find spaces of competitive advantage in global markets.

In What Contexts do Clusters Emerge and Prosper?

The spaces of competitive advantage for clusters are, in general terms, those already defined for clusters rooted in industrial districts. Insofar as clusters do not reduce to business networks led by large companies, such spaces correspond to the worlds of flexible specialisation or of decentralised innovation (Section 2). Mass marketing, mass logistics, mass research, mass production may insert in such worlds in a more or less pervasive way, explaining a more or less strong role of large companies in various types of contemporary clusters and the diffusion of their local and trans-local business networks. In any way, given the existence of open spaces for clusters, their emergence and prosperity in a country or a region have to be explained by specific conditions or strategies.

What about strategies for promoting cluster development?

If cluster and local development would only be a question of location choices by footloose companies, appropriate public incentives would be able to manage and promote development in one single region. The flip side is that, if the administrative skills and the political willingness behind such incentives are diffused in many regions, then we can easily have adverse results. Regions will obtain a negative sum payoff, and positive payoff will accrue only to large companies able to play one region against the other. Furthermore we know that nowadays the access to large reserves of natural resources is no more a necessary source of location advantage for a region (see Argentina and Russia).

The picture is different, but not necessarily more encouraging, when we admit the possibility of cluster and local development in the enriched sense of the terms. Different approaches to the problem are present in the literature. One is 'naive constructivism', which extends the idea of managing cluster development to the constitution of the social relations and attitudes that support local development. A second approach is 'local determinism', or strong path dependency, according to which only localities and regions, endowed with a particular and non-transferable set of appropriate economic and civic traditions, may host virtuous cycles of local development. A third approach stands in the middle.

According to the third way, nuclei of cluster and local development are hidden in the life and job experiences of many localities and regions. Such hidden nuclei may coexist with vibrant clusters or with the networks of large trans-local firms[8] in developed industrial areas. Or, they may be important parts of the stagnant economy of underdeveloped areas. When windows of opportunity open in external markets, one hidden nucleus may flourish, becoming the core of an emerging cluster development. A successful coupling between hidden potentialities and external opportunities is in the empire of luck and uncertainty. However, strategies applied by locally embedded public or private agents may play an important role, making the difference. Cluster development demands collective action for the constitution of (and access to) specific public goods (specific standards, basic training, specific infrastructure, etc.). When present and embedded, leading agents possess the contextual knowledge and the charismatic capacity needed for pushing the community towards the building of the necessary public goods. Negative sum interlocal games are less probable because of the peculiarities of timing and context. Opportunities for interlocal specialisation and collaboration increase.

How do large (trans-local, footloose) companies interfere?

Different views coexist on the possible roles of large trans-local companies. According to the first one, such companies cannot have a positive impact on cluster and local development, but for the few lucky places (the global cities, or the global enclaves of large cities) where most of their central units seem to be based. Their location in other places is decided on the basis of the possibility of extracting local rich resources,[9] and of including them in their global networks. Or they may be attracted by the possibility of acquiring and retaining a relevant local market power.

According to a second view, the increasing importance of flexible specialisation and innovative worlds induces a transformation in the structure and strategies of many large trans-local firms. In order to boast competitive advantage in some spaces of such worlds, they tend to assume a 'heterarchical' structure, including a plurality of home bases and management cultures. They also try to embed many of their units in the economic and social relations of localities where cluster and local development is emerging or is already vibrant. When the embeddedness strategy is successful, reciprocal positive effects result, since the large trans-local companies benefit from and favour trans-local knowledge transfer.

The third view is that large companies may play both ways, according to various opportunities. Therefore, public targeting and antitrust policies, working also at the local level, are important in order to tilt the private corporate strategies towards positive feedback and embeddedness.[10]

4. SOME VIEWS RELATING CLUSTERS TO THE NEW ECONOMY

The bases above allow for some more specific applications. Two of them are envisaged in what follows here and in the next section. The first one concerns some general aspects of the relations between cluster and local development, the new economy, and globalisation. In this regard, let us recall a condensed set of statements concerning the main technological forces acting on industrial structure in the new economy (see the chapter by Nichols and that by Sugden and Wilson in this volume): a) The knowledge intensity of many production processes is increasing. b) The possibility of breaking down such processes in separate parts, organised by means of market mechanisms and digital transactions, is increasing. c) Standards for transferring knowledge through markets are more and more important and pervasive. d) High value added is concentrated in the more knowledge-intensive parts of production processes, like marketing, R&D, logistics, finance, standard setting. e) The more an activity is knowledge-intensive, the more it is characterised by internal economies of scale, since fixed costs are high and marginal costs are low. Such technological forces intrude in different ways in different types of industrial organisation.

How are Large Companies Affected?

The technological forces of the new economy have deep consequences for large companies. The opportunities for enlarging their trans-local structure increase, but the traditional advantages of internal vertical integration in terms of productive efficiency are reduced. Such advantages were based on the management of complex mass production processes through the hierarchical control of private sets of codified knowledge. In the new economy, instead, sets of codified knowledge are easily broken down and transferred. As a consequence, large companies tend to concentrate on a few core businesses, according to one of two main strategies or to a combination of them. The first strategy is proprietary control of the standards necessary for transferring knowledge. The second one is private control of methods for tapping and combining the information flowing in the digital nets (engines of research, brokers of e-markets, etc.). Even the large companies are not able to retain complete control of the resources needed for such strategies. In these cases they tend to make alliances with other big players or to extend their external networks of dependent suppliers and buyers (Shapiro and Varian, 1999, Chapter 8). However, it is useful to point out that these views on business strategy reflect just one type of tendency, based on the effects of the new ICT (information and communication technologies) on the transfer of codified knowledge. Sources of competitive advantage and strategies based on contextual knowledge do not necessarily vanish, even if their manifestation may be modified. A quotation from Porter (2001, p. 78) helps to make the point clearer:

> Basic Internet applications will become table stakes – companies will not gain any advantage from them. The more robust competitive advantage will arise instead from traditional strengths such as unique products, proprietary content, distinctive

physical activities, superior product knowledge, and strong personal service and relationships. Internet technology may be able to fortify those advantages, by tying a company's activities together in a more distinctive system, but it is unlikely to supplant them.

What are the Consequences for Industrial Clusters' Development, Structure and Prosperity? Do Trans-local Companies have a Different Role?

It is tempting to assume a business-like view, in order to outline the consequences of the expansion of the new and global relations on cluster development. Like large firms, clusters should: a) shed the activities with lower knowledge intensity; b) focus on some core activities with high knowledge intensity; c) increase the international alliances and networks, for taking advantage of the development of complementary activities in fields related to the core; d) assume a more concentrated but open industrial structure, since innovators in knowledge games have large fixed costs and low marginal costs.

The single consequences are plausible, but the overall picture could be misleading if 'Porter's point' is not considered. Firstly, the core of a developing cluster is represented, as we have recalled, by an evolving set of specialised and interconnected activities that constitute the field where cognitive proximity and common attitudes towards trust and entrepreneurship are applied. Within such a set, not all the strategic activities are necessarily high-tech or knowledge-intensive. Some of them may have a relatively high manufacturing or environmental (natural resources processing and management) content. Various conditions explain this connection. For example, the more operative activities may be the open laboratory where customisation and innovation projects are realised with the help of more knowledge-intensive activities.

Secondly, bigger and trans-local players embedded in the cluster are important, for sure. However, the changing population of smaller players maintains a non-secondary role, inasmuch as quick response, care for detail and diffused creativity should also be requested in the markets where a cluster is able to win a place. Here, the single players contribute to the high fixed cost of the cluster's set of public goods; but, the individual burden for covering general costs, and the private fixed costs of any single venture, need not be particularly high.

Thirdly, the new information and communication technologies (ICT) may have a role in strengthening the relationships internal to the cluster. Some aspects of the activities constituting the core may be routines that are easily transformed in specific standards, or pieces of codified information transferred by email, or portals for aggregating demands, etc. Transaction costs decrease, and the organisational effects are in general consistent with the decentralised structure of the cluster. These last possibilities may also be referred to Italian experiences running within clusters and industrial districts. Such experiences, which are investigated by various centres of economic studies and have the attention of big ICT suppliers, show both the abundance of possible applications and the difficulties of diffusion. Diffused adoption requests the contextual adaptation of codified knowledge and standards; this adaptation may be very expensive, and the decentralised structure of the cluster raises uncertainty about the return on investments made by ICT suppliers. Furthermore, the introduction of new ways of sharing knowledge may affect the local structure of market power, and this implies incentive and strategic problems that demand non-easy solutions (RUR-Censis, 2000; Micelli and Di Maria, 2000; Bramanti, 2001).

Is the Nexus Between Cluster Development and Local Development Modified? Do Localities Change Their Nature?

The considerations above could be modified if the nexus between cluster and local development suffered dramatic changes, as a result of the increasing opportunities for flows of information, persons and capital at the global level. Here two views are confronted. According to the first, the spatial model of the economic and social relations in the new economy is represented by a 'virtual' community, made of linkages among footloose, disembedded economic agents, building an international network within the global village. According to a second view, successful global networks are made up of linkages among agents who are embedded in different localities. Their network skills depend also on their experience of local networking, and their success in global networking depends not only on the excellence of their individuality, but also on their capacity to represent different stocks of local culture. In the second view, the local community is not substituted for the virtual community: they may be complementary. Furthermore, increasing competition in global markets tends to strengthen the need for a well-identified homeland, representing a temporary shell of easy social relations, where the need for complex and changing translations of values and languages is reduced.

Let us suppose that the second view is representative of important trends in the new economy world. The fundamental nexus between cluster development and local development would still represent a key for prosperity in many localities. Some changes are implied, nonetheless. The first one is given by the fact that the flows of persons and information (via transport systems and ICT infrastructure) tend to enlarge the area of daily job and civic experiences. Small localities become parts of strongly interconnected metropolitan areas or regions. Each small locality becomes less socially bounded, but the larger area cannot have the same capacity to produce common experiences and shared values as the old, smaller ones. Diversity increases. This is good for generating hints towards new ideas, but not for reproducing shared attitudes. The larger localities may be seen as the places of local 'societies' more than of local 'communities'. There are somewhat defined thresholds, in size and multiplicity, beyond which the nexus is lost.

A third consideration concerns dynamic problems and change. Globalisation may be seen not only as a result but also as a process of sudden enlargement of the space of economic and social relations. This generates deep challenges for many companies, clusters and localities. The division of labour and the set of specific public goods have to be adjusted in many dimensions. The social sphere is also invested, since old jobs are lost or menaced, the flows of persons may drain skilled people from an area, while new waves of immigration increase the problems of cohesion within and among the localities of one region. Even if new paths centred on the nexus between cluster and local development are possible, the discontinuous and systemic nature of the transition may trap the localities in a path of economic stagnation and social decline or unrest. Leadership and luck are requested for moving the system towards a new high road.

How is Policy for Cluster and Local Development Modified?

In the new economy world, some items included in the policies for local development become more evident. The first one has to do with the necessity of strengthening the identity of the small homeland. Public administrators or private leaders may have a role in this, playing as ambassadors of their localities and regions. Also local economic, cultural and sport brand names acquire a higher symbolic role. On the other side, the dangers of parochialism and racism have to be avoided. Here, national, federal and multinational policies promoting the idea and the practices of a common field of values and interests are extremely important.

A second item is connected to the larger scope for positive and negative interference by large trans-local companies. Targeting and antitrust-like policies sensible to the local dimension are necessary. Of course the local public power is generally not strong enough to counterbalance the strategies of large companies. It follows that local policies should be inserted into larger institutional networks of public power and monitoring capacities (Bailey, Harte and Sugden, 1999; also Connor in this volume).

A third item concerns transition. Various problems could be highlighted and related to strategies for identifying and constituting new specific public goods, and for supporting, through social cohesion, the reproduction of common attitudes towards trust and entrepreneurship. An aspect clearly connected with the new economy is the necessity of upgrading the knowledge intensity of local

activities. Here two polar solutions may be envisaged. One is a dualistic structure, based on the coexistence of restricted centres of scientific and managerial excellence with a large pool of cheap, semi-skilled workers. The other
solution is a new artisan structure, whereby large segments of the workforce
upgrade their skills, with new combinations between operative and tacit abilities, creativity, and control of codified knowledge. Even if public policy has
not the capacity to select, plan and manage any particular solution, still public
leadership and investment may contribute to the movement. For example, if
the second type of solution is preferred, public investments in professional
training, and in social and residential services that help the private investments
in human capital, will have a high priority.

A last item concerns the increasing probability that localities and regions
do not correspond to a well-defined level of public administration. This
requires action by a set of public players (mayors of contiguous municipalities, county representatives, etc.), with a variable institutional geometry
according to the problems.[11] Furthermore, at the local level, there may well be
other important strategic agencies – local business associations and clubs,
trade unions, leading entrepreneurs and bankers, community leaders (for
example the clergy). The result is encapsulated by the concept of multilevel
governance of local development (Garofoli, 2001).

5.   HINTS ON CLUSTER DEVELOPMENT: THE CASE OF
SOUTH-EASTERN WISCONSIN

The framework presented on clusters and local development can be pursued
and illustrated in the context of some aspects of the current debate on the
economic perspectives of South-eastern Wisconsin (USA). Let us consider
some questions in this regard, also borrowing from the previous reflection on
the new economy. (See also the background material and further discussion of
this case in the next part of this volume.)

Are Clusters Important in South-eastern Wisconsin?

A positive answer has been given, see Zimpher et al. in the Appendix to
Chapter 11 of this volume, and Mone et al. (2000). Ten clusters have been
identified in Wisconsin; some of them probably have an important core in
South-eastern Wisconsin. There is some reason for suspecting that some
among the so-called 'ten clusters' identify just a concentration of firms and
employment in particular sectors. For others, the information given is closer to
the definition of a cluster. The 'machinery' cluster and the agro–food–beverages cluster seem to have a basis of dense interrelationship among firms that

is not governed by pure market or hierarchical mechanisms. This is also at the core of the paper by Whitford et al. (2000): institution-making for the specific needs and advancement of such relations is strong. Furthermore, the Milwaukee metropolitan area, a focal-point in South-eastern Wisconsin, emerges as strongly specialised in parts of such activities at the national (USA) level (see Peoples in Chapter 7 of this volume).

Clusters and Localities

It is not clear if such clusters have a geographical core, with a regional and state corolla, or if the activities are just dispersed all around the state. In both cases, it has to be clarified, if and to what extent one or more localities and local communities take the destiny of each cluster as strongly connected to the welfare and destiny of their workers, entrepreneurs and families. In other words, how strong is the nexus between industrial clusters and local develop-ment? In particular, what is the role of the metropolitan area of Milwaukee in shaping the main features of such a nexus in South-eastern Wisconsin? Let us elaborate a bit on the matter.

The metropolitan area is medium-sized in US terms. It has relatively low resi-dential costs; it has a tradition for public administration building and expanding social and urban infrastructure; it has a relatively strong system of public schools, training courses, and university courses in fields also connected to the traditional clusters; within its prevalent tertiary functions, the relative importance of the health care system and of the insurance system suggests the presence of local factors of strength in some activities intensive in codified knowledge. The brand names of local industrial companies are clearly present in social events played in the city. The brewery museum is just an example of social connection not with a single company, but with a local industry. The linkages of the metropolitan area with the other counties of South-eastern Wisconsin are strengthened both by intense commuting, and by the proximity of the city with the rural atmosphere prevalent in the other counties. Let us suppose that this set of facts defines an image of the area shared by important segments of the population. It would appear a promising situation for finding a relatively strong nexus.

On the other side, Milwaukee, as many other US metropolitan areas, seems to have heavy problems of urban and social segregation. This tends to increase the separation between the networks of business relations and the networks of social relations. Important sources of trust, entrepreneurship and cognitive proximity are lost. Regional governance is very difficult. Market and hierar-chic relations are predominant around some isles of industrial cooperation (see Section 3). This second set of facts induces the image of a weak nexus. However, it could be that the first image is more important in relative terms (i.e. against US standards).

Clusters and the New Economy in South-eastern Wisconsin

Let us suppose that: a) some nuclei of dense relationships exist and that they define one or more vital clusters in South-eastern Wisconsin; b) such clusters are still connected, directly or indirectly, to the manufacturing and rural tradition of the region. If that is the case, they are an engine of industrial and social progress that is not strictly dependent on the strategies of transnational companies operating in South-eastern Wisconsin (or which could operate there). They are neither necessarily subservient to the influence of Chicago nor destined to vanish with the progress of the new economy. Some items within the debate on the perspectives of Wisconsin may be reformulated appropriately. A fundamental divide, on community and business options, is represented by the structure of competencies that could and should be supported: more tilted towards dualism, or towards the new artisans? The second option seems more consistent with the current situation. If that would be the case, a list of questions call for an answer:

1. How may support and a new lease of life be given to the relatively diffused capacities of making mechanical goods and growing vegetables and animals? For sure, such capacities have to be enriched with higher knowledge and creative content. This depends on formal training, but also on the organisation and strategies of teams of companies trying to advance quality and innovation with the participation of some important segments of their workforce. The impulse to workforce participation and the network of exchanges among firms tends to support spin-offs.
2. How can large firms' strategies be targeted and monitored, in order to orientate them, or confirm their orientation towards positive local feedback? Anti-business attitudes and regulatory excesses are damaging, but the idea that what is good for the big company is necessarily good for the community could be even more dangerous. In any case, an advancement of thought and administrative skills on local targeting and multilevel antitrust seems useful.
3. How is it possible to preserve the production of social services and public goods that support the welfare of a large class of workers contributing to the traditional clusters? Tax breaks may be important, but the fiscal capacity necessary for supporting public good production and distribution should not be hampered.
4. How can there be an increase in the capacity of the strong university system to produce competencies and attitudes aimed at high-tech products and services whose open laboratory is lent by regional rural, industrial and tertiary activities? The relations between the university, the local levels of government, the business associations and the unions are important to this

end. However, they are easily doomed by the incapacity to define the individual incentives of the participants. The vision of a higher-level equilibrium that can be gained with a clear contribution of the various parts has to be hammered home.

5. Among the young and their families,[12] how can it be made more evident that good economic and social opportunities may still be found in the renewed traditional clusters and in related activities?

Some of these questions are already included in the agenda of some public or collective agencies operating in the area or in Wisconsin at large (for example, Whitford et al., 2000; Zimpher et al. in the Appendix to Chapter 11 of this volume). The framework here presented gives one possible international perspective, among the many, on industrial clusters and local development supporting such types of agenda.

The Emergence of New Clusters

The strengthening of the traditional clusters would make their evolution easier, and improve the growth of the more knowledge-intensive, connected activities. Furthermore, the cultivation of true cluster relations would stimulate the development of a similar logic of development in more dispersed nuclei of economic activities in the regions and in connected areas of the state. In our framework, public action may plant the seeds for entirely new paths of local development, but planning is not possible, and the investments run a high probability of failures or surprises.

6. CONCLUSIONS

Italian experiences in industrial districts have generated, along the years and with international comparisons, some general propositions on local development, more or less explicitly defined in the literature. First, a unique path of economic development does not exist, nor does a uniquely efficient form of industrial organisation. Second, technology and performance are co-defined with the structure of social relations in general, and of local relations in particular. Third, local communities include specific stocks of skills and entrepreneurial attitudes. In the case of economic underdevelopment, such stocks are largely hidden within the fabric of daily life. Take-off and paths of prolonged development are fuelled by an endogenous exploitation of such stocks. Fourth, internal and external factors and influences define windows of opportunity for local development; if the opportunity is taken, the local community enters the international division of labour with an active role (at least partially). Fifth, paths of local development can be based, as far as the industrial structure is concerned, on clusters not dominated by large firms, where various forms of business units work in teams and are embedded in local networks of specific public goods and social relations.

This perspective does not vanish in the new economy world, even if many important qualifications are needed. The application to the territorial and social conditions of some parts of the country (USA) that is leading the New World economy, is an interesting test, which deserves more attention and investigation.

NOTES

*   This chapter comes from two presentations, at the First and the Second L'institute–Milwaukee Workshops. The author would like to thank the hosting organisations for the opportunity, the audiences for useful comments, and particularly Lisa De Propris, James Peoples and Roger Sugden for deep discussions and general help. The usual disclaimer applies.
1.   Like trust within bilateral or team exchanges, and collective action supporting the availability of local public goods.
2.   Robinson (1958); for an explicit connection with Marshallian thought and the industrial district, I would refer to Bellandi (1989).
3.   For more details on this model I would refer to Bellandi (2001).
4.   Some Italian cases can be found in Florio (1996).
5.   The spatial identification of local systems refers to 1991 data.
6.   Of course, plant size and firm size are not the same thing. However, in Italy there is usually a large overlapping between small plants and small firms.
7.   Another term used in the literature is 'local productive system'. Sometimes, the term 'industrial district' is used for indicating an 'industrial cluster'.
8.   Trans-local means that the firm is running activities in different local (regional) systems.
9.   E.g. pools of skilled people, local brand names with national or international appeal, patents of local innovators and producers.
10.   More references on the matter can be found in Bellandi (2001).
11.   For example, local public goods may extend on different optimal areas of service.
12.   In the different communities involved, and elsewhere in the state of Wisconsin and outside.

REFERENCES

Amin, A. and Thrift, N. (eds) (1994), *Globalization, Institutions, and Regional Development in Europe*, Oxford: Oxford University Press.

Bailey, D., Harte, G. and Sugden, R. (1999), 'Regulating transnationals: free markets and monitoring in Europe', in K. Cowling (ed.), *Industrial Policy in Europe*, London and New York: Routledge, pp. 311–25.

Becattini, G. (1990), 'The Marshallian industrial district as a socio-economic notion', in F. Pyke, G. Becattini and W. Sengenberger (eds), *Industrial Districts and Inter-firm Cooperation in Italy*, Geneva: International Institute for Labour Studies, pp. 37–51.

Becattini, G. (2000), *Il Distretto Industriale. Un Nuovo Modo di Interpretare il Cambiamento Economico*, Torino: Rosenberg & Sellier.

Becattini, G. and Rullani, E. (1996), 'Local systems and global connections: the role of knowledge', in F. Cossentino, F. Pyke and W. Sengenberger (eds), *Local and Regional Response to Global Pressure: The Case of Italy and its Industrial Districts*, Geneva: International Institute for Labour Studies, pp. 159–74.

Bellandi, M. (1989), 'The industrial district in Marshall', in E. Goodman and J. Bamford (eds), *Small Firms and Industrial Districts in Italy*, London: Routledge, pp. 136–52.

Bellandi, M. (2001), 'Local development and embedded large firms', *Entrepreneurship and Regional Development*, **13**(3), 189–210.

Braczyk, H., Cooke, P. and Heidenreich, R. (eds) (1996), *Regional Innovation Systems*, Chicago: Jossey-Bass.

Bramanti, A. (2001), 'Nuove tecnologie di comunicazione e cambiamento locale', in G. Becattini, M. Bellandi, G. Dei Ottati and F. Sforzi (eds), *Il Caleidoscopio Dello Sviluppo Locale. Trasformazioni Economiche Nell'Italia Contemporanea*, Torino: Rosenberg & Sellier, pp. 371–91.

Brusco, S. (1996), 'Global systems and local systems', in F. Cossentino, F. Pyke and W. Sengenberger (eds), pp. 145–58.

Brusco, S. and Paba, S. (1997), 'Per una storia dei distretti industriali italiani dal secondo dopoguerra agli anni novanta', in F. Barca (ed.), *Storia del Capitalismo Italiano*, Rome: Progetti Donzelli, pp. 265–333.

Callejon, M. and Costa-Campi, M.T. (1996), 'Geografia de la produccion. Incidencia de las externalidades en la localizacion de las actividades en Espana', *Informacion Comercial Espanola. Revista de Economia*, **754**, 39–49.

Corò, G. and Rullani, E. (eds) (1998), *Percorsi Locali di Internazionalizzazione. Competenze e Auto-organizzazione nei Distretti Industriali del Nord-Est*, Milan: Angeli.

Costa-Campi, M.T. and Viladecans-Marsal, E. (1998), 'External economies and the competitiveness of manufacturing companies. Some empirical evidence and implications for the design of industrial policy', Paper presented at EUNIP 1998 International Conference, Rethinking Industrial Policy in Europe, 1–3 October, Barcelona.

Crevoisier, O. (1999), 'Innovation and the city', in E. Malecki and P. Oinas (eds), *Making Connections: Technological Learning and Regional Economic Change*, Aldershot: Ashgate, pp. 61–77.

Dei Ottati, G. (1994), 'Trust, inter-linking transactions and credit in the industrial district', *Cambridge Journal of Economics*, **6**, 529–46.

Dei Ottati, G. (1997), 'The remarkable resilience of industrial districts in Tuscany', in F. Cossentino, F. Pyke and W. Sengenberger. (eds), pp. 37–66.

De Propris, L. (2000), 'Local systems of production in the U.K.', Paper presented at the First L'institute–Milwaukee Workshop on Enterprise Strategies and Regional Growth Policies in the New Global Economy, University of Wisconsin at Milwaukee and L'institute, Milwaukee, 10–21 July.

Dupuy, C. and Gilly, J-P. (1999), 'Industrial groups and territories: the case of Matra-Marconi-Space in Toulouse', *Cambridge Journal of Economics*, **23**, 207–23.

Florio, M. (1996), 'Large firms, entrepreneurship and regional development policy: "growth poles" in the Mezzogiorno over forty years', *Entrepreneurship and Regional Development*, **8**(3), 263–96.

Garofoli, G. (2001), 'I livelli di governo delle politiche di sviluppo locale', in G. Becattini, M. Bellandi, G. Dei Ottati and F. Sforzi (eds), pp. 213–34.

Johannisson, B., Alexanderson, O., Nowicki, K. and Senneseth, K. (1994), 'Beyond anarchy and organisation: entrepreneurs in contextual networks', *Entrepreneurship and Regional Development*, **6**, 329–56.

Maillat, D. (1998), 'Interactions between urban systems and localized productive systems: an approach to endogenous regional development in terms of innovative milieu', *European Planning Studies*, **6**(2), 117–29.

Marullo, C. (2001), 'L'area di Prato: analisi del sistema innovativo', mimeo, August.

Micelli, S. and Di Maria, E. (2000) (eds), *Distretti Industriali e Tecnologie di Rete: Progettare la Convergenza*, Milan: Angeli.

Mone, M., Torinus, J.B., Blanchard, B., Sheehy, T. and Shepley, J.J. (2000), 'Critical success factors for knowledge-based industrial clusters in Wisconsin', Paper prepared for the Wisconsin Economic Summit, 29, 30 November, 1 December.

Piore, M. (1990), 'Work, labour, and action. Work experience in a system of flexible production', in F. Pyke, G. Becattini and W. Sengenberger (eds) *Industrial Districts and Inter-firm Co-operation in Italy*, Geneva: International Institute for Labour Studies, pp. 52–74.

Porter, M. (1998), *On Competition*, Boston: Harvard Business Review.

Porter, M.E. (2001), 'Strategy and the Internet', *Harvard Business Review*, March, 63–75.

Robinson, E.A.G. (1958), *The Structure of Competitive Industry*, Cambridge, UK: Cambridge University Press, First Edition 1931.

RUR-Censis (2000), 'I distretti produttivi digitali', *Primo Rapporto Federcomin*, www.federcomin.it.

Russo, M. (1996), 'Units of investigation for local economic development policies', *Economie Appliquée*, **1**, 85–118.

Sabel, C.F. and Zeitlin, J. (eds) (1997), *World of Possibilities: Flexibility and Mass Production in Western Industrialization*, Cambridge, UK: Cambridge University Press.

Salais, R. and Storper, M. (1997), *Worlds of Production. The Action Framework of the Economy*, Cambridge, MA: Harvard University Press.

Scott, A.J. (1988), *Metropolis: From the Division of Labour to Urban Form*, Berkeley: University of California Press.

Sforzi, F. (1989), 'The geography of industrial districts in Italy', in E. Goodman and J. Bamford (eds), pp. 153–73.

Sforzi, F. (ed.) (1997), *I Sistemi Locali del Lavoro 1991*, Rome: ISTAT.

Shapiro, C. and Varian, H.R. (1999), *Information Rules. A Strategic Guide to the Network Economy*, Boston: Harvard Business School Press.

Signorini L.F. (ed.) (2001), *Lo Sviluppo Locale. Un'indagine della Banca d'Italia sui Distretti Industriali*, Rome: Donzelli–Meridiani libri.

Solinas, G. and Baroni, D. (2000), 'I sistemi locali manifatturieri in Italia 1991–1996', in G. Becattini, M. Bellandi, G. Dei Ottati and F. Sforzi (eds), pp. 395–417.

Tavares, A-T. (2000), 'Modelling the impact of economic integration on multinationals' strategies: an analysis of four European host countries', Paper presented at the First L'institute–Milwaukee Workshop.

Tessieri, N. (2000), 'Multinazionali e distretti industriali in Italia', *Sviluppo locale*, **13**, 77–99.

Whitford, J., Zeitlin, J. and Rogers, J. (2000), 'Down the line. Supplier upgrading, evolving OEM–supplier relations, and directions for future manufacturing modernization policy and research in Wisconsin', a Report prepared for the WMEP, Center on Wisconsin Strategy, December.

PART III

10. The global economy and manufacturing: the case of Wisconsin

Donald A. Nichols[*]

1. INTRODUCTION

This chapter illustrates and explores the situation facing a traditional manufacturing area looking to prosper in the modern global economy. Its focus is the state of Wisconsin in the US but, at least in its broad terms, the situation faced by that state is not unique in the world. Readers who are particularly concerned about other localities are likely to identify aspects of Wisconsin's past, present and future mirrored and encountered elsewhere.

I briefly sketch how globalisation and technology have affected Wisconsin's manufacturing sector, and I note some of the challenges these forces will pose in the future. While Wisconsin's manufacturing sector is quite diverse, I give most of my attention to the large and volatile machinery industry, which provides over half of Wisconsin's exports and which is the sector most sensitive to export fluctuations and import competition. Different industries face different problems and opportunities, of course, but the effects of globalisation and technology are likely to be quite similar across Wisconsin's major exporting industries.

My intent is to provide an understanding of the challenges and opportunities that Wisconsin manufacturing will face in the new economy. The two features of the new economy that I emphasise are a) it is global; and b) it has been – and is being – reorganised by technological progress, and in particular by developments in information technology. The interplay of these two forces will change the nature of Wisconsin's manufacturing in coming years.

2. THE HISTORICAL ROOTS OF WISCONSIN MANUFACTURING

Wisconsin's speciality is the manufacture of machinery, an industry that requires workers who are skilled in the metal trades. The percentage of Wisconsin's workforce employed in the manufacture of non-electrical machinery (SIC 35) is the largest of any state in America. This industry and the major industries that supply it, such as the foundry industry, consist of a group of small- to medium-sized firms concentrated in South-eastern Wisconsin, and spread across Northern Illinois and neighbouring states.

At the close of the nineteenth century, Wisconsin was already an important site for the manufacture of agricultural machinery, an industry whose location roughly parallels that of today's machinery belt. When automobile manufacturing sprang up in the early twentieth century, it became quickly concentrated in the Detroit and surrounding areas. Many firms in the Midwest became suppliers to both of these industries, as technology that was developed for one often found applications in the other.

As markets for other metal-based industrial and consumer goods developed, the Midwest became the logical place for firms in these new industries to locate in the US because it had the cheapest source of metal, a good transportation network, workers skilled in the metal trades, and also because it was closest to the suppliers of high-quality components.

By the mid-twentieth century, the Midwest had become the home of an interdependent network of firms that comprised the largest and best complex of metal-based manufacturing in the world. While the fortunes of this complex rose and fell with that of the US economy as a whole, its fortunes differed from the rest in two important ways: a) because the purchase of durable goods can be easily postponed, the metal-based industries suffered more than average in recessions; and b) wages paid in manufacturing industries were far higher than wages in non-manufacturing industries.

The Global Challenge to US Manufacturing in the 1970s

The 1970s marked the transition to a global economy. Until 1970, many firms in the machinery industry had not faced serious competition from abroad. But in the decade of the 1970s, the share of US imports and exports doubled from about 5 per cent of GDP to about 10 per cent. In contrast, each of these components had made up about 4 per cent of the total economy in 1950. Imports at a level of 4 to 5 per cent of GDP did not constitute a threat to American manufacturing.

By 1970, not only had Germany and Japan recovered from World War II in the sense of rebuilding their capital base, but in many areas they had completely closed the technology gap as well. Furthermore, the greater attention paid to quality in both Germany and Japan gave them an advantage over US firms in many markets.

The rapidly changing volume of trade flows in the 1970s led the major industrial nations to adopt flexible exchange rates as the way to stabilise their trade balances. Flexible exchange rates help maintain an equilibrium in the trade balance as follows: because domestic costs must be paid in domestic currencies, exporters typically base their international prices on their domestic costs. Then an increase in the value of an exporter's currency will lead it to raise its price in terms of the depreciating foreign currency in order to cover its domestic costs. The higher international price will make the exporter's products less competitive abroad, which will slow the growth in its foreign sales. Through this process, if one country's exports begin to grow more rapidly than those of the rest of the world, the growth in its exports can be slowed by an increase in the value of its currency.

During the 1970s, both the yen and the mark had to be revalued regularly to slow the increase of German and Japanese exports to the US. By the end of the decade, foreign penetration into many US manufacturing markets had become so substantial that many Midwestern firms had to close. The terms 'Rust Belt' and 'Snow Belt' became common in the press at that time. The bad news was that many firms had to close; the good news was that because of competition, it was the inefficient firms that closed while the most efficient firms remained in business. Many of these remaining firms had adjusted to the foreign challenge with an aggressive style, and were subsequently dubbed 'lean and mean'.

Lean manufacturing denotes a mode of production and supply chain management that was developed in Japan, largely by Toyota, and that was responsible in large part for the amazing leaps the Japanese had made in the quality and quantity of their manufacturing output (see also Cowling and Tomlinson in Chapter 2 of this volume). In response to the Japanese challenge, many Midwestern manufacturing firms sought to adopt this Japanese approach. A lean industry is built around the customer. It produces goods to order in relatively small batches, with great attention paid to quality, as little waste is permitted due to error, and with the smallest possible level of inventory in the pipeline. With fewer inventories, production schedules must respond quickly to changes in consumer demand. As an organisational strategy, lean manufacturing leads a firm quickly to identify any problems in its production pipeline.

The term 'mean' reflects a heightened attention to costs. New advances in computers and in accounting practices permitted firms to do their cost accounting in much more detailed and precise ways than before. It became much easier for a firm to determine where it was fat, either in the price or volume of its inputs, and to determine which functions could be shut down or purchased more cheaply from other firms. Downsizing, outsourcing and total quality management became terms of common parlance to describe the ways lean and mean firms improved their competitiveness in the 1970s and 1980s.

Wisconsin fared relatively well in the 1970s, at least compared to the rest of the Great Lakes states. This was due in part to the fact that Wisconsin specialised in machinery rather than autos, and machinery had not been as hard-hit as autos by the huge increase in energy prices. Wisconsin also had an auto firm, American Motors, but that firm built small cars, and sales of small cars rose when energy costs rose. But the US auto industry as a whole had huge labour costs and union work rules that it could not run away from, and it had internal organisational problems. Its inventories were huge, and it was slow to identify problems in its production processes. In the 1970s, the auto industry was simply not built around the customer. It had become the opposite of lean and was not able to respond quickly to the challenge from abroad.

While autos typified in many eyes the problems of US manufacturing and of the Great Lakes 'Rust Belt' states, not all capital goods firms shared in these difficulties. Many capital goods were already being built in small batches, some being built to order, and as a result, many machinery firms already had close relationships with their customers. As the dollar fell in value during the 1970s, though not by enough to protect the auto industry, Wisconsin's capital goods manufacturers were given a temporary respite from foreign competition. In 1979, an article in the *Wall Street Journal* referred to Wisconsin as the 'shining star of the snow belt'.

The Challenge to Wisconsin's Machinery Industry in the 1980s

The bottom fell out of the US machinery industry in the double dip recessions of 1980 and 1981–82. Capital investment of all kinds collapsed as interest rates soared. Between 1979 and 1983, Wisconsin lost over 100 000 jobs in durable manufacturing, an amount equal to 5 per cent of its entire workforce. The tepid recovery that followed brought further problems for Wisconsin's export-sensitive industries because the recovery was accompanied by very high interest rates that led to a strong appreciation of the dollar and to a massive trade deficit. This time the dollar went up, though not because foreigners were trying to buy increasing amounts of US exports. It went up because they were buying increasing amounts of US securities in order to earn the record high interest rates available in the US.

International capital markets had become sufficiently integrated by the early 1980s that differentials in national interest rates could lead to substantial changes in currency values, and because those changes in currency values were not driven by changes in domestic costs or productivity, they could wreak havoc with foreign trade. Rather than view the changing value of the dollar as a stabilising force, it became a source of instability to exporters. Indeed, ever since the mid-1980s, fluctuations in currency values have been related more to trends in capital markets, such as interest rate differentials, than to changes in the relative costs of traded goods. In the new global economy, because of the way exchange rates are set, it is fluctuations in international capital flows that drive the competitiveness of manufacturing exports.

In the recovery that followed the recession of the early 1980s, foreign firms captured a growing share of America's machinery market. This meant that Wisconsin's recovery from the recession would be slow. Meanwhile, the continued, relentless competition from abroad forced firms to change the way they did business. In many cases, the Japanese emphasis on quality became instituted in US firms as ordinary business practice. In addition, costs were scrutinised in new, rational ways and many functions were outsourced.

In some cases, the assembly process itself was outsourced. Manufacturing firms became importers of their own products. Firms that outsourced production and ended up importing their own products were referred to as 'hollowed out'. These corporations continued to add value to their own products, of course, in the form of management, technology and design, and also in the brand names they could attach to the products they imported. But assembly was often outsourced, typically to Asian firms.

One Japanese method proved difficult to copy at first. This was 'just-in-time' inventory management. In lean manufacturing, the lowest possible level of inventory is obtained by producing each component of a product just when it is needed. This method was developed in post-war Japan where it was especially attractive because a shortage of capital and space made it difficult to finance and store inventories that had not already been sold. In the Japanese system, goods were 'pulled' from the manufacturing system by consumer orders, rather than 'pushed' into the system by firms' production plans. In Japan, an assembly line of a complicated product might be located in a central building with the manufacturers of the components in small buildings just across an alley from the assembly line. Components would be shipped across the alley on dollies 'just-in-time'. No warehousing, loading or unloading would be needed, which saved a lot of money. The difficulty with this system is the extreme precision it required in the coordination of production between assembler and suppliers, and also in the atmosphere of trust and cooperation that was necessary for success. But once the system was mastered, the discipline required for the synchronisation of production yielded other benefits, including an emphasis on quality.

In contrast to Japan, Midwestern factories were already spread across the landscape. Factories of suppliers were linked by trucks and trains to central warehouses that stored components for a set of assembling factories. Capital and space were abundant so there was no financial or physical imperative to shift to the just-in-time method. But a shift was sought nonetheless on the belief that it would greatly improve product quality and productive efficiency.

Wisconsin's Response to the Global Challenge of the Early 1980s

How could the Midwest move to a just-in-time method of inventory management with factories so widely dispersed? An answer to this question was found
in information technology. A problem raised by globalisation was solved by
the other dominant feature of the new economy, information technology.

The advent of the cell phone and the placement of a cell phone in each truck
was the crucial development that allowed factories and shipments to be linked
together in a single complicated system. Rather than dollies moving across an
alley, semi-trucks moved across the entire Midwest. It was not proximity that
made the Japanese system work, but predictability of arrival time at the destination. Today shipments leave one factory on a precise schedule, proceed to a
destination hours away and arrive just in time. One truck pulls up to the loading dock just as the preceding truck pulls away.

The new system has many advantages over the system it replaced.
Inventory holding and handling costs are reduced, processes vulnerable to
breakdown are easily identified and strengthened, and producers can respond
much more quickly to changes in consumer tastes. The response of Midwest
manufacturing has been so thorough that a buyer of components can now
routinely put the entire responsibility for timely delivery of zero defect
components on the supplier's shoulders and expect performance. Indeed, more
and more responsibility for product performance, including design, is now
being put on the shoulders of suppliers, and suppliers have increased their reliability in order to meet the new expectations.

As the distances over which products can be shipped on precise schedules
have increased, competition among suppliers has become more intense. If a
cross-town supplier cannot meet the new standard, a new supplier in another
city can be engaged. This has weeded out the inefficient firms and forced the
survivors to get lean and mean. In this way, the cell phone information system
has enabled efficient firms greatly to increase their sales. The result is that in
the last two decades, the machinery industry has been transformed by the first
wave of the information revolution. It should be noted in passing that the
deregulation of the US trucking industry in the late 1970s also facilitated the
transformation in Midwest logistics.

Because of the relatively inefficient system of truck transportation in Japan,
it is hard for the Japanese themselves to recopy the Midwest's version of this
system. Competition among geographically dispersed suppliers in a just-in-
time system requires an excellent highway system. The uncongested Interstate
highway system in the Midwest offers it a distinct advantage with the
predictability of travel times it permits. Offsetting this advantage is the fact that
the distance over which deliveries can be made on a predictable basis is rapidly
increasing. Shipping times are increasingly coordinated on a worldwide basis.

Hence one of the great advantages of the Midwest that led to its resurgence in the last decade and a half will be eroded somewhat in coming years.

Wisconsin's political response to the economic difficulties of the early 1980s was also intense. Notable among the ongoing stream of studies and activities in support of economic development was a major look at the Wisconsin economy by the Strategic Development Commission, which issued its major report in 1984. And following the election of Governor Thompson in 1986, Wisconsin paid much more attention to its business climate. In particular the effect that its tax and regulatory system had on the competitiveness of its businesses got new attention in the late 1980s and these systems underwent some major reforms. Some of Wisconsin's subsequent growth was due to a much higher level of effort to attract new businesses into the state, a task made possible once the business climate had been improved.

For the purposes of this chapter, then, part of the successful Midwest response to the global challenge of the 1980s should be viewed as a product of the first wave of the information revolution. The network of cell phones that links the shipments to the factories enabled a huge reduction in shipment, storage and interest costs. Hence, cell phones should be viewed as an input into the manufacture of automobiles and machinery. They – and semi-trailers – have replaced warehouses and dockworkers. And within firms, logistics management has replaced old-fashioned systems of inventory tracking and verification.

Wisconsin manufacturers have become lean and mean, with an emphasis on quality that might never have occurred without foreign competition.

Wisconsin Manufacturing in the 1990s

The 1990s were a golden age for Midwest machinery manufacturers (see also the Appendix to the following chapter of this volume, by Zimpher et al. on the South-eastern part of the state). More than just the introduction of better management and information technology was responsible for this prosperity. Domestic investment, including the purchase of machinery of all kinds soared in the 1990s. At the same time, purchases of machinery by developing countries, especially those in Asia, also soared. Meanwhile, the dollar had fallen substantially from its mid-1980s peak, and US products were again competitive on world markets.

The huge growth in machinery sales provided the funds needed for the machinery manufacturers to purchase new efficient equipment for themselves. The transformation of the old Midwest manufacturing economy from a group of loosely connected factories into a tightly integrated network of quality-conscious, customer-driven managerial teams was financed by the large profits earned in the 1990s from booming sales.

The Midwest durable goods manufacturers have become a more tightly woven network than ever before. Transport costs have fallen as the management of fleets has become more efficient. Whole new industries of supply chain management have emerged, led by the trucking firms who specialise in minimising the costs of coordinating production activities over great distances. That is, many of the lean and mean manufacturing firms routinely outsource their logistics problems to firms that specialise in these activities.

While outsourcing reduces employment within manufacturing, it should not be confused with a decline in the importance of manufactured products in the economy. There was no decline in the value of automobiles or of machinery as a share of the GDP in the US. In fact, there seems to have been a modest increase in the percentage of consumer and business spending on the Midwest's traditional products during the 1990s. But there has been a large decline in the share of workers engaged in assembly, which reflects an increase in productivity, and, because of outsourcing, there has also been a large shift of employment out of manufacturing and into the service sector. It bears repetition, however, that the products traditionally made in the Midwest did not decline in economic importance.

As the 1990s came to an end, the only clouds on the horizon for US machinery manufacturers seemed to be that the value of the dollar had again risen somewhat. The opportunity for investment provided by the US stock market in recent years led to a huge inflow of funds into the US causing the dollar to rise in value. As a consequence, a trade deficit emerged by the end of this period at a rate of over $400 billion per year. Machinery manufacturers were among those who suffered the most.

3.   THE CHALLENGE OF THE NEW ECONOMY TO WISCONSIN MANUFACTURING

But Wisconsin will be challenged in coming decades by the changing nature of the economy. One symptom of that challenge has been widely publicised, namely, the relatively small percentage of college graduates employed in Wisconsin. Another symptom is the continued purchase of Wisconsin's small- and medium-sized companies by firms headquartered out of state, and in many cases, out of the country. Are these two challenges related?

In what follows, I provide a strategic overview of the new economy into which both of these challenges fit. Other problems and possibilities are also identified in the overview.

The first step in addressing the problems and opportunities faced by Wisconsin or indeed by similar regions in the world is to have a cohesive strategic overview of the new economy. Is there really such a thing as the new economy, and if so, how does it differ from the old economy (see also Sugden and Wilson in Chapter 1 of this volume)? Where are the openings into which a set of old economy industries can be plugged into the new economy? Do these openings provide an opportunity for a state like Wisconsin to enjoy the benefits of the new economy?

Some Features of the New Economy

Midwest manufacturing overcame the challenge of the early 1980s in several ways, but one of them was to use information technology to lower the cost and improve the quality of its products. A view of this process was provided above, and it provides a way to understand how the new and old economies are linked. In that view, the old economy buys inputs from the new economy. In this subsection, I expand that view and then consider its implications.

In describing how the Midwest met the challenge of the 1980s, the substitution of information technology for warehouses was emphasised. In looking to the future, we must remember that it is not just information technology whose role is expanding, but that the role of industrial technology is accelerating as well. The automobile I buy differs in fundamental ways from the automobile my grandfathers bought. My car has less steel but better technology. Over the years, brainpower has been substituted for both brawn and raw materials, and this substitution has occurred within the individual automobile firms as well as within the Midwest's factory network. The substitution of technology for other inputs is likely to continue and it will remain an important feature of the new economy in many industries.

Technology is but one form of information. Other forms of information are increasing in importance as well. Branding and consumer information is important. The practice of business management is increasingly complex and is dependent on information. And the linking of all these kinds of information through information networks is growing.

Taken together, it is this group of inputs, all based on information, that define the new economy, and it is the growing roles of these inputs that will dominate the character of the economy in coming years. To think of them as inputs is the key to understanding the new economy. To say that an automobile is made out of information to a greater extent than it is made out of steel may violate our intuition about the physical character of a product, but it is not misleading in an accounting sense because information now makes up a greater share of the cost of a new automobile than raw materials do. Economists would use the term 'value added', and would note that the share of value added in final output that is provided by information exceeds the share of value added provided by physical materials and possibly even of the whole process of assembly.

Because the slice of the economy I have emphasised in this chapter is the manufacture of machinery, it would take me too far afield to describe information as a final consumer product. But a brief consideration of how little consumers actually spend on information compared to how much they spend on durable goods – their phone bills, their cable TV bills and their Internet connections combined are less than a car payment – tells us quickly that the major role of information in the new economy is to add value to the whole pipeline of production, rather than to be a consumer product itself.

This tells us that from the perspective of the Wisconsin economy, the threat of the new economy is not that consumers will stop buying lawn mowers made in Wisconsin and start buying 'information' made in California. The threat is that an increasing share of the cost of a Wisconsin lawnmower will be the cost of California information, while a shrinking share will be spent on Wisconsin-made inputs and workers. New, more intelligent ways to make lawn mowers will reduce the cost of lawn mowers and improve their quality. The question for Wisconsin's future is whether the college graduates who contribute to these new information systems will live in Wisconsin or somewhere else.

Economies of Scale in Information

An important feature of the new economy is that there are enormous economies of scale in the field of information. An investment in technology is just as expensive if it will be used to produce 1000 or 2000 farm tractors, but the cost of the invention per tractor will be half as large if production is twice as large. Technology, branding and systems of management are forms of information that have large economies of scale.

This insight predicts that a consequence of the growing importance of information will be a drive toward large-scale production in all industries, as companies try to expand in order to spread their information costs over a larger volume of production. One way to expand is to export – better to sell on two continents than to sell on one. Hence the growing importance of information is one of the forces driving the move toward a global economy. Foreign producers will feel these same forces, of course, and they will try to expand into US markets.

A second way to spread information costs over a larger volume of production is for firms to combine. This insight suggests that we will see a continued move toward consolidation of many manufacturing companies in the new economy. This consolidation will take place on a worldwide basis. This means that mergers and buyouts will continue to be a feature of Wisconsin's economic news in coming decades. Wisconsin's machinery manufacturers will be targets for foreign buyers who need to spread their technology costs over a larger volume of production. Because of the growing importance of technology, and because of the economies of scale in the development and application of technology, consolidation can be expected to accelerate in the future.

In terms of consolidation, other industries are further along than the machinery industry. This may be because the scale of production in machinery is small enough that automation has not been as economical in machinery as it has been in some other industries. For example, while a single auto assembly plant may turn out 300 000 copies of the same car each year, the entire market for farm tractors in the US is only about 100 000 per year, and this is divided among several brands, each offering many models with enormous variations in size and specifications. In many machinery industries, volumes have remained small enough and the variety of products large enough that skilled handwork has remained a major input. Because of the low volumes and necessary handwork, the assembly costs are likely to remain high in the machinery industry in the future, so that even after machinery feels the full impact of the information revolution, manufacturing cost will remain a relatively substantial part of the final costs of the product. But despite the importance of assembly costs in the machinery industry, it remains the case that an important effect of the increasing role for information as an input will be a strengthening of the forces of consolidation.

To gain insight into the possible structure of the machinery industry in a mature knowledge economy, it is helpful to note the organisational patterns of some other industries in which knowledge is a larger share of the final costs than it is in machinery. Three industries in which information plays a moderate, large and dominant role, respectively, are autos, pharmaceuticals and Internet technology. These three industries have large dominating clusters of activity in Detroit, New Jersey and Silicon Valley respectively. Each can tell us something about the complicated interactions among regional economies, industrial clusters and the forces of consolidation in the new economy (and see also other contributions to this volume, including Husbands in Chapter 3, Schweitzer and Di Tommaso in Chapter 8, and Bellandi in Chapter 9).

Industrial Clusters: Autos, Pharmaceuticals and Internet Technology

Detroit became the headquarters of auto manufacturing in the first decade of the twentieth century when manufacture and assembly was the most advanced sector in the economy. The clustering of manufacturing activity reduced the supply lines and increased the transfer of manufacturing skills and expertise across firms. As the volume of production of a single model increased to the extent that more than one assembly plant was needed, plants were spread across the country to be near consumers in order to minimise transportation costs. But with the proliferation of models over the last few decades, volumes no longer justify several plants for the same model, so coastal plants have been closed and assembly returned to the Midwest, again to minimise transport costs, but also to be near the engineers and laboratories, as the importance of technical information has grown within the auto industry.

Today, Detroit has a bigger share of the development of auto technology than it has of auto manufacture. Many foreign auto manufacturers have opened labs in Detroit to take advantage of – but also to contribute to – the cluster of engineering talent and technology that are growing in Detroit and whose role in the auto industry has increased in importance in recent years. Technology has become so important and so large a share of costs in the auto industry that firms the size of Saab and Volvo are no longer able to afford to develop their own technology. This is the major reason why the number of auto manufacturers has shrunk in recent years. The major auto firms are now demanding a similar rationalisation from their suppliers, which is leading to a consolidation at that level. Competition among suppliers who sell relatively uniform products to manufacturers is likely soon to be organised through auctions on the Internet.

Pharmaceuticals is a more information-intensive industry than autos, and perhaps even more can be learned about how the knowledge economy will affect industries in the future by looking at how the pharmaceutical industry is organised today. In pharmaceuticals, the ratio of the costs of technology to the cost of manufacturing is extremely high. In such an industry, large volumes of sales are essential if development costs are to be recovered. The important part of the pharmaceutical company for a region to attract is its headquarters and its research and development labs, not the factories that manufacture the pills. Pharmaceutical research centres have enriched New Jersey, while the pills are made in Puerto Rico.

Software is an even more knowledge-intensive industry than pharmaceuticals, and it provides an extreme example of the same economic force. Seattle has Microsoft's headquarters and its major research and development centre. Where the disks or CDs are burned and put into mailers – the physical part of software manufacture – is not the valuable part of the software industry for a region to attract.

Networks of Business Professionals

A final feature of the new economy, the functioning of a vigorous professional network, can best be observed in Silicon Valley. Young engineers move to Silicon Valley because that is where the jobs are, and firms move to Silicon Valley because that is where the engineers are. Employee turnover is high and firms seem to divide and recombine around new functions quite rapidly. Corporate structures are fluid. Networking among these engineers and their employers provides an important source of information flow. The glue that holds this cluster together are the economies that derive from having one job market instead of two, and the more rapid rate at which information flows through a local network than through distant networks, possibly because of the rapid rate of employee turnover.

While most analysts of the new economy emphasise the flow of information among the scientists and engineers of Silicon Valley, it is important to remember that the valley is also the home of a thriving network of business professionals who staff not only the headquarters of the corporations located there, but who also include entrepreneurs and venture capitalists, along with a group of lawyers, accountants and bankers who specialise in financing the information technology industry.

Note that it is the latter group who decide where the money will go, which means they decide which ideas are to be developed, which new products are to be created, which companies are to merge, which new ventures can be spun off from existing companies, etc. In the new economy, capital is directed decentrally by a network of legal and financial professionals and entrepreneurs, typically outside the walls of any manufacturing company. A truly vigorous industrial cluster requires not only a network of engineers and scientists to work on the technology, but also a strong network of business professionals and venture capitalists to provide direction to the industry. Corporate headquarters of medium- to large-sized firms, and the business professionals who provide expert advice to those headquarters, provide an important breeding ground for these professionals and potential entrepreneurs.

Machinery in the New Economy

The same forces that drive autos, or even pharmaceuticals and software, are at work in the machinery industry, though their implications to date have been softened because the costs of assembly of machinery remain relatively high. Wisconsin should learn the lesson, however, that global consolidation of machinery manufacture is likely because consolidation will spread the cost of information and technology over a larger volume of production and in this way increase a firm's competitiveness and brand image. This is probably the force that lies behind the purchase of many of our machinery companies by foreign manufacturers. This force is likely to accelerate with the increasing importance of information as an input.

Machinery is likely to develop into an industry where a few large firms in each industry have assembly operations on all continents, but a headquarters in one of them. To become a local assembler is to accept a role that is likely to diminish in importance in coming years. Wisconsin's strategy should be to see that the corporate headquarters and the research function

remain here for a large percentage of its firms. Far better for Wisconsin, for
example if Case had bought New Holland than that New Holland bought
Case. Far better for Wisconsin, for example, if Giddings and Lewis had
purchased the machine tool division of Thyssen than that Thyssen bought
Giddings and Lewis. How to retain corporate headquarters in Wisconsin
remains part of the challenge of the new economy to Wisconsin manufacturing.

4.   A VISION FOR THE TWENTY-FIRST CENTURY

Imagine South-eastern Wisconsin, the heartland of Wisconsin manufacturing,
as the Silicon Valley of the machinery industry. As a worldwide hub, it would
include in its region not only the headquarters of some newly consolidated
worldwide firms, but it would also include many small entrepreneurial firms
– perhaps spin-offs from the larger companies – revolving around a few
bright inventors, who would sell specialised components or licences to the
original equipment manufacturers or who might consult with them or work
jointly with them on special projects. There would be excellent links to basic
university research on materials science, hydraulics and electronics. Perhaps
a large independent lab with public/private funding on machinery-related
science would be nearby. Sematech in Austin provides the best example of
such a lab.

The engineers of both the small and large firms would be networked,
perhaps through their professional associations, perhaps through their links to
university faculty, or perhaps through their accountants and consulting firms.
A vigorous professional network would have all three of these links, possibly
more, and it would provide enough information about job vacancies to support
employee turnover of the kind that would bring the most able brains to work
on the most rewarding problems. A network of this kind would offer exciting
opportunities to the best young professionals, and would attract many of the
best to live in Wisconsin.

This vision suggests that it will not be enough just to keep the factories in
Wisconsin, though assembly will remain important in the machinery industry
for a long time. It will also be important to sustain a substantial research and
development function. A network of the best scientists and engineers moving
quickly from assignment to assignment would offer excellent careers to individuals, and it would also provide a formidable hub of technical know-how
and fast-moving technological developments that would make South-eastern
Wisconsin one of the best places for a machinery firm to locate on a worldwide basis. How difficult it would be to locate somewhere else and have to
compete with South-eastern Wisconsin in developing new products, or in

solving new technical problems, when one's competitors in South-eastern Wisconsin had access to the world's best talent.

I have argued that it would also be important to keep many of the corporate headquarters in Wisconsin. They, and the outside professionals they use, would provide an important breeding ground of the small businesses who would invigorate the local economy and who would team with the larger firms to develop new products and technologies. Perhaps Milwaukee, the metropolitan centre of Wisconsin (and located in the South-eastern part of the state), would relate to Chicago, Illinois in the way Silicon Valley relates to San Francisco in its use of business professionals. A strong presence of professionals on the ground in Milwaukee would be supported by some of the world's best in Chicago. Wisconsin needs its machinery manufacturers to be entrepreneurial and on the prowl for foreign acquisitions rather than just to consider the offers they receive to sell to foreign headquarters. Entrepreneurial venture capitalism cannot be sustained without these business professionals. It is in the state's interest to try to provide a congenial headquarters city for these firms.

And the state need not give up on firms that have already sold themselves. If Wisconsin develops the right environment of exciting new engineering technology, New Holland will find it to be in its own interest to have its technology development remain in the state.[1] (See also Husbands on Mexico, Chapter 3 of this volume.) Just as many foreign computer manufacturers have long had labs in Silicon Valley, and just as foreign automakers maintain labs in Detroit, Milwaukee and South-eastern Wisconsin should seek to become the worldwide centre of machinery technology and expertise. This would not only protect its remaining blue-collar jobs, but it would provide exciting employment opportunities to Wisconsin's best young engineering students as well.

In my view, we need not even give up on information technology. Granted, Silicon Valley would sell many products to a vigorous Wisconsin-based machinery industry. But the pipeline between the two industries can be owned and developed from either end. It is as natural to develop information technology for the machinery industry at the home of the machinery industry, as it is to develop it at the home of the information technology industry.

Success at developing an information technology industry is much more likely if it is based on a strong vigorous base of customers than if an attempt is made to develop it as an island in competition with Silicon Valley and its many would-be imitators. If Wisconsin is to retain and attract its share of highly educated people, it will need to have centres of entrepreneurial activity and centres for research and development. Wisconsin has a base of strength in its machinery industry that others cannot match. The surest future is to build on that advantage.

NOTES

* This is a slightly revised version of a paper prepared for the Wisconsin Economic Summit that was held in Milwaukee from 29 November to 1 December 2000. The views expressed are those of the author and are not necessarily held by the University of Wisconsin System or by Jay Smith or Katharine Lyall. While the views are my own, I have benefited from the comments of participants of the Policy Analysis Workshop at the LaFollette Institute and of the Great Lakes Economic Development Researchers annual meeting. Helpful comments were provided by David Audretsch, Jeff Bernstein, Mark Mone and William Testa.

1. New Holland technology development currently takes place in Racine, in South-eastern Wisconsin.

REFERENCES

Arthur, B. (1990), ' "Silicon Valley" locational clusters: when do increasing returns imply monopoly', *Mathematical Social Sciences*, June, **19**(3) 325–51.

Arthur, B. (1994), *Increasing Returns and Path Dependence in the Economy*, Ann Arbor: University of Michigan Press.

Audretsch, D. (2000), *Creating a New Economy for the Midwest: A Research Proposal*, University of Indiana.

Black, D. and Henderson, V. (1999), 'Spatial evolution of population and industry in the United States', *American Economic Review*, May, 321–7.

Dalton, D.H. and Serapio, M.G. Jr. in conjunction with P. Genther Yoshida (1999), *Globalizing Industrial Research and Development*, US Department of Commerce, Technology Administration, Office of Technology Policy, September.

De Vol, R.C. (1999), *America's High Tech Economy: Growth Development and Risks for Metropolitan Areas*, Santa Monica: Milken Institute.

Doeringer, P.B. and Terkla, D.G. (1996), 'Why do industries cluster?', in U.H. Staber et al. (eds), *Business Networks*, Berlin: Walter de Gruyter, pp. 175–89.

Hammer, R.B. and Blakely, R.M. (1999), *Migration and Educational Attainment in Wisconsin: 1990–1998*, A presentation to the UW Board of Regents, Madison: Applied Population Lab, December.

Henton, D., Melville, J. and Walesh, K. (1997), *Grassroots Leaders for a New Economy: How Civic Entrepreneurs Are Building Prosperous Communities*, San Francisco: Jossey-Bass.

Klier, T. (2000), 'Structural change and cyclicality of the auto industry', *Chicago Fed Letter*, Number 159, The Federal Reserve Bank of Chicago.

Krugman, P. (1991), 'Increasing returns and economic geography', *Journal of Political Economy*, June, **99**(3) 483–99.

Krugman, P. (1994), *The Self-Organizing Economy*, Oxford: Blackwell Publishers.

Mahroum, S. (1999), 'Europe and the challenge of the brain drain', *IPTS Report 29*, Institute for Prospective Technological Studies, European Commission.

Nichols, D.A. (1993), *The Growth of Business Services in Wisconsin*, Madison: LaFollette Institute.

Shapiro, C. and Varian, H. (1999), *Information Rules: A Strategic Guide to the Network Economy*, Cambridge, MA: Harvard Business School Press.

Slater, C.M. (ed.) (1999), *State Profiles: The Population and Economy of Each U.S. State*, Washington, DC: Bernan Press.

Slater, C.M. (ed.) (1999), *Foreign Trade of the U.S., Including State and Metro Export Data*, Washington, DC: Bernan Press.

Ward, D.J. (1999), 'Note on the Wisconsin economy', a presentation to the Board of Regents of the University of Wisconsin System, May.

Winters, D., Strang, W. and Klug, J. (2000), *Wisconsin's Economy in the Year 2010*, Wisconsin Economy Study No. 32, Madison: University of Wisconsin, School of Business.

Zucker, L-G., Darby, M.R. and Brewer, M.B. (1998), 'Intellectual human capital, and the birth of U.S. biotechnology enterprises', *American Economic Review*, June, 290–306.

11. Reflections on a university's role in regional economic development

Mark A. Mone

1. OVERVIEW

The purpose of this chapter is to reflect on recent efforts by the University of Wisconsin-Milwaukee to enhance regional economic development in South-eastern Wisconsin. The time frame covered in this narrative parallels approximately the same two years that the L'institute workshops were being convened in Milwaukee, Wisconsin. I first describe efforts leading to the campus's significant involvement in a variety of local community and regional initiatives – beyond economic development – as these set a stage for how and why the campus became involved in regional economic development efforts. Based on the description of this recent set of events and related outcomes, I draw conclusions and offer suggestions that may be relevant to other regions and their economic development initiatives.

During the time frame described, I was involved as the university's director of TechStar, a business development project involving five leading academic institutions in South-eastern Wisconsin. This position became an economic development point role for UW-Milwaukee, positioned jointly between and directly for both the Chancellor and the Dean of the Business School. This narrative and my reflections represent my own views as a participant observer; they are not meant to represent the perspectives of the university, faculty, or administration. These views also do not necessarily represent the views of any of the academic institutions, associations, municipalities, or other organisations with which the university was involved.

2. UW-MILWAUKEE'S HISTORIC ECONOMIC DEVELOPMENT EFFORTS (PRE-1999)

Historically, being located in the urban, commercial, and population centre of the state of Wisconsin, UW-Milwaukee has always undertaken economic development initiatives. Most of these were in individual academic units, such as in the School of Business (e.g., Center for Business Competitiveness, Bostrom Entrepreneurship Center; Minority Entrepreneurship Program), the College of Letters and Science (e.g., Small Business Development Center, Center for Economic Development, Work Force Development Center) or the Schools of Education, Social Welfare, and Information Science. While conceptually overlapping, each of these efforts targeted and, ultimately, reached somewhat different audiences. Operationally, both faculty and administration were sensitive to criticism that more efforts should be undertaken for these initiatives to work more closely together and concentrate their efforts on specific outcomes. Such criticism was frequently encountered in times of resource scarcity, when so-called efficiency pushes were made to consolidate or centralise such efforts.

However, it was not budgetary crises or efficiency mandates that ultimately led to a greater integration of campus economic development initiatives. With the arrival of a new Chancellor, Dr Nancy Zimpher, in the fall of 1998, efforts were begun from a different perspective to concentrate and coordinate the activities of numerous UWM schools and colleges. In a broader effort to aim many of the campus's faculty and administrative efforts toward community engagement, a major transformation was begun.

Compared to all previous change efforts in the history of UW-Milwaukee, the involvement – in terms of number of people, constituencies represented, amount of time involved, and the systematic discipline employed – was colossal. Collectively, these efforts became known as the 'Milwaukee Idea', with implications for the economic development efforts for the region.

The roots of this thinking and similarity in associating university initiatives with geographic regions go back to the turn of the twentieth century. At that time, the University of Wisconsin, located singularly in Madison, coined the term, 'The Wisconsin Idea'. Recognising the role of a major land-grant institution, campus administrators were concerned with the question of how the university could make a difference to the state – in terms of agriculture, economics, politics, social development and numerous other areas. In the more recent context, the Milwaukee Idea was to be UW-Milwaukee's variant on this theme, focusing on 'Three Es: Education, Environment and Health, and Economic Development'. Through these umbrella concepts, the university began focusing some of its efforts on local and regional initiatives.

In brief, these three areas ('Es') became umbrella concepts under which similar activities across different academic units would be coordinated. More than just a concept, budgetary decisions soon became aligned very clearly with the Milwaukee Idea over the next two years. Critically important to the implementation of the first 11 themes of the Milwaukee Idea, several key staffing decisions were made to support the initiative. Specifically, a provost, several academic deans, and some faculty members were hired with backgrounds consistent with and supportive of the Milwaukee Idea. Thus, by virtue of the faculty engagement and community constituents with whom relations were more firmly established, the stage was set for the campus to become more involved in regional economic development efforts.

3.   UW-MILWAUKEE'S REGIONAL ECONOMIC DEVELOPMENT EFFORTS (*ca* 1999–2001)

While the Milwaukee Idea work was proceeding on campus with the involvement of more than 200 faculty members, administrators, and members of the Milwaukee community, the Chancellor was also holding significant meetings in the community relating to economic development. In particular, a meeting was held in early 1999 in which a vision was established for creating a university-led regional economic development initiative: TechStar. The vision for TechStar at that time was broad, encompassing workforce development, business incubation, venture capital formation, technology transfer, and technology-related education, among other areas. In this meeting, five CEOs from large, area businesses pledged funds to assist in the development of this initiative. Present also was Tim Sheehy, the President of the local business chamber of commerce, the Metropolitan Milwaukee Association of Commerce (MMAC). This organisation and its president would come to play a key role in working with the university on regional economic development. Following this meeting, efforts were begun to develop a proposal and staff the initiative. Several campus deans were involved in these efforts, with the result being a draft proposal for the economic development initiative and a campus director in place.

The next step was to initiate two series of meetings, one with the presidents of the leading academic institutions in Milwaukee County and the other with an existing group of administrators from these schools. This latter group had been meeting monthly for approximately the last year to discuss technology transfer issues at their respective campuses. The campuses included UW-Milwaukee, the Medical College of Wisconsin, Marquette University, and the Milwaukee School of Engineering. Engineering or Graduate School deans primarily constituted the membership of this group. In a pivotal meeting, these two groups were brought together with the Mayor of Milwaukee, with the result being the official formation of a campus-designated TechStar initiative that would focus on regional economic development, in the broadest sense.

Following the meeting with the Mayor, the formal establishment of meetings and a structure to fully develop the proposal was initiated. The UW-Milwaukee campus TechStar director held numerous meetings with CEOs, presidents of academic institutions, and city, county, and regional economic development groups and business associations. As these meetings were being held, the formal designation of key people from each campus was established. These individuals were appointed by their respective academic institutions' presidents, authorised to speak on their behalf, and charged with representing the interests of their campus's faculty members and administration.

It soon became evident that if the TechStar initiative was to have any meaningful impact, it would need to receive significant funding. Locating such funding, beyond the seed funding enabled by the CEO's initial commitment, became a primary objective. Given UW-Milwaukee's lead role, the fact that the private sector had already committed seed funding, and the hesitance of the academic institutions to commit their own funds, the state became the primary resource to be considered. It was clear from UW-Milwaukee's perspective that the TechStar initiative should not interfere with its traditional state support. While the state funding was important to get TechStar to an operational stage, it was planned even at the beginning that the initiative would become self-funded relatively quickly.

A concurrent development was the study of other regions in which economic development was flourishing. In particular, campus-led initiatives became the focus of this study. Efforts such as the Houston Applied Research Center, an initiative involving several southern US-based campuses and the Monterrey Institute (in Mexico), were studied. Rensselaer Polytechnic Institute, in New York State, was examined closely due to its successes in starting businesses. The University of Texas Austin's campus received a great amount of attention, given the rise of technology-related business in Austin, including the success of Dell Computers and its many suppliers and spin-offs. The University of Washington's close relationship with GE Medical Systems in Seattle was a natural model as well, given the headquarters of GE Medical in South-eastern Wisconsin. Of importance also was the Silicon Valley's relationship with Stanford University, the University of California-Berkeley, and other campuses, as well as Massachusetts' Route 128, with all of its campus technology-related initiatives.

The key ideas gained from this examination of other campus-based economic development initiatives were threefold. First, universities appeared to play a key, substantive role in regional economic development. It seemed that every successful regional initiative in the US and abroad (e.g., notably in Berlin, Germany and throughout Finland), universities played key developmental roles. Frequently, an important element seemed to be the technology transfer or business involvement based on faculty members working with local businesses. Second, there was a sense of urgency imparted by this study, as it was evident that the then-successful regions had begun their economic initiatives often decades before material results occurred. Finally, between this research and the meetings being held with business, government and university leaders, it became clear that for both funding and measurement success, a clearer focus of the TechStar initiative was needed.

Through considerable discussion, it was agreed that the focus of TechStar would become campus involvement in business start-up, primarily through the development, commercialisation and, ultimately, the transfer of campus technology into new and existing businesses. It was determined that TechStar would develop an infrastructure in South-eastern Wisconsin to marshall the technology-focused intellectual capital in the participating educational institutions in order to advance the economic and societal well-being of the region and the state. TechStar would provide the necessary infrastructure to create new jobs by bringing together South-eastern Wisconsin academic institutions and the business community. We argued that universities drive industry and business competitiveness in the new high-tech economy, as exemplified by Palo Alto, Boston, Austin, San Diego and Durham/Chapel Hill. Key targets for TechStar included fostering technology-related economic development, stemming the loss of highly trained and skilled people, and increasing the number of high-paying jobs – all of which are critical issues for Wisconsin's future. TechStar's founding structure relied on strategic partnerships among universities, the business, financial and labour communities, and civic leadership. Finally, one of TechStar's strengths would be its focus on technology transfer and related application to new start-ups and existing industry.

For the purposes of this chapter, the remaining TechStar story will necessarily be brief. TechStar established an objective of raising approximately $2 million from the state, with some expectation that the initiative would become self-funded by its third year. After a lengthy process of courting business, lobbyists, local and state government officials, and university regents, and with considerable assistance from the MMAC, the TechStar initiative received government funding of $1 million over a two-year period (2001–03 state fiscal years). A director was hired from the technology sector, and he narrowed the focus further to technology-related new start-ups, and has been involved in working primarily with medical technology applications.

The realisation that TechStar needed to focus its efforts marked, arguably, the most significant turning-point for TechStar's development at that time. This was not only significant as a turning-point for the TechStar initiative, but for UW-Milwaukee's efforts to affect the larger region's efforts in terms of broad economic development, workforce training, and numerous other aspects originally envisioned by the Chancellor and the core group of CEOs involved in seed funding TechStar. The strengths of the narrower focus for TechStar were that it increased the likelihood of targeted funding (necessary for certain aspects of state spending) and enhanced the measurability of outcomes. The focus also increased the chances of meeting campus objectives pertaining to technology transfer and economic business development. However, the broader campus objectives for TechStar were, in fact, diverted, because TechStar no longer seemed viable as the mechanism for addressing regional economic development issues (e.g., workforce development, economic planning, attracting and retaining technology talent and businesses, etc.).

4. STATE OF WISCONSIN ECONOMIC SUMMIT AND THE JOINT VENTURE FOR SOUTH-EASTERN WISCONSIN

This diversion of TechStar was soon alleviated by the announcement in spring 2000, that a statewide Economic Summit was being planned. The governor of the state announced concerns that given the economic boom occurring nationally, the state of Wisconsin must plan and take action so as to not be left behind in terms of wage growth, employment, employees and businesses developed, attracted and retained, and other markers of economic development. Because the University of Wisconsin System would be leading and coordinating the efforts of the Summit, it was evident that UW-Milwaukee could play a key role in shaping the Summit activities in South-eastern Wisconsin. In fact, the UW-System President and the UW-System Board of Regents President asked UW-Milwaukee Chancellor Zimpher to chair the South-eastern Wisconsin regional planning subcommittee for the Economic Summit to be held in Milwaukee in 2000. The goals of this regional subcommittee included but were not limited to the following:

- Hosting at least one high-profile public forum, to generate ideas around each of seven key topics to be examined at the Summit. Members of the Summit Executive Committee were available to serve as guests/presenters/keynoters.
- To raise awareness for the Summit through public events, opinion columns, letters to the editor, media interviews, guest columns in company and institutional newsletters, etc.
- To be attendees to the Wisconsin Economic Summit, 29 and 30 November and 1 December 2000 at the Midwest Express Center in Milwaukee.
- To gather information and offer recommendations for the region at the Summit. A complete copy of this regional report is included as an Appendix to this chapter.

Listening Groups Leading to the Formation of the Joint Venture

Following the appointment of Chancellor Zimpher as the South-eastern Wisconsin region's chair, a series of six listening sessions and two regional planning advisory groups were held. These sessions were held throughout the region to obtain an understanding of peoples' perceptions of these seven themes from the Summit:

- quality jobs;
- venture capital;
- regulatory climate;
- educating the workforce;
- fiscal future and entrepreneurial climate;
- key infrastructure;
- distinctive brand image.

The listening sessions were held in autumn 2000 in Milwaukee, Waukesha, West Bend, Racine/Kenosha, and Mequon, and were attended by a total of over 300 representatives of business/labour, education, non-profit agencies and government. A summary of the thoughts expressed at these sessions follows. Additional opinions were obtained a) from student focus groups on the UW-Milwaukee campus, and b) from the results of a study on issues of importance to the region's technology community conducted by the Metro Milwaukee Technology Alliance in summer 2000. The narrative describing the contents of the sessions, including key ideas aggregated across the listening sessions and recommendations advanced, is found in the Appendix.

Clearly, the region saw both challenges and opportunities lying ahead. Integrating regional demographics, definitional characteristics, and the perceptions generated across the listening sessions and other sources, we offered specific recommendations, found in the Appendix, pertaining to themes raised in the Summit. These were by no means independent activities, but rather ones that will necessarily have spillover benefits that we thought could address sequentially (and simultaneously) several of the Summit's themes. For example, recommendations for building quality jobs, if successful, will also serve to reverse the 'brain drain' as skilled workers will have relatively more attractive employment options in the state.

We suggested that a group of key regional leaders in business/labour, education, non-profit agencies and government be convened by 30 January 2001, with the charge of examining the key questions enumerated above and creating a comprehensive business plan for the region's future economic growth that highlights early and ongoing successes. To take advantage of the momentum of this Summit, we suggested that the review process and strategic plan be accomplished within the following six months.

We envisioned a model in which leaders in business, labour, education, the non-profit community and government would form a 'Joint Venture', working together to identify and address common issues that have been raised in the

Economic Summit. Figure 11.2A in the Appendix illustrates the proposed components of the joint venture. The joint venture would have a broad focus in that it would be setting the agenda and addressing common issues pertaining to the six-county region across the entire spectrum of themes raised in the Summit. TechStar, as earlier described, became an example of how the regional collaboration would work, especially because as TechStar became operational it grew to include more universities and business-related sectors. The general charges for this new entity were to accelerate the region's efforts:

- to become aggressive economically;
- to expand workforce opportunities that meet personal, social and economic needs;
- to enhance the overall quality of life and regional prosperity.

To accomplish these objectives, the South-eastern Wisconsin Joint Venture's initial task was to examine several key questions:

1. Who should work together? Business, labour, education, non-profit agencies, government, etc.
2. Why should we work together: what's in it for us to work together versus the separate geographical, industrial, or functional paths we're now on?
3. What barriers to working together must be overcome?
4. What are specific examples of regions working together, and how have they overcome barriers inherent in regional cooperation?
5. How would the group be best structured to manage the tension between the high degree of participation required for buy-in versus the need to be small enough to move quickly and get the job done?
6. How can this initiative link us beyond the borders of the South-eastern region, to the state, the country and internationally?
7. What are our key objectives and how will we know if we've achieved success in the short- and long-term?
8. What is our action plan for going forward (sequence and specific actions taken by whom)?
9. Who is responsible for coordinating our activities?

The reason why the Joint Venture made sense to the players in the region at the time included the idea that South-eastern Wisconsin is in a strong and unique position within the state for economic growth. Consider the facts at that time. Within the six-county region, there existed:

- 35 per cent of the state's population and 36 per cent of the state's employees;

- 80 per cent of the state's minority population, creating opportunities to capitalise on the region's diversity;
- 48 per cent of the state's high-tech jobs;
- 40 per cent of the state's college-educated population (the sixth highest ranking of North American cities in per capita population with higher education credentials);
- access to the intellectual capital of over 2300 faculty from more than 16 colleges and universities, and to the 10 000 graduates produced by those institutions each year;
- a 1999 GMP of $61.15 billion;
- 52 per cent of the state's publicly traded corporations;
- seven Fortune 500 companies;
- core businesses in manufacturing, data processing, insurance, business services, mutual funds and printing;
- 54 per cent of the state's registered patents;
- close proximity to US and Canadian markets;
- strategic location in the Chicago, Milwaukee, Madison and Twin Cities corridor, which features excellent transportation systems;
- daily flights out of Milwaukee to 50 major business markets;
- the value of goods and services exported from the region exceeded $5 billion;
- an international port on a major waterway.

These were seen as over a dozen compelling economic indicators for South-eastern Wisconsin. While these lay a foundation and a profound sense of opportunity for the region and the state, they alone do not make an economic future. Hence, although it was felt that the region possessed several criteria essential for economic growth, the region had not capitalised on these strengths.

Equally important, it was seen that many regions were positioning themselves for an even brighter economic future. What was typical in these areas is how local and state government, higher education, industry and labour collaborate on a host of issues across regionally limited borders. Similar to Silicon Valley's Joint Venture for 2010, we believed that without greater regional coordination, we were not likely to successfully address many of the themes raised in the recent State of Wisconsin Economic Summit. It was clear that regional economic development requires systemic thinking, behaviour and concrete actions. It was determined that 'now would be the time' for business/labour, education, non-profit agencies, and government in South-eastern Wisconsin to come together, plan, and activate a strategy that takes advantage of these assets and create a South-eastern Wisconsin Joint Venture.

Thus, the South-eastern Wisconsin Joint Venture for Economic

Development was born. This Joint Venture was to be a regional task force that would work together on critical issues common to the region. The premise for the Joint Venture model in South-eastern Wisconsin was supported by the fact that several key regional players recognise the value in working together for the region's greater good. It was believed that these objectives could only be realised through partnerships based on commitment and mutual collaboration, and by capitalising on the unique assets to the region. There were many coordination efforts occurring within the region at the time of this proposal, and we saw the Joint Venture as building upon and working with these efforts. Without that commitment, we would continue to 'go it alone' in terms of different players not working across either region or functionality.

As a dynamic, forward-looking structure, we suggested that the Joint Venture's coordinating body be unconstrained, free to look at both contemporary and future challenges facing the region. Indeed, if we simply examined other high-growth regions in the country and aimed to mirror their achievements, our region could very well be behind yet another set of challenges.

5. PLANS FOR AND RESULTS OF THE ECONOMIC SUMMIT, JOINT VENTURE AND TECHSTAR

As a result of the Joint Venture, several initiatives were worked on in this six-county region, many of which received a significant boost from the Wisconsin Economic Summit. These included:

- TechStar being launched (assessment found below);
- UW-Milwaukee and UW-Madison partnerships being discussed;
- workforce development partnerships (including the pk-16 initiative, and doubling information technology graduates);
- increasing economic opportunities for disadvantaged populations, and a host of other commitments and possibilities related to the Milwaukee Idea.

Given the expectations from the Summit and the vision underlying the set of initiatives, in the South-eastern Wisconsin region there was a desire to coordinate our strategy with a specific timetable, and attention to structure, selection of members and support. The umbrella for all of our activities was to be the Joint Venture. To build on the listening sessions, we involved many of the participants involved in earlier listening sessions. Beyond that, we attempted to involve many people who had not previously had the opportunity to participate. We also attempted to draw from all of the seven themes identified for the State Economic Summit.

In March 2001, we took a step toward building a regional economic strategy for South-eastern Wisconsin. Nearly 200 representatives from business, labour, education, non-profit, economic development and government sectors participated in an inaugural plenary session for the Joint Venture. With the sponsorship of the Wisconsin Electric Power Company, Richard Florida, Heinz Professor at Carnegie Mellon University, kicked off the meeting with an address to the group about regional economies and the importance of collaboration.

Following Florida's keynote address and the question and answer session that followed, a smaller group of regional leaders then met as a steering committee to create a plan for an economic development agenda for our region. The plan was to bring the larger group of people together quarterly for plenary sessions and convene the steering committee bi-monthly. To guide ongoing efforts between meetings, we identified five task/issue areas and leaders for each of the groups: a) Recruiting and Marketing; b) Ideas to Jobs; c) Education; d) Connecting Commerce; and e) Asset Analysis.

The objective of this plan became the development of a blueprint for the economic competitiveness of our region, with possible next steps including:

1. Regional leaders will assemble a list of attributes for a marketing campaign.
2. Get the media to the table and think about media in a new way.
3. Market Milwaukee to ethnic communities and promote it as a new kind of melting pot.
4. Connect the Greater Milwaukee Convention and Visitors Bureau to the Joint Venture Steering Committee.
5. Play up national images of regionally rooted highlights such as Harley-Davidson, Violent Femmes, BoDeans, Hispanic Community, among others.
6. Use benchmarks for infrastructure for technology in the South-eastern Wisconsin region.
7. Identify 'Quick wins' and 'Low-hanging fruit'.
8. Continue efforts similar to the College Collaborative.
9. This steering committee will meet every other month, schedule large group plenary sessions quarterly, with task groups working in between.
10. Conduct a similar session at the colleges and within the ethnic neighbourhoods.
11. Take Richard Florida's advice, which is: Be with young people. Party. Engage people. Have fun! Become the example of what you want to become in the new Milwaukee. Blur the boundaries of our work. Cultivate folks. Have a better strategy for accountability. Create a listserv. Rotate leadership.

Additionally, the South-eastern Wisconsin Joint Venture for Economic Development, representing business, labour, government, education, non-profit and financial communities, co-chaired by Chancellor Zimpher, MMAC President Tim Sheehy, and Firstar Wisconsin President Jay Williams, began to address the 'image' and 'brand concept' of South-eastern Wisconsin. The Joint Venture strategic alliance aimed to bring together leaders from groups that can work together on common infrastructure challenges facing the region and state. Energy and other natural resources were to also be a high priority, as well as air service and road transportation. Another issue that emerged is the level of connectedness or how well wired the region is for Internet capacity.

The plans for this Joint Venture were ambitious, but the progress has not been realised as fully as some had envisioned. As I understand it, the Joint Venture is now led by MMAC President Tim Sheehy, and the focus has been narrowed to four of the counties central to the South-eastern Wisconsin region.

With respect to TechStar's measurable outcomes, more time is necessary to determine if it will successfully launch businesses from university-derived technologies. At this time, the Medical College of Wisconsin has been involved in two TechStar-related initiatives, but the businesses are not yet launched. Time is needed also to inform us of the effectiveness of both the campuses working together and the ability to start successful businesses from campus research and technologies that may apply to existing businesses.

6. CONCLUSIONS

From my involvement in the development of TechStar, the role that I played in being an economic development key person for UW-Milwaukee, writing the South-eastern Wisconsin regional paper and a clusters study paper for the State Economic Summit, and coordinating the formation and establishment of the Joint Venture, I will offer some observations. These reflections are arranged around themes such as universities' role in regional economic development, the meaning of leadership in the context of forming and sustaining a catalyst for regional economic growth, the regional qualities that seem useful in supporting such initiatives, and the extent to which the experiences in South-eastern Wisconsin might be generalisable to other regions. As implied by these headings or thematic questions, my comments will reflect on issues at both the university and broader regional level. Consistent with the preceding narrative, these are my own views, not meant to be representative of any particular institution or person other than me. There are many individuals and organisations working diligently on economic development in this region, and my comments should in no way be seen as critical of their substantial efforts.

My critical evaluation and reflections begin with the question: what is or should be the role of a university, or higher education in general, in regional economic development? It might be useful to reflect briefly on the different ways that community participants answered this question. Our examination of other successful regional economic development initiatives revealed that universities can and do play significant roles. Consider, for example, the undeniable association in California's Silicon Valley between prominent universities, the silicon chip, and other technological industrial developments. Likewise, during the formation of TechStar and during the planning and listening sessions for the State of Wisconsin Economic Summit, the role of UT-Austin in boosting that area's emergence as a leader in high-technology industrial growth was frequently cited. It is clear to me that the assets of higher education in terms of research, both applied and basic, the community involvement and leadership roles, objectivity and renown, can all be significant levers to influence regional economic initiatives. (See also Schweitzer and Di Tommaso in Chapter 8 of this volume.)

Such arguments were generally recognised and respected as UW-Milwaukee increased its engagement in regional economic development. However, just as in other regions, we were not without critics. For example, the Silicon Valley's Joint Venture 2010, which relies heavily upon university involvement, met with criticism in its early years. One critical perspective on our efforts in economic development was that voiced by a business reporter for the largest newspaper in the state. At a listening session in Milwaukee, he challenged the University of Wisconsin's role in leading the State Economic Summit, asserting that, 'We all know the universities' involvement is a sham, simply a ruse to boost public support to advance your own budgets from state government'. From my own involvement, working at that time with business, local and state government, education, and other sectors, I was surprised to hear this perspective expressed so vehemently. While there may be some legitimacy to this claim, certainly our chancellor believed that by boosting the health of the local region all would benefit.

Another comment on university involvement in regional economic development, generally, and TechStar, specifically, involved the credibility of the universities involved. When we exhorted the role of universities in other regional economic development efforts, a few people noted that the university involvement in many of those instances was of a world-class or at least nationally prominent academic institution. To counter this criticism, we bolstered our case with substantive facts concerning the level of federal funding associated with our research, the corporate-supported grant activity, and the leadership role the academic institutions played in regional education, executive training, medical and engineering research discoveries, and other indices of regional and national prominence. The easiest deflection of this criticism, of course, and the underlying premise of UW-Milwaukee's efforts, was the spirit of collaboration that we attempted to engender.

As a specific example of this collaborative approach, we presented to the governor of Wisconsin proposed biomedical engineering research that involved the work of the engineering faculty from two universities working in conjunction with the medical school. In this TechStar example, a working hip or knee joint would draw from metallurgy, motion mechanics, rapid prototyping, and surface coating fields, using expertise found in the participating academic institutions. We were guided by the vision that by working together, we would be able to contribute to technology transfer to a much greater degree than by working alone.

What I observed in South-eastern Wisconsin was that whoever took the lead, or attempted to take the lead, in regional economic development, often encountered resistance. Much like the reaction that Milwaukee-led initiatives have in the larger seven-county region, UW-Milwaukee, for example, would find that there was often a turf issue, political challenge, or other point of resistance in bringing potential participants together. This challenge would face any person or entity attempting to bring the different parties together, so this, to me, is no reflection on the university's role.

On balance, it is very clear to me that universities can and should play a role in at least local if not regional economic development. Logic suggests and much evidence demonstrates that local talent is the basis for the formation of any type of industrial cluster (see also contributions to Part II of this volume): companies will not be able to grow businesses in regions in which the workforce lacks the necessary skills and talents. Higher education plays a critical role in this as well as in the ability to create and deliver new technologies (e.g., as in the Seattle-Redmond area in Washington State or the Research Triangle in North Carolina). I would not go so far as to say that there is a moral imperative that they must (some make this claim), but I think out of a sense of social responsibility and self-preservation universities ought to engage in local economic development issues.

At the same time, it seems worth pondering whether universities can *lead* this effort, as in pushing economic development at the business development and public policy level, or do universities operate better if they are responding to corporate or business-led pull activities? One senior vice-president of technology for one of the state's Fortune 100 firms located in Milwaukee argued that a university's role should be that of an educational provider. He asserted that a university's role was simply to attract students, educate them and place them in industry. In his view, educated labour, not universities, would lead the development, implementation and production of technology products and services. Certainly we and others in the region disagreed with this provocative perspective, but it was useful to consider because it showed that no matter how the question is answered, universities play an important role in economic development.

The next issue is: if the university's role is legitimate, what else must be involved to successfully launch and sustain regional economic efforts? In comparison to other successful regional economic development efforts, we lacked some of the corporate top management voice. As a natural outcome, items that were identified as priorities for economic development in the region became a function of who was present at the meetings. To a large extent, this same phenomenon occurred in the listening sessions and during the State Economic Summit. However, if those priorities – the ones listed by the participants at the key meetings – did not coincide with the priorities or 'hot buttons' of top business leaders, government officials, or other organisational or community leaders responsible for them, they will not be as likely to successfully lead to change.

To our credit, as we formed regional efforts we typically attempted to err on the side of inclusiveness. This meant inviting and attempting to involve as many constituents as possible. Throughout our work in the era described, we had the President of our local business chamber (Tim Sheehy, MMAC) as a co-leader with our Chancellor. However, representation of business leaders in large group settings, where different constituents aired their views and regional economic development efforts were being discussed, often lacked the input of CEOs of the leading firms.

For a focused initiative like TechStar, the CEOs had input and financially supported the undertaking. This was pivotal support that helped create the momentum for TechStar. In turn, enough CEOs valued its potential payoff and were able to support this initiative at the different levels of state budgetary approval. The efforts of Tim Sheehy in this regard cannot be over-emphasised, as he both collected the input of the key business leaders and was able to effectively communicate with legal, finance, academics, and state and local government officials.

In contrast, for a more ambiguous and arguably more ambitious initiative like the Joint Venture, the CEO involvement was more absent. There was no question that CEO input was provided in the beginning stages of the Joint Venture. For example, in the context of UW-Milwaukee's Chancellor's corporate board or the MMAC's board meetings, the Joint Venture was reviewed and supported as an important endeavour. These boards, collectively, included the CEOs and presidents of perhaps 75 or more of the largest firms in the region, including such notable firms as Johnson Controls, Inc., Miller Brewing, Rockwell Automation, GE Medical, Northwestern Mutual, Briggs and Stratton, Harley-Davidson, Manpower Inc., and so forth. However, despite the sanctioning of the Joint Venture, the missing ingredient was the CEOs sitting on the board of and actively participating in the Joint Venture.

Another question concerns the extent to which the issues we faced and how we approached them are generalisable to other regional economic development initiatives. My reflections on this question exceed the activities of just UW-Milwaukee or education in general and speak to the more collective efforts of the Joint Venture. For the benefit of drawing further conclusions, it seems necessary to anchor the issue of regional economic development leadership firmly into the context of both a general dilemma facing any regional effort, and the particulars of Milwaukee in its role in South-eastern Wisconsin. At the broadest level, most regions will have, inevitably, tension over who takes the leadership role. Within this region, Milwaukee County has been described as the 800-lb gorilla in regional decision-making concerning the airport, transportation, law enforcement, sewage and numerous other regional issues. Efforts to bring about greater regional cooperation on numerous fronts have been stymied by this perception (and sometimes participants acting the part), despite there being many regional economic development bodies involving elected and appointed officials (e.g., Regional Economic Partnership group, South East Wisconsin Regional Planning Commission [SWRPAC]).

As an example, tensions surfaced over something as basic as naming rights, which contain implications for the image or brand of the region. Those outside the region (and certainly most within Milwaukee County) argued that we should harness the name of the region based on the Milwaukee image, supporting this locale as the heart of the region and encouraging others to benefit from Milwaukee's growth. Subsequent efforts by the city of Milwaukee Economic Development officers toward this objective would then be questioned by those in Waukesha, Racine, Kenosha or other counties, as they would feel potentially slighted by marketing or substantive efforts in which they perceived lesser benefits. If this tension were only at an abstract or conceptual level, this resistance would simply be a nuisance. However, this tension undercut the ability to fund and implement collaborative issues, as questions of identification (i.e., regional identity versus local identity) prevailed.

A related issue concerns the availability of leadership talent in any given community. During the time frame of this narrative, an ongoing saga was being reported in regional news media concerning the City of Milwaukee's Mayor allegedly having an extramarital affair with a key office aide. In terms of subsequent events, including a settlement on behalf of the Mayor and his withdrawal from future mayoral races, his effectiveness and involvement in regional economic development seemed limited. Subsequent to the era described in my narrative, Milwaukee County was rocked by a so-called 'pension scandal', resulting in the resignation of the Milwaukee County Executive and the recall of seven County Board supervisors. The Superintendent of the Milwaukee Public Schools, the largest K-12 system in the state, and the head of the Greater Milwaukee Committee (an exclusive, prominent group of CEOs, university, legal, financial and social service agencies) resigned. The local archbishop also resigned before retirement amid a scandal concerning an affair and a considerable sum of so-called 'hush money'. Prior to this set of events, and during the era I described, there had already appeared a series of articles and much local media attention on the paucity of leaders (referred to as a 'crisis of leadership') in the region. Importantly, the two leaders who consistently were mentioned as highly effective and most likely to be able to manage necessary change in the region were the Chancellor of UW-Milwaukee, Nancy Zimpher, and the President of the Metropolitan Milwaukee Association of Commerce, Timothy Sheehy. In the context of a larger leadership vacuum, these two individuals stepped into the roles of regional economic development leadership.

In retrospect, Nancy Zimpher and Tim Sheehy deserve a great amount of credit for their efforts. They are both exceptionally effective in their own spheres of influence and they have both grown those spheres over the past five years. By bringing higher education and business together, they will more likely effect positive change. I believe the community sees them as having a partnership that works and it is a significant asset for the community.

The final question I address is: who can effectively lead regional economic development and what does leadership mean in the context of regional economic development? Based on the experiences described in this narrative, one conclusion that I draw is that the initial leadership for such broad-based initiatives as a Joint Venture needs a relatively small core of committed, senior people. It is not as important whether they are the president of a university, the CEO of an 'anchor' or 'pillar' firm, or the leader of the largest business association in the region. Rather, they need to be associated with or leading one of the key groups that are critical in any region (e.g., business, labour, education, finance, non-profit association, chamber of commerce, etc.). Then, they need to undertake a set of actions that include developing a vision, structuring a clear division of labour, and dedicating themselves and their staff to specific time frames and obligations. In this context, I think our Chancellor and the MMAC President were the best candidates for leading this initiative.

Commonly discussed in management literature are the different skill sets required to launch a business versus those required later to expand and manage a business. In a similar way, I think starting a regional joint venture needs a visionary champion, someone capable of marshalling the different constituents, gaining commitment to overarching themes and goals, and having connections to bring the necessary resources to bear. To then sustain these efforts, an infrastructure needs to be created and staffed, all of which requires significant resources. In some communities this may be lessened through networking if essential components are in place. Even that lesser role, however, can be burdensome for those attempting to coordinate the regional activities.

We learned that the responsibilities for logistics, communication, and even a minimum of a quarterly meeting structure, if added to peoples' inevitably already full schedules, could be overwhelming. A lesson I think many people gained through this experience is just how much of an undertaking true regional economic development is. Indeed, without the sustained support and follow-through of key individuals and their organisation, based on commitment of time, staff and resources, I think it is difficult – if not impossible – for any regional economic efforts to succeed.

In that context, given how daunting the task is concerning regional collaboration, one has to ask about the motivation or rationale behind such efforts. What would compel counties (in this case) in a defined region to 'submit' to the larger identity or efforts typical in most regional collaboratives? I suppose this question falls into the realm of organisational change efforts and, accordingly, back into the issue of leadership, and what it means in the context of regional economic development.

Specific to this region, but perhaps in any region, a leadership challenge also becomes how to include the right people at meaningful (substantively, politically, credibility, etc.) levels, without being superfluous to what those people already do. In light of many people already employed in positions of economic development responsibility, this will be difficult. We encountered a phenomenon in this regard in that people would attend meetings, but would later explain they participated out of defensiveness, to be sure that their county or economic development agency was not adversely affected by the larger Milwaukee regional decision-makers.

In some rare cases, I think massive change efforts can be led or motivated by a champion with significant charisma or so-called 'visionary leadership'. Without anything else, though, these qualities alone are perhaps necessary, but not sufficient for sustained motivation. I believe that there needs to be the perception by key stakeholders that, without a conviction and practical form of collaboration, the region will be worse off than it is by working alone, regional collaboration efforts are doomed. I think that the job losses in certain counties in this region have compelled them to work better together with each other (e.g., Racine and Kenosha counties). Sometimes, job losses have motivated counties to look outside this region for ways to cluster or grow economically (e.g., Washington county). However, I think it is difficult for counties to unite, without a common perceived crisis that will be addressed to each county's benefit if they work together. I do not think this means that regional economic development cooperation efforts are doomed without a pressing crisis, but it makes the leadership challenge much more daunting.

In a way, the answer to the question of regional economic development leadership may be that it is a classic case of managing a geographically dispersed team, not uncommon in many of today's matrix-structured organisations. It is classic in the sense that in regional economic development, there are many intra-regional players with their own agendas, goals, time frames and budgets that, to be effective regionally, must work together. At the same time, these players are not accountable to the larger entity, nor does the so-called leader have any authority to lead, in any formal sense. Hence, balancing persuasion, communication skills, and the earlier-mentioned assets of credibility and interpersonal relations is a skill I think necessary for this type of leadership role.

In retrospect, I think it's fair to ask if there was anything that could have enhanced the success of UW-Milwaukee's regional economic development efforts. Similar to the Milwaukee Idea, the campus's and Chancellor's efforts were inclusive, which can be a real strength. However, universities are, by nature, bodies filled with diverse perspectives. More inclusion brings more likelihood for conflict and debate. In planning and general direction setting, this can be very effective and has been a hallmark of the decision-making in this era. The Chancellor is also to be credited with bringing faculty, staff, and key administration to economic development meetings and providing them with the responsibilities necessary for campus involvement. All these things worked to benefit the regional economic development efforts.

Critically, if any academic institution is going to be involved in regional economic development efforts, I suggest the need to understand that it is taking on a significant responsibility. As opposed to the involvement at a planning or on a committee level, the real, substantive changes that are involved in economic development require a significant, sustained commitment. Such commitment needs to be matched with the resources and restructuring of campus activities to support this initiative. The risk of not meeting this commitment is that of not meeting the expectations created in the larger community, as well as at the campus level. As noted earlier, efforts toward regional economic development take many years, often decades, to measure.

If a campus is to make a commitment to regional economic development initiatives (or any substantive community change), then faculty and administration need to understand and accept the necessary roles. I think it is fair to say that if there is not a natural embracing of economic development efforts, there is less likelihood for success. This notion suggests that there exists a ceiling or threshold of activity that any campus cannot exceed: it needs to work within the abilities and interests of its faculty and administration. Drawing from the experiences we examined of regional economic development initiatives in which universities are credited, it is most commonly the faculty contributions in basic and applied research that sustain the contributions (e.g., patented, commercialisable inventions, applied research with policy implications, advisory and board involvement, etc.). The challenge is how to simultaneously reward faculty for their work for their academic field as well as their engagement to their professional area.

In sum, I think that there are several regional economic development efforts that have been enhanced by UW-Milwaukee's involvement and leadership efforts. While we may not be playing the largest leadership role in ongoing regional economic development efforts, we have had many positive effects. For example, the region would not have TechStar, it is likely that we would not have the Regional Joint Venture, and we would not have the increased understanding of the dynamics underlying regional economic development in this region. Aside from the broad efforts described in this narrative, UW-Milwaukee has numerous departments, centres, and faculty initiatives through which it is assisting and leading economic development initiatives. These initiatives have benefited from our involvement at the broader regional level, and the initiatives themselves have had positive, lasting impact on the community and region.

APPENDIX: WISCONSIN ECONOMIC SUMMIT – SOUTH-EASTERN WISCONSIN REGIONAL PAPER *(Nancy L. Zimpher, Mark A. Mone, Sammis White, Timothy R. Sheehy and Kris Piwek)*[*]

Introduction

The purpose of this paper is to review discussions and recommend possible strategies pertaining to economic development in South-eastern Wisconsin. We begin by defining and describing the region. Next, we review information generated during a series of regional listening sessions and from other data collected in the last year from a variety of regional sources. These data are categorised according to the seven themes of the Summit: enhancing the regulatory climate, educating the workforce, building quality jobs, improving the entrepreneurial climate, building venture capital capacity, enhancing key infrastructures and building a distinctive brand image. We conclude with recommendations and a plan of action for addressing key economic challenges in South-eastern Wisconsin.

Beyond specific strategies that might be helpful to each theme, we suggest that the region's future, like many other regions with more advanced economies, is highly dependent on the ability of key players to coordinate their activities around common economic development goals. Specifically, we articulate a vision for how business/labour, education, non-profit agencies and government can work together to develop a coordinated strategy and planning team for this region. TechStar, a proposed collaboration between four research academic institutions, industry and state government – aimed at technology transfer for new start-ups and existing industry – is but one example of how local cooperation could enhance the greater good of the region. In turn, we suggest that greater regional coordination and cooperation in the form of a regional 'Joint Venture' formed by key regional leaders could serve as a catalyst for greater economic activity, increased employment in high-paying jobs, and a positive brand image for the entire state.

Key Economic Indicators

The region

For at least the last 30 years there has been a common definition of South-eastern Wisconsin. It has included the seven counties that geographically fill the south-eastern corner of the state. For the purposes of the Economic Summit, the region has been slightly redefined. It includes the three metropolitan areas of this corner of the state: Kenosha, Milwaukee and Racine. The area includes six counties, the three just mentioned and Ozaukee, Washington and Waukesha. Walworth County, a county without a major metropolitan area, has been ceded to Dane County for purposes of analysis (see Figure 11.1A).

The South-eastern region is dominated by Milwaukee in the north and Chicago in the south. Metropolitan Milwaukee has approximately 1.5 million

Figure 11.1A   The South-eastern Wisconsin region

people and metropolitan Chicago has 8.9 million. Kenosha is now being called part of the greater Chicago area by the US Census Bureau because of its increasing ties to the Chicago economy. Kenosha is served by Chicago's commuter railroad, and many of Kenosha's citizens work in Illinois. Although we include Kenosha in our definition of the South-eastern region, Kenosha's economy is increasingly influenced by that of Chicago.

Population and workforce
The South-eastern Wisconsin region has an estimated population of 1.8 million people. They collectively constitute one-third of Wisconsin's population, although the region is but 6 per cent of the acreage of the state.

Unlike much of Wisconsin, the South-eastern region's population is diverse; it is home to about 410 000 African American, Hispanic, Hmong, Native American, and other minority residents. They collectively constitute over two-thirds of the state's minority population and almost one-quarter of the region's total population.

The South-eastern Wisconsin population is committed to work. In fact, the state has one of the highest labour force participation rates, the proportion of adults who work or are looking for work, in the nation. The state's average is 74.7 per cent while the nation's is 67.1 per cent. In counties such as Waukesha and Ozaukee, the participation rate is over 80 per cent. On the other hand, Milwaukee and Racine Counties have rates that are just above that of the nation. Thus, there is some room for greater participation in the South-eastern region. The greatest room for growth in participation is among the minorities who constitute 23 per cent of the population and only 15.8 per cent of the region's labour force.

Another concern facing the region is the age distribution of the region. The population is ageing. An increasing proportion is reaching retirement age and a similar portion is reaching the age to enter the labour force. Current projections vary by county, but the overall impression is that of near parity between those entering and leaving the labour force, indicating little room for growth.

Employment
The economy in South-eastern Wisconsin accounts for just over one-third (37 per cent) of the jobs in the state. Milwaukee metro accounts for the bulk (87 per cent) of the region's total of close to 960 000 jobs. Racine's economy is about 8 per cent of the region's total jobs, and that of Kenosha, 5 per cent of the total.

The job distribution by industry largely matches that of the state. Services (30 per cent) are more concentrated here than in the state as a whole (25 per cent). But manufacturing (23 per cent), retail (16 per cent), and government (11 per cent) are very similar to that in the entire state. Notably, the distribution of

Table 11.1A   Distribution of employment by industry, South-eastern region, 1999

Industry	Workers	%
Agriculture & mining	5 681	1
Construction	34 364	4
Manufacturing	216 316	23
Transportation/utilities	44 071	5
Wholesale trade	55 584	6
Retail trade	153 116	16
Finance, insurance, real estate	59 949	6
Services	285 443	30
Government	102 640	11
Total	957 241	

jobs in manufacturing is 1.5 times that in the US. The South-eastern region and the state are still much more dependent on manufacturing than the nation as a whole (see Table 11.1A).

Despite reflecting state distributions, the South-eastern region varies from other areas such as Dane County. Dane, for example, has but 11 per cent of its employment in manufacturing, 24 per cent in services, and 25 per cent in government (counting the University of Wisconsin). Regions of the state do differ in terms of their industries.

In the 1990s, Wisconsin experienced rapid employment growth (21 per cent). The South-eastern region did not grow as fast, 15 per cent, but it was still faster than the growth of the US (13 per cent). In terms of absolute number of jobs added, services (business, health, education and social) was clearly the leader with a gain of 72 003 positions. In second place, far behind, was manufacturing (+12 210). No other industries added more than 8000 jobs. In relative terms the winners were: services (+34 per cent), construction (+24 per cent), and wholesale trade (+17 per cent). (See Table 11.2A). Manufacturing employment grew by 6 per cent, and retail grew by 3 per cent. (We should note that many new manufacturing jobs were created in the decade, but that over 12 000 disappeared in the region, about half through firm death and half through downsizing.)

To better understand current trends, we should note the years in which employment growth occurred. For example, services grew evenly at about 15 per cent in both the first and second half of the decade. Manufacturing realised 90 per cent of its modest growth by 1995. Retail trade realised all of its growth before 1995. The only industry that did well in the second half of the decade

Table 11.2A   Change in employment by industry, South-eastern region, 1991–99

Industry	Absolute change	% change
Agriculture & mining	1 903	50
Construction	6 632	24
Manufacturing	12 210	6
Transportation/utilities	5 462	14
Wholesale trade	7 907	17
Retail trade	4 818	3
Finance, insurance, real estate	4 938	9
Services	72 003	34
Government	6 091	6
Total	122 041	15

was construction, growing by 18 per cent compared to only 5 per cent in the first part of the 1990s. Overall growth occurred at 8 per cent in 1991 to 1995 and 6 per cent for the 1995–99 period. A similar, slowing pattern prevailed for the state as a whole.

When one looks at the more detailed descriptors of industries (Table 11.3A), we can see more specifically in which industries employment growth has been occurring. A key to comprehending South-eastern Wisconsin's role

Table 11.3A   Fastest growing industries (two-digit SIC), South-eastern region, 1991–99

Rank	SIC	Industry	Gain
1	73	Business services	31 771
2	80	Health & allied services	14 755
3	83	Social services	10 054
4	82	Educational services	7 709
5	50	Wholesale trade, durable goods	6 896
6	45	Air transportation	6 183
7	17	Special trade contractors	5 276
8	87	Engineering & management services	4 390
9	37	Transportation equipment	3 925
10	36	Electronic & other electric equipment	2 968
Total			93 927

in high-tech is to understand the use of SIC codes, which are a common way of identifying industries, and are referenced frequently throughout this section.

Far and away the fastest growth has been in business services. This industry accounts for 34 per cent of all recent employment growth. Within business services the largest gainers have been temporary help, computer programming services, and data processing and preparation. Together, these four specific industries account for 25 per cent of all growth in the region.

Beyond business services a good deal of growth (27 per cent of the total growth) has occurred in three industries: health & allied services (14 755), social services (10 054), and educational services (7709). The baby boomlet moving through the schools has fuelled the demand for additional teachers. The increased demand for health care has forced expanded employment in that industry in both hospitals and doctors' offices. And the expanding economy has increased the ability of the area to pay for and deliver social services. The fastest growing social services are those in job training and residential care.

High-tech employment

As most people know, high-tech employment is highly prized today. We look to Silicon Valley with envy in terms of employment and incomes. We tend to think of Wisconsin as way off the mark. But are the state and this region behind the curve? The answer depends in part on how one defines 'high-tech'. There is not one definition. One of the most highly publicised is the one used in 1998 by the Milken Institute. It uses 14, three-digit SIC codes. By this measure some 4.7 per cent of the employment in South-eastern is high-tech. That is below the national rate of 5.8 per cent, but above the Wisconsin rate of 3.5 per cent. The vast majority of this employment in the region is concentrated in metropolitan Milwaukee.

We must note that the Milken definition of high-tech is not a very inclusive one. In fact, it overlooks many industries that hire a large number of IT (information technology) workers. An example here in Milwaukee is the 'quiet company'. Northwestern Mutual has almost a one-to-two ratio of IT employees or IT consultants to its non-IT consultants. The firm is counted as FIRE, 'Finance, Insurance and Real Estate'. Metavante, a part of a bank, is almost exclusively IT, but that is not how one counts it using traditional Standard Industrial Codes, as Milken does. In other words, there is more IT here than meets the eye: IT is being applied in a variety of settings. It is critical to the region that it be applied in more such settings.

The region's high-tech employment is concentrated in a few industries (Table 11.4A). The most important is SIC 737, computer programming, data processing and other computer-related services. Some 36 per cent (16 168) of the region's high-tech employment (45 449) is in this one industry. The next largest is SIC 384 surgical, medical and dental instruments and supplies with

Table 11.4A Distribution and change in high-tech employment, South-eastern region, 1991–99

SIC	Industry	1999 employment	Absolute change	% change
737	Computer programming, data processing, & other computer-related services	16 168	8812	120
384	Surgical, medical & dental instruments & supplies	6235	113	2
871	Engineering, architectural, & surveying services	5417	1373	34
481	Telephone communications services	3880	-1451	-27
382	Laboratory apparatus and analytical, optical, measuring & controlling instruments	3506	94	3
367	Electronic components & accessories	3421	1302	61
Other	**	6872	1325	24
Total		45 499	11 568	34

Note: **Others include SIC 283, 357, 366, 372, 381, 781 and 873.

6235 employees in 1999. Not far behind in third place is SIC 871 engineering, architectural and testing services with 5417 employees.

In terms of growth in the 1990s, the growth is largely confined to SIC 737 programming and data processing. This industry added over 8800 workers (+120 per cent) in the 1990s. Virtually all workers were added between 1995 and 1999. Electronic components and accessories (SIC 367) grew by 61 per cent or 1302 employees and engineering and related services (SIC 871) added 1373 employees, growing by 34 per cent. The overall growth rate in the 14 high-tech industries was an enviable 34 per cent in the region, more than twice the overall growth rate.

Number of employers
In 1999 there were almost 48 000 employers in South-eastern Wisconsin. Some 2 per cent were governments (local, state, federal and schools). The rest were private sector employers. The number of employers in the region grew by 19 per cent between 1991 and 1999. The majority of the growth came from services employers. But manufacturing added 305 employers, construction added 842, and wholesale trade added 905 employers. The number of employers in retail actually declined as the industry consolidated.

The employers varied in size. Those with fewer than 100 employees accounted for 48 per cent of the employment in 1999. Those with 500 or more employees employed 24 per cent of all employees. Growth in employment in the last decade, however, does not reflect this distribution of employees related to company size. Most growth occurred in employers of fewer than 500 employees, with 56 per cent of the employment growth for the decade in firms with fewer than 100 employees. Those with between 100 and 500 were responsible for 41 per cent of the growth. The largest employers added just 3 per cent of the total, in comparison with their 24 per cent share of all employees.

Two other dimensions of employment growth are worth mentioning. First, employment growth is coming from newer entrants to the region. Some 60 per cent of the net employment growth in the region came from employers that were not in existence in 1991. That suggests the importance of new business activity. Second, all of the net growth is coming from employers that have multiple locations. Single-site employers are losing ground in the current economy. Mergers, acquisitions, expansions to new sites are the game that is now being played. The new economy is about more employers that are smaller and that have multiple locations. Most services require access to clients, hence the generation of multiple locations closer to the customer.

Unemployment rates
The region maintains its long streak of having an unemployment rate below that of the nation. In August 2000, the region's unemployment rate was 3.8 per

cent. The good news is that most of those looking for employment are finding opportunities. The bad news is that within the region some areas have unemployment rates below 2 per cent, indicating difficulty for employers who are looking for additional workers. The low unemployment rate is a constraint on the growth of the regional economy.

Earnings per worker

One of the most critical measures of the economy is the earnings of the workers. Table 11.5A shows the average earnings per worker by industry and the change in those averages over the 1990s. The good news is that real earnings per worker are reasonably high ($31 445 in 1999 – higher than anywhere else in the state), and they have been rising in South-eastern Wisconsin in the last decade. The average worker has experienced a $3008 gain in real income (in constant dollars) over the decade. That is quite different from the experience in the 1980s.

Unfortunately, the gain in income amounts to a little over 1 per cent per year. What we are finding is that more of us are working than in 1991, but we are not earning that much more. The true charge for the Summit is not so much more jobs for South-eastern Wisconsin, or the rest of Wisconsin, as it is more income earned from those jobs. Our labour force is not increasing. What is needed is more productivity and value added, so that earnings of workers can rise more rapidly.

Table 11.5A   Distribution and change in average earnings per worker by industry, South-eastern region, 1991–99

Industry	1999 average	Absolute change	% change
Agriculture & mining	$19 565	$52	0.3
Construction	$36 350	$2252	7
Manufacturing	$40 048	$2654	7
Transportation/utilities	$35 623	$1754	5
Wholesale trade	$40 136	$5157	15
Retail trade	$15 246	$1777	13
Finance, insurance, real estate	$49 468	$14 548	42
Services	$26 300	$3140	14
Government	$33 789	$21	0.1
Total	$31 445	$3008	11

Summary of key economic indicators

In summary, following are the key indicators related to the South-eastern region's economy that are important to understanding the region's position, the areas that will challenge us, and where we may find pockets of opportunity:

1. The region is growing in terms of employment, just not as fast as the rest of the state.
2. The growth is coming largely in the service sector (SICs 4–9).
3. Business services is the single industry with the greatest employment growth. The single largest component of that growth is attributable to temporary help firms.
4. Manufacturing continues to be important to the region, even if employment has remained relatively steady in recent years. The industry demands services from other industries and is still a major piece of the foundation of the regional economy.
5. High-tech employment is present, at rates higher than the state's, although below national levels.
6. Employment growth in the region slowed over the decade; only construction employment grew faster after than before 1995.
7. Unemployment rates are lower than the nation's, but this does vary within the region.
8. There are more employers today than there were in 1991, and the average size of employer is smaller than it used to be.
9. Some 56 per cent of the employment growth came from firms with fewer than 100 employees; only 3 per cent came from employers with 500 or more employees.
10. About 60 per cent of all net, new jobs were added by firms that came into being after 1991. That means that the majority of net employment growth came from entities that did not exist at the start of the decade.
11. All of the net employment gain in the region occurred in employers that have multiple sites. Employment in single location entities decreased over the decade.

Qualitative Analysis of Economic Conditions

Listening groups

A series of six listening sessions and two regional planning advisory groups were held throughout the South-eastern region to obtain an overview of the region's perceptions of these seven themes:

•   quality jobs;
•   venture capital;

- regulatory climate;
- educating the workforce;
- fiscal future and entrepreneurial climate;
- key infrastructure;
- distinctive brand image.

The listening sessions were held in autumn, 2000, in Milwaukee, Waukesha, West Bend, Racine/Kenosha, and Mequon, and were attended by a total of over 300 representatives of business/labour, education, non-profit agencies and government. A summary of the thoughts expressed at these sessions follows. Additional opinions were obtained a) from student focus groups on the UW-Milwaukee campus, and b) from the results of a study on issues of importance to the region's technology community conducted by the Metro Milwaukee Technology Alliance in summer 2000.

Quality jobs   There was a general perception among listening session participants that there is a lack of quality jobs in the South-eastern region. Three distinct themes emerged:

1. The region needs more high-tech job opportunities.
2. The region needs more skilled workers.
3. The region needs to do more to enhance job quality for the entire spectrum of the working community.

First, there was a definite consensus that the region needs more high-tech jobs. Despite this consensus, there was a division as to where the regional community feels high-tech jobs could and should be created. Participants throughout the region agreed that one of South-eastern Wisconsin's current strengths is in the manufacturing sector. Some participants believed that the region should take advantage of and build upon this strength, investing in high-tech innovations in the current industrial sector. They saw clear opportunities to enhance productivity in existing industries. Another viewpoint was held by others, who believed that Wisconsin has to break out of its 'manufacturing mentality', be more forward-thinking, and create and attract new businesses that will offer high-quality, high-paying employment in the technical arena.

Lack of high-tech jobs was not the only issue of concern related to high-tech. Lack of sufficient high-tech talent was of great concern, especially to those trying to hire technical employees. The region is clearly perceived to be suffering from 'brain drain', where top talent leaves the state in pursuit of better opportunities. Listening sessions throughout the region, as well as focus groups with graduating students, showed that the area is not perceived as a good place for fast-track careers nor as a high-level career destination. The region's businesses that currently offer high-tech job opportunities are often frustrated by their difficulty in recruiting and retaining employees in the South-eastern region, as cited in the results of a survey of metropolitan Milwaukee technology business leaders in summer 2000, conducted by the Metro Milwaukee Technology Alliance.

It was also evident from the listening sessions that the term 'quality jobs' does not necessarily mean high-tech jobs to everyone. There were recurring comments that the South-eastern region needs to do more to allow all workers to advance in their positions, thus increasing income potentials across the board, particularly for the minority population. As one participant put it, 'Addressing the issues of social equity cannot be overlooked. The central cities need to be revitalised to bring work to where many unemployed and underemployed live.'

Indeed, a number of participants felt that the region needs to 'make an asset' of its diverse population by increasing efforts to diversify the workforce. In addition to the dearth of quality job opportunities for the minority population, it was noted that there is a marked under-representation of minorities in upper-level jobs. More needs to be done to support education and training that allows greater diversification and better advancement opportunities for minorities in the workforce.

Venture capital   Comments throughout the South-eastern region consistently pointed to a lack of adequate venture capital, or early money, to fund new business start-ups and to support business growth. This was a problem cited throughout the whole region, and was of particular importance to the minority and small business communities. Almost 95 per cent of high-tech businesses surveyed by the Metro Milwaukee Technology Alliance whose businesses are currently seeking growth capital indicated that access to growth capital to the future of their business is 'somewhat important' or 'very important'.

Listening session participants were keenly aware that Wisconsin's slow or negative response to funding business ventures means that high-tech businesses in particular will move on to other states for their funding and operations. In Wisconsin, said one participant, 'it is an eight- or nine-month process. By that time, somebody else is already providing that high-tech service in another state.'

To underscore this, UW-Parkside Chancellor Jack Keating drew from David J. Ward's South-eastern Wisconsin Regional Advisory presentation to compare changes in per capita venture capital in Wisconsin, Minnesota, and nationwide between 1988 and 1998. In 1988, Wisconsin's per capita venture capital stood at $7.44, Minnesota's was $16.35, and the US average totalled in at $21.48. By 1998, Wisconsin increased to $14.30, the US average climbed to $71.79, and Minnesota skyrocketed to $137.19. Although the figures speak for themselves, Keating summarised, 'Venture capital equals high levels of technically skilled jobs equals good income equals tax base.'

Regulatory climate There was an evident sense of frustration by business-people at listening sessions in the South-eastern region that government doesn't understand business, and that tax and regulatory policies are overly burdensome. Clearly, the region's businesses felt that taxes are a major barrier to expanding their operations, as well as to attracting new businesses to the area. Wisconsin's tax structure was described as 'onerous'. One participant stated, 'State and local taxing entities need to understand the enormous imped-iments they present for businesses seeking to expand.' Wisconsin needs to 'level the playing field' with regard to taxes, said some businesspeople, who are concerned that Wisconsin can't compete with other states that have much more favourable tax structures for businesses.

In addition to burdensome taxes, the regulatory climate in Wisconsin was called 'atrocious'. Government is viewed as having 'no understanding of time', with a few participants citing the extraordinary amount of time it takes to obtain permits as an example of government not adequately responding to the needs of business. On a positive note, it appears that business has a sincere desire to work together with government bodies for the betterment of the econ-omy. 'Let's get together', was a repetitive theme at listening sessions in the region. Kenosha County was cited as a 'textbook case' of how government and business can work cooperatively.

Educating the workforce The listening sessions elicited comments about the strengths in the education system and in the quality of the workforce, but also highlighted ideas on improving education in the state. In general, people felt that the South-eastern region's public school systems are good, but acknowl-edge that major problems exist in some of the larger districts. Area universi-ties and colleges were viewed as excellent, providing good educational value and quality graduates. Respondents to the Metro Milwaukee Technology Alliance's summer 2000 survey indicated that the quality of technology employees in the Milwaukee area is good as well. Graduating students commented in focus groups that they felt well-prepared for their chosen careers, including in areas of technology.

Still, there were perceptions that education of the area workforce needs to be improved. First, participants called for both better general training and better skilled training of the workforce. Members of the Business Council, an association of African American business owners, ranked as a 'top priority' issue the lack of competent, well-trained staff, and the need for training programmes to prepare individuals ('particularly those from lower income black neighbourhoods') to be successful in their jobs. Opportunities

Industrialization Centers of America (OIC) was cited as a prime example of a successful job training programme aimed at African Americans. OIC Greater Milwaukee is one of the largest training sites in the OIC network. In addition, there were numerous comments in the region indicating that the workforce is 'not skilled or technically competent enough' to support high-tech companies.

Second, continuing education was viewed as vital to the improvement of the workforce. Participants wanted to see companies value the continuing education of their workforce, and government to back such initiatives through tax breaks.

Third, participants indicated their desire for government to provide greater support for education in the state. It was noted that funding for education is not keeping pace with increased costs; at the same time, businesses are calling for more qualified workers. 'Funding for education in Wisconsin needs to be restored and enhanced.' Government was also called upon to provide tax incentives for continuing education to both businesses and individuals. Participants also felt that the state could take steps to keep our 'best and brightest' in the region by increasing the number of Wisconsin students who are admitted to Wisconsin universities and colleges, and by providing more honours opportunities for high-achieving students.

Last, the listening sessions looked to the educational system itself to take steps to better prepare the future workforce. Building on the recurring theme of communication and cooperation, participants felt that both K-12 schools and universities/colleges 'need to have a better understanding of the needs of business' and need to coordinate better with business and each other. Specific suggestions included developing and providing specific job training tracks to meet employer demand, providing practical application of skills at all levels of education, providing more internship opportunities, and creating an educational focus on entrepreneurship. Education was also asked to increase awareness and knowledge of technical and professional training opportunities among school guidance personnel so that they can share this information with students and parents making education and career decisions.

Fiscal future and entrepreneurial climate   Opinions about the fiscal future and entrepreneurial climate of the South-eastern region pointed to the need for a change in the way things get done. The perceived economic climate of the South-eastern region is that of a 'traditional' or 'conservative' economy that relies on its past strengths, rather than an innovative economy that seeks out new opportunities. 'Wisconsin seems to look backward for our growth.'

A number of comments were made about the lack of a strategy or incentive system for both attracting new companies and retaining current industry and jobs. 'Milwaukee leadership needs to go after business to stay and expand', said one individual. Again, participants cited the need for coordinated effort among business/labour, education, non-profit agencies, and government to set an agenda to solve economic issues.

Again, the topic of social equity was addressed during discussions about the economic future of the region. Participants urged that the region take advantage of the diversity of its population. A number of participants discussed the lack of opportunities for the economically disadvantaged, particularly minorities residing in central cities. It was felt that for these areas and individuals to be able to improve their economic future, they require educational support, worker training and funding to revitalise business.

Key infrastructure   While infrastructure was not a predominant theme, it is clear within our region that these issues are key to our future growth: air, energy, roads and mass transit. The authors also note that a paper written for the Metropolitan Milwaukee Association of Commerce by Dr Eric Schenker, emeritus professor and dean at UWM, identifies future energy sources as a major issue to be dealt with given Wisconsin's economic growth and increasing demand for power.

More interesting were perceptions on what could be viewed as non-traditional infrastructure, or 'people and idea' infrastructure. Throughout the many listening sessions, people pointed to the need to better coordinate the efforts of business/labour, education, non-profit agencies, and government. Common themes surfaced regarding improving communication among the major players. There were numerous appeals for government and business to work together on issues of regulation and taxation. Other comments called for business and education to work together to ensure that tomorrow's workforce is trained in the areas that business needs. Education was urged to coordinate its various levels, from elementary school to high school to technical college or university. Entrepreneurs stated the need for an avenue to network together. The message was clear: 'We need to work together.' As such, improving this type of infrastructure carried considerable weight at the listening sessions.

Distinctive brand image   Wisconsinites are proud of who they are, and the South-eastern region is no exception. It boasts a high quality of life, a strong work ethic, and a good place to raise a family. That said, the region also realises that it is perceived as traditional, resistant to change and risk-averse. Participants recognised that this is a serious impediment to attracting new, innovative firms to the area. There was strong opinion that the region needs to 'break out from the beer and brats image to technology and modern day manufacturing'. 'The Dairy State image is not high-tech', said one participant.

Technology leaders agree. The findings of a survey of metro Milwaukee technology business leaders conducted by the Metro Milwaukee Technology Alliance in summer 2000 indicate that 'enhancing the image of the area as a technology center is paramount in growing their businesses', and would lead to both increased business for their own operations, and attraction of other technology businesses to the area.

An enhanced business image, however, may not be enough. Milwaukee's lifestyle image is 'not glamorous enough' for younger people in information technology fields – people who earn high salaries, stay single longer, change jobs frequently, and want a dynamic lifestyle.

Listening session summary

Clearly, the region sees that both challenges and opportunities lie ahead. Integrating regional demographics, definitional characteristics, and the perceptions generated across the listening sessions and other sources, we offer the following specific recommendations pertaining to themes raised in the Summit. These are by no means independent activities, but rather ones that will necessarily have spillover benefits that can address sequentially (and simultaneously) several themes. For example, recommendations for building quality jobs, if successful, will also serve to reverse the 'brain drain' as skilled workers will have relatively more attractive employment options in state. Our suggestions include:

1. Focus on workforce development; we have to be able to do more with fewer worker additions. Simply put, the existing workforce is stretched to its limit, which creates a ceiling on both existing industry and the prospects for new business start-ups.
2. Look to 'New Manufacturing' for growth in the region. While it is recognised that traditional manufacturing has historically been the heart of the regional economy, the South-eastern region needs to 'break the mould' in order to move the economy forward and remain competitive.
3. Stress the *application* of technology to make employers in all industries efficient. This involves infrastructure, workforce development, and fostering competition.
4. Encourage new business development by creating the appropriate climate, eliminating regulatory barriers, and attracting venture and seed capital.
5. Increase the representation of minority populations in both the general workforce and in upper-level positions.
6. Take steps to ensure a stable power supply and reasonable energy prices.
7. Address the brain drain and build quality jobs through several mechanisms:
   - Encourage job growth in high-tech and so-called 'new economy' organisations.

- Provide tax breaks and reduce regulatory bureaucracies that impede start-ups.
- Encourage and develop state-sponsored productivity boosters: answer the question, how to do more with less? Provide governor's awards and other recognition programmes that foster productivity enhancements.
- Challenge manufacturing firms to demonstrate they how they have moved up the value chain. Increased wages will follow if value is being added; conversely, jobs will leave the area and real wages will decline if the status quo is maintained.

8. Encourage all (and particularly state-supported) higher education institutions to work more closely to develop specific centres of academic excellence that promote economic opportunity and workforce development. Examples of areas in which centres and skill development could be promoted:
   - high-technology engineering applications;
   - biomedical and bioengineering areas;
   - printing industry;
   - entrepreneurship in business schools.

9. Provide state tax incentives for employers with educational assistance programmes. Additional incentives could be provided for close collaborations with educational partnerships that are either focused on specific industry consortia or working in tandem with multiple education levels (e.g., 2-plus-2-plus-2).

Positioning South-eastern Wisconsin for the New Economy

South-eastern Wisconsin is in a strong and unique position within the state for economic growth:

- 35 per cent of the state's population and 36 per cent of the state's employees;
- 80 per cent of the state's minority population, creating opportunities to capitalise on the region's rich diversity;
- 48 per cent of the state's high-tech jobs;
- 40 per cent of the state's college-educated population (the sixth highest ranking of North American cities in per capita population with higher education credentials);
- access to the intellectual capital of over 2,300 faculty members from more than 16 colleges and universities, and to the 10 000 graduates produced by those institutions each year;
- a 1999 GMP of $61.15 billion;

- 52 per cent of the state's publicly traded corporations;
- seven Fortune 500 companies;
- core businesses in manufacturing, data processing, insurance, business services, mutual funds and printing;
- 54 per cent of the state's registered patents;
- excellent proximity to US and Canadian markets;
- strategic location in the Chicago, Milwaukee, Madison and Twin Cities corridor, which feature excellent transportation systems;
- daily flights out of Milwaukee to 50 major business markets;
- the value of goods and services exported from the region exceeds $5 billion;
- an international port on a major waterway.

These are over a dozen extremely compelling economic indicators for South-eastern Wisconsin. They lay a foundation and a profound sense of opportunity for the region and the state. Yet these variables alone do not make an economic future. Although we have the key criteria that are essential for economic growth, we have not capitalised on these strengths. Consequently, it is clear that regional economic development requires systemic thinking, behaviour and concrete actions. *Now is the time* for business/labour, education, non-profit agencies, and government in South-eastern Wisconsin to come together, plan and activate a strategy that takes advantage of these assets.

Highlighted below is an example of regional coordination, TechStar, which is currently being developed, followed by a general strategy and call to action for regional thinking and coordination – nothing short of a regional Joint Venture leading to robust economic growth and development in South-eastern Wisconsin.

TechStar

Because Wisconsin industries often employ mature technologies, they are continually challenged to sustain long-term competitiveness in the market-place. To maintain and improve long-term economic health, South-eastern Wisconsin needs to pump emerging technologies into its business community. Universities drive industry and business competitiveness in the new high-tech economy, as exemplified by Palo Alto, Boston, Austin, San Diego and Durham/Chapel Hill.

One answer to this challenge is the regional coordination exemplified in the recently announced TechStar initiative. TechStar represents an infrastructure that will be developed in metropolitan Milwaukee to marshall the technology-focused intellectual capital in the participating educational institutions in order to advance the economic and societal well-being of South-eastern Wisconsin and throughout the state. TechStar directly addresses three statewide economic development needs:

1. greater access to intellectual capital;
2. increased competitiveness of existing businesses and industries in the marketplace;
3. more new technology-based businesses.

TechStar provides the necessary infrastructure to create new jobs by bringing together South-eastern Wisconsin academic institutions and the business community. Key targets for TechStar include fostering technology-related economic development, stemming the loss of highly trained and skilled people, and increasing the number of high paying jobs – all of which are critical issues for Wisconsin's future – in addition to being among the key themes of this statewide economic summit.

TechStar's founding structure relies on strategic partnerships among universities, the business, financial and labour communities, and civic leadership. Several models have been studied, including the North Carolina Research Triangle, Houston Advanced Research Center, and Rensselaer Polytechnic Institute. Their best practices have been identified and adapted to Wisconsin's business climate. As a result, the appropriate intellectual, fiscal and personnel resources have been identified to meet the primary TechStar goal: *turn ideas into companies and jobs.*

Since start-up businesses and existing firms have different technology or general assistance needs, TechStar will have two main cornerstones: an Established Business Technology Service Center and a Startup Business Commercialization Center. This approach is also consistent with the rest of our study in which we call for enhancement to existing industry and promulgation of practices that facilitate new business start-ups.

Beyond this specific initiative, we suggest a broader, more inclusive umbrella organisation be formed. TechStar's strength is in its focus on technology transfer and related application to new start-ups and existing industry. However, it is not enough, as examples of other booming regional economies show. What is typical in such areas is how local and state government, higher education, industry and labour collaborate on a host of issues across regionally limited borders. Similar to Silicon Valley's Joint Venture for 2010, we believe that without greater regional coordination, we are not likely to successfully address the themes raised in this Summit. Accordingly, we present an outline below for such coordination.

A South-eastern Wisconsin Joint Venture
We submit that there is an urgency to forge our future together *now* if do not wish to allow other regions in the US and abroad to eclipse us. We envision

Figure 11.2A   A Joint Venture for regional economic development

a model in which leaders in business/labour, education, the non-profit community and government would form a 'Joint Venture', working together to identify and address common issues that have been raised in this Summit. Figure 11.2A illustrates the proposed components of the Joint Venture. Using TechStar as a building block, the Joint Venture would have a much broader focus in that it would be setting the agenda and addressing common issues pertaining to the six-county region across the entire spectrum of themes raised in this Summit.

The premise for a Joint Venture model in South-eastern Wisconsin is supported by the fact that several key regional players recognise the value in working together for the region's greater good. Without that commitment, we would continue to go it alone in terms of different players not working across either region or functionality. And, as dynamic, forward-looking structure, we suggest that this coordinating body not be constrained with just these issues. Indeed, if we simply examine other high-growth regions in the country and aim to mirror their achievements, our region could very well be behind yet another set of challenges. Thus, the charge to their new entity would be to accelerate the region's efforts:

- to become aggressive economically;
- to expand workforce opportunities that meet personal, social and economic needs;
- to enhance the overall quality of life and regional prosperity.

These objectives can only be realised through partnerships based on commitment and mutual collaboration, and by capitalising on the unique assets to the region.

The South-eastern Wisconsin Joint Venture's initial charge would be to examine several key questions:

1. Who should work together? Business/labour, education, non-profit agencies, government, etc.
2. Why should we work together? What's in it for us to work together versus the separate geographical, industrial, or functional paths we're now on?
3. What barriers to working together must be overcome?
4. What are specific examples of regions working together, and how have they overcome barriers inherent in regional cooperation?
5. How would the group be best structured to manage the tension between the high degree of participation required for buy-in versus the need to be small enough to move quickly and get the job done?
6. How can this initiative link us beyond the borders of the region, to the state, the country and internationally?
7. What are our key objectives and how will we know if we've achieved success in the short- and long-term?
8. What is our action plan for going forward (sequence and specific actions taken by whom)?
9. Who is responsible for coordinating our activities?

Next steps

We urge that a group of key regional leaders in business/labour, education, non-profit agencies and government be convened by *30 January 2001*, with the charge of examining the key questions enumerated above and creating a comprehensive business plan for the region's future economic growth that highlights early and ongoing successes. To take advantage of the momentum of this Summit, we suggest that the region process and strategic plan be accomplished within a six-month period.

Conclusion

In conclusion, the regional demographics and comments from regional leaders that were summarised earlier in this report point to a wealth of both challenges and opportunities for South-eastern Wisconsin. It is now up to our regional leaders to answer the call to action, to come together as representatives of the regional economy, and to decide upon and embark on a course of action that will position South-eastern Wisconsin for growth. We submit these recommendations and pledge our support and involvement for the benefit of all.

NOTE

* The authors gratefully acknowledge the assistance of Karla Ashenhurst, Ron Heilmann, Sandra Hoeh, John Keating, Tom Luljak, Mary Mulroy, Shelia Payton, Joel Rodney, Allison Rostenkowski, Eric Schenker, Kathryn St Clair, Brad Stewart, and Linda Stewart in the data collection and preparation of this paper.

12. International perspectives on the prosperity of a region: a personal reflection*

J. Robert Branston, Roger Sugden and James R. Wilson

1. INTRODUCTION

For two weeks in July 2001 a group of around 20 scholars from Wisconsin, other US states and Europe had a unique opportunity to interact with each other, and with public officials and businesspeople from surrounding localities. The purpose was to collaborate on their research, and to think about development in a globalised new economy. As explained in the Foreword, this volume derives directly from that two-week experience,[1] the preceding chapters having been debated, developed and worked on during the Second L'institute–Milwaukee Workshop on 'Urban and regional prosperity in a globalised economy'.

In this final chapter, we aim to provide a personal reflection on the *process* of the workshop itself. We see this as having been positive; with flaws but also with valuable lessons for the future. The chapter explores the aims of the process as it was initially conceived, and asks whether these aims have been realised. We seek to identify problems that were encountered, and make tentative suggestions as to how these might be overcome in the future. The motivation for such an analysis lies in a view that the workshop, and indeed this volume, are merely dimensions of an ongoing concern to become part of the process of economic development (in regions or, in the language of Chapter 1) in localities such as Wisconsin. In this regard, the workshop in itself is not an end-result, and neither is this volume. Crucially, then, we conclude with thoughts on how and where the process might develop from here.

The chapter is structured in three sections. Section 2 describes the aims of the workshop, and Section 3 explores the reality. Section 4 turns to the future, and to the steps being taken to learn from and carry forward the process. Included as an Appendix to the chapter is a report entitled 'International perspectives on South-eastern Wisconsin's economic development'. As will be detailed, this was first-drafted and debated by participants during the course of the workshop. From the outset, the report was conceived as an important output of the process.

2.   THE AIMS OF THE WORKSHOP

This was the Second L'institute–Milwaukee Workshop, the first having been held at the University of Wisconsin-Milwaukee (UWM) in July 2000. The idea behind initiating this series of events has its origins in two similar activities hosted jointly by the Universities of Warwick and Birmingham in the UK during the early 1990s.[2] Following the experience of these earlier workshops, an explicit aim was to emphasise the relevance of interaction amongst scholars in different contexts, not confined solely to formal sessions and presentations. Thus, both L'institute–Milwaukee workshops were of significant length (two weeks), and their schedules were designed to leave a large amount of time free for different types of activities and interaction. Moreover, sessions were deliberately timetabled to finish in the early afternoon and early evening, so as to encourage debate that extended into lunch and dinner in a different, more informal environment. Participants were also given shared office space and computer facilities, so that research could be carried out, alone or with others, during the course of the two weeks. Thus the ideas emerging from interaction with colleagues could contribute to and enrich ongoing work, and participants' current research could itself fuel discussion and interaction.

A first aim of the 2001 workshop was hence to facilitate research relationships among a group of scholars with interests in related fields, extending the process initiated the previous year. The workshop was envisaged as being part of a continuing, dynamic networking in research activity. The hope was that debate and writing initiated (and in some cases continued) during the two weeks would extend to form the basis for future work and projects among and between, though by no means exclusive to, those involved. The importance attached to different types of interaction – in particular the fusing of social and professional activity – was seen as a route to achieving this end. Moreover, it is derived from a parallel view that economic development necessitates a fusing of economic and social interests. The success of local development in the 'Third Italy', for example, is arguably rooted in the way in which social and economic relationships are forged together, based on values of trust, respect and appropriate cooperation, existing alongside appropriate rivalry.[3] Importance was also attached to furthering the network of researchers and maintaining a dynamism and freshness of ideas – again parallel to similar concerns in economic development processes. In this regard, the Second L'institute–Milwaukee Workshop invited a mixture of participants, drawn from its predecessor and from scholars new to the process, and ensured that new/young researchers (including PhD students) were integrally involved.

A second aim of the 2001 event differentiated it quite substantially in nature and scope from the First Workshop. Its broad topic was 'Urban and regional prosperity in a globalised economy', and within this a key objective was to address local 'prosperity' under 'globalisation' in the specific context of South-eastern Wisconsin. This did not mean that each of the papers presented by participating scholars had to be explicitly focused on South-eastern Wisconsin. Rather, it meant that discussion around the different ideas and experiences presented would be geared towards their implications for local economies in general. These consequences could then be drawn out for Wisconsin in particular. Moreover, the aim extended further than this. It incorporated a fundamental concern with becoming part of the development process itself; interacting with local academics, businesspeople and public officials in seeking to learn from each other how different ideas might be applied to South-eastern Wisconsin.

This concern was again rooted in a certain perspective on development. In particular, the view that development is a process of determining, and then seeking to move towards, the goals and desires of the people that live in a particular locality. It is thus inappropriate for development objectives and policy solutions to be set by people from outside of a locality.[4] Corresponding to this view, great care was taken to avoid a situation where a group of largely 'external' academics discussed, formulated and then prescribed various courses of action to be followed by a locality. The emphasis instead was on presentations of perspectives on different issues by each of the invited scholars, with reference to their own experience and research interest. Parallel with this, there were sessions given by businesspeople, academics and public officials from the Wisconsin area. The intention was that these would provide different perspectives on specific economic development issues affecting the locality. It was envisaged that the discussion in and around both types of session – as well as in specific time allocated solely for considering the implications flowing from all sessions – could result in the development of ideas relevant to the local economy. The objective was essentially for the workshop to provide a learning forum for local and external participants, with knowledge flowing in both directions. It would thus become a small part of the process of determining and seeking to move towards development goals. It would be a contribution benefiting from international experience and expertise, but one that was, vitally, rooted in the aims and views of people within Wisconsin.

More specific objectives in this regard included the hosting of a public panel session on 'University and community partnership in building a sustainable regional economy'. This was in line with drawing wider groups into the debate, and with emphasising the continuing involvement of the University of

Wisconsin-Milwaukee in the development of the locality, but in partnership with other interested groups (business, government, local community). Also central was the proposed production of a report during the course of the work-shop.

It was envisaged that the report would draw together the experiences of participating scholars to comment on the development of South-eastern Wisconsin, but do so in a non-prescriptive way that fundamentally incorpo-rated and reflected the input of local actors. Besides providing a focal point for discussions at the workshop, this report was intended to feed into future discussions within South-eastern Wisconsin, perhaps stimulating ideas and possibilities that could contribute to the state's development, thereby leading to new initiatives and activities. In particular, at the time of the workshop the state was planning the Second Wisconsin Economic Summit. It was thought that this Summit might provide an ideal opportunity to interact with others who were attempting to stimulate and contribute to new ways forward, not least because material prepared for the previous year's First Wisconsin Economic Summit had provided an important influence on the design of the workshop.[5] Accordingly, an objective was to circulate and 'present' the report at the Second Summit, but also to disseminate it more widely on the Internet and among other interested parties within the region.

Finally, perhaps the most visible aim of the workshop was to produce this volume, documenting both the ideas that emerged from participants based on their own specific expertise (comprising the main body of chapters), and the experience of the process itself (essentially the Foreword, part of the first chapter and this final chapter).

3.   THE REALITY OF THE WORKSHOP

It is clear from the aims and objectives outlined in Section 2 that the workshop was concerned primarily with the *process* of research and learning, and with rooting that process within the context of ongoing local debate and concerns around the development of a locality. In this section we explore the reality of that process. Where we do discuss the more visible *outcomes*, in particular the report that was actually written (see the Appendix to this chapter), we do so in terms of their contribution to the ongoing process rather than as outcomes in their own right.

In many respects the workshop can be seen to have broadly fulfilled the aims described in Section 2. In terms of facilitating long-term and evolving research relationships among a group of scholars with related interests, it provided an academic and social environment that allowed the continuation of the process that had begun (as far as Milwaukee is concerned) at the 2000 workshop. Debate on a range of issues, within and without the sessions, was healthy, vibrant and at times fierce. Moreover, the achievement of this volume is a testament to the ongoing research stimulated by the workshop, as is the further commitment of many of those involved to future projects and initiatives that we will return to in the next section. Regarding the invigoration of the network, the workshop can also be viewed as a success. Participation by a number of academics new to the network and not involved in the previous event has stimulated fresh research relationships, and several young/new researchers have been integrally involved both during the workshop and in discussions around future projects.

However, a slightly more critical perspective is warranted regarding the second aim, that referring to the local development process in South-eastern Wisconsin. At a somewhat superficial level, there was again a good degree of success. Interesting sessions were given by local business people, academics and public officials on the problems and reality of the local economy, which in turn stimulated a great deal of insightful debate, both at these and other times. Discussions around the sessions given by 'external' participants, for example, frequently shifted towards marrying the various specific concerns of the presenters with the context of local development provided in the more Wisconsin-oriented sessions. There was also a great deal of interesting debate around applying the different perspectives of participants to the specifics of South-eastern Wisconsin in the times allocated for debating and preparing the report, a process that is elaborated on below. In terms of the more specific outcomes, the public session was well attended, although the audience was perhaps not as broad as was envisaged, and a report was produced that genuinely fused the expertise of scholars with the development concerns recounted by local actors involved in the process.

Nevertheless, examining the reality more deeply, it is clear that severe limitations were uncovered in the way in which the workshop sought to become part of the development process. There are consequently lessons to be learned from the experience. These can be explored particularly in terms of the writing of the report and its subsequent role in South-eastern Wisconsin, although the arguments also pertain to the process more widely.

The designers of the workshop were extremely conscious of the 'insider'/'outsider' issue; that it is not for outsiders to come into town for a couple of weeks and pretend to understand local conditions and desires, let alone attempt to start telling local people how to run their economy.[6] The report attempts to reflect this, in its style, structure, wording and content. It is also reflected in the choice of authorship. There was a decision to deliberately opt for collective authorship under L'institute – rather than naming the particular people involved – because the report was not conceived as from a set of individuals, rather from an activity and process involving many participants, both internal and external to the locality. Even so, it is instructive that throughout the process sensitivity about the role of 'outsiders' was strongly evident. For example, even amongst the participants there were suggestions that the process of writing the report was flawed because it implied outsiders presuming to tell 'locals' what to do.

The lesson we draw from this sensitivity is the following. If development is to be based on the aims, objectives and actions of the people of a locality, but if those outside the locality might be able to contribute ideas and suggestions for locals to act upon as they decide, then the ways in which the outsiders conduct themselves is crucial. There needs to be conscious awareness of sensitivities and concerns, of the economic, political and social characteristics of the locality. Related, there needs to be sensitivity on the part of local people, for example a refusal to jump to the depiction of interfering outsiders when that is not accurate. Both insiders and outsiders need to be aware of each other's roles, respectful of each other, and willing to learn together as the process unfolds.

The reality of the workshop was certainly a step towards such a situation. However, it is likely that a fuller awareness of sensitivities and a greater degree of comfort with each other's roles in the process can only evolve over a longer period of time. This would be similar to the way in which knowledge, awareness and trust emerges in individual relationships. In addition, this conclusion has wider relevance for the role of multinational relationships in development processes more generally. For example, a common criticism of the World Bank in its dealings with less developed countries is that development professionals arrive, stay in top hotels, and then return after a few weeks or months to their career paths in Washington; they are distant from the actual process of development.[7] Combine this with the charge that the World Bank is highly prescriptive in its advice,[8] a one-way rather than two-way flow, then it becomes clear why the Bank is often viewed as an 'outsider'; it is often seen as having a stake or interest in the local development process that differs markedly from that of the local people. In this sense we argue that it forges development relationships that are 'international' (cross-border) but not 'multinational' (integrated across nations, rooted in all constituent localities). That workshop participants were explicitly conscious of such difficulties from the outset, took great care to avoid being prescriptive, and yet encountered similar problems, highlights the difficulties inherent in genuinely multinational interaction where issues of 'development' are concerned. It suggests the need for relationships to emerge over time, a perhaps lengthy process of learning, evolving the trust and knowledge about each other that can yield a truly productive cooperation.

Indeed, the intention was that participants at the workshop would see themselves as part of the ongoing process, contributing to refinement of the report and to future activities in Wisconsin beyond the immediate two weeks spent in Milwaukee in July 2001. In practice, they have contributed in terms of 'routine' academic activities, the sorts of concerns that they are used to having as academics; for example, developing their chapters for this volume. However, there is a question over their role with the report and the development process within Wisconsin. Subsequent to the period in Milwaukee, some participants have been active in their input, but not others. In part this is a reflection of the type of self-selection that takes place in much cooperative activity. It also stems from a lack of clarity amongst some participants about expectations and aims, which suggests that they require more effective communication. This is a lesson for the future, and although perhaps obvious, it warrants emphasis. Moreover, a further explanation is probably a lack of belief, a view that the workshop and the report, no matter how well-meant or how well-executed, could not succeed in their aims. In part (and assuming the aims are desirable and can be realised), the remedy for this is learning from experience. Success will breed success, and mistakes that are addressed in appropriate ways will yield greater confidence.

The role of the report following the workshop has also been, at least for us, disappointing in terms of its impact in Wisconsin itself. Despite initial intentions, as it emerged the report was never circulated beyond personnel at the University of Wisconsin-Milwaukee, and even there the distribution was not widespread. The basic reason was that it was concluded that the report would not impact on the audience of policy-makers, public officials and businesspeople concerned with economic development in the state, nor would it impact on the sorts of university personnel involved in the process. This was in essence a judgement call on the part of those concerned. The specific difficulty was thought to be that the report reads as if there exists some form of 'planning' or coordination mechanism for economic development in Wisconsin, a process that was judged to be non-existent.[9] If that judgement is correct, it is an attempted contribution that fails to take adequate account of the economic, political and social reality to which it is directed. No matter how well-intentioned it might be, a report or any other contribution to economic development that misjudges or fails to take account of realities is bound at best to have no impact unless it is lucky, and at worse to have adverse consequences.[10] Of course, one conclusion from this train of events might be that it points to a need for an appropriate planning process in the state; we suggest that it might be an institutional omission if there is no natural recipient of the report.

Wisconsin clearly has a very active concern with its economic development, but at formal, pan-state levels that concern appears to be channelled from and through many independent actors. Admittedly, this impression is gained from discussions at the workshop amongst a limited group of people, mostly from South-eastern Wisconsin, and none of whom included 'official' representatives from the state. A report written (deliberately) in terms of 'might' and 'maybe', 'perhaps' and 'possibly', could be too weak and tepid, lacking in a hard-hitting approach that is relevant to the sort of urgency and immediacy that many of the independent actors seem to be demanding. For example, as the Appendix reveals, there is considerable interest in Wisconsin on 'clusters' as a means of promoting its economic development. The report urges caution, suggesting that 'clusters' is a concept that encompasses many possibilities. This might be a message too easily dismissed as the luxury of academics, locked into their own timescale when Wisconsin's reality is seen to be far more immediate, at least by some of those pushing the process of debate.

Recognition of a possible demand for immediacy does not imply that the workshop ought to have glossed over the potential inadequacies in the ways in which 'clusters' might be conceived and therefore pursued in Wisconsin. An outcome of the workshop, not previously appreciated, is that those inadequacies might exist, and this is potentially important. However, the workshop failed to enable such concerns and their consequences to feed into the Wisconsin development process.

In our view, the workshop was not necessarily ill-conceived. Perhaps the institutions of development ought to have been considered more carefully before a workshop on issues such as clustering. Had that occurred, either it would have been possible to comment on institutional developments that could provide a favourable climate for the sort of report that was to be written, or knowledge of the institutional conditions would have enabled the writing of a very different and thus more appropriate report. Similarly, another possibility would have been to have an open, public session towards the end of the workshop, designed to feedback the report to the local academic, business and policy-making communities.[11] This would have deepened the two-way interaction, perhaps creating a more favourable outcome; for example, we might have been able to persuade some political constituency to 'buy' our general views, and/or we might have been able to revise the report appropriately. As it was, the design of the workshop was fitted around issues that certain (academic and business) insiders had identified as crucial for the state. In that sense it was relevant, and was an attempt not to rely on a long-run academic timescale, but instead to contribute on the issues that others were addressing. In doing so, those involved have learned more about Wisconsin's development process, and learning was one of the aims. For us, it is perhaps disappointing that the report has found no 'natural' recipients; that there appears to be no connection between the way the report was written and conceived, and the apparent reality of the development process in Wisconsin. But the learning was necessary, and can now inform the way in which such initiatives are pursued in the future.

4. WHERE FROM HERE?

As is clear from Section 3, some of the aims of the workshop have been met more impressively than others. In particular, an evaluation of the aims and reality of the workshop has highlighted difficulties and limitations associated with its effective integration with the development process of South-eastern Wisconsin. These, we believe, are largely attributable to two factors. First, the need for further learning regarding the sensitivities surrounding 'insiders' and 'outsiders' where local development issues are concerned. Second, a report that failed to find an appropriate audience within the region. Both factors can be related partly to an insufficient initial understanding of the institutions and context in which the region's development is rooted.

The question now is where to go from here? We suggest that there are many things to be learned from the experience, both for application within South-eastern Wisconsin, and for more general consideration in future initiatives that aim to fuse academic research with local economic development, particularly in a multinational context.

In terms of South-eastern Wisconsin, the experience of the workshop and the report has highlighted what is perhaps an institutional omission. Amid a seemingly great desire among some to address various local development problems, there appears to be no body or process within the state that can act as a focal point, coordinating the different ideas that stem from these concerns. There are, however, the possible beginnings of various such focal points. One in particular might be the Wisconsin Economic Summit, the second of which took place in November 2001. The focus of the second Summit was on clusters, an issue that also emerged as a fundamental concern at the workshop. Hence the debate and research that took place at the workshop, and the analysis contained in the report, are of relevance to ongoing activities in Wisconsin. Whilst they have yet to find a specific way into that process, there is a chance that they may do so in the future. What would be required is continued and appropriate evolution in the focal points for discussing, coordinating and planning solutions to Wisconsin's development problems, or a new presentation of the workshop debate, research and analysis.

From an academic perspective, one of the most important issues to emerge from the process of the workshop was the local concern with clusters as a catalyst for economic development. One of the key arguments made in the report is that there are, however, significant differences in what is meant by clusters, and that certain forms of clustering may be more desirable than others. A main conclusion was the need for care in embracing clusters as a solution to problems of local economic development; a questioning of what is required from economic development, and subsequent determination of what form of clustering might best realise those aims. Similar arguments are made with regard to other development issues, such as entrepreneurship. Linked to these conclusions is a need for wider involvement and debate as integral to the development process, perhaps reaching broader groups than was achieved at the workshop. Again, we can point to the ongoing development of the Wisconsin Economic Summit as a starting-point in this regard, although with a hint of warning that perhaps this is not yet an inclusive enough process. In that case, it might run the danger of leading to an inaccurate and inefficient identification of problems and solutions.

L'institute intends to pursue the clusters issue further in a project focusing on experiences and impacts in different aspects of economic and social life.[12] Many of those contributing to the Milwaukee Workshop will also be involved in this project, although again the network will be widened to include researchers new to the process. While the context initially takes a more European focus – specifically, workshops in Catalonia (Spain) and Toulouse (France) – the findings will be applicable to the ongoing concerns in South-eastern Wisconsin. Indeed, it is hoped that the research undertaken in this project will enable a follow-up to this volume, where findings from a different context can be related back to the ongoing process of research, debate and policy formation around clusters in South-eastern Wisconsin. The intention is to create and nurture, in the context of academic research, the type of 'democratic globalisation' that is suggested as a positive way forward for multinational relationships by Sugden and Wilson in Chapter 1 of this volume. By taking the lessons from activities undertaken in one locality, seeking to learn from them in projects conducted elsewhere, and then relating those findings back to the ongoing process of the original locality, we offer the scope for forging influential relationships; it may be possible for knowledge and cooperation over certain issues to flow across localities in a way that maintains its roots in the specific interests of each locality.

While problems were encountered in achieving the aims set out prior to the L'institute–Milwaukee Workshop, we do not believe that these are insurmountable in the longer run. Clearly there is much to learn about genuinely 'democratic', multinational relationships, both what they are and how they are attained. In this regard the workshop can be seen as a positive step, the beginning of a learning process that many of those involved intend to pursue in different contexts and different ways in the future.

APPENDIX: INTERNATIONAL PERSPECTIVES ON SOUTH-EASTERN WISCONSIN'S ECONOMIC DEVELOPMENT (*L'institute*)

Foreword

This report is intended to contribute to debate on future economic development in Wisconsin, especially South-eastern Wisconsin. Most notably, it is based upon ideas and experiences offered by scholars that participated in the Second L'institute–Milwaukee Workshop on 'Urban and regional prosperity in a globalized economy'. This was a meeting of scholars, public officials and business people. The scholars came from Wisconsin, elsewhere in the US, and from Europe (including England, Italy and Finland). The workshop was held at the University of Wisconsin-Milwaukee (UWM) in July 2001 and was hosted by the Department of Economics (College of Letters and Science) and the School of Business Administration. The event was part of the programme of L'institute, a joint venture between UWM (where L'institute is part of the Center for International Education) and the Universities of Birmingham (UK) and Ferrara (Italy).

The origins of the report lie in the First L'institute–Milwaukee Workshop, held in July 2000. This event brought together scholars from different parts of the US and Europe to analyse and discuss their research. It was decided that the Second Workshop would not only invite scholars to participate on a similar basis, but would also attempt to give something further to the local community, based on the scholars' fields of expertise. These included the analysis of clusters, entrepreneurship, governance, Japanese industrial development, labour markets, antitrust, supply chain management, technology and innovation and public policy.

The report is a result of discussions that included various commentators on economic development from the region; it is not merely views from outsiders, rather it is a product of discussions with some of those living and working in Wisconsin. However, the report is neither the outcome of exhaustive discussions with all interested parties in South-eastern Wisconsin, nor the outcome of our own research on the area. Our aim is far more modest; to discuss some options that might be relevant for the region's future economic prosperity, based on a very limited set of comments, observations and largely anecdotal evidence presented at the workshop. Of course, the choice from amongst those options is not a matter for outside observers. That is for the people living in the area.

The aim is to include international scholars in the process of regional economic development; to incorporate not only Wisconsin-based faculty members but also faculty from around the world who are networked into UWM. The foundation for this aim is three propositions:

- Universities are in a position to contribute to the process of economic development because of the expertise embodied in their scholars.
- The most effective contribution from universities implies the possibility that scholars be incorporated into the economic process, rather than that they be asked to provide inputs as 'external' commentators.
- Appropriate internationalisation in universities can lead to a situation where a university is a meeting place and conduit for expertise from around the world.

It is an aim of L'institute to pursue activities that put these propositions into practice. This report represents an outcome of those activities. It is intended as a useful contribution in its own right, and to be part of a learning process that might foster a more effective involvement of international scholars in the process of Wisconsin's economic development in the future.

Summary of the Issues and Responses from Anecdotal Conversations

Emerging public discussion has identified various issues for Wisconsin to address. Among these are concerns with alleged low per capita wealth, foreign ownership of companies and a perceived 'brain drain' of college graduates. We would doubt the validity of some assertions on these issues and suggest that they warrant further clarification.

Whilst there is a lack of skilled labour in certain respects, the proportion of college graduate jobs in the state is argued to be relatively low. If there is a problem, to refer to it as a 'brain drain' may be somewhat confusing, given the way that this term has been used elsewhere. Nevertheless, the notion of a 'brain drain' appears to be viewed as both an emotional and an economic issue in practice. The emotional argument is that a lack of employment opportunities for college graduates disturbs the social balance in ways that are undesirable. The economic issue is associated with a desire to create more high-quality and high-value jobs, and linked to the concerns over low per capita wealth. All of this might be representative of a more general perception of a threat to the quality of life in Wisconsin. A highlighted question, therefore, is how might the demand for college graduates be increased, and movements towards a more dynamic economy be made?

Suggested and current steps to address these problems include:

- the stimulation of public debate, searching for new ways forward;
- the identification of 'clusters' of firms, in particular, productive sectors as important focal points for attention;
- the introduction of classes in entrepreneurship, in an attempt to foster the emergence of new firms;

- a greater role for Wisconsin's colleges and universities as dynamic actors in the local economy, including encouragement of university–business partnerships;
- the establishment of Techstar, a business/academic/government consortium designed to support high-tech activity;
- the use of firm incubators, particularly to stimulate the emergence of high-tech activity;
- the attraction/creation/access to greater venture capital;
- the development of a network of 'angel investors' across the state, drawing especially on experienced businesspeople who are withdrawing from full-time involvement in the running of their own enterprises.

While many of these steps are being undertaken, we urge caution. Possible confusion around key issues implies the need for processes of clarification and investigation. In particular, this implies that continued public debate might take particular prominence in determining ways forward. There is a danger that attempting to focus solutions on currently identified concerns may miss the point and potentially lead to error.

Summary of Tentative Discussion of Ways Forward in South-eastern Wisconsin

Public debate

1. One view is that successful economic development requires the participation of all interested parties, suggesting that all should be fully involved in determining the aims and objectives of economic development in a particular region. If that option were to be adopted in South-eastern Wisconsin, it would be important that debate on the economy included all constituents (or at least that it evolved to do so). This might be achieved with the stimulus of different arenas that bring together different but overlapping interest groups for discussion and debate. A series of arenas can offer platforms for the various interest groups, which might then come together in particular meetings. Perhaps this is how the annual Wisconsin Economic Summit is conceived, for example.
2. We have heard in our discussions concern that the culture of South-eastern Wisconsin needs to change in order to embrace the challenges facing the region. Perhaps what is happening is that people are becoming conscious of their region and are looking to build a local identity. This is in line with more general trends in a globalised new economy, where regional identity is often perceived as important. With this in mind, one view is that it may be important to stimulate and promote a culture of engagement, concern being with the process of engagement in addition to

the specific results arising from discussions within and across arenas. This argument also has implications for education, both in schools and beyond; if the people of South-eastern Wisconsin are seen as engaged citizens, then this needs to be reflected in education that encourages and enables such involvement. South-eastern Wisconsin's place in a globalised new economy does not on that view depend merely on, for example, the number of college graduates studying high-tech science and engineering; it also depends on education at all levels to facilitate an active citizenry.

3. Another choice that might be made is the following: to focus on the region in terms of its being engaged in competition with elsewhere, and thus to frame policies and ways forward in light of this competition; or to focus on the potential of the region in terms of what it wants and what it can do, which might imply competition but which might also imply cooperation and linkages with elsewhere. Where interests coincide, South-eastern Wisconsin might attempt to learn from and with Chicago, for example, or other Midwestern regions. There might also be potential for effective cooperation between South-eastern Wisconsin and other localities in the world.

Clusters

1. Various approaches to clusters can be identified, implying that there are various options for a region that is looking to them for a focus. This would perhaps suggest that clusters are an issue that would benefit from extensive analysis within the South-eastern Wisconsin region, drawing on experience in other places, for example Italy and Japan.

2. Italian experiences in recent decades, for example, suggest that some successful clusters are made up of a network of economically independent agents, also connected by market exchanges, but fundamentally sharing a non-market mechanism of governance. This non-market mechanism is collective action to produce public goods. Such goods are specific to the needs of the cluster and to the various interest groups – teams of agents – operating in its context. For example, the public good might focus on joint initiatives in marketing, research and development, finance, training and/or infrastructure. Such initiatives have depended critically on common attitudes towards trust and entrepreneurship among the peoples of a region. Evidence suggests that these conditions are more easily produced when economic relations overlap with a dense network of social relations, suggesting another reason why engagement might be seen as especially important.

3. Are the clusters existing in South-eastern Wisconsin of this type and might they be a basis for future economic success? Or are they different? Answers to these questions might be used to influence the form and therefore the impact of clusters in the future.

Lessons from Japanese experiences?

1. Like Wisconsin, the Japanese economy has a strong tradition in manufacturing, and in particular, the machinery industries. With this in mind, it might be interesting that Japan actively encouraged the development of clusters at the regional level. These clusters became known as 'company castle towns', since they predominantly consisted of thousands of small Japanese firms supplying intermediate goods and services to Japan's major corporations. Relations between Japan's large corporations and the smaller firms were seen to be long term, and involved the fostering of mutual trust and close cooperation amongst all parties. For a considerable period of time, these arrangements appeared congruent with Japan's economic development. However, it has been argued that by the 1990s the traditional relationships began to break down and decline has set in. It has also been argued that the situation has been exacerbated because the majority of small firms are 'locked in' to specialised relationships with their main contractor. Following the case of Japan, it might be suggested that clusters that involve networks of small firms dependent on the global interests of larger corporations are unlikely to provide long-term, sustainable economic prosperity.

2. Japan has tried to nullify its hollowing out problem through its Technopolis Project. This has involved the creation of advanced technological production sites with close linkages with universities and research centres. However, the project has been unable to negate the effects of globalisation. One reason appears to have been its over-reliance upon attracting major corporations to the cluster, rather than using resources to encourage a greater degree of diversity and embeddedness within Japan's industrial regions.

Entrepreneurship

1. Entrepreneurship is generally seen as a generator of prosperity, but there may also be a conflict between enterprise formation and other desirable social objectives. For example, regulations on redundancy may increase the risks of initiating business activity, and tax-financed public services and social protection are often seen as indirect impediments.

2. It is perhaps worth remembering that enterprise formation is not an end in itself. It is desirable insofar as it creates employment opportunities, provides consumers with greater choice and leads to innovation and growth. However, the way in which it takes place may be problematic. Employment generation, for example, might be biased towards low-skilled workers, who are often seen as vulnerable.

3. Robust applied research provides an input to innovative business activities. But this should not mean an exclusive focus on research with immediate

commercial applications, because good applied research also requires good basic research. The opportunities to communicate provided by a university that is strong in both types of research may be more successful than if it specialises on issues with immediate practical applications. Moreover, business enterprises are known to be attracted to universities with academic excellence in all areas.

4. Competition policy may be an important component of a strategy that reduces the contradiction between different economic objectives. For example, a reduction of artificial barriers to entry can stimulate the emergence of new entrants.

5. The fact that enterprise formation might not be seen as an end in itself also means that policy-makers might want to encourage activities that are not solely dependent on profit opportunities. The presence of a non-profit sector can also be a complement to an antitrust policy, because it becomes difficult to charge excessive prices in competition with non-commercial providers. In addition, non-commercial providers in the cultural sectors affect both the quality of life and the demand for highly skilled employees.

Conclusion

1. In raising questions and queries about the future for South-eastern Wisconsin, we are pointing to various possibilities and options. Although we have been far from exhaustive, it seems clear that choices are there to be made.

2. As the region looks to go forward we would urge that there is no search for a unique and simple answer. If any are hoping for a single step that will provide a panacea, they are likely to be disappointed. Likewise for any that might look for a blueprint that can be simply copied. Evidence from around the world suggests that there is no such thing, which is not to say that there are no lessons to be learned from others in similar and related circumstances.

3. South-eastern Wisconsin is part of a globalised new economy. In that context, it might seem prudent for the people of the region to be prepared to sow many seeds in their search for economic prosperity, to introduce pilot projects and to experiment so as to find what best serves their own aims and objectives. This might require the people to look for the best way forward for themselves, to seek what is appropriate for this region based upon its own characteristics and desires.

Introduction

The starting point for our discussion is a presentation of some of the key issues that South-eastern Wisconsin is said to be facing, and a listing of some of the responses that are being suggested. These issues and responses have been brought to our attention as potentially important by various commentators from the region, but they are not necessarily all of the considerations that matter. We are reporting our understanding of views that have been expressed. This understanding might be flawed, not least given that it results from preliminary and quite brief discussions, where the evidence is often anecdotal. We have not had the opportunity for research that might verify or contradict this evidence. In addition, it is not being claimed that we have been presented with views that are exhaustive of all the considerations facing the people of South-eastern Wisconsin. Indeed, we would suggest, for example, that it is particularly important to ensure that all issues are identified and that processes are put in place to achieve this result. That is one of the points that we make in the third section of the report, when we offer tentative discussion on ways forward.

Economic Development in South-eastern Wisconsin: Issues and Responses

An emerging public discussion in Wisconsin – surrounding, for example, the first Wisconsin Economic Summit, held in November/December 2000 – has identified various issues that seem to be shaping current debate. These include alleged low per capita wealth, a concern about foreign ownership of productive assets and, linked to both, an apparent 'brain drain'.[13] However, we would doubt the validity of some assertions on these issues and suggest that they warrant further careful investigation to clarify the key points.

The debate about wealth, for example, draws upon the view that Wisconsin ranks forty-first in the nation and seventh in the Midwest on an assets per capita basis. The implication is questionable, given that Wisconsin ranks thirtieth nationally and fourth in the Midwest in the median value of owner-occupied housing (US Census Bureau, 1990). As for the 'brain drain', it refers to a net out-migration of college graduates. It has been argued that while 'Wisconsin retains a good percentage of its own college grads (ranking as high as 7th in recent years), it does not attract college grads from other States' (see Torinus, 1999 and Ward, 2000). The problem is argued to be that the region 'ranks 29th in the nation with 23% of its citizens holding a four year degree and . . . is in the bottom quarter of States in terms of net migration of college graduates. Wisconsin's net migration (loss) of college grads results from a very low (as low as 50th in the nation in recent years) in-migration of college graduates'. Yet it is also reported that Wisconsin experienced 'modest net in-migration of college graduates from 1990 to 1995'.[14] As for South-eastern Wisconsin, 73 per cent of alumni from the University of Wisconsin-Milwaukee are retained in the area, marginally higher than the US average (71 per cent) and considerably higher than the Wisconsin average 62 per cent (*Milwaukee Journal Sentinel*, 22 August, 1999). To us, this implies a confusion that necessitates clarification.

In fact, any notion of a 'brain drain' in Wisconsin seems to be misplaced given the usual way that the term has been used. 'Brain drain' typically refers either to a situation where a person leaves a region to obtain education elsewhere and does not return, or to circumstances where a person is educated in a region and then leaves. It is not typically applied to a case where a person from one region obtains education in another, for example Wisconsin, and then returns to their home state. Moreover, situations in which people are coming into a region to obtain education could be argued to offer opportunities to that region, because it may then be able to encourage them to stay and draw upon their expertise in the future.

Nevertheless, our limited discussions certainly revealed that in practice importance is attached to Wisconsin's ability to maintain and create employment opportunities for college graduates. This seems to be from both an economic development perspective and an emotional perspective. The latter is interesting in that it was framed in our conversations in terms of people's children leaving the state, particularly those that are college graduates. This raises a set of questions as to how cities, regions, localities can hold on to people, maintaining a strong 'society' in a 'global' economy where mobility is a key feature. Indeed, is it desirable to try to do so? These issues are also prominent in European countries – for example, Spain. Moreover, perhaps the real issue is the age distribution of the population and the subsequent demographic structure of the area. There are also questions about whose concerns are being represented; are worries about children leaving the state confined to those whose children attend college, or are the concerns wider?

One possibility is that the issue regarding college graduates is representative of fears that current lifestyles in South-eastern Wisconsin are under threat in the medium term. The area is often described as a good place to live, but perhaps it will start to decline because of economic threats from other localities with different lifestyles, including differences in job quality, leisure activities and environment. South-eastern Wisconsin in certain respects appears to be economically successful. For example, it experienced 21 per cent employment growth in the 1990s, including 6 per cent growth in manufacturing, has been said to have high earnings per worker for the types of jobs available, and has a high labour force participation rate, 75 per cent compared to a US average of 67 per cent (for data, see Appendix, Chapter 11). An implication of fears of threat from elsewhere might be a desire (amongst some?) for new ways forward, because existing lifestyles might be perceived as unsustainable in the medium term, given 'competition' from other economies that adopt different approaches. A further implication might be a call (from some?) for protection, in some sense, in an attempt to preserve a way of life. If this is the case, however, there is a danger that focusing solutions on the specific concern over college graduates will miss the point and lead to error. There are also crucial questions as to whether everybody in South-eastern Wisconsin sees the current position as desirable, and why this is (or is not) the case.[15]

From an economic perspective the position is complex. Unemployment remains low, at 3.8 per cent (see Appendix, Chapter 11), and there are reported shortages of 'skilled' labour, although to us it is neither clear if this is a worse problem now than before, nor if it is a worse problem than in similar states. From this viewpoint, it might appear that there is a need for more people to develop intermediate and higher-intermediate skills, through perhaps vocational courses, and for fewer to proceed through channels that lead to college graduation. However, a second challenge identified by some in Wisconsin is the pursuit of high-quality jobs, namely those in high-tech industries and those that lead to enhanced job quality in general.[16] This is related to the perception that Wisconsin is characterised by low per capita wealth. It could be argued that a focus on intermediate and higher-intermediate skills is unlikely to be conducive to an increase in higher-income and higher-quality jobs. The perceived economic concern is thus geared towards ways in which to maintain more college graduates, and in doing so to create a dynamic and 'higher-value' local economy. This is associated with the concern for the future, as identified above. Integrated within this is another query that was raised in our conversations; the claim that Wisconsin is effectively subsidising other state education systems through the emigration of its college graduates (although if this is the case education might be seen as a beneficial export – see Krauss, op. cit.). Related to these issues are concerns with ensuring a more dynamic role in the local economy for Wisconsin's educational institutions, attracting greater venture capital, improving infrastructure and enhancing the regulatory and entrepreneurial climates. Connected in particular with the desire for high-tech activity is the establishment of Techstar, a consortium of business, academe and government.

One view is that there are potentially two broad approaches to the so-called 'brain drain'. The first is to seek ways in which to *change* the Wisconsin economy to attract and maintain more graduates. This might involve a reorientation to more high-tech activities, or perhaps to services and away from basic manufacturing. The second is to question whether it is possible to attract these people while *maintaining* manufacturing as the base of the economy. One suggestion put to us is that manufacturing is in fact changing 'naturally' in becoming more knowledge-intensive. Thus it may be possible to refocus activities *within* manufacturing so as to attract more graduates. Initiatives currently under discussion in Wisconsin that are in line with these approaches include the introduction of classes in entrepreneurship, in an attempt to foster the emergence of new firms, and the use of firm incubators, particularly to stimulate the emergence of high-tech activity.

A related issue is the notion of 'place'. It was argued by some commentators from the region who were talking to us that graduate students no longer target a career path with a particular firm. Instead they determine a 'place' where they will seek employment. This is associated with the emergence of specific localities as clusters in certain sectors. An implication is that Wisconsin needs to develop acknowledged clusters of firms in activities/sectors that are attractive to college graduates. Again, this is an issue currently under discussion amongst some in the area. However, perhaps there is a further dimension in terms of a particular place being a 'hot spot' for young people to want to live. While this is strongly related to the clustering of particular activities, it is also associated with the existence of 'trendy' and 'vibrant' arts, sports, leisure and residential scenes (themselves related to clustering of economic activity, but possibly not exclusively). This is associated with analyses of indices representing some notion of city 'vibrancy' and attractiveness to young people, particularly young professionals.[17] It also has two further implications that relate to issues identified in the ongoing debate in Wisconsin. First, identifying the distinctive brand image that Wisconsin wishes to pursue, if any. Second, the significance of social equity, which has been identified to us as important in the context of creating an entrepreneurial culture, but which has wider implications for how Wisconsin is perceived as a place to live and work.

As for the particular focus for the more immediate way forward, current thinking in the region emphasises 'clusters', planned as the central theme of the second Wisconsin Economic Summit. In particular, there is to be a focus on knowledge-based clusters, which in turn is related to the approach that Wisconsin can be successful in manufacturing if it moves towards a knowledge-based model. Questions remain, however. For example, how should the clustered sectors be identified? One possibility is to analyse how currently successful manufacturing firms are succeeding, noting the other firms that are emerging around this, and to base a cluster process on these experiences. Is that approach desirable? There is also the notion of networks between businesspeople and others with interests in the development of the Wisconsin economy. This is linked to the idea of a network of 'angels' supporting new enterprises with finance, and also to the establishment of the Techstar initiative.

Tentative Discussion of Ways Forward in South-eastern Wisconsin

Public debate

One view is that successful economic development requires the participation of all interested parties. This might be said to follow from an analysis of key decision-making in production and from the suggested desirability of decentralised, democratic involvement. These points have been argued to be significant in a globalised new economy, both for particular regions that have been successful and for regions that have failed yet to realise their full economic potential. Such an approach suggests that all parties should be fully involved in determining the aims and objectives of economic development in a particular region. If that option were to be adopted in South-eastern Wisconsin, it would be important that debate on the economy included all constituents (or at least that it evolved to do so). This might be achieved with the stimulus of different arenas that bring together different but overlapping interest groups for discussion and debate. These arenas might exist around, for example, the business community, the education community and residents' associations. There is no need to jump to a solution that attempts to involve all interest groups on the same footing in one arena. Indeed, such a jump may be undesirable. Rather, a series of arenas (that may be to a degree competing) can offer platforms for the various interest groups, which might then come together in particular meetings. Perhaps this is how the annual Wisconsin Economic Summit is conceived, for example; an arena where different groups meet for discussion, analysis and identification of ways forward, those groups having participated in other arenas throughout the year. Moreover, it is likely to be important that there is fluidity and flexibility, avoiding rigidity that prevents arenas from changing, converging and diverging over time.

We have heard in our discussions concern that the culture of South-eastern Wisconsin needs to alter in order to embrace the challenges facing the region. Perhaps what is happening is that people are becoming conscious of their region and are looking to build a local identity. This is in line with more general trends in a globalised new economy, where regional identity is often perceived as important. With this in mind, one view is that it may be important to stimulate and promote a *culture of engagement*, concern being with the *process* of engagement in addition to the specific results arising from discussions within and across arenas. It is possible, for example, that engagement occurs only when there is perceived to be a problem. It may then quickly dissipate when the perception changes or the problem is being addressed. An alternative would be to view the *process* of engaging in debate as fundamental to future development, thus to view the evolution of a culture of engagement as an aim in itself. The significance of this process does not turn on the existence of real or alleged problems. In addition, we would not see this process as taking place at the expense of solving immediate problems. Advantages of such an approach include the potential for debate and strategy to evolve as problems are evolving, in a sense to stay ahead of the game. A culture of engagement that diffuses across society may also be advantageous in the sense that it promotes engagement by all groups. It thus avoids the potential that only a subsector of society participates in debate and accordingly benefits, addressing issues that might not be wholly representative of wider concerns.

The discussions in which we have participated appear to demonstrate a desire to promote engagement, and there has been explicit recognition of the need to involve particularly young professionals. This argument also has implications for education, both in schools and beyond: if the people of South-eastern Wisconsin are seen as active citizens, members of social, economic and political communities, then this needs to be reflected in education that encourages and enables such involvement. South-eastern Wisconsin's place in a globalised new economy does not on that view depend merely on, for example, the number of college graduates studying high-tech science and engineering. It also depends on education at all levels to facilitate an active citizenry.

This approach is associated with the idea of a region deciding for itself what it wants from its economy. It would be for the people of South-eastern Wisconsin to determine what they desire from their economy, to decide how they see themselves as a community or communities. Moreover, this leads us to another choice that might be made: to focus on the region in terms of its being engaged in competition with elsewhere, and thus to frame policies and ways forward in light of this competition; or to focus on the potential of the region in terms of what it wants and what it can do, which might imply competition but which might also imply cooperation and linkages with elsewhere. For example, one possibility is that Chicago is seen as a metropolitan area drawing economic activity from Wisconsin, especially South-eastern Wisconsin, which is a competitor for the same activity in a zero sum game; what one region gains, another loses. Alternatively, the people of South-eastern Wisconsin might focus on their own potential to produce, their own innovative capacity, looking to pursue that to the full rather than be concerned about others in a negative sense. Concern with others might instead arise in a positive manner. Where interests coincide, South-eastern Wisconsin might attempt to learn from and with Chicago, or other Midwestern regions. It might also see opportunities arising as a result of successful economic activity in, for example, Chicago, benefiting from proximity without being a satellite.[18] This is analogous to the choice facing individuals: to see themselves as being in competition with others, or to focus on the fulfilment of their own selves, the determination of their own potential as human beings.

This process need not be confined to the Midwest. There might be potential for effective cooperation between South-eastern Wisconsin and other localities in the world. For example, there has been concern expressed about the impact of some transnational corporations producing in the region. Perhaps some fears over this issue could be allayed by cooperation with other regions where these transnationals also produce. There is also a potential to link with other regions in a mutually beneficial learning process. Not least, the people of South-eastern Wisconsin might be able to discover beneficial ways forward in conjunction with regions facing similar or related problems. This is not a matter of copying from elsewhere or adopting another region's model. Rather, it might be part of the process of the people of the region finding their own way forward, founded on their own concerns, desires and traditions.

These options might be argued to overlap with a fundamental issue at the root of economic development in the region. On the one hand, in our conversations and anecdotal evidence we have heard genuine concern about the future of the communities and societies in South-eastern Wisconsin. On the other, when this has been translated into possible suggestions for the future, it is not clear that the focus has been communal and social. This point can be illustrated by the discussions that we have had surrounding clusters. There are hints that initial discussion of clusters has been concerned with a group of individual firms that produce in the same sector, focusing perhaps on policy initiatives that are directed at each firm in isolation. While this is one view of clusters, there are others that might be considered.

Clusters

Various approaches to clusters can be identified, implying that there are various options for a region that is looking to them for a focus. This would perhaps suggest that clusters are an issue that would benefit from extensive analysis within the South-eastern Wisconsin region, drawing on experience in other regions, for example Italy and Japan. There are choices to be made regarding the types of clusters that the region might be able to nurture in the future. These choices also depend on the types of clusters that currently exist.

As an illustration, one definition of a cluster, suggested in particular from experience of economic success in Italian industrial districts, might be the following. A cluster is made up of a network of economically independent agents, connected by market exchanges, but fundamentally sharing a non-market mechanism of governance. This non-market mechanism is collective action producing specific public goods, more or less consciously. Such goods are specific to the needs of the cluster and to the various interest groups – teams of agents – operating in its context. Thus the term cluster is attached to the idea of an evolving set of private and public activities. For example, the public good might focus on joint initiatives in marketing, research and development, finance (through mutual guarantee schemes), training and/or infrastructure (perhaps including investment in new communications networks). Experiences elsewhere imply that such initiatives have depended critically on common attitudes towards trust and entrepreneurship among the peoples of a region. Evidence suggests that these conditions are more easily produced when economic relations overlap with a dense network of social relations, hence another reason why engagement might be seen as especially important.

Notably, cooperation along these lines need not be at the expense of effective competition, a requirement that might be seen as important if efficiency is to be ensured.

The potential importance of cooperation in a market context is also illustrated by observations on organisational solutions found in the new economy, such as: 'many commentators have likened cyberspace to the Wild West, where old patterns of behaviour no longer apply and everything is up for grabs. Perhaps, but the lone cowboy approach rarely works in the information age. Network economics and positive feedback make co-operation more important than ever. Most companies need to cooperate with others to establish standards and create a single network of compatible users. But as soon as the ink is dry on the standards agreement, these same companies shift gears and compete head to head for their share of the network' (Shapiro and Varian, 1999). It should be appreciated that this illustration is quite narrow, however, and that it points to potential problems; cooperation may extend to more than the establishment of infrastructure or standards, and it is important that these are not used as a barrier to the dynamism of the industry.

One specific question is whether clusters with the dense form and processes suggested above exist in South-eastern Wisconsin, and whether they might provide a basis for the region's economic success. We have heard in our discussions that clusters are present in South-eastern Wisconsin, with around ten specific clusters identified. It may be, however, that some of these are pure geographical concentrations of firms and markets. Nevertheless, it is likely that some of those identified are closer than are others to the characteristics of successful cluster experiences in other parts of the world. In particular, the machinery and agro–food–beverages clusters seem to have strong traditions and provide a basis for dense inter-relationship among firms. It has also been argued that institution-building for the specific needs and advancement of such relations is strong within the region (Whitford et al., 2000).

For us, this raises various questions. It is not clear, for example, if such clusters have a geographical core, with a regional and state corolla, or if their companies are dispersed throughout the state. In both cases, it would need to be clarified if and to what extent one or more localities and local communities within the state take the destiny of one cluster as strongly connected to the welfare and destiny of their workers, local entrepreneurs and residents. In other words, from where do the institutions and public goods that are shared by firms in one cluster derive? Are they solely the result of strategies enacted by, for example, leading firms? Or is there a greater involvement of local public, social and economic organisations that take care of aspects connected to social and environmental sustainability? Answers to these questions might be used to influence the form, and therefore the impact, of the clusters.

More generally, suppose that some nuclei of dense relationships exist and define one or more vital clusters in South-eastern Wisconsin. If that is the case, they might be seen as engines of industrial and social progress and further questions arise as to the ways forward. For example, how might the clusters be enriched with higher knowledge and creative content? How might the growth of specialised knowledge activities be supported so that they can be harnessed to service the specific needs of the clusters? Is it possible to communicate to the young and their families, in the different communities involved, that good jobs and the sort of lifestyles that they desire may be available in the renewed clusters and the dynamism of the region? Positive answers might facilitate the development of a similar logic of development in more dispersed nuclei of economic activities in South-eastern Wisconsin. Moreover, in the search for answers and to avoid potential pitfalls, it might be useful to consider experiences from elsewhere, for example Japan.

Lessons from Japanese experiences?

Like Wisconsin, the Japanese economy has a strong tradition in manufacturing, and in particular, the machinery industries. Moreover, one view is that Japan's post-war industrial strength has resulted from a combination of an active industrial policy and an institutional approach to economic development.

Japanese industrial policy has been the responsibility of the Ministry of International Trade and Industry (MITI) and has focused upon targeting 'strategic industries' for future economic and industrial development. The machinery sector received specific attention and, at various times over the last 50 years, has benefited from measures such as direct subsidies, discriminatory tariffs, preferential commodity taxes and favourable industry regulation. To complement these measures, MITI actively encouraged the development of clusters of industrial activity at the regional level. These clusters became known as 'company castle towns', since they predominantly consisted of thousands of small Japanese firms supplying intermediate goods and services to Japan's major corporations. Relations between Japan's large corporations and the smaller firms were seen to be long-term, and involved the fostering of mutual trust and close cooperation amongst all parties. For a considerable period of time, these arrangements appeared congruent with Japan's economic development.

However, it has been argued that by the 1990s the traditional relationships began to break down, as Japan's larger corporations substantially increased overseas production and began to use their global supply networks for the outsourcing of intermediate goods and services. Consequently, Japan's smaller firms began to feel isolated, and felt under pressure to accept lower profit margins and falling order books, resulting in an unprecedented rise in the number of small firm bankruptcy cases (*Nikkei Weekly*, 19 October, 1998). It has also been argued that the situation has been exacerbated by the hierarchical nature of industrial production in Japan, where the majority of small firms are 'locked in' to specialised relationships with their main contractor. This has left Japan's small firm base with little scope to diversify. At the regional level, the result has been a significant decline in business activities and industrial vitality, reducing the potential for economic regeneration, productivity growth and development. Commentators have raised serious concerns that Japanese industry is now facing a crisis of hollowing out.

Interestingly, Japan has tried to nullify the hollowing out problem through its Technopolis Project. This was launched in the 1980s and has involved the creation of science parks – advanced technological production sites – with close linkages with universities and research centres. The aim has been for Japan to establish a number of high-tech cities that could encourage and retain major investors. By the mid-1990s, approximately 30 projects had been instigated. However, while the project has had some minor successes, it has been unable to negate the effects of globalisation and the problems of hollowing out on the wider scale. One reason for this relative failure appears to have been the project's over-reliance upon attracting major corporations to the cluster, rather than using resources to encourage a greater degree of diversity and embeddedness within Japan's industrial regions. The major corporations have taken a global perspective for their operations and they appear to have regarded their regional activities as little more than footloose investments.

The Japanese experience therefore provides a potentially important example for economic policy-making. Perhaps the Techstar project in South-eastern Wisconsin shares a number of similarities with Japan's Technopolis project, particularly with its emphasis upon new economy initiatives. There is also the interest in encouraging industrial clusters. However, it is important that such initiatives should take full account of the global activities of the larger corporations that the region might wish to encourage and the types of industrial linkages that they are likely to build with the state's indigenous firms. These are important considerations since, as we have seen in the case of Japan, clusters that involve networks of small firms dependent on the global interests of larger corporations are unlikely to provide long-term, sustainable economic prosperity.

Entrepreneurship
Entrepreneurship is generally seen as a generator of prosperity, but there may also be a conflict between enterprise formation and other desirable social objectives. Insofar as employment and enterprise formation are dependent on profit opportunities, social objectives that are seen as associated with higher direct or indirect labour costs might be *harmful*, because of their impact on profits. For example, high wages may make it more expensive to be an

employer. It may also decrease the incentive to become self-employed, as high wages increase the attraction of paid employment. Regulations on redundancy may increase the risks of initiating an activity, and tax-financed public services and social protection are often seen as indirect impediments. This may leave decision-makers with a stark choice. Either focus on a business-friendly policy that excludes large parts of the working population from the prosperity that is created, because it implies low wages; or focus on a welfare-oriented policy that excludes a section of the population from employment, because of low business activity.

This conventional view is too simplistic, because social insurance may offer a protection that encourages risk-taking. A well-developed public infrastructure is also often seen as crucial by the business community. Moreover, empirical evidence suggests that high profitability has a slow and limited effect on entry into an industry, and that the non-pecuniary benefits associated with being an entrepreneur are also important. While an increase in direct and indirect labour costs can drive firms out of business and cause unemployment, it is not certain that a reduction will stimulate the emergence of new enterprises.

However, it seems unwise to ignore the contradiction between enterprise formation and other social objectives. It may therefore be worthwhile to explore how public policy can increase economic activity without excluding the least well-off employees from prosperity. Similarly, if equality is seen as a desirable social objective, it may be worthwhile exploring how public policy might achieve greater equality without reducing entrepreneurship.

It is perhaps worth remembering that enterprise formation is not an end in itself. It is desirable insofar as it creates employment opportunities, provides consumers with greater choice and leads to innovation and growth. However, the way in which it takes place may be problematic. Employment generation, for example, might be biased towards low-skilled workers and low-quality jobs. Such workers are often seen as vulnerable, and other undesirable social outcomes associated with inequality might result. Education may then be argued to play an important role in reducing the dependency on low-skilled jobs but, in its turn, this may create other problems. For example, our discussions reported in the second section suggest that there may be a shortage of job opportunities for the highly skilled in South-eastern Wisconsin. In this case, one response would be to stimulate enterprise growth particularly in the high-tech sector. More generally, regions might want to consider their options in terms of the different forms of enterprises that might be created.

The research sector appears to play an important role in Wisconsin. Robust applied research provides an input to innovative business activities. But this should not mean an exclusive focus on research with immediate commercial applications, because good applied research also requires good basic research.

The opportunities to communicate provided by a university that is strong in both types of research may be more successful than if it specialises on issues with immediate practical applications. Indeed, sound basic research can often have unintended commercial applications, and as such might be seen as valuable in itself. Moreover, business enterprises are known to be attracted to universities with academic excellence in all areas, as highlighted by the experience of commercialising research findings in, for example, the University of Warwick, UK.

Markets are rarely perfectly competitive in practice. Competition policy, therefore, may be an important component of a strategy that reduces the contradiction between different economic objectives. For example, a reduction of artificial barriers to entry can stimulate the emergence of new entrants. Another case in point is provided by antitrust policy. If firms are forced to reduce their profit margins, an implication is that a given level of direct and indirect labour costs becomes consistent with a higher level of economic activity, and therefore higher employment.

The fact that enterprise formation might not be seen as an end in itself also means that policy-makers might want to encourage activities that are not solely dependent on profit opportunities. The non-profit sector has traditionally been an important provider of, for example, education and health care in the US, and there may be other sectors where an increased role can be explored. The presence of a non-profit sector can also be a complement to an antitrust policy, because it becomes difficult to charge excessive prices in competition with non-commercial providers. For example, the cooperative retail movement in Sweden has been seen as a way to affect the pricing policy of its more commercial rivals. Firms and organisations in public ownership might provide a similar role, but they may also provide a valuable complement, and not only in cases of natural monopoly. Infrastructure industries, for example, have often been in public ownership. A high quality of life may be important for attracting highly skilled employees who may be in high demand elsewhere, and a working public transport system may then be of vital importance, not least for environmental reasons. The experiences of privatised public transport in Britain have not been encouraging, and suggest that conventional views on public ownership may be prejudiced. Similarly, the privately-owned electricity system in parts of California has experienced recent difficulties, indicating that debate over public–private provision is far from closed. Moreover, non-commercial providers in the cultural sectors affect both the quality of life and the demand for highly skilled employees.

Conclusion

In raising questions and queries about the future for South-eastern Wisconsin, we are pointing to various possibilities and options. Although we have been far from exhaustive, it seems clear that choices are there to be made. We suggest that it is important to be clear about the perceived problems; to establish their exact nature and precisely why they are of concern. Related to this, it might be appropriate to nurture a culture of engagement, in order to identify and understand the region's nature and identity. We have also indicated that clusters and entrepreneurship are likely to be significant issues that warrant active attention, each implying options that deserve to be addressed. Clusters, for example, can be found in many forms throughout the world. Which sorts do the people of South-eastern Wisconsin desire? Are they attainable and, if so, how?

As the region looks to move forward we would urge that there is no search for a unique and simple answer. If any are hoping for a single step that will provide a panacea, they are likely to be disappointed. Likewise, any that might look for a blueprint that can be simply copied. Evidence from around the world suggests that there is no such thing, which is not to say that there are no lessons to be had from others in similar and related circumstances.

South-eastern Wisconsin is part of a globalised new economy. In that context, it might seem prudent for the people of the region to be prepared to sow many seeds in their search for economic prosperity, to introduce pilot projects and to experiment so as to find what best serves their own aims and objectives. *The need is for the people to look for the best way forward for themselves, to seek what is appropriate for this region based upon its own characteristics and desires.*

NOTES

* We would like to thank Marco Bellandi, Susan Donohue, Rita Hartung Cheng, G. Richard Meadows, Stan Siebert, Marcela Valania and Ping Wei for their valuable comments and suggestions. The responsibility for errors, however, is entirely our own.

1. As well as from its predecessor, the First L'institute–Milwaukee Workshop on 'Urban and regional prosperity in a globalised economy', July 2000.

2. For more detail on the Warwick–Birmingham workshops and their wider contribution to the ongoing evolution of a European Network in Industrial Policy (EUNIP) and L'institute itself, see Sugden (2000).

3. See, for example, the volume edited by Pyke, Becattini and Sengenberger (1990), in particular the contribution by Becattini. See also, Bianchi (1993).

4. See Sugden and Wilson (2002a) for a detailed background to this perspective on development. See also their discussion of 'globalisation' in this volume (Chapter 1).

5. For example, a paper by Don Nichols presented at the first Summit, the substance of which is reproduced in Chapter 10 of this volume, was very influential in preparing the questions and topics that workshop participants were asked to consider (see also Chapter 1).

6. Consciousness around the insider/outsider distinction also stemmed partly from previous experience with public sessions at the L'institute–Ferrara Graduate School in Industrial Development Policy (see www.linstitute.org/ferraraschool/ for further information). These sessions have attempted, on a smaller scale to the workshop, to fuse the expertise of visiting participants with that of local actors. The insider/outsider distinction at these school sessions

has been very marked, with most of the 'real' business and discussion taking place privately amongst local actors away from the public space; literally, in the adjacent corridors.

7. See, for example, Taylor (1997, p. 151). He draws a parallel with the criticism of von Mises (1935) of socialism 'on the grounds that "as if" planners could never improve upon capitalism because they would just "play" a market game without being disciplined for their mistakes. The same doubts apply to bureaucrats "playing" at running national economies with their attention focused on career advancement in the institutions back in the United States'. See also Stiglitz (2002) on the International Monetary Fund (IMF).

8. Again, see Stiglitz (2002) and also 'IMF's four steps to damnation', an interview with Joseph Stiglitz by Gregory Palast, reported in *The Observer*, 29 April 2001.

9. By 'planning' we do not imply 'central planning', for example of the type that used to characterise Central and Eastern Europe.

10. Sugden and Wilson (2002b) argue in the case of Argentina's economic crisis, for example, that a contributory cause has been the failure of the IMF to appreciate the economic, political and social reality in which its 'free' market policies were seemingly to be introduced.

11. For example, students at the L'institute–Ferrara Graduate School in Industrial Development Policy are asked to prepare a report on economic development in the province of Ferrara, which is then communicated to a wide audience at a public session at the end of the School. The intention is to interact with the local community, and thereby increase the local relevance of the School's activities.

12. More information about this project can be found at L'institute's website, www.linstitute.org.

13. See, for example, Bill Krauss, 2001, 'The Great Wisconsin Brain Drain', *Wisconsin Academy Review*, spring. It is argued that 'Wisconsin seems to be destined to become a State of branches, not headquarters. The best and the brightest gravitate towards headquarters, not branches.'

14. Reported, with the caution that estimates were based on small samples, in Rick Romell (1999).

15. See, for example, Krauss, *op. cit.*, 'Milwaukee is a city on a Great Lake and features short commutes, an active cultural life, good clubs, access to country living, and good schools. It features these things, unfortunately, for the settled economic elite who can afford to live in the suburbs that ring the city.'

16. According to Romell, *op. cit.*, 'Competitive Wisconsin, Inc., a group of business, labor, agriculture and education leaders, is calling for the State to shift its economic development emphasis "from the quantity of jobs created to the quality of those jobs" '.

17. These ideas are associated with the work of Richard Florida, who recently met with Southeastern Wisconsin civic leaders to discuss the issues, see *Milwaukee Journal Sentinel*, 11 March 2001.

18. Recent debate around the possibility of a high-speed train link between Chicago and Milwaukee has suggested that there is potential for greater cooperation along these lines, although opinions differ on the impact of such a venture.

REFERENCES

Bianchi, P. (1993), 'Industrial districts and industrial policy: the new European perspective', *Journal of Industrial Studies*, **1**, 16–29.

Krauss, B. (2001) 'The great Wisconsin brain drain', *Wisconsin Academy Review*, Spring.

Pyke, F., Becattini, G. and Sengenberger, W. (1990), *Industrial Districts and Inter-firm Co-operation in Italy*, Geneva: International Institute for Labour Studies.

Romell, R. (1999), 'As economy goes digital, state leaders fear brain drain', *Milwaukee Journal Sentinel*, 15 August.

Shapiro, C. and Varian, H.R. (1999), *Information Rules. A Strategic Guide to the Network Economy*, Boston, MA: Harvard Business School Press.
Stiglitz, J.E. (2002), *Globalization and its Discontents*, London and New York: Norton.
Sugden, R. (2000), 'Small firm networking and the internationalisation of universities: a multinational approach', L'institute Discussion Paper 11, Universities of Birmingham, Ferrara and Wisconsin-Milwaukee, www.linstitute.org/papers/.
Sugden, R. and Wilson, J.R. (2002a), 'Development in the shadow of the consensus: a strategic decision-making approach', *Contributions to Political Economy*, **21**, 111–34.
Sugden, R. and Wilson, J.R. (2002b), 'Cambiando attitudini alla cooperazione: Il fondamento per una nuova struttura industriale in Argentina', *L'industria*, **XXIII** (3), 529–38.
Taylor, L. (1997). 'Editorial: the revival of the liberal creed – the IMF and the World Bank in a globalized economy', *World Development*, **25**(2), 145–52.
Torinus, J.B. (1999), 'The great brain robbery', *Corporate Report Wisconsin*.
US Census Bureau (1990), Summary Tape File.
Von Mises, L. (1935), 'Economic calculation in the socialist commonwealth', in F. Hayek (ed.), *Collectivist Economic Planning*, London: Routledge.
Ward, D.J. (2000), 'High income strategies for the Wisconsin economy', Paper presented at the first Wisconsin Economic Summit.
Whitford, J., Zeitlin, J. and Rogers, J. (2000), 'Down the line . . . supplier upgrading, evolving OEM–supplier relations, and directions for future manufacturing modernization policy and research in Wisconsin', Report prepared for the Wisconsin Manufacturing Extension Program (WMEP).
Winters, D.J. (2000), 'Help wanted! Sustaining Wisconsin's economic prosperity', Paper presented at the first Wisconsin Economic Summit.

Index